Communicating Gender

Communicating Gender

Suzanne Romaine
Oxford University

LEA
LAWRENCE ERLBAUM ASSOCIATES, PUBLISHERS
1999   Mahwah, New Jersey   London

Lawrence Erlbaum Associates, Inc., Publishers
10 Industrial Avenue
Mahwah, New Jersey 07430

Library of Congress Cataloging-in-Publication Data

Romaine, Suzanne, 1951–   .
    Communicating gender / Suzanne Romaine.
      p.   cm.
    Includes bibliographical references and index.
    ISBN 0-8058-2925-3 (alk. paper). — ISBN 0-8058-2926-1 (pbk. :
alk. paper).
    1. Language and languages—Sex differences. 2. Communication—Sex
differences. 3. Gender identity. 4. Feminism. I. Title.
    P120.S48R66 1998
    306.44—dc21   98-17562
                                                                CIP

Books published by Lawrence Erlbaum Associates are printed on acid-free paper,
and their bindings are chosen for strength and durability.

Printed in the United States of America
10 9 8 7 6 5 4 3

*To some women friends with thanks for their support
and friendship, and lots of interesting conversations!*

Birgit
Dorothy
Fiona
Isabel
Karen
Leialoha
Mitzi
Nancy
Sherryll
Shinae
Tomi
Urmi

Contents

Preface

This book is about how we communicate gender and why language and discourse play such important roles in the process. Because my own intellectual training lies primarily in linguistics, that has to some extent led me to look at gender primarily through the lens of language. However, I think a good case can independently be made for the centrality of language and communication to any discussion of gender, or for that matter virtually any discipline. If you accept my arguments that what we call "society," or even more grandly, "reality" itself, is largely constructed and represented to ourselves and others through language, then language and discourse are paramount. In the first chapter I explain why "doing" gender is a dynamic and inherently communicative process and why language is so fundamental to understanding our gendered selves.

Certainly another indication of the centrality of language is its frequent mention in the popular debate on sexual difference. This can be seen by picking up almost any contemporary magazine where articles on topics such as differences in male–female conversation, body language, advice on how women should speak in the workplace, and so on, have become increasingly frequent. Sociolinguist Deborah Tannen's book, which was a best seller for several years, dealt with problems in male–female communication.

The many popular articles and books now being published about the topic of cross-gender communication suggest that men and women are having a hard time communicating with one another. At home, women complain that their husbands do not really talk to them. Men complain that women talk constantly, but have nothing important to say. At work, men say that women get intimidated and offended too easily. They do not

speak up or they back down even when they have a good point. They tend
to be more emotional and to personalize business matters. Women say that
men leave them out of shop talk, and informal talk, where the "real"
business gets done. The misunderstandings are often so severe that they
give rise to the complaint that men and women do not even speak the
same language. As Suzette Haden Elgin (1993) pointed out, this is the
ultimate disclaimer. Here again, there is a wealth of material aimed at a
popular audience. Bestselling author John Gray (1992) claimed that men
and women are so different, they even behave as if they live on different
planets: Men are from Mars and women, from Venus.

Language is key too in the campaign for language reform, where I show
that the debate is really about issues of race, gender, class, or culture. To
advocate deliberate change is to threaten the status quo, the prevailing
moral order, and a particular view of the world. Whose values will prevail
in public discourse? If "only" words were at stake, why is there so much
resistance?

Because the gender and communication interface impacts across such a
broad social, cultural, and political spectrum, I believe its study must be
truly cross-disciplinary. In writing this book I have necessarily had to poach
on the terrain of a great many other disciplines such as anthropology,
biology, communication, education, economics, history, literary criticism,
philosophy, psychology, and sociology. I was particularly concerned to
bring a linguistic perspective to bear on central issues in feminist theories.
I have learned a great deal by reading through the continually expanding
literature on gender and sexuality, written primarily by feminist scholars
over the past 25 years. Similarly, within the field of postcolonial studies,
I have benefited from the work of Edward Said, which has led me to see
more clearly how deeply embedded in racism and colonialism is the "master" narrative underlying the Western liberal humanist tradition.

Because modern linguistic theory is essentially a product of 19th-century
European scholarship, some notions basic to linguistic analysis, such as the
arbitrariness of the linguistic sign and theories of markedness, are also
embedded in this master narrative of masculinist science. Writing this book
has been a fascinating, yet sometimes depressing, experience. Although I
was well aware of the more obvious ways in which language has discriminated against women as well as how the discipline of linguistics has tended
to marginalize the study of language and gender, I was at times surprised
at how deeply ingrained such prejudice is in the intellectual discourses and
metaphors of the Western and other traditions.

The limitations of this viewpoint lead me to reject essentialism and to
adopt a rather broad definition of feminism that goes beyond the subject
of women. An examination of bipolar categories such as *men* and *women*
is necessary, but does not exhaust the issue. The categories are not the

ultimate loci of experience reducible to some essence, but represent changing subjectivities over time and space. In much of the linguistic research on language and gender linguists have looked for correlations between sets of people pre-grouped into male–female and other categories (such as social class, ethnicity, etc.) and features of language (e.g., vocabulary, pronunciation, etc.) as well as language use (e.g., politeness). This approach has limited explanatory power because it starts with the categories of male and female as fixed and stable givens rather than as varying constructs themselves in need of explanation. The standard sociolinguistic account of the relationship between language and society often seems to suggest, even if only implicitly, that language reflects already existing social identities rather than constructs them. There is a lot more to the study of language and gender than that.

As far as feminist theories are concerned, I believe the way forward in discussions of women's equality, and so forth, lies in moving away from sexual polarization. Here I align myself with scholars such as Sandra Bem (1993), Judith Butler (1990), and others who have taken a constructivist view of gender. Gender is above all dynamic and changes in response to cultural and historical forces. Gender is doing and not just being. Even though our culture treats the gender identities of male and female as if they were essentially real and stable components of personal identity, we are never passive victims of culture or history.

Finally, I am aware of the dilemma faced by many gender scholars of having their work dismissed as "unscientific" because it appears to have clear political implications and objectives. As one man wrote to the *Times Higher Education Supplement* (Feb. 18, 1994): "Gender studies, women's studies, feminist writers etc. are all faces of an essentially political agenda which should no longer be treated as a serious academic discipline." I accept the charge that those of us interested in gender issues have a political agenda. Feminism, however defined, is a political position. It would be lack of a political agenda that would be intellectually suspect, and not to acknowledge one, which is dishonest—hence my statement of my position in the above paragraphs. Like E. Jane Burns (1993, p.xi) I would say that my interest in this topic is not purely theoretical but also "personal and political." I do not accept the accusation, however, that personal and political commitment to a topic means it cannot be treated as a serious academic discipline. There is a double standard at work here that must be acknowledged: Criticizing the status quo is seen as political but accepting it is not.

Susan Douglas (1994) summed up well how I myself feel when she pointed to the ambivalence toward femininity and feminism she felt: "Pulled in opposite directions—told we were equal, yet told we were subordinate; told we could change history, yet told we were trapped by history—we got the bends at an early age, and we have never gotten rid of them" (p. 9). In this book I've tried to get rid of some of my bends. I hope others will find it "unbending" too, but not in the conventional meaning of the term as dogmatic and inflexible. I do not expect all readers to agree with me!

ACKNOWLEDGMENTS

Some of the material I include here comes from a series of lectures and practical classes I gave on the topic of language and gender at Oxford in Michaelmas Term 1993 and Hilary Term 1994. In preparing these sessions I was greatly aided by consulting the Language and Gender Syllabi Collection edited by Elizabeth Hume and Bonnie McElhinny and published by the Linguistic Society of America's Committee on the Status of Women. The collection contains 26 syllabi from courses on language and gender offered in a variety of departments, including linguistics, anthropology, English, and education. From them I got many references, ideas, and material for exercises.

I am also grateful to a number of colleagues such as Bernd Heine for the Ewe examples in chapter 4, and to Lou Burnard of the Oxford University Computing Services for help with the British National Corpus, an early pilot version of which I have used to collect some of the material in chapters 4 and 5. I would also like to thank Judi Amsel for her assistance and her comments on an early version of chapter 9.

To facilitate the use of the book as a textbook, I have tried to avoid cluttering the text itself with detailed citations and I have avoided footnotes altogether. I have mentioned some additional sources of reading at the end of each chapter and given full bibliographical details in the references at the end of the book. In the text itself, I have used specific dates after the names of scholars for whom I have cited more than one reference in the bibliography in order to make clear which particular work provided the source for what I say. Where I have quoted directly or paraphrased a particular point, I have given the date and page number in the text. Each chapter ends with discussion questions and exercises, many of which involve readers either in collecting their own data for analysis or analyzing data.

—*Suzanne Romaine*

1

Doing Gender

Language is part of man's nature, he did not create it. We are always inclined to imagine naively that there was some period in the beginning when a fully evolved man discovered someone else like him, equally evolved, and between the two of them language gradually took shape. This is pure fiction. We can never reach man separated from language, and we can never see him inventing it. We can never reach man reduced to himself, and thinking up ways of conceptualizing the existence of someone else. What we find in the world are men endowed with speech, speaking to other men, and language gives the clue to the very definition of man. (Benveniste, 1971, p. 224)

DOING AND DISPLAYING GENDER

Our biological sex is determined at birth by factors beyond our control, yet being born male or female is probably the most important feature of our lives. The first question generally asked about a new born baby is whether it is a boy or girl, just as the first thing we notice when we see someone for the first time is whether the person is male or female. Almost every official form we fill out requires us to say whether we are male or female. Physical appearance, dress, behavior, and language provide some of the most important means of identifying ourselves daily to others as male or female. When we see a baby dressed in pink with a frilly bonnet, we conclude it must be a girl. Even though unisex fashions have made gender boundaries increasingly less rigid, gender is still one of the most visible human traits; 80% of U.S. 2-year-olds can readily distinguish males from females on the basis of purely cultural cues like hairstyle and clothing.

1

These clues are *gender displays or indexes*, whose surface manifestations may alter culturally and historically. Such displays may also be intertwined with and reinforced by other distinctions—for example, titles like *Miss* or *Mrs.*, which mark someone not only as female, but also as single or married, or by different items of clothing worn by girls/boys, or married/unmarried women. Among the Bedouins of the Egyptian western desert, for example, married women wear black veils and red belts, whereas unmarried girls wear kerchiefs on their heads and around their waists.

Gender is thus an inherently communicative process. Not only do we communicate gender in these ways, but we also "do it" with our words. Because we construct and enact gender largely through discourse, this book is about the crucial role of language in particular and communication more generally in doing gender and displaying ourselves as gendered beings. If we hear someone talking about children named *Tommy* and *Jimmy*, we assume they are boys. When we read about scientists in the newspapers, most of us still have mental images of men, even though there are now many women scientists. When we hear someone describe a color as "baby blue," "carnation pink," "lavender," or "mauve," we imagine the speaker to be a woman rather than a man. When most people read a newspaper headline *Doctor seduced patient*, they assume the doctor is male and the patient, female (see chap. 4 for further analysis). When you read the opening epigraph to this chapter about language being part of "man's nature," did you think of women being included or excluded? Did "man" create language?

The use of the term *man* instead of a more gender-neutral term such as *human(s)*, *humanity*, *people*, and so on obscures women's contributions to language and its evolution. Yet even seemingly gender-neutral terms such as *person, member of society*, and so forth are often still interpreted as masculine by default, as in this example from sociolinguist William Labov (1972a, p. xiii), where he urged linguists to turn their attention to studying "language as it is used in everyday life by members of the social order, that vehicle of communication in which they argue with their wives, joke with their friends, and deceive their enemies." Nowadays, such usage would be called "sexist" and many publishing houses have specific guidelines telling authors how to avoid language that either excludes women or stereotypes them in negative ways. These are conscious choices we as language users can make, and thanks to several decades of feminist reform, decisions not to make them increasingly stand out. During O. J. Simpson's trial in Los Angeles the courtroom paused to consider whether a male defense attorney was being sexist when he accused a female prosecuting attorney of acting "hysterical" (see chap. 2). Conversely, to accuse a male of hysteria (or being a wimp), as the press did George Bush in his unsuccessful campaign for reelection to the presidency in 1992, was to suggest he was effeminate and therefore unfit for the office. In many areas of public life so-called "gender-neutral" language now prevails. University departments now have *chairpersons* or *chairs*, and some restaurants have *waitpersons* or *waitrons* (see chap. 10). Challenging naming practices symbolic of male possession and dominance of women, such as titles like *Mrs./Miss*, are part of women's linguistic revolt.

The claim that language is sexist is by no means new. In 1895 Elizabeth Cady Stanton rewrote the Bible to highlight the unjust ways in which women were spoken and written about. Nearly a hundred years later Dale Spender (1980a) brought the association between language and patriarchy to the media's attention with the claim that language is man-made. Similarly, Robin Lakoff's (1975) arguments about the political implications of what she called "women's language" put the study of women and language on the map. Lakoff showed how language served to keep women in their place. Women inherit their subordinate place as each new generation inherits sexist words. Dictionaries, grammars, and even artificial languages have been made primarily by men. What if language were "woman-made" instead of man-made? (See chap. 10 for discussion of feminist dictionaries.)

There is still no agreement on the question of whether language is sexist, and if so, wherein the origins of its sexism lie, or on the directions reform should take. Languages may vary in terms of the amount and type of sexism they display, which implies they will require different types of reform. Although English-speaking feminists have paid critical attention to language, it has been at the very heart of the French feminist debate. If the world is constructed and given meaning through language and language is "man-made," then our history, philosophy, government, laws, and religion are products of a male way of perceiving and organizing the world. Because this knowledge has been transmitted for centuries, it appears "natural," "objective," a "master" discourse beyond question. Language thus holds the key to challenging and changing male hegemony.

If women's oppression has deep linguistic roots, then any and all representations, whether of women, men, or any other group, are embedded first in language, and then in politics, culture, economics, history, and so on. This is at least one interpretation I make of Donna Haraway's (1991, p. 3) claim that "grammar is politics by other means." Howard Bloch (1991, p. 4) pointed to the central role of language when he said, "misogyny is a way of speaking about, as distinct from doing something to women." Within the approach I take here, I would claim, unlike Bloch, that speaking *about* as well as *to* women in a misogynistic way is equivalent to *doing* something harmful to them. The harm done does not need to be physical, but can arise from the creation of a hostile verbal environment. Indeed, this view now receives support from legal definitions of the term *sexual harassment* (see chaps. 7 and 8). In a 1984 report on women in the courts Robert N. Wilentz, then Chief Justice of New Jersey, noted:

There's no room for the funny joke and the not-so-funny joke, there's no room for conscious, inadvertent, sophisticated, clumsy, or any other kind of gender bias, and there's certainly no room for gender bias that affects substantive rights. There's no room because it hurts and it insults. It hurts . . . psychologically and economically. (cited in Troemel-Ploetz, 1991, pp. 455–456)

Yet we needn't speak in words in order to do harm. A popular perfume advertisement showed a woman wearing a miniskirt and high heels (and presumably also the fragrance being advertised). The caption read: "Make a statement without saying a word." The proverbial expression about a picture being worth a thousand words applies here. The ad glamorizes the woman as a sexual object, suggesting her availability, and how her attractiveness can be enhanced if she but wears the right perfume. The ad also conveys the message that a woman's appearance and her scent communicate her sexual intent. She does not need to say anything: Her consent is implied in the way she dresses and the perfume she is being urged to put on. She has "asked for it" without saying anything (see chaps. 8 and 9).

In focusing attention on gender as a dynamic process that people index, do, display, communicate, or perform, gender itself has become a verb. This active view of gender is also consistent with bell hooks's preference for talking about "women's movement" (or "feminist movement") without the definite article, rather than "the women's movement," to emphasize activity and becoming rather than static being. Likewise, Judith Butler's (1993) notion of performance is central to the idea of gender as something we do (see chap. 2). Both talk and actions can be gendered. Although we sometimes think of communication in a narrow sense as being focused on language in its spoken, written, or even signed forms, my approach in this book takes a much broader view. Conversations, newspapers, television, advertisements, scientific and academic journals, literature, popular music, and movies are all forms of communication that send messages about as well as shape our understandings of gender. They are in effect all languages or discourses of gender involving more than words; they may include gestures or "body language," images, and ways of dressing.

When we see or hear gender being indexed or displayed through any channel of communication, our stereotypes may be activated. Gender stereotypes are sets of beliefs about the attributes of men or women, such as that men are stronger and more aggressive, women are passive, talk more than men, and so on. Stereotypes are often associated with and not easily separated from other salient variables such as race, class, culture, age, context, and so forth. Stereotypes about how men and women speak reveal insights into our attitudes about what men and women are like or what we think they are supposed to be like. Perceived gender differences are often the result of these stereotypes about such differences, rather than the result of the actual existence of real differences. The linguistic basis for the media's accusation that George Bush was a wimp rested on the claim that he used words stereotyped as "feminine," such as "splash" of coffee and "having a chat." The image of the gossiping woman shows how easy it is to confuse expectations with actual behavior. How is the supposedly overly talkative woman to be reconciled with women's claims that they have been silenced? Who really talks more: men or women?

Much of the early research on language and gender devoted a great deal of energy to addressing the issue of "women's language" using laundry lists of specific linguistic features such as hedging (e.g., it's *kind of* late, *you know*), the use of tag questions (e.g., we're going at 6 o'clock, *aren't we?*), and so on, believed to be tied to women's subordinate status. This approach is doomed to naiveté and circularity unless it acknowledges that the same linguistic features can, when used by different persons in different contexts and cultures, often mean very different things.

This is so because different cultures vary in their expectations about what it means to be a man or woman. Western societies have a long tradition of handbooks written by both men and women showing what women had to do to be good housewives and mothers, or what it meant to be a gentleman. Women today are still faced with a barrage of advice from women's magazines, TV talk shows, and popular books. Certainly in the 19th century gender determined more of an individual's options than it does today, but even now gender can affect our expectations, as well as our activities, manners, and almost everything else.

Although language is central to our constructions of the meaning of gender, much of language is ambiguous and depends on context for its interpretation, a factor far more important than gender. On closer examination, there are few, if any, context-independent gender differences in language. In some instances men talk more than women, whereas in other situations women talk more then men. As I show in chapter 6, silence can be both a sign of oppression and resistance to it. The same words can take on different meanings and significance depending on who uses them in a particular context. Imagine the words "How about meeting for a drink later, honey?" said by a male customer to a waitress he does not know, or said by a woman to her husband as they talk over their schedules for the day. Such examples suggest that we need to seek our explanations for gender differences in terms of the communicative functions expressed by certain forms used in particular contexts by specific speakers. They also point to the complexity involved in reforming sexist language. We cannot simply propose to ban words like *sweetie* or *honey* from public communication because they can be construed as offensive in some contexts. Some words such as *lady* (and even *gender* itself) are in certain contexts euphemisms, terms coined to avoid embarrassment at reference to the unmentionable (i.e., *woman* and *sex*), whereas others are instances of public name-calling (see chap. 5). What we must try to change are the conventional uses of language in sexist ways. Otherwise, we get trapped in a circular argument: Men have power because men define meanings and men define meanings because men have power.

Many questions come to mind about how everyday talk and action get gendered. From a linguistic perspective, we must consider at the very least how sex and gender are actually marked in language (see chaps. 3, 4, and 5), how men and women speak across a range of different settings (see chap. 6), how children acquire whatever linguistic differences we may find (see chap. 7), how language can be sexist and how it can be reformed (see chap. 10). Many studies have identified systematic male–female differences in many languages. These range from differences in vocabulary, to differences in linguistic forms (e.g., phonology and syntax), to whole communicative styles, such as politeness, directness, and silence.

Although I give English more detailed treatment than other languages, I look at evidence from a number of languages, including other European languages such as French, German, Italian, the Nordic languages, as well as a variety of non-Western ones such as Japanese, Chinese, and Dyirbal, and even invented languages like Láadan. Japanese, for instance, is often presented as an example of a language showing extraordinary sensitivity to the social context in which it is used. There is also a long tradition of belief that Japanese has a true women's language, going back to studies of the language used by ladies of the imperial court. Much of the discussion focused on certain words having to do with food, clothing, and other domestic concerns. For example, the male word for *rice* is *mesi* and the female word *gugo*. These forms are believed to have spread out from the court into more general usage among Japanese women. Yet alleged differences in male and female speech represent only part of the picture. We must also look at how men and women are spoken about, how they are portrayed in cultural discourses in the wider sense I referred to earlier, and how ways of speaking and acting fit into cultural beliefs about the roles of women and men.

GENDER IN CROSS-DISCIPLINARY PERSPECTIVE

It is no accident that many of those engaged in the study of language and gender are in fact not linguists by training, but practitioners of other disciplines. We can see from this range of questions I have raised that gender is so pervasive a feature of our everyday lives that we cannot study it comprehensively without reference to a number of scientific disciplines such as anthropology, biology, communication, education, economics, feminist theory, history, linguistics, literary criticism, philosophy, psychology, and sociology. Although each field of study has made important contributions to our understanding of the complexity of gender, it is all too easy to lose sight of the whole picture. We must work to make the connections between these different disciplines and not simply try to graft gender onto already existing fields of research, as suggested by titles of countless books such as *Gender and X*, where X can be anything ranging from anthropology to history, race, language, and so forth. Such titles suggest an additive rather than integrative perspective. In order to be coherent theoretically, the study of gender must involve a dialogue across disciplines, and that is the perspective I have adopted in this book.

Each of the disciplines I mentioned has naturally had its own concerns and tackled the study of gender in different ways. Anthropology, for instance, has been devoted to the study of cross-cultural differences in human behavior, which has led to skepticism about the extent to which men are "naturally" stronger, more aggressive and dominant than women. Indeed, one of the best ways to examine the interaction of society with gender is to look at other cultures with quite different arrangements for the sexes where the arrangements are regarded as equally as "natural" as our own. Despite prevailing beliefs in Western culture that have conceived of male superiority and dominance in both religious and scientific terms, male dominance is not universal or inevitable. There are both human and animal groups among which neither males dominate females, nor females dominate males. There are also societies in which women have both political and economic power, and cultures where there is minimal differentiation of gender roles. In short, there is an astonishing variety of family forms and child-raising arrangements.

If biology alone were responsible for behavior patterns, then we would not find such great cultural diversity. Being male or female is done differently in different cultures. In her work in Papua New Guinea, for example, Margaret Mead (1949) observed both Arapesh men and women behaving in a way we would think of as feminine by western standards. Other cultures are much less gender polarized than our own. Clifford Geertz (1995) described Balinese society as "unisex" and "egalitarian." Men and women wear almost identical clothing, and even though each sex has different tasks, the male/female distinction is largely irrelevant in everyday life. Within Balinese cosmology male and female creative forces stand in complete and perfect unity within the supreme deity, Siwa.

Balinese society contrasts sharply with our own, where both religion and science have sought to provide support for long-standing cultural beliefs that people are either male or female, but not both or neither (see chap. 2). Some cultures readily allow individuals to assume gender identities opposite to their biological sex. On Pohnpei in Micronesia, Ward (1979) described how after a teenage girl named Maria began to behave like a boy, family and community met and held a feast to declare her a boy. They cut her hair, dressed her as a boy, and called her Mario. The Tewa people of the U.S. Southwest recognize a category of individuals labeled *kwidó*, who have androgynous personalities. Within Sambia society in New Guinea engaging in what many Westerners would call homosexual sexual activity is considered part of normal male sexuality (see chap. 8). A preoccupation with sexual performance in Western culture has made outward erotic behavior the basis for the dichotomy between heterosexual and homosexual as identities. Yet the sexual self defined externally is not necessarily the same as the internally identified gendered self (see chaps. 2 and 11 for some of the linguistic consequences). Morover, the self can be composed of multiple identities, such as woman, feminist, Native American, and so on.

Even though a person's membership in other categories such as ethnicity, religion, nationality, and such is generally much more ambiguous, some-times even readily changeable, and not always so openly displayed, most of us have grown up believing everyone is male or female. Monique Wittig shocked some delegates to an international women's conference when she declared she was not a woman but a lesbian. A lesbian, she said, had no sex and was beyond the binary categories of man and woman. In her 1981 autobiography, *Né homme, comment je suis devenue femme* ('Born man, how I became woman'), Brigitte Martel told of her experience as a trans-sexual male who became female. The French title underscores her shifting gender allegiance in a way that the English translation does not fully convey (see chaps. 2 and 11 for further examples of this kind). The past participle meaning 'born' appears in its masculine form (*né*) reflecting her previous existence as a man, whereas the past participle 'become' (*devenue*) is marked as feminine through the addition of an *-e* (see chap. 3 for further discussion of how French marks gender).

Although a broader view of sex and gender would recognize a continuum, the polar opposites of male and female have defined the basic categories. Gays, lesbians, and transsexuals have ideas about their gender identity that defy mainstream ideology that the categories are binary. There is still very little agreement on what constitutes the gender categories we label as *man*, *woman, lesbian*, and so on. The fragmentation within the women's move-ment over issues such as sexual orientation, lesbianism, and so forth raises questions about what feminism is, whom it claims to represent, and what counts as "women's experience," if indeed such a term is meaningful.

These examples suggest that our readiness to see "reality" naturally carved into male and female as polar opposites is culturally and linguistically conditioned. Gender is more a cultural performance than a natural fact: doing rather than being. Yet biology cannot be totally dismissed as a factor in the production and reproduction of gender. The biological division into male and female is found in humans as well as many other species. Clearly there are some biological bases for defining men and women, although scientists are still not sure of the extent of biological differences (see chap. 2).

Despite its contributions to a cross-cultural understanding of variability in human sexuality, anthropology has only just begun to tackle what Edwin Ardener (1975a, 1975b) called "the problem of women." For a long time most anthropological research was men's work, based on the study of men by men. Claude Lévi-Strauss's study of the Bororo done in the 1930s provides a striking example of the invisibility of women to many of the founding fathers of anthropology. He noted how "the whole village left next day in about thirty canoes, leaving us alone with the woman and children in abandoned houses." As modern readers we may wonder how it can happen that a "whole" village can be said to have left when the women and children are still there, or that the European anthropologists are described as "alone," despite the presence of the women and children, or indeed how the houses can be thought of as "abandoned" if they are filled with the women and children. Anna Livia Brawn (1995, p. 117), who cited this example, pointed out how Lévi-Strauss made it clear three times in one sentence that he did not consider women and children to be fully human.

The availability of women as subjects of investigation was often limited in some cultures, where women were kept separate from men. Even where anthropologists could have consulted women, however, they tended to dismiss their information. Thus, in trying to understand other cultures, many anthropologists overlooked at least half the "members of society." Even one of the most important journals in the discipline still carried the title *Man* when I began writing this book in 1993! Moreover, I find it telling that Ardener labeled this failure on the part of male anthropologists to include women's voices "the problem of women"; why not call it "the problem of or with anthropology/anthropologists," or indeed, "the problem of men," or "the problem *with* men"?

Culture has also been prominent in the work of sociolinguist Deborah Tannen (1990a), who explained differences in male/female conversational style as the result of men and women being members of different cultures. Hence male/female conversation becomes cross-cultural communication, and is potentially fraught with misunderstandings (see chap. 6).

Nevertheless, gender is not just about biological and cultural difference; it is also about power. Much of this power and symbolic domination is achieved and validated through talk across a range of contexts, for example, at home, in school, in court, in the workplace, in academic journals, and so on. Crucial decisions are often arrived at on the basis of verbal interaction in interviews, meetings, and other public encounters. Society is composed of competing discourses speaking from different perspectives and articulating different points of view. In the words of Russian literary critic Mikhail

Bakhtin (1929/1973), society is *heteroglossic* (i.e., has different languages or voices). Those in power determine whose version of reality prevails, whose ways of behaving and speaking will be seen as normal, and whose ways deviant. The maxims of the dominant culture are presented as timeless truths of human experience. All of us are taught in school to accept the beliefs of the dominant culture. In this way male values become the values of society at large. Our ideas about what is "normal" are deeply embedded in linguistic practices. Men have the right to be referred to as *writers* or *doctors*. Women who occupy these professions are marked with special titles such as *lady/woman doctor* or *female/woman writer*. Because language is connected with the construction of our identity, questions about identity and self-definition have been at the forefront of women's movement and have focused on the right to be named as part of the struggle for self-determination. Women wish to decide how to represent themselves.

Difference tends to be defined negatively and carries with it assumptions about a hierarchy of traits associated with "Ourselves" versus "Others." Women share in common with other subordinated groups the fact that they have been persistently seen as Others (see chap. 2), for whom the traditional remedy has been assimilation to the norms of the dominant group. All subordinate groups in society, such as the working-class and ethnic and racial minorities, share similar problems. Their ways of communicating and behaving are described as deviant and illogical in relation to some other norms of behaving, which define the socially powerful. The language of the dominant group is the standard against which all other speech forms are measured. Male privilege sustains the myth that male talk is not gendered, just as those who speak Oxford English claim that it is others who speak with accents.

Whatever singles out a subordinate group will be used to justify treating its members as inferior. In this way differences, whether real or imagined, get politicized. Lack of confidence, hesitancy, and silence, for instance, are all familiar traits of oppressed and subordinated groups in their encounters with a more powerful majority. Some White educators, for example, have said that Black children are "nonverbal." Deborah Cameron (1990a) drew an analogy with sociologist of language Basil Bernstein's use (1973) of the term *restricted code* to describe the language of children of non-White and working-class origins. In both cases the judgments arose at least partly from lack of access to the so-called elaborated code, or the standard. However, if we accepted such negative beliefs about the inferiority of the language of women, Blacks, the working class, and so on, then we would have to conclude that there is something wrong with the way the majority of people speak.

Within sociolinguistics, Charles Ferguson (1959/1972) coined the term *diglossia* to refer to a situation in a multilingual community where each language or variety serves a specialized function and is used for particular purposes. An example can be taken from Arabic-speaking countries such as Egypt, in which the language used at home may be a local version of Arabic. The language recognized publicly, however, is modern standard Arabic, which takes many of its normative rules from the classical Arabic of the *Koran*. The standard language is used for "high" functions such as giving a lecture, reading, writing, or broadcasting, while the home variety is reserved for "low" functions such as interacting with friends at home. The high (H) and low (L) varieties differ not only in grammar, phonology and vocabulary, but also with respect to a number of social characteristics, namely, function, prestige, literary heritage, acquisition, standardization, and stability. L is typically acquired at home as a mother tongue. Its main uses are in familial and familiar interactions. H, on the other hand, is learned later through schooling and supported by institutions outside the home. The separate domains in which H (public/official/formal) and L (private/domestic/informal) are acquired immediately provide them with separate institutional support systems. Entry to formal institutions such as school and government requires knowledge of H. Speakers regard H as superior to L in a number of respects. In some cases H is regarded as the only "real" version of a particular language. There is also a strong tradition of formal grammatical study and standardization associated with H.

In other instances of diglossia two completely different languages are involved, such as in Peru, where colonialism has imposed Spanish onto an indigenous and largely Quechua-speaking society. Because more men than women are bilingual, Penelope Harvey (1994) found that men's greater access to the new prestige language gave them far more autonomy and power than women. Women are silent at public, formal meetings conducted in Spanish because they know only Quechua or have extremely limited Spanish skills.

By substituting "women's language" (or, for that matter, the language used by any subordinate group) for the low variety and men's for the high, we can see the relevance of the analogy (see chap. 10 for another example). Women have generally had less access to the contexts and institutions where the more prestigious H variety/language is acquired. Even though sociolinguists have often found women's speech to be closer to the standard in Western urban societies, women have still generally been excluded from public discourse with its formal styles of speaking and writing such as political speech making, conducting of religious services and media broadcasting (see chap. 6). It is a myth that language is equally available to all. Moreover, in societies with inequality between men and women, whatever women do will be devalued. Hence, in Western culture, sociolinguists have documented the indirectness, standardness, and conservatism of women's speech, while in Madagascar women speak directly and are innovative. In both cases, however, women's language is seen as deviant. Societies define prestige in relation to socially and sexually dominant groups. Women in neither culture participate fully in public ceremonial domains in which H is spoken.

The onus is therefore on women to become bilingual, just as it is on less powerful groups more generally. English speakers in Wales do not need to learn Welsh, but Welsh speakers cannot do without English. So women have had to talk like men in order to be heard. Yet even when women adopt men's voices, they can be silenced with ridicule (see chap. 6).

This example shows that what is important is not the differences themselves but how they are perceived in a particular society, how they fit into a society's beliefs and stereotypes about men and women. Male dominance has often been supposed universal because we tend to equate dominance with roles played in public and official life. Men's location and activity in the public rather than domestic sphere has defined society as masculine. Hence, anthropologists such as Lévi-Strauss found nothing remarkable in defining the locus of their investigations into culture as synonymous with what men do. Women may be publicly represented as subordinate but still wield considerable political and economic power. Yet the organization of life into domestic or private and public or official domains of power so fundamental to modern Western society reflects a male perspective on social life.

Language has helped to gender the way we think about space; men's space is public, in the workplace, whereas women's place is private and in the home. This difference is encoded discursively in expressions such as *working mother, businessman, housewife,* and so on, making it easier to accept as "natural" the exclusion of women from public life (see chap. 4). In Japanese these views are embodied in the terms used by husbands and wives to refer to one another. A married woman is called *Okusan* 'Mrs. Interior', signifying that her place is in the home. Japanese men call their wives *kanai* 'house insider'. Women speak of their husbands as *shujin* or *danna* or the more informal *teishu,* which means 'master of an inn or tea house'. These terms of address reflect the traditional wisdom embodied in two English proverbs: *A man's home is his castle,* and *A woman's place is in the home.* Traditional norms dictate that the husband is the bread-winner, whereas the wife is the bread baker. This is reflected historically in the Old English words *hla:fweard,* 'loafkeeper', and *hlaefdige* 'loaf-kneader', which became modern English 'lord' and 'lady', respectively (see chap. 4 for further discussion of pairs like *lord/lady*).

Significantly, as late as 1979, a series of letters to the editor of one of Japan's major national newspapers questioned the propriety of women reading newspapers in public while riding on trains, subways, and such. Because the subject matter of newspapers concerns public affairs, which women have traditionally had nothing to do with, some writers felt that female passengers should confine themselves to reading paperback novels or magazines while on public transport. When Margaret Thatcher became Prime Minister, the media routinely identified her as a housewife. Although Thatcher was running her own household at the time, she had also served as a Cabinet Minister and could just as well have been referred to in that capacity. It is hard to imagine a similar context in which a male would be referred to with no mention of his public accomplishments or position (see chap. 4).

Discrimination against women is built into such divisions between the workplace and home, between production and reproduction, all of which are reinforced by the way we talk about them. Not only in Western cultures, but in other parts of the world, there has been a persistent misrecognition of women's work as somehow less than work. The dichotomy is reinforced linguistically by the distinction between *housework* and *work*. Only work done to produce a profit in the public sector counts as work and goes by the name of *work*. The "work" women do at home is invisible (or what Ivan Illich, 1982, called "shadow work"), unpaid, not counted in the gross national product, and goes by the special name of *housework*. Men have not only control of the marketplace, where the "real" work gets done, but also control over women's sexuality and their labor in the home. In France, until quite recently bakers' wives who sold bread all day long were classified as "unemployed" and received no pension. Their labor was expected as part of their wifely duties and therefore did not officially count.

Feminist analyses have pointed out how housework makes the modern capitalist economy feasible because it frees the man to work in the public sector by relieving him of domestic work, which has to be done and which would otherwise have to be paid for. Because women on average work 20 hours more a week than men, sociologist Arlie Hochschild (1989) referred to the "second shift" that women put in at home. The cumulative effect of the work women do is that they produce time for men. In Western culture, time of course is money.

Feminist research of the last few decades has been responsible for its critical stance toward gender as an analytical category. Indeed, the very term *gender* in the contemporary senses in which I have been using it in this chapter is a product of this research; previously, it was seldom used outside linguistic discussions of noun classification (see chap. 3). Now many universities offer courses on the topic of gender, gender and language, and so forth. Some have established programs and award degrees in a field variously called "women's studies," "feminist studies," or "gender studies." The choice of names for such new programs of study may reflect differences in content and focus. While I was working on this book the University of Oxford decided to establish a master's (!) degree in women's studies from 1996. Although *gender* is not synonymous with *female*, it is sometimes construed that way. Similarly, feminism is often taken to be synonymous with the study of women, rather than constituting a more encompassing inquiry into constructions of femaleness as well as maleness (and much more, in my view; see chap. 2).

Like any new field, the study of gender has faced opposition from critics who have tried to dismiss it as an empty discipline, motivated by politics rather than scholarship, as I said in my preface. It is worth remembering, however, that even in the 19th century the study of English language and literature was not considered a legitimate discipline at the University of Oxford. James Murray, editor of the *Oxford English Dictionary*, actually credited the women's movement directly for the appearance of English studies at Oxford in the 19th century. The enlargement of the state education system made the classics-based curriculum increasingly unsuitable for the many new pupils to be encompassed within it. Women and the working classes of both sexes would find the classics too intellectually demanding and needed an "easier" subject. What is deemed to be worthy of study is always subject to political interests. Universities have traditionally been organized in terms of disciplines and departments with little overlap, rather than in terms of cross- or interdisciplinary programs. This too has been responsible for lack of a truly integrative perspective.

Many aspects of gender are more often studied by women than men. When writing his book on gender, Ivan Illich, for instance, found himself in a "double ghetto." He was unable to use many traditional words because they were sexist. Never before had so many colleagues and friends tried to dissuade him from his work with suggestions that it was trivial and ambiguous. Talk about women was not for men. Within sociolinguistics both mainstream men and women have taken up the cause of working-class speech, the languages of minority groups, and so on as central problems of the discipline, but women's words are still studied largely by women. Talk about women's talk is not for men either. In a similar vein, anthropologist Edwin Ardener (1975b, p. 20) recalled a female colleague saying "no anthropological book with 'women' in the title sells." Worthwhile intellectual discourse has been assumed to be male (see chap. 11 for similar reactions to feminist science fiction).

Penelope Eckert and Sally McConnell-Ginet (1992) pointed out that the effect of a new research focus on women has perpetuated a long-standing view of men as normal, and women as deviant. Indeed, much of the early work on gender focused on finding differences and highlighted, in particular, women's deviance from a supposed male norm. There are dangers involved in looking at women's language and behavior as having special status. In the next chapter I look at some of the repercussions of this thinking in the fields of biology, linguistics, philosophy, and psychology. A good illustration from the field of linguistics is philologist Otto Jespersen's inclusion of a chapter in his book on language (1922) devoted to "The Woman." There was no corresponding chapter on "The Man." The assumption is that men's language is simply language and requires no special discussion. Since then the focus has moved from "women's language" to a broader consideration of gender and language. The titles of more recently published books and collections reflect this change in emphasis. For example, Jennifer Coates called her 1988 book *Women, Men, and Language* (similarly, Joan Swann, 1992, wrote about *Girls, Boys, and Language*); Dennis Baron (1986) called his book *Grammar and Gender*. This shift reorients the field away from documenting women's supposed deviance from male norms, not merely to a study of differences and what they mean but to understanding interactions between men and woman. The concepts of both masculinity and femininity are in need of critical evaluation, as I show in the next chapter.

THE WORLD OF WORDS: COMMUNICATING GENDER THROUGH LANGUAGE

I have already mentioned many of the reasons why language is so central to the study of gender. As my opening epigraph says, "We can never reach 'man' separated from language. . . . language gives the clue to the very definition of man." Language is a uniquely human trait. When children learn to talk, they learn to create a linguistic sense of self. This self is gendered from a very early age. The conventional approach to meaning within linguistics is that we use language to describe the world, but we use it to do much more than that. With language we bring different worlds into being. I have already given many examples of how language plays an active role in the symbolic positioning of women as inferior to men. It both constructs and perpetuates that reality, often in obvious ways, but at other times in subtle and invisible ones. The verbally represented world is gendered.

Language is the primary means through which we understand the world and our place within it. "In the beginning was the word" (Genesis 1:1). It is the world of words that creates the world of things and ideas. We do things with words. The Bible relates how even before God created Eve, he brought all the animals to Adam to "see what he would call them: and whatsoever Adam called every living creature, that was the name thereof" (Genesis 2:19). If the world is brought into being through acts of naming, then naming a thing is the first stage in appropriating it and assuming power over it (see chap. 5). Language can alter reality rather than simply describe it. When a minister or judge says "I now pronounce you man and wife" to a man and woman legally entitled to be married, they do indeed become for legal purposes husband and wife. Persons with the appropriate authority to perform a marriage ceremony do more than just describe a situation when they utter those words. They actually perform the wedding. Saying so makes it so. Note too how recent changes in laws in states such as Hawaii recognize so-called *same-sex marriage*. Here the special term marks the union as different from our conventional understanding of *marriage*.

Linguists, however, have paid far more attention to the descriptive rather than to the more performative, social functions of language. In doing so, they have emphasized the basic arbitrariness of the linguistic sign. In other words, there is no physical correspondence between linguistic signals that make up a name and the things they refer to. The animal that English speakers call *pig* is what speakers of the Manam language in Papua New Guinea call *boro*. Conversely, the Danish word for 'girl' (*pige*) sounds very similar to the English word for 'pig'. Nevertheless, we all have a deeply ingrained feeling of inherent aptness in the words of our own language and that a particular word expresses exactly how we feel or think about something. As Aldous Huxley's character Old Rowley commented while pointing to swine wallowing in the mud, "Rightly is they called pigs" (Huxley, 1921). Yet the fact that other languages have completely different words shows that there is nothing in the words themselves bearing a necessary relationship to the animal.

If this principle of arbitrariness were absolute, what can we make of Dale Spender's (1980a) claim that English is a "man-made language" in which women are systematically marked as deviant and deficient? Moreover, other languages not related to English show similar patterns reflecting negative cultural beliefs about women (see chaps. 3, 4, and 5). Can it be accidental that language ignores and deprecates women, defines women as secondary to men, and names women's experiences as trivial or even denies their very existence?

Probably at one time or another we have all been lost for words to express a particular feeling or experience we have had. Betty Friedan (1963), founder of the National Organization for Women (NOW) and sometimes called the "mother of the modern women's movement" in the United States, raised the consciousness of women with her detailed discussion of what she called "the problem that has no name." More recently, she wrote (Friedan, 1981) of new problems that have no names. Although Friedan in 1963 was not primarily concerned with linguistic issues, her book underlined the inadequacy of language to name and discuss women's experiences. There are still no names for some of the problems Friedan discussed more than 30 years ago, but bringing them into people's consciousness by writing about them can be a liberating experience in itself (see chap. 9). Silence is itself a form of oppression. Women such as Mary Daly have created numerous terms for areas of female experience which have no names (see chap. 10). English has no expression corresponding to *virility* to refer to female potency. Elsie Clews Parsons observed that the sexual vocabulary of women was inadequate for discussing their own sexuality, let alone that of men. We see an interesting case of this in chapter 8.

Language can make social inequalities visible or invisible. As I have shown, some problems have been stigmatized as "women's problems" through the names given to them, such as the *feminization of poverty*. This label refers to the prediction that by the year 2000, 90% of all people living below the poverty line in the United States will be older women and young women with dependent children. Here only the name is new; the problem itself is old. Economist Claudia Goldin observed that poverty has always been feminized. Why do we not refer to it as the *masculinization of wealth*?

Language has surely been a significant rhetorical weapon in what Susan Faludi (1991) called the "backlash" against feminism. In the rhetorical battle about reproduction the stakes are high because all of women's aspirations and struggles for self-determination rest on having the right to decide whether and when to have children. The issue of women's reproductive freedom has thus been the target of the most severe backlash. Although communication between parties with conflicting views and interests is the first prerequisite for containment of conflict and the possibility of resolution, each side uses different language to stake a claim on a particular version of reality. The Mandate for Leadership II, a right-wing group opposed to women's rights, realized that

> the most important battle in the civil rights field has been for control of the language—especially, such words as "equality" and "opportunity." The secret to victory, whether in court or in congress, has been to control the definition of these terms. (Butler, Sanera, & Weinrod, 1984, p. 74)

A combination of slogans, advertising, and semantic obfuscation lies at the heart of the anti-abortion campaign. Anti-abortionists describe themselves as "pro-life" and "pro-family," whereas those who advocate women's right to abortion call themselves "pro-choice." By appropriating the positive member of an opposition between *pro* and *anti*, they want us to believe that if we don't agree with them, we are therefore against family and against life.

The New York Archdiocese of the Catholic Church proposed establishing a new order of nuns, to be called "Sisters of Life," who would devote themselves exclusively to opposing abortion. The Catholic Church promoted the slogan "The Natural Choice is Life," suggesting that proponents of abortion were advocating something unnatural. No doubt the church was very much aware that people would remember how advertisers had exploited the connection between popular products like Coca-Cola and the words *natural* and *life* in catchy slogans such as "Coke is natural" and "Coke adds life." Robin Lakoff (1992) pointed out how effective the juxtaposition of the words *life, natural,* and *choice* is. The slogan exploits the fact that these are among the words that provoke the strongest possible positive response in people (see chap. 9). Yet the choice supposedly offered by the slogan is a real choice only if abortion is freely available and women have the information necessary to make an decision as well as access to medical facilities.

Feminists who are "pro-choice" are branded as "child killers" and against the "rights of the fetus." They are accused of hating motherhood and children. Thus, their opposition to women's entry into the work force is called "pro-motherhood" and "pro-family," and anger at women's sexual freedom is called "pro-chastity." Conservatives lobby against women's rights by saying they are for "family rights." Some of the backlashers were women who claimed to be feminists or even "neofeminists." New labels were created to refer to "old feminists" who were overambitious career women. They became in the new rhetoric "macho feminists" or victims of what Betty Friedan called "female machismo."

Similarly, the Pro-Life Action League realized the strategic significance of language in the debate about abortion. When speaking to the press, its director Joseph Scheidler advised in his book *Closed: 99 Ways to Stop Abortion* (1985), use the word "baby" or "unborn child" instead of "fetus." "You don't have to surrender to their vocabulary. . . . They will start using your terms if you use them" (p. 53). The book urged opponents of abortion to be positive and to present themselves positively as being "for protection for the unborn," rather than negatively as "anti-abortionists." In slogans such as "Baby-killing is murder," the use of humanizing terms such as *baby* and *child* instead of technical, medical terms like *embryo* and *fetus* served to conceptualize abortion as equivalent to murder. Other slogans, such as "Everyone deserves to be born," presuppose and assert that the unborn are persons too, with rights equivalent to those who have already been born. Thus, the campaign sets up an equation where fetus = baby = person. In this rhetoric of reproduction, women's bodies are passive. They are simply the containers for new life. Scheidler, for instance, spoke of a woman's body after abortion as a "haunted house where the tragic death of a child took place." When the woman is portrayed as simply the vessel carrying the child, the child's rights as a person appear to be morally greater than those of the mother.

Conversely, by using technical terms from the medical domain such as *embryo* and *fetus,* those in favor of abortions could try to focus the discussion on abortion as a surgical procedure with no moral implications. Embryos and fetuses have no independent existence outside the mother's womb, whereas the term *baby* conjures up an image of a human being with a separate body and life of its own. Abortion then becomes a willful taking of the life of a child.

Another book advocated using the language feminists used in their fight for the right to their own bodies. "The baby has to have a choice" and "Equal rights for unborn children" became slogans at demonstrations. Margaret Sanger, birth control pioneer and founder of Planned Parenthood, was called a "whore" and an "adulteress" by Randall Terry, founder of Operation Rescue, dedicated to blockading abortion clinics, counseling women against abortion, and providing homes for unwed mothers. Terry opposed any form of contraception as well as sex education.

Slogans and slick rhetoric obscure what are actually complex and controversial issues about the meanings of the words *life* and *human*. As can be seen in the debate raging about euthanasia or assisted suicide and other terms such as *brain-dead*, the opposite end of the human life continuum is equally problematic: When does human life end? Who decides? The moral, medical, and legal ambiguities surrounding both the beginning and end of life are considerable. The anti-abortion campaign makes use of pictures of late-term fetuses, which are more clearly human like, although only 11% of abortions in the United States occur after the first trimester. Although a fetus during the first trimester of development has many of the characteristics of a baby, the central nervous system has not yet matured to the point where the fetus can feel pain or have other human-like qualities. If we define "life" in terms of possession of human-like qualities, then the fetus has not yet reached that stage, even though it has the capacity to do so.

Danet (1980) discussed a case involving a doctor convicted of manslaughter after he carried out a late abortion. Vocabulary became an explicit topic of negotiation and conflict in the trial. Although sentences such as *the fetus was aborted* and *the baby was murdered* can be used to describe the same event, the choice between them reflects crucial difference in world view that can have legal implications. If no "person" existed, then no crime of manslaughter could have occurred. Notice too how the passive construction does not name the person who commits the murder or performs the abortion (see chap. 4).

Both Robin Lakoff (1992) and George Lakoff (1996) pointed out semantic and moral inconsistencies in the conservative pro-life campaign. One would logically expect someone who is "pro-life" to also be in favor of tighter gun control laws, to be against the death penalty, to oppose war, and possibly even to defend animal rights. Yet most conservatives share none of these causes, which also aim to preserve life. It is at the very least inconsistent to be against abortion, but at the same time not provide people with the information and medical services available to prevent unwanted pregnancies. The majority of pro-lifers also would admit abortion if a woman has been the victim or rape or incest. These inconsistencies all indicate that pro-lifers are not really pro-life or pro-children as much as they are against women's rights to control their sexuality and reproduction.

Because some men feel they will lose in the short term from women's equality, they oppose any measure that will give women a greater say in determining their own lives.

Nevertheless, there are also many women who are pro-life. Robin Lakoff believed such women may be motivated by fear at the prospect of choice itself because they have been socialized into a world where women are passive. Having choices to make is a frightening prospect because you may make the wrong choice and have to take responsibility for your decisions. Lakoff wrote that for such women "pro-choice" rhetoric is terrifying. According to Lakoff, Attorney Elizabeth Bader has suggested reconceptualizing the debate by referring to the pro-life camp as being for "forced motherhood" and the pro-choice camp as being for "voluntary motherhood." Lakoff herself suggested that the pro-choice movement ought to use similar visual campaign tactics and air commercials showing terrified teenagers seeking illegal abortions from unqualified back-alley practitioners. They could also adopt slogans such as "Life is love" and "Choose to live" or "Forced motherhood: the choice of the past."

LANGUAGE: LOADED WEAPON OR BROKEN TOOL?

The discourse in which the debate on abortion has been carried out shows clearly how different versions of reality are constantly being negotiated. There is no such thing as neutral or objective language. As Dwight Bolinger (1980) suggested, language is a loaded weapon. Words clearly have the power to influence our thinking and to direct our consciousness to certain areas of our experience at the same time as they take our attention away from others. The ability to impose one particular view of reality while suppressing others derives not from language itself, but from the power of the dominant group.

No particular language or way of speaking has a privileged view of the world as it "really" is. The world is not simply the way it is, but what we make of it through language. The domains of experience that are important to cultures get grammaticalized into languages. All languages give names to concepts of cultural importance and mark certain categories in their grammars, such as male versus female, one versus more than one, past versus future, and so forth. Yet no two languages are sufficiently similar to be considered as representing the same social reality. The many languages of the world are therefore a rich source of data concerning the structure of our conceptual categories. Much has been made of superficial linguistic facts such as that English has no word corresponding to German *Schadenfreude*, "happiness about someone else's misfortune," or that in many languages spoken in Papua New Guinea the same word is used for *hair*, feather, and *fur*, or that in Russian *mir* can mean both *peace* and *world*. When the language we acquire as children makes certain distinctions in the world around us, our conceptual system pays attention to them. We see the world through the categories of our native language. In this respect the concepts we learn to form and the categories we construct are influenced by the language we learn. This idea is often attributed to Benjamin Lee Whorf (1956), who compared the world views held by speakers of English and Hopi (a Native American language). He argued that speakers were led to very different conceptual systems by virtue of the different structures of their languages. We can now understand another sense in which we cannot "reach man separated from language, and we can never see him inventing it," as the epigraph to this chapter suggests. Each of us inherits the language of the community into which we are born. As philosopher Ludwig Wittgenstein (1958) put it, "the limits of my language are the limits of my world" (p. 10).

A useful way of conceptualizing some of the structural differences is to think of languages as varying not so much in what it is possible to say, as in what it is unavoidable to say. In Spanish and many other European languages it is not possible to say something such as *you are tired* without indicating the sex of the person spoken to and the relationship the speaker has to the addressee. To say *estas cansada* means not simply *you are tired*, but that the addressee is female (compare masculine *cansado*) and the speaker knows her well enough to address her in the intimate second person singular form (compare the polite form *esta*). The different male and female endings -*a*/-*o* are gender displays or indexes. Comparing English and Spanish in this regard, we can say that Spanish speakers are obliged by virtue of the fact that they speak Spanish to make such distinctions of status and gender. These distinctions have been "grammaticalized," or made obligatory, in Spanish, whereas they have not in English. It is not possible to translate a sentence such as *I hired a new worker* into Russian without knowing whether the worker was male or female.

It is not true that English speakers cannot make the kinds of distinctions made in Russian and Spanish. We can, but we have encoded them in other ways such as through the use of titles, and such distinctions are not obligatorily encoded for second-person pronouns. English does, in fact, encode gender in its third-person pronouns, that is, *she/he, her/him, hers/his*, whereas Finnish does not. Japanese men and women use different sets of first- and second-person pronouns. Just where in a language gender or other differences will turn up is an interesting empirical question that still needs much more investigation. Javanese has no inflections for gender but is grammatically stratified into minutely graded hierarchical speech registers, whereas Moroccan Arabic has gender inflections, but little in the way of status marking. The linguistic markers of gender often index other social distinctions such as status and vice versa. Thus, gender cannot be considered separately from social status.

Certainly pronoun systems are one strategic site in languages where social information of various kinds is often grammaticalized and can be used to maintain, create, or transform social relations, as we see in chapters 4 and 5. This is why pronouns along with occupational titles and other forms of address are frequent targets of language reform.

Because language and language reform have played crucial roles in feminist theories and in the struggle for gender equity, clarification of the relationship between language, thought, and reality is essential. As Deborah Cameron (1990a) pointed out, what we believe about the debate on language makes a big difference. If we say women lack the means for expressing their world view in language and are therefore silenced, the problem is linguistic. If, however, women are muted because the language they speak is unacceptable to men, the problem is one of power.

According to one view on the question of the relationship between language and reality that has informed the task of reform, language attaches labels to things that are already there. Therefore, language simply reflects the society and culture of its speakers—a view I refer to as *language as symptom*. Casey Miller and Kate Swift (1991), for instance, are typical of those who see their job as reforming language so that it catches up with the new nonsexist society being created. They focus their attack on providing gender neutral alternatives for sex-differentiated job titles, masculine pronouns used as generics, and a few other key areas where male bias is particularly visible.

Others, however, such as Spender, see the relationship as being the other way around—that is, language determines, causes, or at least influences or shapes society and our perception of the world—a view I refer to as *language as cause*. The language-as-cause position credits language with a more active role in creating gender divisions and, accordingly, in being able to remedy gender-related inequalities. If you believe that language determines reality, then changing language offers a way of altering reality. The dream of a common language has enticed women such as Andrea Dworkin, for whom language is still a broken tool, sexist and discriminatory to the core (see chap. 11 for an example of how this dream has figured in feminist science fiction). The special problem for women is that they can only express themselves in the language that symbolizes the way men have perceived the world to be, a language Julia Penelope has called PUD (patriarchal universe of discourse; see chap. 4). Women have no way of understanding what their own experience is, because the very tool they must use to express themselves is biased against them.

Women like Dworkin and Wittig feel that their inner female selves are not in synchrony with their verbal selves—they are selves divided by language (see chap. 11). Women have to search for the words that give meaning to their existence, which in the male world and ways of talking has been unspoken and nameless. In a man-made language you either see yourself through male eyes and become alienated, or you become silent. Opting for the former is the equivalent of becoming bilingual, an all too common solution advocated in the advice industry in the form of seminars teaching women to behave and speak like men in order to succeed in the business world (see chap. 6). This means accepting as normal and legitimate a male point of view, one of whose central principles is misogyny. Writers such as Dworkin and Daly have pointed to Chinese foot binding, which maimed women for 1,000 years, and witch hunting, which may have killed as many as nine million women, as examples of men's systematic oppression of women on a massive scale.

For French feminists in particular, the task is to deconstruct the patriarchal vision by focusing on the processes by which language creates meanings. Any attempt to speak within current discourse structures will merely reproduce them. Women cannot simply mimic a language we have had no share in creating. Targeting reform in a piecemeal fashion will not rid a language of sexism. Cosmetic changes such as replacing *chairman* with *chairperson*, which are characteristic of the Anglo-American women's movement, are not sufficient. For French feminists such reform is even dangerous because it encourages women to believe they can work within the existing system. As I show in chapter 10, some of these reforms have not actually eradicated sexist distinctions in language use. It is still possible to use reformed language without changing one's thought processes. The preoccupation with equality in the Anglo-American struggle does not effectively challenge the patriarchal construction of society. Women merely equal to men would be like them. In this way differences between men and women don't count or are ignored. To use a gaming metaphor, women would be simply equal players in a predominantly male game still played by male rules. But many women would prefer to change the rules of the game.

MULTIPLE JEOPARDY: GENDER, RACE, AND CLASS

As I have already said, it is not only women who are excluded from the institutions of power and their discourses. Gender inequality is never independent of hierarchies based on class, race, and ethnicity. This reminds us that the androcentric world is primarily a construction of upper middle-class, White, heterosexual men. Generic "man" thus stands for White men, and all others are lesser men.

The apparent universality and uniqueness of women's oppression has nevertheless led some feminists to argue for the primacy of gender over race, class, and other variables, which are all components of our identities. As far as language is concerned, Donna Haraway (1991, pp. 241–242) observed interestingly that there is no linguistic marker to distinguish biological and cultural race as there is for biological sex and cultural gender. She wrote that the absence of a linguistic marker for race underlines the fact that race, unlike gender, is a totally arbitrary cultural construction with no biological foundation. Nevertheless, race and class, like gender, are lenses through which we understand social patterns. The gap in school achievement between high- and low-income children, for example, is greater than that between low-income boys and girls. Even wealthy women's money does not guarantee them access to power. In some societies the constraints on upper class women could be even more severe than those on their working class counterparts. In 16th-century Guatemala and Mexico, for example, many daughters of ruling families never left home until the day of their wedding. Moreover, they never spoke while eating or raised their eyes above the ground. In 18th-century England it was still considered unseemly for a titled woman such as Lady Mary Wortley Montagu to publish her views on scientific topics such as the desirability of smallpox inoculations. Nevertheless, the constraints on women of her class and color were and still are of a different nature from those of her less privileged sisters, whether they are factory workers or housewives.

A Native American woman, for instance, is oppressed both as a Native American and as a woman, a condition sometimes called *double* or *multiple jeopardy*. Although both racial and sexual difference marginalize Black women, for many minority women the issue has been one of priorities. Where do the loyalties of an African American woman lie? With women who fight male dominance, with African Americans more generally, who fight White racism, or with women of color who fight both? Within discussions of race, gender often takes second place, whereas within gender studies, race often gets short shrift. As I observed earlier, the discourses of racism and sexism share much in common in terms of their arguments and style of argumentation (see chap. 3).

When bell hooks began research in the 1970s about the place of Black women in discussions of feminism and racism, she recalled being ridiculed by both friends and strangers. One person asked her what there was to say about Black women. When hooks brought up the topic of racism at White middle-class feminist gatherings, she was accused of changing the subject. She noted that no other group had their identity so socialized out of existence as had Black women, who had been brought up to regard racism as the most important dimension of their identity. Thus, they tended to devalue femaleness and did not identify with White feminists' ideas about womanhood, even though some White feminists associated themselves with Black advocacy on the grounds of a shared experience of slavery. For many women marriage has been a form of domestic servitude—as conveyed in the term *wedlock*. Both slaves and women have been victims of paternalism. Slave owners in the southern United States claimed it was as impertinent to criticize slavery as it was to tell a White man how to treat his wife and children. Father always knew best.

In fact, the women who organized the Seneca Falls convention in 1848, generally regarded as the official beginning of the women's rights movement in the United States, had long been active in the antislavery movement. Their political commitment to abolition of slavery and to women's rights was founded on the similarity between the legal status of married women and that of slaves as male property (despite the obvious contradiction implied by the very real differences in the daily experiences of female slaves and White housewives).

hooks (1981, 1989) also pointed out how historians have more often emphasized the emasculating effects of slavery on Black men while ignoring the plight of Black women who were victimized by Whites, male and female alike, as well as by Black men. While Black men were primarily exploited as field labor, Black women did conventional women's work in White households and performed men's heavy field jobs. They were also assaulted by White masters and forced to breed. This contributed more generally to a devaluation of Black womanhood by American society at large (see chap. 8). Black women were even denied the titles *Miss* and *Mrs.* White men jeered at Sojourner Truth that they didn't believe she was really a woman when she addressed the second annual convention of the women's rights movement in 1852. Speaking just after a White man had told the audience there could be no equal rights for women because they were too weak to perform their share of manual labor and therefore innately inferior, she told them how she had plowed and planted as well as given birth to five children, most of whom had been sold into slavery.

When the question of Black suffrage became a political issue, many White women realized that for the majority of White men, Black suffrage meant male suffrage, and the issue was polarized along the axes of sexism and racism. Language played a key role in making Black women invisible. hooks showed how statements about "Blacks" or "Negroes" were really about Black men, whereas references to "women" focused on White women. As an example, she cited (1989, p. 7) a passage explaining White feminists' reaction to White male support of Black male suffrage in which the author writes about how shocked the women were that "men would so humiliate them by supporting votes for Negroes but not for women." What hooks failed to note about this statement, however, is how it also demonstrates that the default interpretation of the word *man/men* is "White man/men." Black women faced a double bind: To support Black male suffrage was to endorse a patriarchal social order in which they would have no voice, but to support women's suffrage would ally them with White women, who abandoned the Black cause once they realized that Black men might get the vote, whereas they would not. Despite the outspokenness of activists like Sojourner Truth, who recognized that sexist oppression was just as much a threat to Black women's freedom as racism, Black men were given the vote.

Although sexism prevented White women from playing the dominant role in racism, it did not exempt them from participating in it, and racism has tended to preclude any significant bonding between Black and White women on grounds of sex. When the civil rights movement began in the 1950s, racism was the most prominent issue, but it was understood more specifically to be concerned with Black men. Black male leaders were reluctant to acknowledge the ways in which they along with White men had oppressed Black women. The Black Muslim movement, for example, accepted many of the founding myths of Muslim belief about the impurity and sexual inferiority of women that I discuss in the next chapter. The movement defined Black liberation as being synonymous with entry into the existing patriarchal nation, demanding elimination of racism, but not sexism or capitalism. Once again, for Black women to side with "women" meant in effect accepting racism and betraying the cause of Black liberation, whereas to side with "Blacks" meant endorsing patriarchy.

It is nevertheless predictable that within the Black rights movement racial liberation should be conceived of as the restoration of Black masculinity. Because subjugation has been associated with femininity within the Western cultural tradition I discuss in the next chapter, it has seemed "natural" that the focus should be on transcending what is perceived as feminine rather than on rethinking not just the foundations of racism, but the notions of masculinity and femininity. Thus, White politicians such as Daniel Patrick Moynihan (1986) argued that a matriarchal family structure was what prevented Blacks from assimilation into mainstream American life. Working Black women who were heads of households were blamed for castrating men through their refusal to allow Black men to assume the traditional patriarchal role of providing for their families. This approach seeks a cure for racism in restoring sexist views of masculinity rather than challenging them.

hooks's (1995) analysis exposed the fallacy behind essentialism with its assumption that we can divorce the issue of race from sex, or either of those from class. Crenshaw (1989) used the term *intersectionality* to examine how class, race, and gender are intertwined in African American women's lives today. She pointed out that in most legal decisions involving Black women, African American women's issues are still not considered typical of women's issues because they are Black and at the same time are not viewed as typical of Black issues because they are women. Sexual orientation and gender identity pose additional variables.

Audre Lorde (1982, p. 203) wrote about her reaction to her White female partner's claim that as lesbians they were "all niggers" and therefore all equal in their outsiderhood because gays were just as oppressed as Blacks in general. She noted, however, that in the 1950s lesbians were the only women who were engaged in trying to build solidarity of the type the women's movement in the 1970s was trying to promote. Among White lesbians, Black lesbians faced a slightly less hostile world than they did in the outer world, which defined them as nothing because they were Black and female. Yet even within this group there was competition for partners, and beauty was defined according to White standards. Lorde felt that her nonconformity to norms within the gay community at times marginalized her. She wasn't cute or passive enough to be a conventional "femme," nor tough enough to be a "butch." For Lorde, it was hard enough to be Black, let alone being Black and female or Black, female, and gay. She had this to say on the position of Black lesbians vis-à-vis feminism (Lorde, 1982, p. 226):

> Being women together was not enough. We were different. Being gay-girls together was not enough. We were different. Being Black together was not enough. We were different. Being Black women together was not enough. We were different. Being Black dykes together was not enough. We were different. . . . It was a while before we came to realize that our place was the very house of difference rather than the security of any one particular difference.

Although Lorde agreed with Daly and Dworkin that the oppression of women knows no ethnic or racial boundaries, she stressed the many ways in which patriarchy's tools of oppression varied within those boundaries. A view of sisterhood founded only on shared victimization and male dominance is limiting. Although solidarity is often rooted in shared history, it can also be based on political choice and commitment. Women who fear giving up on the idea of essential femaleness fear that in doing so we will lose a basis for organized resistance.

In this chapter I have touched on the three so-called *gender lenses* through which Sandra Bem (1993) said our own culture has viewed the world: gender polarization into male and female, androcentrism (i.e., male-centered), and biological essentialism (i.e., belief that biology overrides culture). These lenses conspire to make the present inequalities between the sexes seem natural and inevitable rather than historically and culturally constructed. I have indicated how language assists in this conspiracy.

Bem (1993, p. 169) also pointed out that every "otherized" group needs to look *at* the lenses of a dominant culture rather than *through* them in order to develop an oppositional consciousness. In this way the group can challenge the marginal position assigned to them by the dominant group as well as the seeming neutrality of the dominant perspective. In the next chapter I deal with some of the central issues in feminist theory seen from the vantage point of language and communication. This is necessary due to the emphasis within the study of language and gender on the issue of whether there are systematic differences between male and female language, which is really to ask a more specific version of the central question in the debate on female inequality, namely, whether men and women are fundamentally the same or different.

EXERCISES AND DISCUSSION QUESTIONS

1. Examine some personal dating ads, which often appear in a variety of newspapers, to see if there are patterns in the way in which gender is displayed. How do men and women describe themselves? What do men and women say they want in a partner? What labels do people use to describe their sexual orientation, race/ethnicity, and so on? Here are four rather conventional examples from the *Los Angeles Times Classified Datelines* (February 26, 1995, pp. 5–7) to get you started.

Under the heading *Women seeking men*:

> pretty Calif.[ornia] lady, 22, blnd [blond]/blu[e-eyed] true romantic ISO [in search of] a sweet charming cute sucsfl. [successful] SWM [single white male] 23–32 4 [for] poss.[ible] rel.[ationship]

> feminine, funny, caring, classy JF [Jewish female] ISO N/S [nonsmoker] tall, romantic, sucsfl. SJM [single Jewish Male] who's serious about love.

Under the heading *Men seeking women*:

> affluent DWM [divorced white male], seeks slim, fit female 25–35 with a sense of humor who enjoys Santa Anita races fine dining & sports. Prefer long hair and buxom.

> cute sweet fun guy in mid 20s looking for someone with sense of humor/smile.

2. Some critics of gender studies and feminism have claimed that the issues they raise are of relevance only to White middle-class women. What do you think? Is there a distinction between gender studies and feminist research?

3. In the introduction to her book *Perceiving Women*, anthropologist Shirley Ardener (1975a, p. xviii) wondered whether our own category "women" might not be "an entirely intellectual creation which one day

may disappear." If there is so much variation in our present-day models of women, do women have anything in common that makes them distinctly female?

4. Judith Butler (1990, 1993) used the drag show to illustrate the performative nature of gender, a practice that many women consider to be misogynist and degrading. Discuss the implications and meanings of the drag show for concepts of the sexed and gendered self.

5. Many greeting cards are addressed to persons of a particular sex ("For a wonderful father," "To a loving aunt," "For a very special person," etc.). Examine the kinds of messages that are sent about the recipients of such cards on the basis of their sex. Look not just at the words, but also at the designs, images, and colors used in the card. How do these (implicit or explicit) messages about the roles, activities, or behaviors of men compare to those of women? Are these gender messages conveyed via some linguistic means more than via others (e.g., metaphors or particular words)? Are there any hidden messages?

ANNOTATED BIBLIOGRAPHY AND SUGGESTIONS
FOR FURTHER READING

The idea of displaying, doing, or indexing gender as an ongoing activity can be found in articles by Sally McConnell-Ginet (1983), Elinor Ochs (1992), Candace West and Don H. Zimmerman (1987), and the work of Erving Goffman (1976). The idea of doing things with words can be found in philosopher of language John Austin's book (1962). The manifesto for the Mandate for Leadership II is authored by Stuart Butler, Michael Sanera, and W. Bruce Weinrod (1984). Feminist analyses of housework have been conducted by Anne Oakley (1975a, 1975b), Ivan Illich (1982), Betty Friedan (1963), Glenna Matthews (1987), and Susan Strasser (1982).

There are a number of interdisciplinary anthologies that treat language and gender from a broad perspective, for example, Shirley Ardener (1975a, 1975b); Deborah Cameron (1990b); Sally McConnell-Ginet, Ruth Borker, and Nelly Furman (1980); Barbara Miller (1993); Sherry Ortner and Harriet Whitehead (1981); Joyce Penfield (1987); Susan Philips, Susan Steele, and Christine Tanz (1987); Camille Roman, Suzanne Juhasz, and Christanne Miller (1994); Michelle Rosaldo and Louise Lamphere (1974); Peggy Sanday and Ruth Goodenough (1990); Barrie Thorne and Nancy Henley (1974); and Barrie Thorne, Cheris Kramarae, and Nancy Henley (1983). Textbooks, anthologies, and books with a more specifically linguistic focus include Dennis Baron (1986); Deborah Cameron (1990a, 1990b); Deborah Cameron and Jennifer Coates (1985, 1988); Jennifer Coates (1988); Suzette Haden Elgin (1993); David Graddol and Joan Swann (1989); Marlis Hellinger (1990); Janet Holmes (1994); Mary Ritchie Key (1975); Cheris Krama-rae (1975, 1980, 1981, 1992); Anne Pauwels (1987); Cate Poynton (1989); Philip Smith (1985); Joan Swann (1992); Deborah Tannen (1993c, 1994a, 1994b); and Marina Yaguello (1978). Nancy Henley's (1995a) article contains a good discussion of the intersection between the categories of ethnicity and gender. Walter Williams (1988) treated multiple gender arrangements in Native American cultures as did Suzanne Kessler and Wendy McKenna (1978).

Authors of other useful books not specifically cited here include Lila Abu-Lughod (1986), Elizabeth Fay (1994), Henrietta Moore (1989), Robin Morgan (1982), Peggy Reeves Sanday (1981), and Marilyn Strathern (1988).

CHAPTER

2

Boys Will Be Boys?

What are little boys made of?
Frogs and snails,
and puppy dogs' tails.
That's what little boys are made of.
What are little girls made of?
Sugar and spice,
and all things nice.
That's what little girls are made of. (traditional English nursery rhyme)

The familiar nursery rhyme telling us what little boys and girls are made of suggests that each sex is made of fundamentally different things. When we say "boys will be boys," we generally mean there are certain ways we expect boys to behave simply because they are male, for example, to be high-spirited, aggressive, and so on. On what do we base such expectations and beliefs? Are there sex-specific ways of behaving that are acquired by being born male or female or through growing up as a boy or girl? If there are differences, are they biologically determined or socially constructed?

The debate about what is innate versus what is learned, often called "nature versus nurture," has been going on for centuries. As is the case with most questions posed in such a blunt either/or fashion, complex issues get oversimplified and the answers are not always decisive in favor of one extreme or the other. Popular as well as scientific opinion seems to have seesawed back and forth between these two poles in the search for explanations. In the 1970s feminists were taking a minimalist position, but now the tide seems to be shifting back to emphasizing both biological and cultural differences. In 1992 a cover story for *Time* magazine (1992a) suggested that men and women were different because they were born that way. Meanwhile, in linguistics, Deborah Tannen's (1990a) best-selling book claimed that men and women had different styles of communicating due to socialization in single-sex peer groups. Despite the fact that Tannen herself made no claims for the superiority of male style, her research has been co-opted in various ways. Her findings have been taken up in popular magazines and training courses aimed at improving women's communication skills. Within certain quarters of feminist theory they have bolstered the so-called celebration of difference approach, which grew out of the desire to revalue and reclaim what is perceived as feminine in a culture where femaleness has generally been devalued.

Chris Weedon (1987, p. 98) observed that the nature of femininity and masculinity is one of the key sites of discursive struggle for the individual. Although the terms *masculinity* and *femininity* are widely used in everyday discourse, and psychologists have paid a good deal of attention to measuring them, they are difficult to define and use as scientific concepts. One psychologist commented that these two constructs were "both theoretically and empirically among the muddiest in the psychologist's vocabulary" (Constantinople, 1973, p. 390). Linguistically speaking, the inadequacy of these terms, along with pairs such as *male/female* and *man/woman*, to refer to the varied spectrum of human sexuality can be seen in the existence of a large number of other terms such as *transsexual, homosexual, lesbian, hermaphrodite, transvestite, tomboy, sissy,* and many others. At the same time, the very existence of these terms serves to mark the persons referred to by them as deviating from the norms implicit in the terms *masculine/feminine, male/female, man/woman,* even though the meanings of these terms have undergone change too. Psychologists' early attempts to formulate and measure concepts such as masculinity and femininity were based on the assumption that these notions were the endpoints of a single bipolar continuum. Here too, dichotomization has obscured a more complex picture.

In this chapter I examine how the male self has been constructed as the subject of discourse, and what consequences this has had for our understanding of masculinity and femininity. In tracing some of the prominent themes in feminist theories of relevance to the study of language and communication, I also show how this male subjectivity is inscribed in sciences such as biology and psychology as well as other disciplines like philosophy, and, of course, linguistics, where much of the early research on language and gender tended to reinforce the dichotomy between men and women by presupposing that each sex spoke differently. Theories across a wide range of disciplines embody what I call discourses of gender and sexuality in the larger sense. As Foucault (1972, p. 49) noted, "discourses . . . [are] . . . practices that systematically form the objects of which they speak." Just like the nursery rhyme at the outset of this chapter, they serve to construct what it means to be female or male, at times reifying stereotypes that are taken for granted rather than challenged.

IN THE FIRST PERSON MASCULINE

The masculinity of the subject in everyday as well as scientific discourse has profound repercussions and is at the heart of feminist theory and debate. Andrea Dworkin (1981) writes that the first tenet of male supremacist ideology is that men have this self and women, by definition, lack it. He is subject and she, object. She attributes male power to men's assertion of self as subject whose subjectivity is not merely felt but protected by beliefs, customs, and laws, as well as proclaimed in science, art, and literature. This self cannot be eradicated, and when it falters, institutions devoted to its maintenance buoy it up.

The innatist position was summed up very well by John Stuart Mill in 1869 when he wrote:

> What it is to be a boy, to grow in the belief that without any merit or exertion of his own, by the mere fact of being born a male he is by right the superior of all of an entire half of the human race. (p. 27)

Because reproduction has been seen as the source of women's symbolic and actual oppression, the sexual division of labor as well as the basis for different ways of thinking and behaving, it has been a central topic in feminist theory. Much of the early research on female/male differences was undertaken primarily to try to validate biological differences. Women stand to lose much from such research because it tried to prove scientifically that differences were universal and therefore "natural," that is, biologically based, and therefore, inevitable and beyond questioning. As late as 1873, for example, men argued that higher education for women would shrivel their reproductive organs and make them sterile. A woman's developmental energy had to be channeled into reproduction at the expense of her intellectual advancement. Even in the early part of this century it was suggested that allowing schoolgirls to play hockey would impair their ability to breast-feed in later life. Men measured the size and volume of women's brains and when they found them to be smaller than men's, they took this as a sign of female genetic inferiority. Thus, men have used the observed differences between the sexes to justify their dominance and priority in the human scheme of things. In short: Being female is assumed to pose a problem, but being male is just normal.

This kind of circular argumentation is at the roots of Western philosophy, religion, and science. Believing male superiority to be a scientific fact, men constructed theories to explain women's inferiority. Invariably, the evidence centered on what the woman lacked: She was less moral, less evolved, less rational, and so forth. Conversely, whatever traits women exhibited or were believed to have were devalued, such as women's alleged greater emotionality. The intellectual world of ideas is masculine, whereas the internal world of emotions is feminine. To the extent that certain values and beliefs about sex inform and reinforce scientific thinking, we can consider science gendered. This is at odds with prevailing views that science is objective and impartial. As I demonstrate later, this supposed neutrality is a pretense. Science always operates in someone's interests. Gender is a lens through which scientists have explained biological and social patterns by weighting the differences in favor of men. Scientists, who have been predominantly male, White, educated, and upper class, have used their theories of women's innate inferiority to disqualify women who would have been competing with them for education and professional status. In this scientific discourse the Other is constructed with contradictory images of being both weak and dangerous.

Aristotle, Thomas Aquinas, and more recently Sigmund Freud all regarded women as defective men. Aristotle, for instance, said that women were deformed men, and for Aquinas, they were "misbegotten males." Observing that the female matured more quickly than the male, Aristotle claimed this demonstrated women's inferiority because inferior things all reached their end more quickly. Haste made waste. Yet, as far as Schopenhauer was concerned, women were immature in their powers of judgment. He claimed that women lived in a state of moral infancy. The view of women as children has been a persistent one, as I show in chapter 9 on the images of women in advertising. Before Charles Darwin's theory of evolution became widely accepted, scientists considered variability to be a liability to a species, and women were thought to be the more variable sex. After Darwin showed biological benefit in variability, males were thought to be more variable.

As far as linguistics is concerned, I mentioned in chapter 1 that philologist Otto Jespersen (1922), who was one of the first linguists to comment on differences between men's and women's language, included in his book on language a chapter on "The Woman." His views were not based on actual systematic observations, but his own personal prejudices, as were those of another early commentator, Gustav Cederschiöld (1900). Jespersen claimed that women were quicker to learn, hear, and answer than men, but predictably it was the slowness of men that he valued. He turned this seemingly negative quality into a positive one. Similarly, with respect to hesitancy, when thought to be a male trait, Jespersen attributed it to a greater desire for accuracy and clarity, which led men more than women to search for just the right word. He also believed women were more indirect than men, which made them ineffective. Cederschiöld noted that women had trouble with the genre of political language due to their emotionality and spontaneity (see also chap. 6). The message here is quite straightforward: If you're a woman, you can't win. Damned if you do, damned if you don't.

THE FEMALE EUNUCH: THE SECOND SEX?

French theorists such as Simone de Beauvoir and Luce Irigaray have shown how women have been constructed as "Other" and that femininity is masculinity inverted. She is [−male] (see chap. 5 for further discussion of its repercussions for linguistic theory and the negative meanings associated with terms for women). Linguistically speaking, women are indeed, as de Beauvoir (1968) put it, "the second sex," as can be seen in a variety of naming practices symbolic of an order in which men come first, going back to expressions such as *Adam and Eve, man and woman/wife, husband and wife, boys and girls, guys and dolls, his and hers,* and so on (a notable exception being *ladies and gentlemen,* but more on that in chap. 5).

Male grammarians tried to rationalize men's priority in the linguistic scheme of things. Thomas Wilson's *Art of Rhetoric* (1553) had this to say about order in language, which he believed should be logical and natural. The preferred order for co-occurring male and female entities is "the worthier is preferred, and set before. As a man is sette before a woman."

> Some will set the carte before the horse, as thus. My mother and my father are both at home, euen as thoughe the good man of the house ware no breaches, or that the graye Mare were the better Horse. And what thoughe it often so happeneth . . . yet in speakinge at the leaste, let us keep a natural order, and set the man before the woman for maners sake. (cited in Coates, 1993, p. 24)

Germaine Greer (1971) described the woman as "the female eunuch," a person castrated at birth, doomed to be inferior because she does not have a penis. Men appropriate women's sexuality, like their domestic labor, for their own benefit. She argued that women's freedom was dependent on a positive and active definition of female sexuality. Within the Western scientific tradition, women's sexual organs were for a long time thought to be simply underdeveloped forms of male sexual organs. A number of cultures attribute male superiority to male sexual anatomy. In Burmese culture the penis is characterized as a noble organ, a golden flower, whereas the vagina is seen as polluting (Spiro, 1993, p. 317).

It was Freud, of course, who made explicit a connection between female inferiority and the lack of the penis, resulting in both shame and envy at the lack of a penis. Interestingly, no one argued that males were deformed or embarrassed because they lacked wombs and could not bear children. This would have meant defining woman in a positive way as those who had wombs, and men in a negative fashion as those who lacked them. Things might have been different if psychoanalysis had been founded by a woman instead of "fathered" by Freud. Vagina gratitude might have characterized females, or vagina envy might have been seen as a problem for male psychological development.

Freud's emphasis on the father rather than the mother as the pivotal point of the child's development and his claim about penis envy being the core of female identity have angered many women. Freud's ideas have had enormous repercussions in psychotherapy for many years. His analysis of hysteria (a neurosis in which a person responds to stress by developing physical symptoms not traceable to a physical cause) as a predominantly female disorder is another example of male refusal to pay attention to what women are saying. It was part of the effort to persuade women that the cause of their unhappiness is themselves. Even before Freud, however, classical medical theory defined hysteria (from the Greek word *hystera*, meaning womb) as a disorder caused by disturbances of the womb, more specifically by the dislocation and wandering of the womb around the body. Biomedical discourse tried to validate a biological basis for women's emotionality by tying women's moods to their wombs, hormones, and menstrual cycle. When emotionality is associated with women's irrationality, mental disturbance, and so on, this reinforces a hierarchical view of male–female difference. Women's moodiness is in need of control. Even now there are complaints that too many unnecessary hysterectomies are being performed.

A famous case treated by Freud that became the subject of much subsequent discussion and analysis was that of a young woman named Dora. A certain Mrs. K. was having an affair with Dora's father, whereas her husband, Mr. K., was pressuring young Dora to become romantically involved with him. Dora's father in effect handed over his daughter to Freud for treatment when she would not respond to Mr. K.'s advances. Although Freud did not accept a conspiracy interpretation, he did acknowledge an implicit understanding that Mr. K. could pursue Dora if he did not interfere in his wife's affair with Dora's father. Because Mr. K. was the major threat to the affair going on between his wife and Dora's father, a sexual relationship between himself and Dora would have restored equilibrium to a messy domestic situation in both households. However, after Mr. K. failed to seduce Dora, both men had at stake the portrayal of Dora as a hysterical young girl who did not know what was good for her. Freud at various times referred to Dora as a "girl" and a "child," yet assumed at the same time that she possessed the understanding and sexual responsiveness of a mature woman.

In their analysis of the Dora case, Robin Lakoff and James Coyne (1993) wrote that Freud acted as an apologist for the Victorian patriarchal family and Dora was at his mercy. They have drawn more general attention to the potential abuse of power when the therapist is male and the patient female. The therapist makes interpretations of and to the client, not vice versa. Telling people what they mean and denying the legitimacy of their distress by dismissing it as neurotic behavior is the prerogative of the analyst.

Other male-oriented psychological theories have played a big role in the oppression of women. Most theories of family "normalcy" rely on gender-biased criteria. In studying personality, psychologists have used scales that stereotypically labeled some behaviors as feminine and others as masculine. For example, on one such scale subjects received "masculinity points" for disliking babies and nursing and "femininity points" for disliking soldiering and hunting. Another gave points for "masculinity" if a woman reported that she was self-reliant or ambitious. On another scale, femininity points were subtracted from masculinity points to arrive at a person's overall score.

Similar tests based on suspect notions of masculinity and femininity have been used in hiring and screening the suitability of job applicants for certain positions. Until the 1980s, for instance, Sears Roebuck Company's hiring procedures for retail sales required applicants to take a "vigor" test. Among the questions asked were: "Do you have a low-pitched voice?" "Have you played on a football team?" "Have you ever done any hunting?" "Do you swear often?" These questions were asked despite an in-house study at Sears that actually linked higher scores with poor sales results! Until the Equal Employment Opportunity Commission (EEOC) filed a discrimination suit against Sears in 1979, the company assigned women employees to women's departments, selling women's clothing, cosmetics, and so on, while men sold the big-ticket items like appliances, televisions, boats, and furniture, which earned them more in commissions. As part of its defense in the 1984–1985 trial, Sears claimed that women weren't interested in the higher paying "rough and tumble" jobs.

For a woman to be considered "healthy," she must conform to a largely negatively defined feminine stereotype. With male-biased measures it is no surprise that more women will be classified as neurotic than men, because neurosis is defined as a deviation from the norm. So-called *obsessive-compulsive* behavior is an exaggeration of our culture's preferred masculine presentation of self, whereas hysteria is an exaggeration of the feminine. Yet because being feminine is in itself an aberration, to be a hysterical woman, one need only be a "good" woman. A woman cannot be a healthy woman at the same time as she is a healthy human being.

In its *Diagnostic and Statistical Manual of Mental Disorders*, the standard reference book mental health professionals use in diagnosing patients, the American Psychiatric Association (APA) listed nine characteristics of masochism. They defined as masochistic a person who worries excessively about troubling others, who rejects help, gifts, or favors, so as not to be a burden on others. All of the behaviors listed are of the self-sacrificing sort that generally typify the ideal feminine character. In effect, the APA branded conventional female socialization as a pathological disorder. Dictionaries reinforced stereotypes by defining terms such as *feminine* and *effeminate* in terms of negative character traits such as weakness, softness, and so on, inappropriate to a man.

Women unable to conform to male definitions of femininity were labeled *neurotic, perverted,* or *schizophrenic.* A study of women in the San Francisco area hospitalized for schizophrenia in the 1950s revealed the use of shock treatment for women who sought abortions or who could not accept their domestic roles. Psychiatrists regarded the battered woman as a masochist who had provoked her husband into beating her. When girls or women reported cases of incest and sexual abuse, they were often told they were fantasizing, much as law professor Anita Hill was accused of imagining U.S. Supreme Court Justice Clarence Thomas's sexual interest in her (see chap. 8 for discussion of the way in which women are blamed for provoking male sexual desire). Toward the end of the 1950s tranquilizers were developed in response to a need that doctors explicitly saw as female (see chap. 9 for discussion of gender bias in the marketing of such drugs to physicians). bell hooks (1993) examined the connections between psychological trauma and mental disorders among Black women as a response to the problems of forming identity and selfhood under White supremacist patriarchy.

Such measures and scales reified masculinity and femininity by treating them as if they were real rather than culturally constructed. They reinforced beliefs that the sex of the body should match the gender of the psyche and polarized the distinction between masculinity and femininity by treating them as opposite endpoints of a scale. On every item people must be either masculine or feminine, not both, and thus individuals could be ranked on a continuum corresponding to their degree of masculinity or femininity. To be normal meant being close to the two extremes. Everything other than conventional masculinity or femininity was rendered pathological. Homosexuals, lesbians, transsexuals, and transvestites are "unnatural" and therefore not "real" men or women.

These views have significant repercussions for social policy, some of which I spell out later in this chapter. In many places same-sex sexual activity is still a criminal activity and marriage is denied to same-sex couples, as are spouse benefits that come with heterosexual marriages, not to mention the right to serve in the armed forces, to be members of other organizations, or to adopt children. Yet the very existence of groups such as transsexuals is a powerful challenge to the alleged naturalness of the link between sex of the body and the gender of one's psyche. One minister who objected to Erin Swenson's retention of her ministry after her transsexual surgery stated, "You can't father two children without being male," suggesting that once a biological male, always a male.

Modern feminist research on gender has offered quite a different perspective from that found in traditional psychological theories. Carolyn Heilbrun (1973), for instance, suggested that individuals who conformed to conventional gender stereotypes might actually be the ones who were least mentally healthy because they were prisoners of their gender. At the same time as the privileging of masculinity condemns women to second-class status, it generates male insecurity about being a "real man." Both Heilbrun and Adrienne Rich (1978) advocated genderless standards of mental health in their notion of *androgyny* (a Greek word combining *andro* 'male' and *gyn* 'female'). Androgyny is based on the idea that masculinity and femininity are not opposites but can coexist. The liberation of men and women from rigidly defined sex roles and freedom to show both masculine and feminine qualities at the same time became favorite themes of women's speculative fiction (see chap. 11). In an androgynous world we would no longer think it is natural for boys to be strong and active, and girls to be passive and weak. Because distinctions of gender would not matter in an egalitarian society, they would be superfluous in language too.

Sandra Bem (1993) called attention to the existence of men and women whom she called non-sex-typed, that is, those who score high on both masculine and feminine traits, and those who score low on both. It is those who score high on both that she called androgynous, even though both groups conform much less to conventional gender ideology than do masculine men and feminine women. Bem felt that she herself had been miscategorized by earlier measuring instruments in which she could be classified only as masculine or feminine.

Another effect of the assumption that men are normal but women are deviant can be seen in the fact that much of the research on medical conditions affecting both sexes has also been carried out on men. Heart disease and high blood pressure are two such examples. Despite the fact that heart disease has killed more women than any other single cause in Britain, the government's "Look After Yourself" campaign targeted men. Women were mentioned only insofar as they were seen as a means of improving men's diets and contributing to factors lowering male risk, a fact reflected in advertising strategies used to market margarine and low-fat foods (see chap. 9). British and American women with heart disease are still underdiagnosed and undertreated compared with men. When the first artificial hearts were invented, they were too large to fit within most women's bodies. They were man-made hearts indeed—made by men for only one half the human race! At the same time, medical conditions or diseases specific to women, such as breast cancer, or parts of the female life cycle, such as menopause, are much less researched and less well understood. Sometimes these are euphemistically referred to as "women's troubles."

Men's bodies are taken to be the norm not just in medical research and treatment, but also in terms of insurance coverage. Pregnancy is often excluded from insurance coverage whereas prostatectomies and circumcisions are included. Even coverage itself in the United States is largely determined by employment in certain types of jobs. Ginzburg (1989) contrasted the midwife's view of pregnancy and childbirth with that of the medical profession, where childbirth is seen as an abnormal state of health with the potential to develop into a serious emergency. Doctors have generally dismissed midwifery as unscientific because it is practiced mainly by women, while obstetrics is seen as a science because it is part of the male medical establishment. Other bodies of knowledge practiced largely by women at home, such as cooking, housekeeping, and so on, are, like midwifery, labeled *arts* rather than sciences.

Similarly, other changes and phases constituting part of the normal female life cycle have been labeled *syndromes* and are thus rendered dysfunctional and pathological. An example is premenstrual syndrome (PMS), which the popular press has held responsible for everything from murder to irritability. As Zita (1989, p. 189) observed, however, the step from observable cyclicity in certain aspects of female behavior and physiology to the presumption of pathology is a leap requiring careful scrutiny of the evidence. Within the literature on PMS there are two implicit norms: One is noncyclical male physiology, and the other is stereotypical feminine behavior. Certain symptoms of PMS such as irritability, aggression, and violence deviate from the perceived female normal emotions of caring, nurturing, and so forth. These deviations, along with their cyclical occurrence, are then problematized, and made into a disabling disease in need of treatment by health professionals. Women are susceptible to emotional breakdown by virtue of their own biological weakness.

Even today, however, not everyone agrees on what precisely the differences are between men and women and what they amount to. This is another way of asking, what difference does difference make? Maccoby and Jacklin, for instance, authors of a classic study of sex differences, claimed that language is the only area of cognition in which there is evidence of sex differentiation. Yet their extensive survey of hundreds of studies identified only four differences that they took to be fairly well established. Perhaps the one that has been made most of, but that is nonetheless still controversial, is women's alleged superior language abilities, and men's supposed advantage in visual–spatial skills. In various tests women have shown greater achievement in a variety of verbal skills, whereas men do better in math. Sociolinguist Jack Chambers (1995) has recently tried to explain why women supposedly speak more standardly than men by appealing to women's innate superior verbal ability.

Scientists have also debated for a long time whether there are sex differences in the functional organization of the brain. A long-standing hypothesis has it that language functions are more likely to be highly lateralized, that is, located in the left hemisphere, for men, but represented in both hemispheres for women. A 1995 article in *Nature* claimed to provide support for this using neural imaging techniques that make it possible to see which areas of the brain are activated while people are engaged in certain tasks. Bennett Shaywitz and his colleagues (1995) found that during certain phonological processing tasks more than half of the females showed a different pattern of brain activation involving parts of both hemispheres, while men used only the left. This would supposedly explain why men are more likely than women to stutter, and to have reading disabilities such as dyslexia and speech disorders after brain damage. Damage to one part of the brain is less likely to disrupt women's language abilities, because another part of the brain may be more easily able to take over the functions lost from the damaged area.

Although the scientists did not discuss what general implications their results might have for everyday language use, media reports used the article to explain why men and women cannot be like one another because they use their brains differently.

SEX AND GENDER: WHAT'S THE DIFFERENCE?

In the early years of the women's movement much energy was devoted to countering such biological arguments that had long been used to justify women's subordination to men. This drew attention away from biology to the powerful role of society and culture, and, in particular, to male dominance rather than difference as a source of many gender differences. Gender is not simply something passed on from one generation to another, but actively constructed in a particular context. Its meaning changes not only from context to context but also over time and place. The division into male and female also has different consequences in different settings such as home and school, and even within our life span (see chap. 7 for a discussion of adolescence as a particularly crucial period).

Studies have shown, for example, that people attribute men's success more often to skill and talent, and women's more to hard work or luck. Male accomplishments are taken to be caused more by inherent qualities whereas female performance is attributed more to elements outside her control. People looking at photographs of men and women sitting around a table are asked to rate the people on leadership and dominance. When seeing a male at the head of the table, they considered him the leader of the group, but did not regard a woman seated in the same position as a leader. This reflects our cultural expectation that women are not leaders.

Scholars such as Anne Fausto-Sterling have pointed to the many flaws in both design and interpretation of studies claiming to find significant differences between men and women. In some cases the differences could have been explained by other variables that were not controlled. Stereotypes about math being a male subject discourage girls from taking courses. There was a big outcry when one of the talking Barbie dolls was programmed to say that math homework was difficult. Critics complained that this gave girls the idea that they weren't suited for math and science, traditionally seen as male subjects. Researchers have known for a long time that a loss of confidence in math usually precedes a drop in achievement, rather than vice versa. Thus, the poorer performance of girls on standardized tests could be the result of a confidence rather than an ability gap (see further in chap. 7).

Cross-cultural studies also illuminate the extent to which some research findings may be specific to Western contexts, and therefore socially rather than biologically determined. American mothers are more likely to try to distract a male infant by dangling objects in front of him. This may promote the development of visual–spatial skills. Jack Berry (1966), however, found no differences in spatial ability among the Eskimo population. Generally speaking, sex-related differences in visual–spatial skills were strongest in societies where women's social roles are more limited. Most importantly, however, many of the traits that are supposed to differentiate women from men vary more within the sexes than between them. When girls are exposed more often to spatial tasks, the gender difference declines sharply. If these differences were biologically determined, they would be largely immune to training. Girls' achievement in math is also subject to variation according to ethnicity. Non-Caucasian girls, for instance, outperformed and outnumbered boys in top-level math classes in Hawaii. Yet there has been a persistent belief in a so-called "math gene." Similarly, cross-cultural research shows that women do not always speak more standardly than men (see further in chap. 6).

The interaction between culture and biology has led scholars such as Anne Oakley to make a distinction between *sex* and *gender*, despite the fact that in popular usage the terms are often used interchangeably. Deborah Cameron (1995, p. 127) noted how *gender* has now become a polite synonym for *sex*. Sex is a biological term, and gender a psychological, social, and cultural one. Although the distinction between *sex* and *gender* is becoming well established at least in English usage, it presupposes that we can distinguish between innate and environmental differences. That is far from the case at present. The

nature–nurture issue has been raised not just in connection with the differences between the sexes, but also with respect to many other things such as
the relationship between intelligence and race. The assumption underlying
the testing of intelligence and the notion of IQ was that intelligence is innate
and transmitted genetically. Research on this topic has long been used for
political purposes, such as to exclude certain categories of immigrants to the
United States on grounds of race or nationality.

Here are two interesting examples that offer some evidence of how much
is learned through socialization as a male or female child rather than
encoded as part of genetic inheritance. Although the first case comes from
an experiment, both show how adults behave differently toward babies of
the opposite sex. In the experiment researchers had men and women look
at a videotape of a baby reacting to a jack-in-the-box. The first time the
jack pops out of the box, the baby appears startled; the second time it
appears upset, and before the jack comes out again, the baby starts to cry.
The experimenters told some of the observers that the baby was a boy,
and they told others it was a girl. The words the observers used to describe
what they saw were influenced by whether they thought the baby was a
boy or girl. Those who thought the child was male described the baby as
being "angry." Those who thought the baby was a girl described her as
"afraid." The experiment activated stereotypes about male and female emotions, according to which we expect women to be weak and fearful, and
men, strong and aggressive. Moreover, it illustrates our belief that anger
is the one emotion we expect women to display less of than men due to
the premium society places on women to be nice, as encoded in the nursery
rhyme at the beginning of this chapter (see also chaps. 4, 5, and 7). These
stereotypes in turn were translated into a discourse for talking about male
and female babies.

The second example concerns a pair of identical male twins, one of
whom was eventually raised as female. At the age of 7 months the twins
were circumcised by electrocautery and one of the boys had his penis burned
off by an overly powerful current. A consultant plastic surgeon recommended raising "him" as a girl. When the child was 17 months old, they
changed "his" name, clothing, and hairstyle. Four months later "he" underwent surgery to reconstruct "his" genitals as female. When the twins
were 4 years old, their mother remarked of the girl that she was amazed
by how feminine she was. She said, "I've never seen a little girl so neat
and tidy as she can be. . . . She is very proud of herself, when she puts on
a new dress, or I set her hair. She just loves to have her hair set; she could
sit under the drier all day long."

This example shows that the gender identity of "female" does not necessarily get associated only with biologically female bodies. Although the
distinction between sex and gender takes us some way toward accommo-

dating transsexuals, for instance, it does not resolve the fact of considerable chromosomal variation and that sex too is at least partly culturally constructed. Thus, in the words of Simone de Beauvoir (1968), "One is not born, but rather becomes, a woman." Nothing guarantees that the person who eventually becomes a woman was or is anatomically, hormonally, or chromosomally female. The anatomy of the performer and the gender being performed are not necessarily the same, a fact well illustrated by cultural practices such as drag shows and cross-dressing. Likewise, because becoming a woman is an ongoing process in time, it can be continually subject to redefinition because it is never finished. Judith Butler (1990, 1993) thinks of gender as emerging through repeated acts or performances which congeal over time. Being a woman in the 1960s is different from being a woman today. In my own lifetime I have seen many changes in how gender is constructed. Nowadays, dress codes and fashions have changed so that girls can wear jeans to school, something not allowed in my day, and women no longer are expected to wear dresses to work. Both boys and girls can take mechanical drawing and typing classes. Many more occupations that were formerly male only or predominantly male have become much more integrated, such as the police force.

However, the performative aspect raises the question of what a person was before becoming a woman, and how such a person would be referred to—he, she, or something else? Still another dichotomous way of thinking underlies this question, namely, our assumption that what is constructed is in some sense free, but what is determined is in some sense fixed (see Butler, 1993, p. 94).

Questions such as these are disturbing to those who have tried to define gender in terms of sex, and to dichotomize what is in fact a continuum of biologically differentiated types. As far as we know, all cultures sort people into at least two categories based on anatomical distinctions relevant to their role in sexual reproduction. Nevertheless, every biological correlate of sex, from chromosomes to secondary characteristics such as facial hair, is much less bimodally distributed in the population than we popularly believe. At least 10% of the population has chromosomal variations that do not fit neatly into the classic XX female and XY male dichotomy. I mentioned at the outset of the last chapter that 80% of 2-year-olds in the United States can distinguish males from females on the basis of purely cultural cues such as hairstyle and clothing. What is more significant is that 50% of 3- and 4-year-olds fail to distinguish males from females if all they can see are biological cues such as genitalia. In other words, young children are much more sensitive to cultural than biological differences. This is because American parents, unlike Balinese parents, dress male and female children in very different ways so that their sex is indexed by these superficial clues even when their genitalia cannot be seen. Children are in effect taught a cultural definition of sex. The ancient Aztecs did the same when they put a tiny sword and shield in a newborn baby boy's cradle and a toy shuttle and loom in a baby girl's.

According to Julia Epstein, who cited a medical textbook (1990, p. 104), there is no standard legal or medical definition of sex. There may be as many as 70 types of intersexed individuals. External genitalia are not a sufficient criterion for assigning an unambiguous sex to all newborn babies. Yet Judith Butler (1993) and Anne Fausto-Sterling (1985) wrote that when biomedical researchers "decide" that an anatomically ambiguous or in-tersexed XX individual is male, they take external genitalia to be the definitive sign of sex, even if all the component parts do not add up to our dichotomous definitions. If an XX baby has a penis, then doctors should not amputate it, but should instead remove the female internal organs, implant prosthetic testes, and regulate the child's hormones through-out life. Although such a baby could be made female in a far less radical and invasive way simply by amputating the penis, the medical profession appears to be concerned that the child might suffer psychic trauma from castration. In forcing this binary opposition onto newborn children who do not already fit these categories, science has decided in effect with Freud that masculinity is marked by the presence of the penis and femininity by the lack of it (even if hormonal and chromosomal evidence say otherwise).

Although surgery can "fix" sex and thus restore dichotomy, our identity is more complicated. Despite Butler's more open-ended approach on the issue, many psychologists believe that our gender identity becomes fixed during the first 3 years of life, depending on whether a child is raised as a boy or girl rather than on genetic details such as the presence or absence of a Y chromosome. According to this view, gender identity is one of the earliest, most central and enduring aspects of our self-conception. Others, however, claim that gender identity is flexible throughout childhood, but becomes fixed at puberty through the regulation of hormones. In this view biology overrules whatever upbringing the child might have had. Although most children form a gender identity in line with their biological sex, others do not. The standard sociolinguistic account of variation in urban societies has also tended to assume that identity is more clear-cut and straightforward than it is. In correlating membership in groups such as middle class versus working class, male versus female, and so forth with the use of certain linguistic features, it presents an account of the relationship between lan-guage and society that suggests that language reflects already existing iden-tities and group allegiances rather than constructs them.

Where pronominal systems are sex differentiated, languages too, like the surgeon's scalpel, impose a dichotomy into male (*he*) and female (*she*), compelling us to choose one or the other in referring to people. Therefore, reformers and writers of speculative fiction have directed much attention to this area of linguistic structure (see chaps. 10 and 11). Not surprisingly, pronoun choice has also been an issue for gays, lesbians, and transsexuals. Brawn (1995, pp. 214–215) related the controversy about Billy Tipton and Teena Brandon, who were anatomically female but lived their lives and were accepted in their respective communities as men. On Tipton's death in 1989 the gay community claimed "her" as a lesbian and passing woman, and the magazine *Transsexual News Telegraph* claimed "him" as a transsexual man. One way in which each group staked its opposing claims was through referring to Tipton as *he* or *she*. The *Transsexual News Telegraph* also claimed Brandon, who was murdered in 1994, as a man, rejecting arguments that "she" was a cross-dressing lesbian.

Although some languages like English have a third person pronoun that is gender neutral (*it*), we do not normally use it to refer to people (see chap. 3) because we assume they are not sexually neuter. Unlike other languages, English lacks a sex-differentiated first person pronoun. Although the pronoun *I* is sex-neutral, we assume by convention that it refers to a gendered subject. Interviews with Maori novelist Keri Hulme have shown how closely she has based the central "neuter" character of her book *The bone people* (1984), Kerewin Holmes, on herself. Both the novelist in TV interviews and her character in the novel described themselves as sexless, sexually drawn neither to male nor female, "neuter." In the novel, Kerewin Holmes commented:

> I spent a considerable amount of time when I was o [sic] adolescent, wondering why I was different, whether there were other people like me. Why, when everyone else was fascinated by their developing sexual nature, I couldn't give a damn. I've never been attracted to men. Or women. Or anything else. It's difficult to explain, and nobody has ever believed it when I have tried to explain, but while I have an apparently normal female body, I don't have any sexual urge or appetite. I think I am a neuter. (p. 276)

Audre Lorde (1982, p. 7), on the other hand, wrote that she "always wanted to be both man and woman."

The status of persons who do not fall into the traditional categories poses considerable linguistic problems. How does one speak about the pregnancy of a female-to-male transsexual? Sylviane Dullak, a male-to-female transsexual, entitled her 1983 autobiography *Je serai elle* ('I would be she'). Brawn's (1995) examination of the autobiographies of four male-to-female transsexuals revealed that the authors alternated in significant ways between male and female pronouns to express differences in attitude and identification. For example, after surgery Gina Noël wrote, "*Avant j'étais un transsexuel, maintenant j'étais femme*" ('Before I was a transsexual, now I was a woman'; cited in Brawn, 1995, p. 219). Here the use of the masculine noun for "transsexual" underscored the transition from male to female. Earlier in her life story, however, Noël referred to herself at times as masculine and at times feminine. The author used the traditional grammatical gender system as a way of dealing with the inadequacies of the concept of gender. The pronouns are used to represent not just anatomy, but a complex and varying concept of oneself as a gendered person. Likewise, *Newsweek*'s article (November 4, 1996, p. 66) about transsexual minister Erin Swenson used *he* to refer to Swenson presurgery and *she* to refer to the minister postsurgery: "Privately, Swenson says, she had struggled with her gender for decades. When he married, he told himself that his confused feeling would go away."

Members of the gay and lesbian community sometimes use the traditional system of pronominal reference in novel ways, as, for example, when gay men refer to themselves and their partners as *she* and on occasion even call them derogatory names for females such as *whore* (see chap. 4 for discussion of how women are talked about). These uses seem to be cases where language serves as a statement of sexual orientation rather than identity. Female designation is not a mark of femininity but of opposition to orthodox heterosexual masculinity. A large majority of homosexuals do not express the wish to become members of the opposite sex, and thus have a male gender identity. Transsexuals, on the other hand, say they feel they are members of one sex trapped in the body of the other. Thus, male-to-female transsexuals construct themselves around notions of femininity, adopting some of the more extreme outer indexes of femininity such as heavy makeup, high heels, and so on, with some even attending workshops on how to speak like a woman. Thus, dress and language converge as male-to-female transsexuals try to uphold a traditional stereotypical construction of femininity, in order to pass as members of the sex in which they feel most comfortable.

Sexually liminal communities whose anatomy and psychology outlaw them from the traditional categories use the binary system of linguistic gender that excludes them in order to generate their own alliances and as parody of the dichotomy between male and female. Yet serious investigation of the question of whether the language of such sexually liminal communities is different is only just beginning, although there has been a long tradition of stereotypes, as can be seen in the following report written in 1709 by a commentator observing a group of gay men in a London bar. Here we have a number of stereotypes, which relate not just to the specific features of language women and gay men are believed to share, but also to some more general characteristics of how they converse and how much they talk. They gossip and chatter, shriek and scold (see chap. 6).

They adopt all the small vanities natural to the feminine sex to such an extent that they try to speak, walk, chatter, shriek and scold as women do, aping them as well in other respects. In a certain tavern in the City, the name of which I will not mention, not wishing to bring the house into disrepute, they hold parties and regular gatherings. As soon as they arrive, they begin to behave exactly as women do, carrying on light gossip as is the custom of a merry company of real women. (cited in Bailey, 1991, pp. 246–247)

There are competing views about the cultural as opposed to physiological basis for certain other observable differences between men's and women's speech. For instance, on average, men have lower pitched speaking voices than women and children. This difference is at least partly due to differences in anatomy as a result of secondary sexual changes taking place at puberty, when the male vocal cords lengthen. Men have larger larynxes and their longer and thicker vocal cords vibrate at lower fundamental frequencies. Fundamental frequency is the main (although not the only) determinant of perceived pitch. Women also use a wider pitch range than men; this has been demonstrated in languages as different as Japanese and English. This is what gives rise to the stereotype that women are more excitable and emotional than men (see further in chap. 6). Similarly, a higher pitched voice is associated with a whining child.

All speakers raise their pitch somewhat in public speaking to make themselves heard, but because most women's voices are already higher pitched than those of most men, they have less leeway to raise their pitch before listeners start to perceive them as shrill and emotional. Women have been typically excluded from media positions as announcers and broadcasters because it was thought their voices lacked authority (see further evidence in chap. 9). Women were therefore seen as unsuitable for conveying information about serious topics such as the news. The voice of rationality and authority is male. Apparently, it is still difficult to convince the BBC to let women produce commentaries or voice-overs. Interestingly, during World War II, it was seen as appropriate and even desirable that women were newsreaders because they were broadcasting to audiences of soldiers deprived of female companionship. On the London and Hong Kong underground systems, the prerecorded voices announcing the names of the stations are now female, and some of the BBC newsreaders are women.

However, male–female differences in pitch cannot be fully accounted for without reference to social factors. Adult Polish men, for instance, tend to have higher pitched voices, on average, than American men. Speakers can also be taught to use pitch levels that are not appropriate to the size and shape of their larynx—a famous case being Margaret Thatcher, whom I discuss in chapter 6. When playing house, even 4-year-old children use deeper and louder voices for Father, higher pitch for Mother, and modified baby-talk-like speech for Child. Studies show also that the voices of adult deaf males who have never heard speech do not "break" at puberty. All these things indicate that pitch is at least partly a matter of cultural convention, even though there may be a biological element to it too. Over time, human as well as animal males have developed low-pitched voices to sound dominant and aggressive, probably in order to compete with one another for access to female mating partners. When animals fight, the larger and more aggressive one wins. It was thus advantageous from an evolutionary point of view for males to try to alter their pitch to signal large body size.

This example, like the two previous ones in this section, indicates a complex interaction between biology and culture. It also shows how extremely careful we must be in interpreting the results from the many studies claiming to show differences between men and women. Most human behaviors and characteristics show quite a range of variability. It is rarely the case that every male differs from every female. Most of the differences separating men and women are frequently small in comparison to the variability found within each sex. What we find is a continuum of variability. On average men have lower voices, are taller, stronger, and more muscular than women, but not every man has a lower voice, or is taller, stronger, and more muscular than every woman. It is only quite recently that women have been employed in any number in broadcasting and that girls have been allowed to roam freely and develop their bodies as trained athletes.

No women were allowed in the Olympic marathons until 1984, for instance, largely due to the belief that biological differences between men and women prevented them from competing athletically. Yet, there are some sports where female body characteristics give an advantage. When Gertrude Ederle became the first woman to swim the English Channel in 1926, the world was not only amazed that she could do it, but that she broke the existing men's record by 2 hours. A London newspaper did not have time to withdraw an editorial claiming that her failure demonstrated that women were physically inferior to men and that women could therefore not hope to compete with men. Women's greater body fat provided extra buoyancy and protection against the cold. Other sports such as tennis and basketball, which rely more on upper body strength, favor men's bodies. As social restrictions on female athletics have loosened, and training facilities for women improved, we have seen tremendous strides in women's performance.

THANK GOD I AM NOT A WOMAN

A major part of the problem in evaluating the so-called biological evidence is that society's views about women have long dictated that men should be regarded as genetically superior to women. Adults react differently to male and female children from the day they are born. Many cultures have proverbs and sayings instructing mothers on the different techniques for handling boys and girls. Beliefs about misfortune, unluckiness, and other negative consequences associated with the birth of girls follow females through their life cycle and are expressed in the discourse of sexuality in the form of proverbs, stories, religious rituals, institutions, and symbols. At Japanese New Year, for instance, it is bad luck if a woman is the first person to enter the house. Many cultures have proverbs expressing beliefs about the inferiority of women, such as these Burmese ones: "Even a male dog is superior to a female human" and "If a woman had no nose, she would eat excrement" (Spiro, 1993, p. 317). In China there is a saying that if you spare a woman a beating for three days, she will stand on the roof and tear the house apart (Zhang, 1992).

Even before birth, girls tend to be less valued than boys in many cultures. Scientists working on the development of the atomic bomb at Los Alamos during World War II took bets among themselves as to whether they would ultimately have a "boy" or a "girl," that is, a success or a dud, respectively. Ultimately, their successful experiments resulted in the "birth" of the bomb nicknamed "Little Boy," "fathered" by J. Robert Oppenheimer. These nicknames reflect widespread preferences in our own and other societies for male children, partly because the male line is guaranteed through sons. In China, for instance, where abortion is readily available, and there is government pressure restricting parents to one child, most aborted fetuses are female and orphanages are filled with unwanted girls. Many more parents hope they will have sons rather than daughters in countries like India, where daughters are an economic liability because fathers have to pay their future husbands a dowry of jewelry, cash, and other goods. A Bedouin midwife recounted to anthropologist Lila Abu-Lughod (1986) how differently people react to the birth of boys. Everyone present rejoices and they run to tell the father. By contrast, if a girl is born, they don't go to tell the men. No one eats dinner. When women come to visit the new mother and her baby son, they offer congratulations. When her child is a girl, they offer formulaic phrases and statements such as "Thank God for your safety," or "Whatever God brings is good."

The Bedouins of the Egyptian western desert value males because they believe them to be morally superior to females. Female inferiority results from women's association with reproduction and sexuality, factors over which women have no control. Women's sexuality poses such a threat to the prevailing social order that it must continually be denied through women's constant show of deference, modesty, and chastity. Women also prefer male children because sons provide their security in a culture organized patrilineally. To the Bedouins, the Western saying that "A son's a son until he takes a wife but a daughter's a daughter the rest of her life" would sound strange. When a Bedouin woman marries, she leaves her own relatives to live with her husband's family. If she lives at a distance from her mother and father, she may rarely see them because her husband determines her rights to visit and be absent from his household. If she divorces, or her husband dies before her, she will depend on her adult sons. When her daughters marry, they will leave home and not be in a position to provide help to their mothers. Their children will be part of her husband's family. The Western saying expresses a belief that the mother–daughter emotional bond remains intact after marriage and is a guarantee of assistance and comfort in old age. Nevertheless, even in Bedouin culture, a woman recognizes that it is her daughters on whom she relies for assistance with day-to-day household chores. Paradoxically, however, the children who secure her position in her husband's household also increase his control over her. She would lose her children if she left, either by choice or as a result of divorce.

Many cultures share the Bedouins' view that it is women's association with nature, emotions, irrationality, fertility, reproduction, and sexuality which dooms them to inferiority. This is why the statement "Thank God I am not a woman" is part of Jewish religious ritual. In the Western tradition, the Biblical account of creation holds Eve responsible for the sin of eating the forbidden fruit. She is the morally weak one who gives in to the serpent's temptation. While both she and Adam are driven from the Garden of Eden, it is she who will be cursed with pain in childbirth and will have her husband rule over her. The fruit, often depicted in paintings as an apple, is, of course, symbolic of larger issues. The tree is the tree of the knowledge of good and evil, and Eve's desire for knowledge is a desire for authority. Her sins are disobedience to God's authority, and giving in to the devil's temptation to satisfy her fleshly desires for knowledge, which will confer power. The price for her sin is the loss of immortality for all humans. Eve's quest for knowledge brings suffering and misery, just as in Greek mythology, Pandora's curiosity leads her to open the box, which unleashes evil into the world. The story of Cupid and Psyche is also a myth of sexual difference. Psyche cannot resist looking at her god lover even though she has been warned not to look. When she does, he vanishes as punishment for her curiosity, her quest for (sexual) knowledge.

Here we see some of the origins for a stereotypical view of women. Because women are weak, they give in to temptation. Because they are unable to control their tongues and their curiosity, they are dangerous and need to be controlled. The New Testament is filled with injunctions against women's speech, dismissed as "old wives' fables" (1 Tim. 4:7), and women who are "tattlers also and busybodies, speaking things which they ought not" (1 Tim. 5:13). (See chap. 6 for discussion of how gossip became associated with women.)

The creation stories of some non-Western cultures such as those of the Maori of New Zealand incorporate similar biases against women, despite a belief in an originally equal male and female force. The primal parents were Rangi awatea, the Sky Father above, and Papatuanuku, the Earth Mother below, who embraced so closely together they shut out the light. When they had children, who were gods, they were born into the darkness until one of them, Tane, stood with his hands on Papatuanuku and thrust against Rangi awatea with his feet to force them apart.

The god Tane wanted to create a race of people to live on earth so he fashioned a mortal woman from the mud and earth whom he named Hine ahuone. She had a daughter, Hine titama, whom Tane married, thus committing incest. When Hine titama discovered that her husband was also her father, she fled to the underworld in shame, where she became *Hine nui te Po,* "Great Lady of the Night," positioning herself at the doorway through which all her earthly descendants would eventually pass. The would-be-immortal Maui tried to defeat death by entering her vagina in order to pass through her body while she was asleep, but she woke up and crushed him with her thighs, thus bringing death and destruction into the world permanently. Female reproductive organs were named *whare o aitua* or *whare o mate,* "house of misfortune/death." In Maori culture, these creation stories give rise to the belief that women are lowly, destructive, profane, but fruitful, whereas men are high and sacred. Thus, the roles of male and female are set apart, and it is again women who are responsible for human mortality, even though only women can give life.

Women are also linked to life in Bedouin cultural practice through the fact that only men slaughter animals. Menstruation pollutes women and prevents them from attaining high moral status because a menstruating woman is not allowed to pray, touch holy objects, or enter a mosque. Her fasts also do not count. Men, however, have no natural restrictions on their performance of religious rituals. The uncleanliness associated with menstruation taints all females from the time they first begin to menstruate until menopause. The red belt worn by married Bedouin women symbolizes women's sexuality and procreation. Men are associated with the color white, a symbol of moral purity. Women never wear white. The wearing of a black headcloth and veil, the other distinctive item of married women's clothing, marks the transition from virgin to woman. To go without a belt is considered indecent, signaling a woman's readiness for sexual activity, because the only time a woman removes it is when she sleeps with her husband. Both men and women cover their heads as a sign of modesty, but a woman also uses her headcloth as a veil to hide her shame and her modesty about her sexuality in front of men. The surest way to protect her modesty is to avoid men altogether and women do not let themselves be seen by men unless it is unavoidable. They do not go to market and don't appear when strangers or guests visit the household. If contact is unavoidable, they use their veils. Women also refrain from talking, eating, or laughing in the presence of men. Even in the company of those in front of whom they would not normally wear their veils, women use their veils to indicate embarrassment at remarks or actions of a sexual nature, for example, at a baby girl who happens to reveal her bare bottom, or talk about marriage.

A "good" woman shows no interest in sexual matters, even to the point of denying her own sexuality (see further discussion in chap. 7 of similar constraints in Western culture). A "good" girl cries at the thought of marriage and the "good" bride screams when the groom comes near her. Yet pregnancy is proof of sexual activity, which has no equivalent among men. Even though childbirth is wanted because men need children to carry on their lineage, and barren women are looked down upon, the act of giving birth is also polluting. Through menstruation and pregnancy, women lose control over their bodies. This is why denial of sexuality is more important to women's virtue than it is to men's. Men's honor also depends on control of natural passions and functions. A man must not give in to fear, pain, hunger, and dependency. Because sexuality leads to dependency, men must deny it by avoiding women.

To be masculine is thus to devalue and reject what is feminine. More specifically, a boy must detach himself from his mother and his dependency on her. The male initiation rituals of Papua New Guinea and other parts of the world make explicit the separation of boys from the domestic sphere and their mothers' influence. Among the Hua people, boys are subjected to nose-bleeding and vomiting to purge themselves of the woman within them. This is what makes them men. Interestingly, the word for "boy" (bade) in the Hua language spoken in Papua New Guinea is composed of the words for "woman" (ba) and "man" (de) (Haiman, 1979, p. 40). The fact that a boy is etymologically half woman and half man encodes a cultural belief that people are not born male and female, but achieve their masculinity and femininity through a series of initiation rituals (see chaps. 7 and 8 for parallels in Western culture).

CHANGING THE SUBJECT

If the achievement of male identity involves a rejection of what is female, for women, the route to transcendence lies only in self-destruction, because to abandon femininity is to destroy herself. This is why some French feminist theories have argued that in order for women to become fully human, we need to grasp the subjectivity that has been appropriated by men for themselves. Some scholars have commented on how the women's movement has seemingly come full circle, starting from an initial denial of the fundamental differences between men and women, to a celebration of difference, and an emphasis on women's superiority. This is a radical discourse because it challenges the dominant ideology of women's difference being interpreted as *inferiority*.

This perspective is gynocentric, stressing that female qualities, whether their origin lies in culture or biology, are superior. At its most extreme, it is the mirror image of traditional androcentrism. Women are not just different but superior to men; they are more caring, nurturing, connected to others. According to some theories, women's nurturing has a biological basis and provides a morally superior basis for society than a male one based on hierarchy and domination.

A number of feminists have written about the different conceptions of self and ways of interacting with others boys and girls they come to have, due to their different relationships with their mothers. All children identify first with their mother, yet both boys and girls must come to reject this identification. A girl must learn to identify with the male point of view at school and in public life (see chap. 7). Boys get their value system reaffirmed and endorsed. In some theories, the fact of being mothered creates a need in men to exert their superiority over women. Boys are brought up to expect nurturing as a natural part of life. Mothers consciously and unconsciously teach their daughters to pay attention to the emotional needs of others. Thus, according to Nancy Chodorow, the basic feminine sense of self is connected to the world while the masculine sense of self is separate. Carol Gilligan, voted Woman of the Year in 1984 by *Ms* magazine, countered many of the traditional views about the development of male and female identity. In doing so, however, she argued for distinct differences in women's and men's moral development and reasoning. She said that women were more likely to make moral choices within the context of particular situations rather than on the basis of abstract and impersonal rules. Some such as Tannen have interpreted differences in patterns of talk associated with all-male and all-female groups as a reflection of women's greater involvement. Holmes argues that there are certain positive qualities in women's style, which are worth adopting more generally (see chap. 6).

Again, however, the role of women in reproduction is central, as can be seen in feminist theory's rewriting and retelling those myths of origin which have tried to justify male priority (see chap. 11). Consider, for example, how some feminist critiques of reproduction argue for "natural" female priority and even superiority to the male. From a biological point of view, the development of the fertilized egg is basically female. All female eggs contain one of the sex chromosomes, X. Male sperm may be either X-chromosome (female) or Y-chromosome bearing (male). Some have, in fact, described the Y chromosome as an incomplete X because it is one of the smallest chromosomes and seems to carry no information other than maleness. For the first 7 weeks in the life of a fetus internal and external genitalia look the same. Biological maleness is brought about when the embryonic gonads, glands which later become either male testes or female ovaries, start to produce the male hormone testosterone. This causes the genitals to assume male form and later is responsible for the appearance of secondary sexual characteristics. Whether the gonads become ovaries or testes is determined by the chromosomes received from the parents at the time of conception.

Traditional embryology textbooks, however, have described this differentiation process as resulting from the "activity" of male hormones, leaving the female to be defined in terms of her "absence" of male hormones rather than as the result of female hormonal activity. Similar conceptions of the active male role in conception and the passive female role portray the sperm as actively seeking out eggs to penetrate. The language used in descriptions of sexual intercourse has likewise emphasized the dominance of the male and passiveness of the female. This is in line with Masters and Johnson (1966) finding that the most common position for sexual activity among heterosexual American couples was the traditional "missionary" position, which gives the male partner more freedom to determine the pace and movement of intercourse.

Recent discoveries and feminist critiques of cell biology, however, challenge the traditional view of conception and suggest that the egg not only guides the sperm with tiny projections on its surface holding the sperm and slowly enveloping it, but also that the sperm must be activated with secretions from the female reproductive tract. This view is at odds with the traditional idea of the female reproductive tract as a passive conduit for male sperm. Even a psychology textbook published in 1993 defined the vagina as "the female canal into which the penis enters during sexual intercourse" and the penis as "the primary male sex organ" (Feldman, 1993, p. 388). Thus, it is not just gender, which is discursively constructed, but sex too, with the prevailing scientific theories assuming that the female is developed passively, and the male actively produced from an otherwise female state. Such theories have in turn reinforced popular beliefs about the primacy of males in reproduction. Archbishop Adrianus Cardinal Simonis, Primate of the Netherlands, cited fertilization as evidence for the passive duties of women. He observed that the egg merely "waits" for the male sperm, the "dynamic, active, masculine vector of new life" (New York Times, March 25, 1987, p. 20).

Many feminists have concluded from these critiques of the traditional view that the basic human form is female and that maleness represents an addition to or deviation from this basically female ground plan. The biological evidence for female basicness and superiority can be further strengthened by the fact that there are some species such as the whiptail lizard in the southwestern United States, which have only females. There are no all-male species. Moreover, in some species males are eaten after they fulfill their role in reproduction.

Other evidence cited by feminists in support of female superiority includes the fact that the lack of a second X chromosome puts men at a biological disadvantage. Some sex-linked diseases are passed through the Y chromosome from fathers to sons. Still others are more likely to occur if there is no counter-balancing X chromosome. Hemophilia and disabilities such as red-green color blindness are among the 100 or more known sex-linked disorders found mostly in males. Women are in many respects more robust than men from the beginning. Female fetuses are less vulnerable to miscarriage, stillbirth, SIDS (sudden infant death syndrome)/cot death, and retardation. Even though women mature more quickly, they tend to live longer. Being male is associated with higher mortality during gestation and afterwards throughout childhood and adulthood. Many childhood diseases affect males more than females, thus suggesting that males are biologically the more fragile members of the human species.

Of course, all this flies in the face of received wisdom handed down culturally, which suggests women are weak, passive, and derivative of men, encoded in a variety of ways in many languages such as English, where suffixes mark feminine terms, for example, *actress*, *majorette*, and so on. Take, for instance, the Biblical account of God's creation of the two sexes, in which Adam is made first and Eve is formed later when God takes a rib from Adam. As Dale Spender (1980a, p. 166) pointed out, this is gross biological distortion since men do not give birth: "She shall be called woman because she was taken out of man" (Genesis 2:23). Yet, as I have argued, creation myths are central to human understanding of the world and the role we have in it. Despite woman's essential role in reproduction, she has her origin in man and owes her existence to him. This idea that women are appendages to men finds a counterpart in many languages such as English, where many feminine occupational terms are formally derived from the male version, for example, *manager/manageress*, and many women's names are diminutives of men's, for example, *Henrietta, Georgette, Pauline*. This is no accident, but I have more to say about that in subsequent chapters. Significantly, God also gave Adam the right and power to name and domesticate the animals. Who names, has power, as I will argue when I talk about naming practices in chapter 5. These are but a few of the linguistic ways in which women are constructed as "other."

If we were to apply the logic often used by men that culture simply mirrors the "natural" state of affairs between the sexes, then it is really surprising that we refer to *mankind* instead of *womankind* and that it is women who are labeled as *authoresses, usherettes*, and so on. Language reform is a large part of the agenda of feminist theorists such as Dale Spender, who believes that men's control over language and meaning creates their power and women's oppression. Mary Daly (1978) says women must also abandon the language of men in order to break the "bonds of phallocracy." They must castrate the male meanings of certain words such as *witch*, *hag*, and *crone*, in order to reclaim them for women's empowerment. Insofar as sexist language practices are symbolic of women's inequality, opposition to deliberate reform has become a strategic site of resistance (see chaps. 4 and 10).

Very quickly, however, it again becomes difficult to disentangle what is innate from what is cultural in some strands of this argument for female biological superiority because one reason for men's greater mortality later in life may be that men seek medical help less readily than females. In both Britain and the United States, more women than men consult their doctors. Greater strength, aggression, and physical activity are part of the male stereotype. Some diseases are more frequently found in men because they are associated with male life styles, for example, lung cancer, heart attacks, cirrhosis of the liver. However, now that it is more socially acceptable for women to drink, smoke, and engage in high-stress executive positions, which have been associated with these illnesses, the gap has lessened between death rates for men and women from these causes. In most of the Third World, women have lower life expectancies than men, whereas in industrialized countries this pattern is reversed. In Britain, a man is twice as likely as a woman to die before the age of 65.

GENES, GENDER, AND SOCIAL POLICY: THE DIFFERENCE THAT DIFFERENCE MAKES

Before concluding this chapter, I want to consider briefly some of the practical consequences of these theoretical debates about the extent to which our genes determine who we are and what we become, and how they are important in determining social policy. Biological reductivism encourages acceptance of the status quo by suggesting that cultural practices follow from biology.

If we believe, for example, that under any circumstances boys will tend to do better than girls at math, then it is easier to accept as "natural" that more boys than girls will pursue careers in engineering and science. Similarly, if differences in verbal ability and visual–spatial skills between male and female are biologically determined, then we shouldn't be surprised that more men are mechanics or contractors and more women are involved in poorly paid service positions. Those who believe that social factors discourage girls from studying math and excelling in science will want to develop special programs to encourage girls to study these subjects.

In 1974, the Women's Educational Equity Act provided funding for projects to expand and improve vocational and career education for women. Since then increasing numbers of women have been enrolling in traditional male fields such as engineering and medicine. The American Association of University Women's (1991) study, *Shortchanging Girls, Shortchanging America* discovered that boys and girls who like math and science have higher levels of self-esteem than other children. For girls especially, these subjects are tied to ambition. Girls who take and do well in these subjects are more likely to aspire to professional careers. Women who have taken more than two math courses in college are the only women who later achieved pay equity and in some cases earned even more than men.

A more dramatic example of how our views on the nature versus nurture controversy may affect policy can be seen in the perception of rape as a crime and handling of rape cases. Is male "uncontrollable mating urge" and "natural" aggressiveness responsible for rape, child molestation, and other similar crimes? California's decision in 1996 to make repeated child molesters undergo weekly treatment during their parole period with the drug Depoprovera to reduce their sex drive is an example of the treatment of sex crimes as a fundamentally biological problem rather than as a social and cultural one motivated by aggression and anger toward women. It is consistent with the "boys will be boys" philosophy, which regards rape as a hormonal eruption of natural male sexual aggression. Again, anthropological studies provide a cross-cultural perspective and show us that rape is not an integral part of male nature, because there are societies which are relatively rape-free in which men do not use sexual aggression to display masculinity and to control women (see Sanday, 1990). Abusive sexual behavior is not a necessary part of male sexual development. In chapter 8, I discuss how talk about rape and sex crimes in the media and courtroom legitimizes verbal and physical violence toward women.

Male violence and its alleged inevitability came to be the focus of radical feminism, with some such as Mary Daly and Jill Johnstone insisting on total separation from men. Daly (1978) provides a detailed examination of various types of cruelty men have inflicted on women, for example, widow burning in India, footbinding in China, genital mutilation in Africa, and so on. Pessimism about male violence has led women like Robin Morgan to say that only women can guarantee the future of life on earth.

A number of feminist utopias, which I discuss in chapter 11, have been built on the premise of women gaining control over their reproductive technology and eliminating men on the assumption that an all-female world based on female values of nurturing and cooperation rather than on male ones of dominance and aggression is essential to the survival of the human species. Of course, it is already possible to contemplate intervening in biological and genetic development. "Biological" solutions to social problems have already been used, for example, sterilization of certain groups of undesirable immigrants to the United States earlier in this century, or suggested, for example, hormone treatments for lesbians and gays to change them to heterosexuals, castration of male sex offenders, and so on.

Even if we accept the view that culture plays a more important role than biology, that does not mean it is necessarily going to be a simple matter to change culturally conditioned ways of behaving and thinking. This is particularly so with regard to power sharing. A more powerful group asked to make more concessions to a less powerful group is quite likely to resist.

I see problems too with the celebration approach to feminism, especially when it appeals to biological or cultural reductivism. Although I think most people would agree that being a woman is not synonymous with being a feminist, if you accept the case for biological essentialism and a limited view of feminism as that which concerns women, then only women can be feminist. Edward Said's discussion of how Western scholars have constructed Orientalism, a discourse about non-Western others, has clarified the discomfort I have felt with the notion of cultural feminism celebrating the universality and uniqueness of women's experience. Like the discourse of Negritude, Afro-centrism, and so on, the language of cultural feminism is one of reverse Orientalism.

This reversal of logic, which privileges the female over the male, does not really take us beyond the negative definition of those we define as "others." Difference continues to be defined in terms of lack and exclusion. It does not really challenge the division of the world into two binary categories of male and female. I am pessimistic about the prospect of avoiding the reproduction of dominance relations in a performance space or on a stage where only the principal players are altered and women simply take the space that men once had. Gynocentrism reproduces the many dualisms pervading Western thought between self/other, male/female, mind/body, subject/object, civilized/primitive, nature/nuture, and so on, which have supported the domination of all those regarded as others on whatever grounds, people of color, women, animals. The opposition between self and other is reinscribed in a variety of other dualities. The self needs an other, just as the subject needs an object, the master needs a slave, and so on.

This is why radical feminism cannot be concerned solely with the elimination of sexism, but must work toward the eradication of all hierarchies of dominance in favor of what Riane Eisler (1987), for instance, calls a partnership model, or *gylany*, a term which links male and female. To some, this agenda goes beyond the label *feminism*, which to many suggests a focus on "women's troubles," often more specifically on the aim of achieving equal rights of middle-class White women, and therefore needs a broader label. Clearly, the worldview so far embraced under labels such as *humanism* has failed to produce a radical critique showing the ways in which sexism, racism, and imperialism are interconnected and do not exist in isolation from one another (see chap. 3).

bell hooks (1984, pp. 25–26), for instance, sees the feminist movement as being directed at the cultural basis of group oppression. Thus, oppression on grounds of race and class would be feminist issues along with the struggle to end sexism. The aim of feminism is not to benefit any particular group of women defined in terms of race or class. Nor should it privilege women over men. I believe she is right that there can be no radical feminist revolution without an end to racism.

Recognizing that gender is culturally and historically constructed goes hand in hand with my belief that the focus on difference is scientifically as well as politically misguided. However, this does not mean we can dispense with many of the current debates about what it means to be a woman, a man, gay, lesbian, bisexual, heterosexual, transsexual, and so on. Nor does it mean that we have to pretend we're all the same and forget about the differences. It means rather that we recognize differences without seeing them as necessary determinants of character traits we have come to associate with femininity and masculinity. Concepts of femininity and masculinity are like other culturally created fictions based on race, such as African American, Native American, Latino, and so on, which come to have psychological reality when institutionalized by the dominant culture and exist by virtue of their opposition to it. They can have an enormous amount of political power both for oppression as well as liberation. What we need to change is the vantage point, or lens, through which we view difference.

Feminist theorist Catherine MacKinnon has cautioned against regarding gender differences as an explanatory "bottom line." Instead, she advocates looking at the difference gender makes. It is no accident that the stereotypical female style of behavior shows the traits it does when the burden of caring for others has disproportionately fallen on women. Greater social sensitivity and politeness are the burden of subordinates in a climate when one has to pay attention to the nuances of the struggle for equality (see chap. 6 on the linguistic hallmarks of politeness). Deborah Cameron (1992a) feels we should not unequivocally celebrate differences that have evolved and been sustained through limiting women's freedom of choice, and through keeping women in a subordinate and economically dependent condition. This does not mean, however, that we need to see women's behavior as being uniformly determined by and indicative of their subordination and powerlessness. Another implication of continuing to believe that men and women are opposites with different traits is that it absolves men from the responsibility of being caring, nurturing, and so on.

Finally, insistence on essential differences between men's and women's experience leaves little scope for transforming the relations between men and women. As long as transcendence is defined as transcendence of what is feminine, there can be no equality. This approach does not permit transcendence of sexist notions of masculinity. Cameron and Frazer (1987, p. 177) argue that we must aspire to a feminist future in which transcendence is not the only possible self-affirmation.

In the next three chapters, I will show how some of the negative cultural beliefs about women and their sexuality I discussed in this chapter have become incorporated into language. The next chapter takes as a specific example some of the metaphors underlying noun classification systems and how failure to take into account the relationship between sex and gender has led linguists to insist on the basic semantic arbitrariness of gender as a grammatical category.

EXERCISES AND DISCUSSION QUESTIONS

1. Examine some of the ways in which gender differences are portrayed in traditional nursery rhymes. Here are a few to get you started.

Little Jack Horner sat in a corner eating his pudding pie
He put in his thumb and pulled out a plum
And said what a good boy am I!

Little Miss Muffett sat on a tuffet
Eating her curds and whey.
Along came a spider and sat down beside her
And frightened Miss Muffet away.

Mistress Mary quite contrary
How does your garden grow?
With silver bells and cockle shells
And pretty maids all in a row.

Compare these with some from the collection called *Father Gander Nursery Rhymes* (Larche, 1986). The aim is to give a parallel female imagery to traditional nursery rhymes. What do you think of them?

Wee Willie Winkie runs through the town,
Upstairs and downstairs in his nightgown.
Rapping at the window, crying through the lock,
"Are the children in their beds.
For it's now eight o'clock?"

Wee Wendy Winkie stands on the stair,
Watching and guarding the townspeople there.

If she sees danger she'll ring the town bell,
When peaceful she shouts,
"Eight o'clock and all's well!"

Jack be nimble, Jack be quick,
Jack jump over the candlestick!
Jill be nimble, jump it too,
If Jack can do it, so can you!

2. Perform the same analysis as in question 1 with at least two traditional fairy tales such as *Cinderella* and *Snow White*, or any others of your own choosing.

3. Judith Butler (1990, p. 147) writes that "the identity categories often presumed to be foundational to feminist politics, that is deemed necessary in order to mobilize feminism as an identity politics, simultaneously work to limit and constrain in advance the very cultural possibilities that feminism is supposed to open up." Do you agree or disagree? Why?

4. Judith Butler (1993, p. 232) describes a cartoon strip in which someone declares of a newborn infant "It's a lesbian." Discuss the assumptions behind the cartoon. Do you agree with them?

5. Examine some dictionaries, old (i.e., pre- 1970) and new, to see what definitions they provide for the terms *sex, gender, man/woman, male/female, masculinity*, and *femininity*. Can you detect changes in how these terms are defined? If so, why and how do you think this has happened?

6. Susan Faludi (1991) says that the meaning of the word *feminist* has not really changed since it first appeared in a book review in the *Athenaeum* (April 27, 1895) describing a woman who "has in her the capacity for fighting her way back to independence." Do you agree? Is there a definition of feminism which all women would accept?

ANNOTATED BIBLIOGRAPHY AND SUGGESTIONS FOR FURTHER READING

Chapter 7 of Donna Haraway's (1991) book traces the history and meanings of the terms *sex* and *gender* in English and other European languages. Nancy Tuana (1993) presents a good overview of scientific, religious, and philosophical conceptions of women. Sherry Ortner's (1974) article proposes women's closer symbolic association with nature as opposed to culture as the explanation for the universal devaluation of females. Riane Eisler (1987) provides a different interpretation of the story of Adam and Eve in which the serpent and the tree are female symbolic remnants of a widespread form of Goddess worship. While Eve's sin still lies in her defiance of a

male God, the vilification of the serpent and the association of women
with evil provide a means of discrediting the Goddess. Jane Caputi's (1991)
article and Brian Easley's (1983) book examine how women have figured
in scientific thinking and metaphors (see also the essays in Tuana, 1989,
especially the critique of cell biology by the biology and gender study
group). Chapter 2 of David Graddol and Joan Swann's (1989) book contains discussion of female/male difference in pitch. Marina Warner's (1994)
book analyzes the symbolism of traditional fairy tales (see also the first
two chapters of Andrea Dworkin's 1974 book), but see P. Gander's (1989)
"Father Goose" rhymes and the collection of feminist fairy tales edited by
Jack Zipes (1986a). The quotation from Thomas Wilson's *Art of Rhetoric*
(1553) is taken from Dennis Baron (1986, p. 3). Arguments for the biological superiority of women can be found in Ashley Montague's (1968)
book. The anthology by Susan Philips, Susan Steele, and Christine Tanz
(1987) contains useful essays addressing the interaction between social,
cultural, and biological processes. The collection by Anna Livia and Kira
Hall (1996) examines the language practices of sexually liminal communities
and William Leap's (1996) book examines gay men's language. Feminist
accounts of women's psychological and sexual development can be found
in Nancy Chodorow's (1978) and Luce Irigaray's (1985) books. Carol
Warren's (1987) book examines the diagnosis of schizophrenia among
women. Catherine Lutz's (1990) article discusses the evidence for women's
supposed greater emotionality. On the gender gap in math/ science achievement and esteem see Phyllis Rosser's (1989) and Peggy Orenstein's (1994)
books (and chap. 7 of this book). Lynn Segal's (1988) book is a useful
overview of some of the issues in contemporary feminism.

3

What's Gender Got
to Do With Grammar?

Gretchen: Wilhelm, where is the turnip? [German *die Rübe*]
Wilhelm: She has gone to the kitchen.
Gretchen: Where is the accomplished and beautiful English maiden? [German *das Mädchen*]
Wilhelm: It has gone to the opera. (Twain, "The awful German language," *A Tramp Abroad*, 1935, pp. 1147–1148)

A cartoon in *Ladies' Home Journal* magazine by Henry Martin depicted a woman pulling up at a service station and saying to the attendant, "Fill him up!"

The two epigraphs to this chapter derive their humor at least partly from a deliberate confusion of the distinction between what linguists have traditionally called "natural" and "grammatical" gender. In his essay Mark Twain goes on to say that in German "a young lady has no sex, while a turnip has," because the word for 'young woman' is *das Mädchen*, or neuter in gender, and the word for 'turnip', *die Rübe*, is feminine. Hence the pronouns that refer to them must be either neuter (*it*) or feminine (*she*), respectively. A linguist would say simply that every German noun belongs to one of three gender categories conventionally labeled masculine, feminine, or neuter. Twain's literal translation sounds comical to English speakers because only persons or other living things with biological sex are usually referred to as *she*. Things such as turnips do not come in male and female varieties and therefore have to be referred to as *it*. Conversely, if the *Ladies' Home Journal* cartoon were translated literally into German, it would not be funny at all. Because the word for 'car' in German (*der Wagen*) is masculine, a masculine pronoun would have to be used in referring to it.

Textbooks generally offer such examples to beginning students of linguistics as an illustration of the basic arbitrariness underlying the category of gender in languages like German, where the fact that a noun is feminine, for instance, is no guarantee that the thing it refers to is feminine. In addition, a noun that is classified as feminine in one language might be masculine in another. In French, for instance, both *la voiture* and *l'auto* 'car' are feminine.

However, there is much more behind these examples than appears at first glance. In this chapter I look at some of the differences between languages like German, where the linguistic category of gender as a noun classification system is said to be "grammatical" and sex supposedly has nothing to do with gender, and others such as English, where it is claimed to be "natural" and to work according to the sex of the person being referred to. I show that languages do not work quite so neatly. There is in fact "leakage" in both kinds of systems. This leakage makes necessary a reexamination of the basis for the traditional distinction between natural and grammatical gender.

My purpose is to provide evidence for the existence of ideological factors in the form of cultural beliefs about women of the kind I discussed in the previous chapter, which enter into gender assignment in systems that are supposedly purely formal and arbitrary as well in systems where gender is supposedly determined by sex. The gender systems of both types of languages support a world view that is inherently gendered at the same time as they allow ideological construction of what is female as Other. As I show also in the next two chapters, the semantic space languages allocate to women is negatively charged by beliefs about what women are like or how they ought to behave.

Thus, it is no accident that women, fire, and dangerous things are classified as feminine in languages like Dyirbal with grammatical gender systems or that hurricanes, boats, cars, and countries are still referred to as feminine in languages like English with natural grammatical gender. This will, I hope, persuade readers who still need convincing that grammatical gender is a feminist issue.

A BRIEF HERSTORY OF GENDER IN GRAMMAR

The first question we need to ask is how gender got into grammar in the first place and what the basis is for distinguishing two types of languages, those with grammatical gender and those without it. Historically speaking, linguists have traced the origins of grammatical gender in the Indo-European languages (which include the present-day European languages) to a system of noun classification based on similarities of sound. Thus, the nouns of a particular gender class belonged there because they shared certain sounds.

The use of the terms *masculine, feminine,* and *neuter* to refer to such noun classes goes back a long time. In the fifth century Protagoras divided the two noun classes of Greek into groups he called masculine and feminine. The grammatical term *gender* is derived from the Latin *genus,* which meant race or kind and had nothing to do with sex. Yet Protagoras was so convinced that sex was inherent in the classification of things he argued that Greek *peleks* (helmet) should not belong to the feminine gender, but should be changed to masculine. Here we can see how sex and gender begin to enter discussions of grammar.

In the 19th century, German grammarian Jakob Grimm, for instance, saw gender classification as the metaphorical extension of sex to the rest of the world. He spoke of the concept of grammatical gender as an extension of a "natural" order onto each and every object. Things named by masculine nouns were, in Grimm's opinion, earlier, larger, firmer, more inflexible, quicker, active, movable, creative; those that were feminine were later, smaller, softer, quieter, suffering/passive, receptive. As I showed in the last chapter, these negative traits stereotypically associated with women have a long tradition in Western thinking. What is masculine is positive, and what is feminine is negative.

Grimm's contemporary Karl Lepsius (1863) believed that only the most highly civilized "races" and "leading nations in the history of mankind" distinguished the genders. This proved, as far as Lepsius was concerned, that speakers of such languages had a higher consciousness of the two sexes. All other languages without gender were "in decline." This fit well with prevailing ideas about the superiority of European cultures and languages, as Judith Irvine (1995) showed in her discussion of how linguists treated the classification of African languages in the 19th century. A 17th-century French attempt by Abbé de Sicard to classify languages and their genetic relationships used a tree with branches of various lengths. Languages spoken by peoples Europeans considered "primitive," such as Hottentot, spoken by African pygmy bushmen, had very short branches, whereas others such as Latin, Greek, or French had long, elaborate branches.

It is quite obvious that Grimm's analysis reflected an underlying belief in male superiority. Other male grammarians attempted to discover a semantic basis for noun classification, even where none was apparent, in order to justify beliefs about women's inferiority. Their examples contained a similar faulty logic with claims to the effect that women's place was in the home because in German and French the word for 'family' is feminine in gender (compare French *la famille* and German *die Familie*). Conversely, men's place was in the affairs of state because the word for 'state' was masculine: Compare German *Staat,* French *état,* Spanish *estado,* and so forth. Although modern linguists have been quick to counter these post hoc rationalizations by pointing to the basic arbitrariness underlying grammatical gender, it is all too easy to throw the baby out with the bath water by going to the other extreme with a claim that grammatical gender has no semantic motivation. Yet at the same time, even contemporary scholars such as Luce Irigaray have been led astray in their efforts to uncover semantic motivation for gender classification. I return to these points after I have examined the linguistic basis for noun classification systems.

Looked at from a modern linguistic perspective, we can say that in some languages gender is a central grammatical category, whereas in others it is completely absent. Despite popular opinion to the contrary, its main purpose is not to classify things according to their sex, but to provide a grammatical system linking nouns with the words modifying them. Anyone who has studied a European language other than English has had to deal with gender as a grammatical category. Languages such as French, German, Spanish, and many others have two or three so-called "genders," masculine, feminine, and neuter. These can be understood simply as noun classes. All nouns, however, not just those referring to males and females, must be either masculine or feminine.

Gender extends beyond those nouns so that articles, adjectives, or other modifiers that go with them must be marked accordingly. This includes pronouns, as we have seen in Mark Twain's story. Thus, in French we have *la semaine dernière* 'the past week' (feminine), versus *le bureau nouveau* 'the new office' (masculine). It would be incorrect to say **le semaine dernier* or **la bureau nouvelle* because feminine nouns must take the feminine form *la* as the definite article (i.e., the word equivalent to *the* in English) and masculine ones must take *le*. The adjectives also have feminine and masculine forms, with *nouvelle* being the feminine, *nouveau* the masculine, etc. In a sentence like *la vielle femme est assise* ('The old woman is sitting down'), the noun *femme* ('woman') is semantically and morphologically feminine, so the adjective *vielle* (m. *vieux*) 'old' has to be feminine, as does the past participle *assise*. It is these modifications in associated words, or "agreement," that tells us we are dealing with a language that has gender as a grammatical category. It is the pervasiveness of gender in such languages that led Monique Wittig (1986, pp. 64, 72, cited in Brawn, 1995, p. 30) to claim that "No other has left its trace within language to such a degree that to eradicate it would not only modify language at the lexical level but would upset the structure itself."

The modern European languages probably inherited this system of agreement from a pattern of noun classification arising in ancient Indo-European, which originally grouped nouns according to phonological or sound-based principles. It then developed into a grammatical system of syntactic concord or agreement. Over time, however, these noun classes acquired a certain amount of semantic motivation by association with certain prominent nouns belonging to them. Thus, classes with a large number of nouns referring to female animates became associated with the female sex, whereas those containing a large number of nouns referring to male animates were associated with the male sex.

We can see from the French example that agreement is highly redundant, affecting as it does a whole range of items. In the last example, *la vielle femme est assise,* gender is marked four times, on every word except the verb. We can also see why French feminists have argued that the grammatical gender system of French treats women as others. The feminine forms are generally marked with an -*e*, whereas the male forms are neutral or unmarked. I explore further ramifications of markedness in the next two chapters. Languages such as German, Icelandic, and Russian have three gender categories, masculine, feminine, and neuter. Compare, for example, German *das Haus* 'the house' (neuter), *die Karte* 'the map' (feminine), and *der Wagen* 'the car' (masculine).

As I show at the end of this chapter, grammatical conflicts arise now that women hold titles or positions that have traditionally been masculine in gender in languages like French, such as *le capitaine* 'captain', *le policier* 'policeman', *le professeur* 'professor', and so on. Neither the masculine nor feminine forms of the adjective (e.g., *nouveau/nouvelle* 'new') or verb form (*assis/assise*) can be used appropriately without resolving the conflict between grammatical and natural gender. Neither *le nouveau professeur est assis* ('the new professor is sitting down'), which necessarily refers to a man, nor *le nouveau professeur est assise/la nouvelle professeur est assise* (which is ungrammatical) is possible according to traditional French grammars.

GRAMMATICAL GENDER

To situate these examples in a larger perspective, we need to look briefly at other languages with gender or noun classification systems that do not rely on biological sex. In principle, many criteria could be used as the basis for noun classification. In practice, however, the most common factors are biological sex (male vs. female), animacy (living vs. nonliving), and humanness (human vs. nonhuman). Ojibwa, a native language of North America, for instance, relies on animacy. Along with many other languages it divides nouns into two basic categories of animate and inanimate. However, what is animate to Ojibwa speakers may not seem so to others who do not share their culture and world view. For instance, snow, snowshoes, and cooking pots are animate. Generally speaking, things that have power are grammatically animate. One cannot always know in advance which things are powerful. Establishing whether some things possess power can mean waiting for a demonstration.

We can see that languages like Ojibwa bring us back to the basic question I raised at the beginning of this chapter. If noun classes in the Ojibwan sense have nothing to do with sex, then where does gender come into the picture? We could just as easily call these noun classes by other names such as "Class I, II, III" and so on. Indeed, some linguists do that, particularly in cases where the language in question has more than three groups, and the basis for classification relies on some principle other than a biological one. In the Tamil language spoken in South India, the two major classes were traditionally called *high caste* (masculine and feminine) and *low caste* (neuter). We could just as easily call Tamil a language with two genders or two noun classes.

Still other languages have more noun classes than German. In such cases the connection between gender, as it is commonly rather than technically understood, and grammar becomes even more obscure and problematic. An example of a language with four is Dyirbal, spoken by Aboriginal Australians in North Queensland. Each noun must be preceded by a classifier telling what category it belongs to. The so-called *bayi* class includes men, kangaroos, possums, bats, most snakes, the moon, and others. The *balan* class includes women, bandicoots, dogs, and anything connected with fire or water, sun, stars, and others. The *balam* class includes all edible fruits and the plants that bear them, ferns, honey, cigarettes, and so on. The *bala* class includes body parts, meat, bees, most trees, mud, stones, and more.

Most of the languages of Africa have even more complex noun classification systems, which could also be referred to as gender systems. In a Bantu language like Swahili, the adjective, numeral, and verb all carry an agreement marker, which is determined by the class of the noun. Thus, all the words in this sentence carry the prefix *ki-*, which belongs to the so-called class 7 nouns:

kikapu kikubwa kimoja kilianguka
[basket large   one   fell]
'One large basket fell'.

Other noun classes have different prefixes. The Bantu languages generally have between 10 and 20 such noun classes.

One interesting question posed by languages with such systems is how children learn them. How do speakers of Russian know, for instance, that the word for 'water' (*voda*) is feminine, while the word for 'house' (*dom*) is masculine and the word for 'wine' (*vino*) is neuter? Although very young children sometimes make mistakes in gender classification while they are learning their first language, mature native speakers typically make very few errors. In some languages the meaning of words provides the primary clue about the class to which it belongs, while in others it is the form or structure of the word that determines what class it will be assigned to. In practice, speakers rely on both meaning and form. For example, in Spanish, nouns ending in -*a* are for the most part assigned to the feminine class (an important exception being the word for 'hand', *la mano*, which is feminine despite ending in -*o*). In German all words ending in -*keit* or -*schaft* are feminine (e.g., *die Gesellschaft* 'society'), whereas those ending in the diminutive -*chen*, like *Mädchen*, are neuter. Borrowed words sometimes cause problems because they have to be assigned a gender class, but usually they are adapted to the rules of the borrowing language. When French Canadians borrowed the English word *lubrication*, it got assigned to the feminine gender because native French words ending in -*tion* are feminine.

The problem of acquisition is even more clear-cut in cases like the Omotic language Dizi, spoken by about 7,000 people in southwestern Ethiopia, where there are only two noun classes. One includes all nouns that are animate and female, such as the nouns for 'girl', 'woman', 'cow', and so forth, as well as all things that are diminutive, such as nouns for 'small pot', 'small broom'. Otherwise, everything else belongs to a category of masculine, which includes men and things not singled out for their small size. Thus, most nouns are in fact masculine. Feminine nouns can also be formally distinguished by the fact that they end in -*e* (*kieme* 'small pot' vs. *kiemu* 'pot') or -*in* (*orce* 'small broom' vs. *orca* 'broom'). Other languages with two classes divide up nouns in a similar way so that the large, more general group includes men, and the other gender class including females is smaller and marked as distinctive in some way (see chaps. 4 and 5 for discussion of the associations between women and small size). This is very similar to the English use of the so-called generic 'he' (e.g., *everyone should get his coat*), which I discuss in the next chapter. Everyone is assumed to be masculine by default unless otherwise stated. In chapter 5 I discuss some of the suffixes found in English and other languages that mark words as both diminutive and female, such as -*ette* in *suffragette*, *kitchenette*, and so forth. We can see this as another manifestation of the ideology I discussed in the last chapter, which regards the female as Other.

However, there are other languages, such as Kala Lagaw Ya, spoken in the western Torres Strait of Australia, in which nouns denoting males are singled out as masculine and all others are feminine (with the exception of the word for 'moon', which is masculine). In such languages we can say that gender is fairly straightforward and is governed partly by semantic principles that select a smaller group of nouns as feminine or masculine and assign the rest to a kind of ragbag category. This residue class includes everything else not in the smaller category.

The Dyirbal system, however, despite having only four classes, is much more complicated than the Bantu system, with many more noun groups. To understand how it is organized, it is not sufficient to look at linguistic structure and formal principles. We must understand something of Dyirbal culture. The first class obviously includes human males and animals, while the second contains human females, birds, water, and fire. The third has nonflesh food, and the last, everything not in the other classes. There is also a general rule at work that puts everything associated with the entities in a category in that particular class. Fish are in the *bayi* class with men because they are seen as animals, and so are fishing lines, spears, and so on because they are associated with fish. This shows that sharing similarities is not the only basis for categorization. Cultural beliefs too affect classification. In order to understand why birds are not in the first category one has to understand that to the Dyirbal birds are the spirits of dead human females. Therefore, they belong in the second class with other female beings. Similarly, according to Dyirbal myth, the moon and sun are husband and wife, so the moon goes in the class with men and husbands, whereas the sun belongs with females and wives.

There is one further principle at work. If some members of a set differ in some important way from the others, usually in terms of their danger or harmfulness, they are put into another group. Thus, although fish are in class I with other animate beings, the stonefish and garfish, which are harmful and therefore potentially dangerous, are in class II. There is nothing in objective reality corresponding to the Dyirbal noun categories in the sense that the classes do not correspond to groups of entities which share similar properties, but the rationale for the categorization tells us something about how Dyirbal people conceive of their social world and interact with it.

Although to English speakers the system might seem quite arbitrary and therefore unlearnable except by memorizing which nouns belong in which class, to children being socialized into Dyirbal culture, it will seem quite natural. Dyirbal is, however, dying out, and the traditional way of life associated with speaking Dyirbal is fast being eroded by English-speaking culture. Children are no longer acquiring Dyirbal as their native language. The remaining speakers speak a much altered form of Dyirbal in which the noun classification system is being restructured. Now only females are assigned to the second class (*balan*). The other members such as water and fire are being reassigned to the residue class IV (*bala*). The mythical associations are now lost, so that birds, which are the spirits of dead human females, are now being transferred from class II to class I. Similarly, the "dangerous items" such as the garfish and stonefish, which formerly belonged to class II by association, are now in class I because they are animates. What has happened is that a system that could be understood only with reference to the world view of its speakers has now become more strictly based on meaning.

Although the Dyirbal system seems exotic to most English speakers, Julia Penelope (1990) in fact commented on the parallelism between it and the English system of classification with respect to their grouping of dangerous things in the same category as feminine entities. The use of *she* in English in connection with hurricanes and such reflects the male point of view. Hurricanes are destructive and irrational forces that "man" needs to subdue. Similarly, cars, boats, and planes, like women, are generally owned and controlled by men. The use of feminine pronouns in reference to them is not unlike the Dyirbal inclusion of women, fire, and dangerous things in the same noun class. I show next that there are deeper metaphors at work here that are motivated in both systems by cultural beliefs about women.

NATURAL GENDER

By comparison with some of the languages I have just discussed, where gender is a grammatical category with syntactic consequences throughout the grammar, English is said to have "natural gender." This means that nouns that English speakers refer to as *she* are in fact biologically feminine in the real world. They include, for example, women, girls, female animals, but not objects such as houses, televisions, and so on. English then relies more or less straightforwardly on the criteria of humanness and biological sex.

Nevertheless, as I just noted, ships, boats, cars, and nations (and, until recently, hurricanes) are often referred to as *she*. The standard view on this, for instance, in authoritative reference works such as Quirk, Green- baum, Leech, and Svartvik (1985, p. 318), who added a short note about it to their discussion of gender, is that the use of personal pronouns occurs with "inanimate entities, such as ships, toward which we have an intense and close personal relationship." Similarly, Otto Jespersen (1949, p. 213) said that the use of the pronouns *he/she* in speaking of inanimate things "always implies a strong personal feeling of affection." Another grammarian wrote that such usages are found chiefly in men's speech and show a "feeling of companionship between a man and his tools" (Svartengren, 1927). This explanation, however, obscures the fact that most cases involve the use of feminine rather than masculine personal pronouns, and that feminine personifications are not arbitrary. Even though Quirk et al. added that "in non-standard and Australian English there is extension of *she* references to include those of antipathy as well as affection, e.g. *She's an absolute bastard, this truck*" (p. 318), they failed to see the larger picture.

Despite several decades of linguistic reform, it is not hard to find ex- amples of female pronouns with inanimates in contemporary usage. A 1994 travel brochure from Sven Olaf Lindblad's Special Expeditions advertising a cruise to Alaska described the ship *M.V. Sea Bird* as follows:

> The Sea Bird, built in the U.S. in 1981, is a one-class ship accommodating 70 passengers in 36 outside cabins. She is 99.7 gross tons, 152 feet long and attains a cruising speed of 12 knots. Her shallow draft of eight feet and bow thrusters provide maximum maneuverability and access to otherwise unreachable waterways and anchorages. She carries a fleet of Zodiac rubber landing craft, extending her reach to almost anywhere.

The United Airlines magazine *Hemispheres* (August 1995) carried an article entitled "Boeing Beauty" in which the author, pilot John Pinter, referred to a Boeing 727 as *she*, "the grand lady of the skies." Indeed, Pinter carried the feminine personification to such an extreme that he called the airplane "the other woman" on first mention, so that it was not immediately evident that the subject of the article was an airplane. He did this presumably at least partly to catch the reader's attention by suggesting the intrigue of an illicit romantic affair. Here are the opening lines of the article (1995, p. 17):

> My wife, JoAnn, met her competition today. She has known about the "other woman" for most of our 31 years of marriage. In fact, JoAnn knowingly drove me into her arms. I planned to introduce the two at the Museum of Science and Industry in Chicago.
> It was difficult to miss such a beauty. She hadn't changed at all, and in fact, she was wearing the same colors she had worn 28 years ago when I fell in love with her.
> Of course, I'm talking about an airplane . . . but what an airplane it is.

When hurricanes had exclusively female names, the associated imagery used in weather reports was stereotypically feminine and often negative. Hurricanes "flirted with the Florida coast" and were "bad-tempered," and so on. When male names were introduced for storms, there were a few "him-icane" jokes at first, but the pronouns used to refer to these storms were neuter, not masculine. I still routinely hear hurricanes with female names referred to as *she*. This is part of a larger metaphor in which nature is a woman.

The idea that nature is female is encoded in expressions such as *Mother Nature*, as for example in this advertisement for villas on the Hawaiian island of Lāana'i, which describes the island as "one of Mother Nature's most beautiful creations . . . with her pristine beaches, tropical forests and romantic upcountry" (*Aloha Airlines Magazine*, April 1996, pp. 21–22).

Female conceptions of nature are also prominent in both scientific and popular discussions of the environment. James Lovelock, for instance, popularized the idea of a biosphere he calls Gaia (from the Greek word meaning earth as both matter and goddess), who is personified as a powerful goddess, following her origin in Greek mythology as Mother Earth. He tells us we need to learn "how to work with Gaia rather than undermining her." Other popular authors such as Norman Myers followed up on this theme of Gaia as female, telling us that "the lady becomes ever more acceptable." The female personification of Gaia suggests some competing images, such as fragility, fickleness, and irrationality, but at the same time capability for great destructive force if not properly controlled and subdued (the implication is of course by men, the male scientists who write in this way).

A science film shown to high school students in the United States in the 1970s, entitled "Nature, a Harsh Mistress," opened with the line: "For centuries man has tried to predict when nature will wreak her havoc." Here the so-called generic *man* contrasts quite dramatically with the feminine *her*, with nature cast as an avenging mistress, a powerful but unpredictable object of force, which the male subject needs to control. A U.S. television commercial for a rust-proofing compound showed a picture of a threatening woman with long red fingernails ready to scratch the finish on a car. The ad said: "Don't let Mother Nature rip you off. She's out to kill your car's new finish." Men have treated nature as they treat women, as a force to be subdued, exploited on the one hand, and as an art object to be admired for its beauty on the other. The emotional female and the natural world are men's resources only if their uncontrollable nature can be predicted and tamed. Knowledge is power, and science is an instrument of conquest that brings aspects of the environment and those we perceive as other under control.

Grammarians have sometimes used terms such as *upgrading* and *downgrading* to refer to cases such as these where a natural gender system is overridden by other factors. Humans may be downgraded, so to speak, by referring to them as *it*, rather than *he* or *she*. A classic case of this occurs with a small child—for example, *The child lost its coat, The baby dropped its rattle.* This usage is more frequent in British than American English. Conversely, upgrading, where an inanimate object such as a boat is referred to as *he* or *she*, is more common. The choice of terms to refer to these processes is, however, questionable. Normally, we have positive associations with 'up' and related compounds, such as *upbeat* and *uplifting*, and negative ones with 'down', such as *downbeat* or *down in the dumps*. Although the downgrading of children with respect to adults can be understood in relation to their age, I do not think women feel "upgraded" when they hear a male teenage surfer yell out in reference to a big wave "Catch her at her height," or a man say about his motorcycle engine, "I had her really revved up." Nor did I feel "upgraded" when I opened a recent issue of United Airlines' magazine *Hemispheres* and saw an ad for a Toshiba laptop computer telling me to "Open 'er up" (see chap. 9 for further discussion of the images of women in advertising). On the contrary, such references are downgrading and degrading to women, however upgrading they might seem from the perspective of the items undergoing the process or the male linguists who write about it! Likewise, it stretches the imagination to think that the use of female personal pronouns in these examples reflects an intense and close personal relationship with these objects, as grammarians have maintained.

It is no accident that children and women, both subordinate groups, are singled out for special treatment (see further in chap. 9), just as it is not a coincidence that more things are personified as female than male. Abstract concepts such as liberty, the soul, and justice are often represented as female along with the moon. Sometimes powerful forces such as time and death are male (although in Russian *death* is grammatically feminine), and occasionally the sun and moon are male too. The Loch Ness monster has been assumed to be female. Towns, cities, and countries are also often referred to as if they were female. Robert Louis Stevenson, for instance, wrote of the Scottish capital that "Edinburgh pays cruelly for her high seat in one of the vilest climates under heaven. She is liable to be beaten upon by all the winds that blow." He also refers to Venice as *she*.

A more extended metaphorical identification of a country as feminine can be seen in this passage about Greenland (*Copenhagen Airport Shopping Center News*, 1995, p. 10):

> Greenland's pride is not only in her links to Santa Claus [sic] but also in the spectacular beauty of her country and the nature of her people. Greenland—a land of immense, floating icecaps—is one of the most unspoilt places on the planet—she has neither witnessed a war, either between her people or between the inhabitants and the environment in which they live.

Sigrid Weigel has explored some of the metaphorical associations between women and topography. She has commented on the tendency for both wilderness (cf. German *die Wildnis*) as well as the town/city (cf. German *die Stadt*) to be conceived of as feminine. Although Weigel is concerned with the ramifications of this within the symbolic system underlying Western history, literature, and art, she does not comment on how this metaphor has been played out in linguistic systems, both in languages like German with grammatical gender, and in languages like English without it. Not only are both concepts grammatically feminine in German (as is nature, *die Natur*), but parallels extend to other European languages (cf. Italian *la città*, French *la ville*, Spanish *la ciudad*, city/town).

Woman is nature embodied, the Other. The underlying concept of woman within this metaphor is that she incorporates a dual nature. She harbors an essentially wild inner nature, although she appears outwardly civilized. Woman is symbolic of the conflict between nature and civilization, tempting men with her beauty, attracting him with her charms, but dangerous and therefore in need of conquest. The idea of woman as wild, in need of taming and domestication, of course provides the theme for Shakespeare's *Taming of the Shrew*. Woman is also symbolic of strange, foreign, and wild territory to be colonized and subject to male conquest, as can be seen in English expressions such as *virgin territory*. Weigel (1990, p. 173) cited references to discourse between military commanders in the Thirty Years' War (1618–1648) in which conquered cities were referred to as conquered virgins.

Cities are conceived of as female because they behave as feminine territory, fortresses to be overcome, harboring within them sensual pleasures as well as the dangers of seduction. The expression *girl of the town* (since given way to *woman of the street*) meant a prostitute. The wrath of God descended on the ancient cities of Sodom and Gomorrah, words that today are synonymous with sexual licentiousness, as punishment for the evil doings of their inhabitants. Weigel noted that in travelogues longing for a distant city is expressed as sexual longing for a woman. The city, however, is at the same time the site of civilization, the place where wild nature has been brought under control and domesticated. Men make their mark on the landscape by erecting cities, which provide refuge from the harsh wilderness.

The idea of female space existing outside or apart from a male-dominated society is played out in some of the feminist speculative fiction I discuss in chapter 11, such as Sally Miller Gearhart's *The Wanderground: Stories of the Hill Women* (1978), where women live in a wilderness, while men control the city. The female space is what Elaine Showalter (1985, p. 262) called "the wild zone," a place where women's values and lifestyle exist outside the dominant male culture.

Because femininity is strongly associated with notions of subordination, conquest, and defeat, there are close parallels between the discourses of colonialism and sexism. The discourse of imperialism is paternalistic; the conquerors are fathers, and the conquered are women and children. As I show in chapter 8, this is one reason why rape is often part and parcel of war: Physical conquest of a territory is metaphorically linked with sexual conquest. Men's right of way to territory amounts to rights to sexual privileges with women.

Rudyard Kipling, England's great poet of empire, portrayed the great cities of the Indian subcontinent as women subjected to their English masters in a kind of acquiescent rape. In his poem "The Song," Calcutta is described as "me the Sea Captain loved," whereas the City of Madras says "Clive kissed me on the mouth and eyes and brow. Wonderful kisses." The Orient is erotic, but submissive, whereas an "at home" English city like Halifax, with its "virgin ramparts," is depicted as the feminine "warden of the honour of the North."

Like women, colonized people are also represented as uncivilized, unclean, morally impure, and therefore dangerous at the same time as they are weak and childlike. In a children's book called *An ABC for Baby Patriots* published in Britain during the Boer Wars in South Africa, the letter K stands for African "kings once warlike and haughty. Great Britain subdued them because they'd been naughty." Seeing the African kings as naughty children who misbehave and are punished provided justification for extension of imperial law and order.

These stereotypes about peoples were projected onto their languages and cultures, as I explained earlier. Europeans dismissed as primitive and barbaric the languages spoken by those whom they regarded as uncivilized. The word *barbarian* comes to us from Greek *barbarus* meaning one who babbles. The Greeks called others *barbarians* if they could not speak Greek or pronounced it improperly. Even before them, the Aztec people of ancient Mexico called those who could not speak their language savages or mutes. Someone who doesn't speak our language is different. Being different condemns the other to being savage, irrational, mute, and female.

Some 19th- and early 20th-century philologists even regarded whole languages as feminine or masculine. Philologist Otto Jespersen (1922, p. 2), for instance, viewed English as a masculine language by comparison, for example, to Hawaiian, which he described as "childlike and effeminate" due to the fact that he found Hawaiian "full of music and harmony." This had to do with the presence of more consonants and consonant clusters in the Germanic languages than the more vowel-like Polynesian languages. English, on the other hand, seemed to him "positively and expressly masculine, it is the language of a grown up man and has very little childish or feminine about it." Max Müller, the first Professor of Comparative Philology at Oxford, had similar ideas. Such beliefs about the masculinity or femininity of languages were really stereotypes about the peoples who spoke them. Jespersen's prejudices about the Hawaiians, as can be seen from his remark that one could not "expect much vigour or energy in a people speaking such a language," clearly provided the source for his disparaging views about their speech (see chap. 5 for discussion of the sound symbolism in English naming practices).

In his discussion of how the foreign and foreigner are conceived as female, Tzvetan Todorov (1984, p. 154) said it is futile to speculate whether the image of woman has been projected on the foreigner or the foreigner's features on women. Both have always been there and what matters is the solidarity of their association, not which came first. The discourse of sexism translates readily and easily into that of racism, and vice versa, because each is in effect a discourse about the Other. At the same time, I think it is not coincidental that sexual difference has provided a powerful metaphor for the representation of other differences. Colonialism relies heavily on sexual metaphor, as do environmentalism and science in general (see chap. 1 for discussion about the debate over the primacy of race, sex, and social class).

Marina Warner (1985, p. 292) concluded that it is because women continue to occupy the space of Other that they lend themselves to allegorical use so well (see chaps. 5 and 10 for more examples). She saw as a principal reason for female allegory the fact that the abstract nouns representing concepts such as *liberty, justice*, and so on belong to the feminine gender in the Indo-European languages. Jespersen too noted some correspondences with Greek and Latin gender for inanimate objects referred to as *she* in English.

In Greek mythology the Muses, for instance, were the nine daughters of Zeus, each presiding over a different art or science. Liberty and the three monastic virtues of Poverty, Chastity, Obedience, the seven gifts of the holy spirit, the heavenly beatitudes, the five senses, the seven liberal arts, and continents, seasons, and months were all feminine in grammatical gender in both Greek and Latin. The allegorical tradition in its Christian form from the Middle Ages into the High Renaissance personified all these concepts in the female form. In influential texts a variety of allegorical figures from Dame Nature to Lady Philology enlivened the lessons.

These metaphors have been encoded into English as well as other European languages, where the distinction has been grammaticalized, or made obligatory in the grammatical category of gender. Historically, English too had grammatical gender, and nouns such as *wilderness* (and a whole range of related abstract nouns ending in *-ness*) were feminine. Similarly, in the Romance languages the cognate (i.e., related) suffixes (e.g., French *-(i)té*, Spanish *-(i)dad*, etc.) are also grammatically feminine and are used to form a class of nouns referring to abstractions such as liberty, charity, and so on. Compare French *liberté* and Spanish *liberdad*.

Another equally fertile and important source of imagery was classical Greek myth itself and the spheres of influence it allotted to its goddesses, especially Athena, who above all influenced the representation of the virtues and all other desired qualities personified in the post-Classical world. The study of Greek and Latin spread through the grammar and public schools in Britain as well as in western Europe ensured that classical myths, texts, and images would gain a greater popularity than they had ever enjoyed before when classical learning had been the privilege of a small group.

We can now return to the claim made by 19th-century male grammarians that men's place was in the affairs of state because the word for state is masculine in languages such as French and German. Although the argument is clearly grounded in a belief of male superiority, I believe there is a discernible patterning in gender assignment in nouns referring to the topographic domain. To illuminate it, however, we need to distinguish between territory as soil, earth, or ground as opposed to territory as country, state, and nation.

Where territory is conceived of in its "natural state," that is, as dirt, soil, earth, and so on from which its fertility arises, by and large the gender assignment is feminine. Compare French *la terre*, Italian *la terra*, Spanish *la tierra*, German *die Erde*, and so on. It is not surprising to find similar patterns in non-Western languages too, given the land's association with fertility. Recall from chapter 2 that within Maori cosmology, for instance, the primal parents were Rangi awatea, the Sky Father above, and Papatuanuku, the Earth Mother below. Here we see quite clearly the metaphorization of nature as the body of a woman. This may reflect a once more widespread form of Goddess worship, subsequently overlain with the negative imageries of more patriarchal religions such as Christianity and Judaism.

Also within this semantic field are terms referring to land in its natural state as landscape and countryside, as in the description of the natural environment of Greenland I looked at earlier, or cultivated as farm land, such as French *la campagne*, Italian *la campagna*, German *die Landschaft* (note, however, Spanish *el campo*). Where land is conceptualized as a politicized entity under the jurisdiction of a nation-state, the nouns referring to it are generally masculine, such as German *Staat*, French *état*, and so on. Masculine personifications of countries, such as Uncle Sam for the United States and John Bull for Britain, represent primarily the country as state, government, and bureaucracy. Here land has been colonized and brought under male control. Yet other symbolic associations of these male-governed nations and countries as abstractions are still feminine, as one can see in the use of female figures to represent them, such as the Statue of Liberty, Britannia, her daughter Zealandia, and Marianne, the symbol of the French Republic, to name just a few. The July 1886 issue of *The Graphic*, an illustrated weekly, had an elaborate pullout map showing its readers the extent of the "Imperial Federation," decorated with female figures representing the colonies paying tribute to Britannia herself. The family is still a metaphor for nation and empire, but in this version we see the glorification of womanhood in symbolic form. Britannia is Queen Victoria, the Great White Mother England with loyal sons willing to fight and die for queen and country.

These feminine abstractions serve as symbolic rallying points of affection and patriotism. Although countries usually have founding fathers rather than mothers, the country itself as "one's native land," in which we are born, is linked with motherhood and the fertility of the land itself, and is therefore often grammatically feminine, such as French *la patrie*, Spanish *patria* (but *le pays*, *el país*), French *la nation*, German *die Nation*, and Spanish *la nación*, as are the names of the countries themselves; for example, France, Italy, Spain, Ireland, and the continents, America, Europa, Australia, Antarctica, Africa, and Asia, are feminine. (Notable exceptions include German *Deutschland* and *Vaterland* 'fatherland', which are grammatically neuter because a compound noun takes the gender of the final element, and the names for Portugal, which are masculine in Portuguese as well as in French, Italian, Spanish, but neuter in German, etc.)

There are naturally some other exceptions, due in some cases to historical irregularities, with the names of some cities and countries being a case in point deserving further examination. Apparently before the Revolution the Russian names of towns on the left bank of the Volga were feminine, and those of the towns on the right, masculine. This may reveal deeper links between women and evil associated with the left hand. In Kamtok (Cameroon Pidgin English), for instance, the word for left is *woman hand*, and the word for right is *man hand*. Marina Warner (1994, p. 90) observed that in an illustration of 1644 two aspects of speech were personified in classical female form. On the left was a plump Natura Eloquens ('natural eloquence') with long unruly hair and many bare breasts, and on the right was the disciplined muse of rhetoric Polyhymnia, with both breasts modestly covered. For the moment, it is important to notice from Warner's example that the woman in need of taming and domestication is the one in a supposedly "natural" state on the left! The rich associations of hair with magic and power, sexual and otherwise, go back centuries, appearing, for instance, in the Biblical story of Samson and the more modern Blue Beard, as well as in Rapunzel, who lets down her masses of blonde hair for the witch and later the handsome prince to climb up (see the next chapter on the associations between women and blonde hair). Hence in Victorian England women kept their hair pinned up neatly. Loose hair was a sign of moral laxity—a wild, unkempt woman. In chapter 9 I show how the cosmetic and fashion industries have produced artificially the so-called "natural woman."

In the next chapter I also explain more of the significance of women's association with language, grammar, and rhetoric: Grammar and rhetoric represent language brought to order and governed by rules (see also chaps. 6 and 10). Languages in their natural state are seen as wild, and so too are the people who speak them, whether they are women in particular, or the conquered more generally. Images of conquered people and their languages and territories share in a symbolic feminism that casts them into opposition with the conquerors and their languages. The title page of James Howell's dictionary of 1659 (*Lexicon Tetraglotton*, London), for instance, depicted the Welsh language as a scared, wild woodland warrior maiden, in comparison with richly clad court ladies representing English and French. Likewise, the province of Brittany in France was romanticized as an untouched virginal beauty, and its language, Breton, associated with rural peasant women (see further in chap. 6 for some of the consequences of this symbolism).

Again, it is not accidental that the words for both grammar and language belong to the feminine gender in the European languages: compare French *la langue/la grammaire*, German *die Sprache/die Grammatik*, Spanish *la lengua/la gramatica*, Portuguese *la lingua/la grammatica*, and so forth. Thus, language too falls into that category of objects including ships, cars, boats, hurricanes, nature, and countries referred to as feminine in English.

The fact that we can also find personification in languages with grammatical gender suggests that such classification systems are not as arbitrary as modern linguists generally claim. In Russian, for instance, there is a superstition predicting the appearance of a male guest if a knife is dropped, or a female guest if a fork is dropped. The word for 'fork' is feminine and the word for 'knife', masculine. Although the superstition seems arbitrary to an English speaker, for Russian speakers it is motivated by grammatical gender. Similarly, French people who watched Ingmar Bergman's film *The Seventh Seal* were struck by the fact that the character who symbolized death was male. In French (as well as Russian) the word for 'death' is feminine, while in Swedish it is masculine. Insulting terms in German for males are often grammatically feminine, such as *die Memme* 'male coward', *die Tunte* 'gay male' (but *der Zahn* 'sexually desirable young girl'). French grammarians have also noted associations between size of objects and gender in sets of related terms such as *la chaise* ('chair')/*le fauteuil* ('armchair'), *la maison* ('house')/*le masure* ('mansion'), *la route* ('road')/*l'autoroute* ('highway'), where the feminine member is smaller than the male one. However, there are a number of exceptions here, such as *la bergère* ('easy chair'), which is more spacious than a chair or an armchair, and *le logis* ('dwelling'), which is less grand than *une résidence* ('a residence').

LEAKAGE BETWEEN GRAMMATICAL
AND NATURAL GENDER

Accepting my arguments about semantic motivation for what I call *leakage* does not mean rejecting out of hand a significant degree of arbitrariness in noun classification systems of the grammatical gender type. I am not claiming, for instance, that German speakers conceive of trees as male, their leaves as sexless, and their buds as female simply because the corresponding words belong to the masculine, neuter, and feminine gender categories respectively (compare *der Baum* 'the tree', *das Blatt* 'the leaf', *die Blume* 'the flower').

Various experiments have, nevertheless, shown regular associations between grammatical gender and connotations of meaning derived from our attitudes toward men and women. In one such experiment the investigator concocted nonsense Italian words ending either in -*o* or -*a*. The former are usually masculine and the latter, feminine. Speakers had to rate the nouns according to whether the imaginary items they denoted were good, bad, pretty, strong, and large. Then the same people were asked to rate men and women in terms of the same criteria. The nonsense words that were feminine in gender were, like women, rated as prettier, smaller, weaker, and better.

Researchers have obtained similar results in related experiments with speakers of Arabic and Hebrew. In Arabic nouns like 'necklace' and 'perfume' are rated higher on a scale of masculinity, which is in line with the fact that these nouns are masculine in gender. When given the same nouns to evaluate on a scale of masculinity, English speakers perceived them as less masculine than did the Arabic speakers.

Another kind of experiment investigated German words ending in -mut, which generally refer to mood and personality characteristics. Historically, words ending in -mut should be masculine, but when the suffix ceased to be productive, some nouns switched to the feminine class, and speakers today show a great deal of variation in gender assignment. When asked to rate words ending in -mut as being active or passive, loud or soft, and so on, which were taken to be facets of a more general scale of introversion versus extroversion, the nouns assigned to feminine gender such as Anmut 'gracefulness', Zagemut 'timidity', and Wehmut 'sadness' all showed introversion. They were rated as passive, soft, and so forth. Nouns such as Hochmut 'arrogance', and Übermut 'bravado', which rated high in terms of extroversion, were assigned masculine gender. Nouns in the same general semantic area, but with different structure, showed similar effects. Thus, nouns referring to emotional states that received introverted ratings were given feminine gender, such as Besorgnis, 'fear'. The word Wagnis 'risky undertaking', however, was given neuter gender. These findings suggest that the reclassification of some of the nouns into the feminine gender is motivated by some of the cultural beliefs I discussed in chapter 2 about the greater emotionality of women. Thus, it will come as no surprise to find that many women reject titles and forms of address that are marked for feminine gender (see chap. 10).

Yet other studies suggest that children may experience their own gender identity earlier if they are born into a community speaking a language with gender as a grammatical category. Päivi and Marc Tukia (1987) studied children between the ages of 16 and 42 months who were speakers of Hebrew, Swedish, English, and Finnish. They chose these languages to represent a range from languages like Finnish, which does not encode gender distinctions in its pronoun system, to those like Hebrew, which marks gender throughout its pronominal and number paradigms. Swedish and English fall in between these two extremes because both have third person masculine and feminine singular pronouns. The children were tested to see at what age they were able to recognize their own gender. Between the ages of 24 and 34 months the Hebrew-speaking children had a much better knowledge of their sexual identity than did the children who came from other language backgrounds. After the age of 3 years (36 months), however, the other children were superior, which suggests that although grammaticalized distinctions such as gender-specific pronouns may influence early learning, culture provides many other clues even where grammar does not do so. Finlayson reported that among Xhosa speakers in South Africa a baby is accorded no gender until it is able to play a role in society. This is indicated linguistically by the fact that the word for 'baby' (*usana*) is assigned to gender class 11, rather than to class 1, which is personal.

We must be careful, however, not to make simplistic equations between categories of the mind and categories of grammar. I showed how the Dyirbal classification drew on perceived as well as culturally derived similarities and associations, which resulted in a grouping of women, fire, and dangerous things into one category. But can we conclude that Dyirbal speakers are induced by this linguistic schema to see a motivation behind these associations? Actually, there is some evidence to support this, because one male speaker consciously linked fire and danger to women in saying, "buni [fire] is a lady. ban buni [class II fire]. You never say bayi buni [class I fire]. It's a lady. Woman is a destroyer. 'e destroys anything. A woman is a fire." Unfortunately, it is no longer possible to probe the extent of influence that the traditional Dyirbal system of noun classification might have had on thought processes.

Even in a language like English with no grammatical gender, there is some evidence for influence on thought processes from gender connotations. Sandra Bem conducted a study in which she showed men and women a list of 61 words including animals, verbs, articles of clothing, and people's first names and asked them to recall as many of them as they could in whatever order. Half the people's names were female, and the other half, male. Within the other category of words, one third had masculine connotations (e.g., *trousers*, *hurling*, etc.), one third had female connotations (e.g., *bikini*, *blushing*, etc.), and the other third had no gender connotations. People who were conventionally gendered, that is, independently showed highly polarized traits, recalled words by clustering them together according to their gender associations rather than by other categories such as names, animal names, verbs, and so forth. Thus, both natural and grammatical gender systems can have consequences for the way we organize our thought processes. What is perceived and classified as feminine carries negative connotations, whether it is overtly marked with sex-specific endings or by association with other concepts having negative meanings. Although I consider the issue of language reform more fully in chapter 10, I now set the stage for this discussion by examining briefly some of the implications for change in languages with grammatical gender.

PROBLEMS AND PROSPECTS FOR REFORM
IN LANGUAGES WITH GRAMMATICAL GENDER

I disagree with Miller and Swift's (1988) claim that the impact of gender is much less sexist than are the blatant generic uses of *man* and *he* in English. I think it is not a coincidence that French feminists have been so concerned with language, and that their arguments about the centrality of language and language reform within feminist theory have taken a rather different turn from those of their Anglo-American counterparts. In languages with grammatical gender like French and Italian, speakers' attention is constantly drawn to the issue of gender in a way that it is not in a language like English. For example, *Elle* magazine carried an article about Charlotte Perkins Gilman, describing her as a precursor of Betty Friedan. The word *precursor* is masculine in French and therefore sounds odd when applied to a woman, especially in the context of a discussion of the women's movement. The neutral English term does not stand out in the same way.

French also has two words meaning 'language', one masculine (*le langage*) and the other feminine (*la langue*). Writers such as Chantal Chawaf (1987) capitalized on this distinction. In her novel *L'Interieur des heures* a woman and her daughter are surrounded by a restrictive masculine space demarcated by language (*le langage*). They dream of another language, which Chawaf calls *la langue*. Similarly, French feminists have appropriated *parole* ('speaking/speech/word'), which is feminine, as opposed to the masculine *mot*, meaning 'word'. Here the dream of a woman-made language is contrasted with that of man-made language.

In French the word for subject is also masculine (*le sujet*). Although theoretically (like the English generic pronoun *he*) it supposedly encompasses both males and females, one of the tenets of French feminist theory I examined in the last chapter is the argument that patriarchy constructs the subject as masculine and effectively excludes women. Paradoxically, its apparent grammatical inclusion of women guarantees their social exclusion. For this reason Hélène Cixous (1975/1986) preferred to stress what is feminine by using the word meaning 'person', which in French is feminine in gender (*la personne*). Likewise, some Spanish feminists prefer to use feminine forms such as *la gente* 'people' which trigger feminine agreement, as in *la gente es muy buena* 'the people are very good'. In this way it is possible to use feminine forms in an inclusive way to refer to people of both sexes, in contrast to the traditional use of masculine forms as inclusives, that is, the so-called androcentric generics I discuss in the next chapter (e.g., *a person left his book on the table*).

In the English-speaking world *person* has of course also been recruited by Anglo-American feminists in new formations such as *chairperson, cleaning person, sales person*, and so on, but in English these are gender-neutral terms (see further in chap. 10 on why it is women who become *chairpersons*, whereas men remain *chairmen*). The political significance of the use of *personne* by French women is lost when translated into English, as is the fact that the French word for 'writing' (*écriture*) is feminine in gender, although the words for writer (*écrivain*) and author (*auteur*) are both masculine. The goal of linguistic reform in French feminist theory has been to transform the subject in its relation to language. Textual politics are in effect sexual politics.

That is not to say that Anglo-American feminism has conceptualized feminist theory in totally different ways or ignored these issues because it has been constructed in a language without grammatical gender. English-speaking feminists, however, have to rely on other textual strategies to draw conscious attention to language, such as the use of respellings like *herstory*, *wombyn/wimmin*, and so forth. In chapter 11 I examine some of the strategies used by creative writers in both French and English to de-gender, engender, or regender the subject.

As I indicated earlier in my example of how one refers to a French woman who is a professor or has a position grammatically classified as masculine, the problems for reform posed by a language with grammatical gender will also be somewhat different from those of a language with natural gender. Marina Yaguello (1989, pp. 73–77) related how the French press reported on the return to France of navy captain Dominique Prieur, who had been placed under house arrest in the South Pacific for her part in the sinking of the Greenpeace ship *Rainbow Warrior*. The Office of the Prime Minister said, "Le capitaine Prieur est actuellement enceinte et l'ac-cord prévoyait que dans ces circonstances, elle pouvait être repatriée a Paris" (Captain Prieur is currently pregnant and the agreement provided that under these circumstances she could be repatriated to Paris).

Here the problem according to traditional French grammar is that the occupation of captain is grammatically masculine and requires the masculine form of the definite article (*le*), even though the person who holds the position is female. A masculine noun also requires agreement of adjectives and pronouns, but in this case there is, for obvious reasons, no masculine form of the adjective *enceinte*, meaning 'pregnant'. It would seem perverse to have used the required masculine pronoun *il* instead of *elle*, when the person referred to is so clearly female, so the report resolved the problem in favor of making the pronoun agree with the sex of its real-world referent rather than the grammatical gender of the job title.

Thus, we have a conflict between natural and semantic gender. *Le capitaine est enceint* is ungrammatical, and flies in the face of biology, but *la capitaine est enceinte* is likewise ungrammatical. Other newspapers dealt with the problem in other ways. One, for instance, did refer to the captain as 'la capitaine', but said that "le" capitaine was pregnant, with the masculine article in quotes. In the face of changing social realities, official authorization was given in 1977 for the use of feminine pronouns with masculine nouns, but this is still disturbing to some French speakers and traditional grammarians, who have resisted adopting feminized nouns such as *la professeur(e)*.

Although such a clash is not grammatically possible in English, it is something akin to what I felt when I was told by a colleague that in writing to Tessa Blackstone I had to address her as "Dear Master" because she was Master of Birkbeck College. The title of Master has not changed since the days when it was assumed that the head of the college would be male (see chap. 11 for further examples in feminist speculative fiction). Although the title Mistress exists, it has become conventionalized in connection with women's colleges at Cambridge, Oxford, and elsewhere, especially in the case of schools, where a woman in charge is referred to as the *headmistress* and a male, the *headmaster*. It is this conventionalization of the terms *mistress* and *master* as titles in the British educational system that made the remark of Geoffrey Warnock (former Vice-Chancellor of Oxford University) so witty (at least by male standards) when his wife, a philosopher who held the title Dame of the British Empire, became head of Girton College, Cambridge: "Once I was married to a Dame; now I have a Mistress." Due to differences in social structure between the United States and Britain, terms like *dame, lady,* and *mistress* have somewhat different connotations in the two countries. The remark sounds much less witty to American women for reasons I explain in the next chapter.

Because traditional French grammarians have been reluctant to accept the use of the feminine form of the definite article before masculine nouns, such as *la professeur*, one way of avoiding the dilemma is to place *madame* before certain titles but to preserve the masculine definite article, such as *madame le juge* 'Madame Judge'. Another possibility would be to place the word *femme* before an occupational title, as in English terms such as *lady/woman professor*, that is, *professeur-femme*. Compare the French possibilities for referring to a woman who is a doctor: *la docteur, la docteure, la doctoresse, la médecin, la femme-médecin*. When in 1984 a woman rode to victory for the first time in a major horse race, the French press did not know whether to call her *le* or *la jockey*. Or should she have been *une jockeyte* or even *une femme-jockey*? Several weeks later when a London policewoman was shot outside the Libyan Embassy, the press did not know whether to refer to her as *policier femme* 'woman policeman' or to coin a new feminine form *policière*. Not surprisingly, feminine equivalents are scarce only for words referring to prestigious white-collar professions, although there are several instances of high titles being feminine in gender while the persons occupying them were male, such as *sa Sainteté* 'His Holiness' and *sa Majesté* 'His Majesty'. However, there has never been a shortage of feminine names for manual jobs. Many women in France are unhappy with coinages such as *policière* or *professeuresse* 'professoress' because they regard them as demeaning and belittling. Many German women, on the other hand, have argued for the use of forms marked for the feminine. I consider these and other aspects of reform in chapter 10. It is obvious, however, that both the extent and type of reform necessary to rid a language of sexist distinctions will vary depending on the type of language concerned.

In the next chapter I look at other ramifications of gender in English relating to both nouns and pronouns. Although English does not have grammatical gender, it does mark distinctions of gender in some of its nouns, such as *actor/actress*, and in its pronouns (*he, she, it,* etc.). These aspects of the language that have made English and other languages "manmade" have also been targeted for reform.

EXERCISES AND DISCUSSION QUESTIONS

1. Examine some grammar books for unfamiliar languages to see whether gender is a grammatical category. If so, how does it work? How many categories are there? Are there rules for determining which nouns belong in which categories?

2. Consider Esperanto (an artificial language invented by Zamenhof in 1878) or any other artificial language to see how it deals with the category of gender.

3. Here are some data from an invented language called Sevarambian as described by Denis Varaisse d'Alais (*A History of the Severambians*) written in 1677. The imaginary kingdom in the Australs, where the Severambians live, is ruled by King Sevarias, who has constructed an ideal language. The king's aim was to create an ideal language free from ambiguity and irregularity. This leads the king to multiply the number of distinctions possible in the language well beyond anything found in natural languages. There are three genders, masculine, feminine, and common, which affect both nouns and verbs. Masculine nouns are indicated by the ending *-a*, feminine by *-e*, and common by *-o*, as in these examples. When one is unsure of the sex of an animal, one says *amboi* denoting 'man and woman', or *phantoi*, meaning 'father and mother'. There are also a series of endings indicating a variety of meanings that in English we would translate with adjectives, such as *-s* meaning 'great, venerable', *-ou* meaning 'disdain, scorn', *-u* meaning 'little', and so on.

	Singular		Plural	
Masculine	amba	'man'	ambai	'men'
	phanta	'father'	phantai	'fathers'
Feminine	embè	'woman'	embei	'women'
	phenté	'mother'	phentei	'mothers'
Common	ero	'light'	eron	'lights'

Examine the effects of gender as illustrated in this verb paradigm for the verb "to love," which has three forms depending on the gender of the speaker: masculine *ermanai*, feminine *ermanéi*, and common gender *ermaói*. The common gender is used if the speaker is neither male nor female, or both at once. There is also a series of endings indicating a variety of meanings that in English we would translate with adverbs, such as *ermanei*, meaning 'to love a little, but nicely', *ermanâffai*, meaning 'to love a great deal and nobly', *ermanoüi*, 'to love crudely', and so forth.

Singular		Plural	
Masculine gender			
Ermana	'I love'	Ermanan	'We love'
Ermânach	'You love'	Ermana'chi	'You love'
Ermanas	'He loves'	Erman'fi	'They love'
Feminine gender			
Ermané	'I love'	Ermanen	'We love'
Ermânech	'You love'	Ermênchi	'You love'
Ermanés	'She loves'	Ermenfi	'They love'
Common gender			
Ermano	'I love'	Ermanon	'We love'
Ermânoch	'You love'	Ermôn'chi	'You love'
Ermanos	'It loves'	Ermôn'fi	'They love'

Translate the following sentences from Sevarambian into English:

a. Ermana embe.
b. Phentei ermenfi phantai.
c. Ermanech ambai.

Translate the following sentences from English into Sevarambian, giving two versions for each, indicating the variant spoken by a woman and the one spoken by a man.

d. The scorned men love the woman crudely.
e. The mothers love the fathers.

**ANNOTATED BIBLIOGRAPHY AND SUGGESTIONS
FOR FURTHER READING**

A good overview of the linguistic issues concerning gender as a grammatical category can be found in Greville Corbett's (1991) book. Istvan Fodor's (1959) article deals with the historical origins of gender in the Indo-European languages. Deborah Cameron's (1985) article and Suzanne Romaine's (1997a) article present a feminist perspective on gender systems. The Dyirbal system of noun classification is discussed by R. M. W. Dixon (1972) and George Lakoff (1987). The examples relating to the personification of Gaia as female are from James E. Lovelock (1985) and Norman Myers (1990). Examples of the myths and metaphors of the British Empire can be found in Robert MacDonald's (1994) book. Suzanne Romaine's (1997b) article on the use of metaphor in environmental discourse gives further examples of the link between femininity and nature. The examples from Robert Louis Stevenson are contained in the collection *The Lantern Bearers and Other Essays* (1988). Articles by T. H. Svartengren (1927) and M. Mathiot and M. Robert (1979) discuss upgrading and downgrading. Information on experiments concerning the connotations of gender can be found in articles by Susan Ervin (1962), M. A. Clarke, M. D. Losoff, M. D. McCracken, and J. Still (1981), A. Z. Guiora, B. Beit-Hallahmi, R. Fried, and C. Yoder (1982), Toshi Konishi (1994), Päivi and Marc Tukia (1987), and David A. Zubin and K. M. Köpcke (1981).

For a discussion of French feminism and the issue of language reform see Hélène Cixous (1975/1986) and Susan Sellers (1991). John Lyons (1968) and Suzanne Fleischman (1994) have discussed the problem of gender clash in French masculine occupational titles used in reference to women. For a popular discussion of the issue, see the article in *Newsweek*, "What is 'le mot juste' in an age of feminism?" (May 28, 1984, p. 23). I have based the exercise from the Sevarambian language on the examples given in Marina Yaguello's book (1991, Appendix 2, pp. 162–166). I have, however, simplified things somewhat because nouns should also have case endings, as in Latin, which I have omitted.

4

English—A Man-Made Language?

The language in which we are speaking is his before it is mine. How different are the words *home, Christ, male, master* on his lips and on mine! I cannot speak or write these words without unrest of spirit. His language, so familiar and so foreign, will always be for me an acquired speech. I have not made or accepted its words. My voice holds them at bay. My soul frets in the shadow of his language. (Joyce, 1917, p. 189)

James Joyce's character, Stephen Daedalus, was not of course speaking here about gender bias in the English language, but instead about the effects of having been colonized by the English language, which replaced Irish as the medium of everyday communication in Ireland after England's conquest. Nevertheless, in line with the connection I noted in the previous chapter between colonized peoples and women, a woman might well express these general sentiments. Gender scholars such as Dale Spender argue that English is a language made *by* men *for* men in order to represent their point of view and perpetuate it. In this world view women are marked as deviant and deficient, or made invisible. Thanks to the women's movement, sexism in language became a political issue. This so-called "sexism in language" can be demonstrated with many different kinds of evidence. In this chapter and the next I look at the main areas of linguistic bias against women and some of the reasons why people have claimed English and other languages are man-made.

The first type of evidence involves asymmetries between pairs of gender-differentiated terms such as *bachelor* and *spinster*, *sir* and *madam*, and so on. The female term has negative associations, while the male term is either neutral or positive. Discrepancies in grammatical forms reflect the tendency for men to be active subjects and women to be passive objects, or simply not mentioned at all. Another piece of evidence is the existence of many more derogatory terms and names for girls and women than there are for boys and men. Finally, I discuss the use of masculine forms such as *he*, *man*, and compounds such as *mankind* in a so-called generic sense to include women.

SPINSTERS, OLD MAIDS, HAGS, AND THE WORD THAT RHYMES WITH RICH: HOW WOMEN ARE SPOKEN ABOUT

Many words for women have negative connotations, even where the corresponding male terms designate the same or similar condition for men. Thus, *spinster* and *bachelor* both refer to unmarried adults, but the female term has negative overtones to it. Such a distinction reflects the importance of society's expectations about marriage, and, more importantly, about marriageable age. The Pope is also technically a bachelor, but by convention, he is not referred to as one since he is obliged not to marry. A spinster is also unmarried but she is more than that: She is beyond the expected marrying age and therefore seen as rejected and undesirable. Like the old grey mare in the song, "she ain't what she used to be." She is an "old maid," an image popularized in a children's card game that carries that very name. No one wants to be stuck holding the card with the picture of the old maid.

These cultural stereotypes about old maids being losers in card games and the marriage market also affect the term *maiden*, as in *maiden aunt* or *maiden lady*, and notably even expressions such as *maiden horse* to refer to a horse that has not won a race. The *Oxford English Dictionary* entry on figurative uses of the term *maiden* defines them as sharing the meaning of "yielding no results." Woman who have not caught a man have lost the race. Other figurative uses such as *maiden voyage*, *maiden speech*, *maiden flight*, and so on, referring to the first occasion or event of a kind, relate to the stereotype that women should be virginal, inexperienced, intact, untried, and fresh in worldly as well as sexual matters. Containers of olive oil claiming to be "virgin," that is, from the first pressing of the fruit and therefore of the highest quality, often show young maidens (see chap. 9 on the use of female images in advertising).

Although some have speculated that the word *spinster* may be dying out, women such as Mary Daly (1973) have been trying to revive it in its original meaning of a woman engaged in spinning (see further in chap. 10). Because these women spinners were often unmarried, this connotation eventually ousted the original meaning and became the primary sense of the word. In the 17th century the term *spinster* became the legal designation of an unmarried woman. Although there are no instances of the word in the Brown Corpus of American English (the first computerized collection of texts compiled in the 1960s), it appears to be still in common use in British English, as can be seen in the British National Corpus (just released in 1995), where I found 156 instances in a sample of one hundred million words. By comparison, the word *bachelor* occurs 479 times, indicating the general tendency that I discuss later, whereby men and their activities are more talked about than women and theirs. Interesting, the term *bachelor girl* (presumably a young spinster?) occurred three times.

If people have any doubt about the negative connotations of *spinster*, all they need to do is look at the range of words with which it is used, or what linguists call its *collocations*. Although there are some neutral descriptive adjectives used with the word, such as *66-year-old, disabled,* or *American,* the majority of words collocating with *spinster* are negative. They include the following: *gossipy, nervy, over-made-up, ineffective, jealous, eccentric, love-/sex-starved, frustrated, whey-faced, dried-up old, repressed, lonely, prim, cold-hearted, plain Jane, atrocious,* and *despised*. By comparison, the collocations of *bachelor* are largely descriptive or positive, with the exception of one occurrence of *bachelor wimp*.

This example shows how the connotations of words do not arise from words themselves but how they are used in context. The meanings of words are constructed and maintained by patterns of collocation. Collocations transmit cultural meanings and stereotypes that have built up over time (see also chap. 8 for discussion of how the media influences our perceptions of rape victims by appealing to the contextual associations of collocations). This sort of bias in the connotations of words for women is far-reaching and applies even to our associations of the basic terms *man* versus *woman,* about which I say more in the next chapter, where I also look at more collocations. No insult is implied if you call a woman an "old man" (if indeed this makes any sense), but to call a man an "old woman" is a decided insult. Because the word *woman* does not share equal status with *man,* terms referring to women have undergone a kind of semantic downgrading or pejoration.

We can also see how the female terms may start out on an equal footing, but become devalued over time, if we examine some more pairs of gender marked terms such as *lord/lady, baronet/dame, sir/madam, master/mistress, king/queen, wizard(warlock)/witch,* and so on. *Lord,* for instance, preserves its original meaning, whereas *lady* is no longer used exclusively for women of high rank. In the 17th century it became a synonym for a prostitute. So did *courtesan,* which originally meant a female member of the court. *Baronet* still retains its original meaning, but *Dame* is used derogatorily, especially in American English. *Sir* is still used as a title and a form of respect, whereas a *Madam* is one who runs a brothel. Likewise, *master* has not lost its original meaning, but *mistress* has come to have sexual connotations and no longer refers to the woman who has control over a household (see chap. 3 for discussion of *mistress* as a title). There is a considerable discrepancy between referring to someone as an *old master* as opposed to an *old mistress*. In Italian the related word *maestro* can mean a 'schoolmaster' as well as a 'great teacher', whereas the feminine form *maestra* refers only to a 'schoolmistress'. In the next chapter I examine in more detail the use of titles such as *Mrs.*, *Mr.*, *Miss*, and *Ms.*

Both *hussy* and *housewife* have their origin in Old English *huswif*, but *hussy* has undergone semantic derogation. *Wife* has negative connotations in expressions such as an *old wives' tale*, *fishwife*, *old wifie*, and so forth. *King* has also kept its meaning, whereas *queen* has developed sexual connotations. *Wizard* has actually undergone semantic amelioration, or upgrading. To call a man a *wizard* is a compliment, but not so for the woman who is branded (or in medieval times burned) as a *witch*. Similarly, in French we have *chef*, which might mean male cook, or *chef d'état*, head of state, to which the female counterpart is *cheftaine*. But *cheftaine* means Girl Scout leader. An analogous English pair would be *governor* compared to *governess*, where the male term refers to a ruler, and the female term to someone who looks after children. The same asymmetry in status is found in Italian. In chapter 10 I discuss the problems these discrepancies pose for language reform. Likewise, other words such as *biddy* and *tart* have changed dramatically since they were first used as terms of endearment. *Tart* meant a small pie or pastry and was later extended to express affection. Then it was used to refer to a woman who was sexually desirable and to a "woman of the street," that is, a prostitute. *Biddy* was a term for a hen, and was subsequently used in colonial America to refer to an Irish maidservant, and a gossiping woman. I say more about the wider semantic associations of these terms later in this chapter.

Historically speaking, we can see the following three trends. First, terms that refer to women gain more negative senses over time. Second, male terms either retain their original meaning or become more positive. Third, terms that were originally generic (such as *girl*) or neutral, such as *tart* or *biddy*, gain more negative connotations when they are specialized to refer to females only. According to the *Oxford English Dictionary* the word *girl*, for instance, in the 13th and 14th centuries was used generically to refer to a child of either sex, usually in the plural form to refer to children in general. Females were called *gay girls* and boys, *knave girls*. The specifically male word *boy* appeared slightly later. Jespersen (1949, p. 195) observed that the word *child* too, although it can be used for either sex, was sometimes used to mean a female child, as in Shakespeare's *A Winter's*

Tale (III.3.7): "A very pretty barne: A boy or a childe I wonder?" He added that he has never found a single instance of words originally designating female beings made into names either for both sexes or specifically for males, just as there are no reported cases of girls' names being appropriated for boys. The same is true, he said, for endings: No endings first used to derive feminine forms are later used to derive masculine ones (see chap. 5). These trends need to be taken into account by language reformers (see further in chap. 10).

Similar asymmetries in meaning between male and female terms can be found in other languages not related to English, like Japanese, where certain adjectives take on a more negative meaning when applied to women. Consider the following examples:

	Meaning	
Adjective	*Applied to Man*	*Applied to Woman*
kareta	mature	withered
kurooto-no	professional	prostitute
zidaraku-na	slovenly	slut

As in English, we see that the concept of a mature woman is associated with a woman beyond her prime. Likewise, to call a woman a professional is to call her a prostitute in Japanese as well as in French and English. The observation that a slovenly woman becomes a slut is paralleled in English by a number of synonyms for *untidy person* listed in *Roget's Thesaurus.* Most of them are words for women such as *slut, slattern, frump, trollop, bitch,* and so on.

MOTHERS AND WORKERS BY OTHER NAMES: THE HOUSEWIFE, THE WORKING MOTHER, AND THE PROBLEM CALLED HOUSEWORK

There are asymmetries in the meanings of terms such as *mother* or *father,* as well as in their collocations, which reflect the fact that the sexual division of labor in our society has placed women in much closer contact with children. As I noted in chapter 2, this reinforced theories about the biological naturalness of the maternal instinct. To say that a woman *mothered* her children is to draw attention to her nurturing role, but to say that a man *fathered* a child is to refer only to his biological role in conception. The notion of mothering can be applied to other people and children other than one's own, whereas fathering cannot. More recently, the term *surrogate mother* has been used to refer to a woman in her biological role as mother.

In the early 1990s such a surrogate mother was the first woman to give birth to her own grandchildren. Now there are many kinds of mothers, as can be seen in the cartoon in Fig. 4.1. We have *biological mothers, surrogate mothers, unwed mothers, single mothers, teenage mothers, welfare mothers, birth mothers, gestational mothers, incubator mothers, adoptive mothers,* and, of course, *working mothers,* and even *natural mothers.* In the famous Baby M case references to the baby's father (i.e., its "natural" or "biological" father) were set against the term *surrogate mother,* suggesting that the woman who bore the child was not as much a mother as the man who provided the sperm was a father. The fact that these notions vary from our cultural stereotype of housewife–mother is signaled linguistically by

FIG. 4.1.   Contemporary motherhood. Drawing by D. Fradon, © 1995, *The New Yorker Magazine, Inc.* Reprinted with permission.

the use of special terms to refer to them. The real liberation of women is inseparable from the creation of different ways of caring for children, a theme played out in feminist speculative fiction portraying worlds where technology or evolution has freed women from their reproductive function (see chap. 11 for discussion of different notions of motherhood).

Then there is the dilemma of what a child of gay or lesbian parents should call the parents. When an interviewer for *Newsweek* magazine (November 4, 1996) asked entertainer Melissa Etheridge and her pregnant partner, Julie Cypher, how they wanted the child to refer to them, Etheridge replied "she's the birthmother, but I am also the mother. We haven't come up with an answer."

We make inferences from terms such as *working mother* or from the absence or rarity of others such as *single father* in our thinking about men and women (see chap. 10 for discussion of gaps in our vocabulary for referring to women's experiences). The Virginia Supreme Court in 1995 ruled that Sharon Bottoms was an "unfit parent" because she was a "lesbian mother." She had to surrender custody of her 5-year-old son to her mother. In 1996 the Florida state appeals court ruled that John Ward, convicted of murdering his first wife in 1974, was a more fit parent than his ex-wife Mary, a lesbian. Here the existence of a term *lesbian mother* and its associated stereotypes can be contrasted with the lack of a term such as *killer father*.

There is no term *working father* because it is redundant. We generally only single out for special emphasis or marking things that are unusual or unexpected, such as the *working mother*. There is a women's magazine carrying the title *Working Mother*, but not surprisingly no new men's magazine called *House Husband* or *Working Father*. The paradox of housework not counting as "real" work and the myth of the "happy housewife" are at the heart of what Betty Friedan (1963) called "the problem that has no name." Because housework doesn't count, it is possible to say that a woman at home doesn't "work." She is included among the "unemployed," a "dependent" for tax purposes, although everyone else in the household is in fact dependent on her. "She's just a housewife" is a familiar refrain, despite the fact that many housewives with children work 90-hour weeks. In 1979 a newspaper article about men who were full-time "homemakers" was headed "The Non-Workers," further reinforcing the misconception that work done at home is not "real" work. A "working mother" does her "work" outside the home. Here we see a double bias against women; a woman who works is marked as deviant with a special name, as is a mother who works. Then of course, there is the "career woman" (a.k.a. "superwoman") discussed in chapter 5.

Conversely, we do not normally talk of *single* or *unwed/unmarried fathers*, for example, because there is no stigma attached to this status for men (see chap. 8 for discussion of a rape case where an unwed mother was cast as a bad mother). The British National Corpus, for instance, contains 153 instances of the phrase *single mother* and only 2 instances of *single father*. There are 68 occurrences of *unmarried mother* (plus 2 of *unwed mother*), but only 6 of *unmarried father* (and none of *unwed father*). We can also compare 59 occurrences of *teenage mother* with only 2 of *teenage father*. Similarly, there are 81 cases of *working mother* and none of *working father*. New gender-neutral terms such as *caretaker/caregiver*, *parenting*, and so on are more recently being used to try to avoid the stereotypical association of women with child care. Yet even the magazine called *Parenting*, which claims to address contemporary parents, displays mothers almost exclusively (Schwartz, 1996). When men are portrayed, they are shown more often in the role of husband rather than father (see chap. 9 for sex stereotyping in the media). I discuss the implications of the linguistic strategy of marking of women with special titles in the next chapter.

Other languages show asymmetries between the meanings associated with the terms *mother* and *father*. In the African language Ewe, for example, the word for 'father' (*tó*) also means 'owner', and the word for 'mother' (*no*) means 'someone suffering from something'. Thus, a 'rich person' is a *ga-tó* ('money owner'), a compound formed from the words *ga* ('money') and *tó* ('father'). A 'sick person', on the other hand, is literally a 'diseased mother' because the word is compounded from *do* ('disease') and *no* ('mother'). Similarly, a 'blind person' is literally an 'eye die mother' (*ngkú-no*) and a 'deaf person' is an 'ear die mother' (*to-kú-no*).

In other languages, however, terms meaning 'mother' have been extended in more positive ways. For example, in some Southeast Asian languages like Thai and Malay the word meaning 'mother' has been extended so that it refers to something large or the main/most important thing. For example, when the Malay words for 'mother' (*ibu*) and 'house' (*rumah*) combine in the compound *rumah-ibu*, the term refers to the 'main part of the house'. Likewise, when the Thai words for 'mother' and 'army' combine, the resulting compound means 'general'/'commander-in-chief'. James Matisoff (1991) showed how the semantic development has proceeded from the meaning of 'mother' to 'origin'/'source' to 'big'/'main'/'most important'. We have a similar metaphor in English expressions, such as 'the mother of all battles', the 'mother board' of a computer, and so on. However, many other languages I discuss next heap ritual abuse and insults on mothers.

WHORES, SEX KITTENS, SLUTS: WOMEN AND BAD WORDS

English has many more terms to refer to a sexually promiscuous female than to a sexually promiscuous male. According to one count made by Julia Stanley (1977), there are 220 words for such women, and only 20 for men. Pierre Guiraud (1978) documented about 600 terms in French to refer to a prostitute. He also found 50 terms to refer to male orgasm, but only 9 to female orgasm. Some of the more common derogatory terms applied to men, such as *bastard*, *mother fucker*, and *son of a bitch*, actually degrade women in their role as mothers. They are insulting when used to men precisely because they are female words. Being a woman is the worst thing a man can think of. Labov's (1972b) early work on so-called Black English vernacular spoken by members of Harlem teenagers revealed a system of ritual insults called sounding, signifying, and playing the dozens, which included insults directed at mothers, such as *your momma got shit on, your mother so old she got spider webs under her arm* (see also chap. 7).

In a cross-cultural study of insults in 103 languages, Edgar Gregersen (1979) found that in 66 of the languages the most abusive curses were those involving mothers. Only 20 languages had father insults. Insults directed against mothers are highly shocking because they heap abuse on one of the roles for which women are otherwise revered in many cultures. The curses directed against mothers are so common that in Spanish-speaking culture even the word *mother* (*tu madre*) suffices as a grave insult on its own, possibly because it alludes to one of the roles in which women are most positively and powerfully active, namely, biological reproduction. Women are the source of life itself. By the same token, however, as I pointed out in chapter 2, it is this power that men have feared. In American English something similar has happened to the word *mother* in expressions such as "what a mother," which is possibly a short form for *mother fucker*. Similarly, the term *bitch* has been extended from its use to refer to an unpleasant woman to anything unpleasant, such as *I had a bitch of a day*. Because the terms *tomboy* and *sissy*, which I discuss in chapter 7, show many of the asymmetries associated with pairs of gender-differentiated terms like *witch* and *wizard*, it is a much greater insult to call a boy a *sissy* than to call a girl a *tomboy*.

Studies of adolescent talk in Britain revealed the tendency for girls to be called names that categorize them according to their sexual attractiveness and availability, such as *dogs, horny birds, whores,* and *sluts*. Girls were aware that they had to walk a fine line between being stigmatized for sexual coldness, or being thought of as a *tight bitch* on the one hand, or too *loose* or a *slag* on the other. These terms again reflect the view of women as sexual commodities: a *loose woman* is too easily available; a *tight bitch* is not available enough; and a *kept woman* is one in bondage to a man. One girl commented that there were simply not very many insulting names you could call a boy. Terms like *prick* or *wanker* didn't seem to have the same force, and there were no derogatory terms for promiscuous boys. There are, however, a few terms such as *gigolo* and *toyboy* to indicate a man kept by a woman as a lover. This reflects the double standard for evaluating male versus female sexuality. Men's sexual activities are highly evaluated, but women's are sanctioned. Being a stud enhances a boy's reputation (see further in chap. 7).

The apparent lesser stigma attached to *prick* as an English term of abuse for men is reflected in the fact that it was included in the *Oxford English Dictionary*, whereas *cunt* and *fuck* were excluded. Yet among the Gurindji Aborigines of Northern Australia the worst possible, but nevertheless frequent, insult is for one man to call another a *stinking prick*. If a woman were to say this to a man, she would be speared.

It should not be surprising that in-group private usage of language is different from what is acceptable in public cross-gender usage. Even in ancient Greece women evidently did swear, although their swear words were different from those used by men. In the play *The Ecclesiazuae* by Aristophanes (393 B.C.), a woman who intends to pose as a man as part of a plot for women to take over the world reveals herself as a woman by swearing "by the two goddesses [Demeter and Persephone]." This was apparently the favorite oath of Athenian women. Ancient Greek men apparently never swore by goddesses. Modern scholars have reported a tendency for women to use different sorts of swear words than men. Stenström (1991), for example, compared men's and women's use of expletives in the London–Lund corpus of spoken English. She found that women used more instances of (*good*) *heavens*, *gosh*, and *blimey*, whereas men made greater use of *bastard*, *damn*, and *devil*.

Our more limited understanding of women's use of derogatory terms for men may well reflect a problem in the methods used for data collection because society places different constraints on men's and women's reporting of such words. Although the whole domain of sexuality is a taboo area, the expectation that good girls and ladies don't swear or use "bad" language makes it much more difficult to collect female usage, particularly if the investigator is male. Gregersen, for example, asked only men for their insults. Insulting terms for males are much more likely to appear in all-female private discourse. Barbara Risch's (1987) study of young women's "dirty words" for men revealed 50 terms in use among university students. She classified the terms into eight categories: birth (e.g., *son of a bitch*), ass (e.g., *dumb ass*, *jack ass*), head (e.g., *shit head*, *jock head*), dick (e.g., *dick*, *prick*), boys (e.g., *mama's boy*, *pretty boy*), animal (e.g., *stud*), meat (e.g., *hunk*, *juicy steak*), and other (e.g., *jerk-off*, *jock strap*). There is some overlap here with terms used to refer to the penis, which I discuss in chapter 8.

In her study of slang in South African English, Vivian de Klerk (1995) found few overall differences between male and female teenagers in terms of the number of words known. Whether the terms were positive or negative, each sex reported knowing more pertaining to the opposite sex. She suggests that although bias toward females may exist in the English vocabulary at large, individuals may be familiar with only a limited range of words (see further in chap. 6 on the connection between males and slang and women and standard speech).

Another productive category of names applied to women and men that are often abusive and derogatory are animal terms such as *bunny, chick, fox, kitten, pig, wolf,* and so on. In French many of the feminine forms of animal names are used derogatorily to refer to women; *guenon,* the long-tailed monkey, has a colloquial meaning of ugly old woman. The association of geese in particular with women, such as through the figure of the storytelling Mother Goose, probably led to the sexual overtones and images the word *goose* took on. In the 17th century it referred to venereal disease and the *goose month* was the period of a woman's confinement before child birth. The use of *duck* (and *hen*) as a term of endearment in British English may be part of this network of associations, as well as the expression *goose and duck* in Cockney rhyming slang, meaning fuck, and the Korean custom of giving the bridal couple a brace of ducks. The duck has her beak tied, while the drake's is free.

Waterfowl like the goose, swan, and stork are symbols of sexual knowledge, as can be seen in Yeats's poem "Leda and the Swan," where the god Zeus in the form of a swan rapes Leda. Yeats asks, "Did she put on his knowledge with his power before the indifferent beak could let her drop?"

In English the names used for women are usually those of small animals, for example, those kept as pets or hunted as prey. The underlying metaphor motivating this extension is man as hunter in search of (sexual) prey to consume. Thus, the traditional gathering that men throw for the bridegroom before the wedding is a *stag party.* A similar women's celebration is a *hen party* (see also chap. 6 on the image of gossiping women as hens and other birds). The fear of being devoured by hairy beasts, bears, and wolves, represents one of the many guises, often the darker side, of male sexual appetite for the female body in fairy tales ranging from that of Little Red Riding Hood, to Goldilocks, to Hansel and Gretel. Early versions of "Beauty and the Beast" assumed a female audience who understood the terror of being given in marriage by their fathers to men who were potential monsters or beasts. The beast represents the mysterious unknown, the danger of sexuality.

The consumption aspect of the sexual hunting metaphor is further played out in terms for food used to refer to men and women as the objects of intercourse, such as *cheesecake, tart, honey(bun),* and *sweetie(pie).* In chapter 8 I discuss some more cases where male sexual organs are conceptualized as food items. Women in the guise of sex objects are associated with sweet food items, especially desserts like cakes and pies. Similarly, "loose women" are easy as pie to seduce; *cherry pie* was used colloquially in the 19th century to refer to an attractive young woman. Places where such baked goods are sold, the cake and tart shop, are also metaphorically extended as slang terms for brothels. Even little girls, according to the nursery rhyme

I quoted at the beginning of chapter 2, are made of "sugar and spice" and therefore thought of as saccharine as in the stereotype of the "sweet young thing." The metaphor is also present in terms of address such as *sweetie* and *honey*, discussed in the next chapter, or expressions such as *give me some sugar*.

Rachelle Waksler (1995), however, found evidence that some abusive words may be losing their gender-specific connotations. For example, *bitch* and *dog(meat)* may be used to refer to men as well as women, and *dick* may be used to refer to women, as in the slang term *honorary big swinging dick* used by London financial traders (the "City Lads") to refer to a successful woman trader.

ONE MAN IN TWO IS A WOMAN

Significant consequences follow from the linguistic fact that certain male terms in English are by convention taken to include females. Grammarians tell us that words such as *mankind, manpower, man-made*, and, of course, even *man*, as in *prehistoric man*, encompass women. Feminists argue that if such terms were truly generic, we would not find sentences such as these odd: *Man, being a mammal, breastfeeds his young.* "Every woman, to a man, became a fierce advocate of admitting women to the suffrage" (an example from 1906 cited by Jespersen, 1949, p. 185). French feminists have seized upon the shock value associated with unexpected usages in their slogans *un homme sur deux est une femme* (One man out of two is a woman), and *cinquante pour cent des hommes sont des femmes* (Fifty percent of men are women).

If the male generics were truly generic, we would expect them to be used consistently across the board. It should therefore not sound odd to say, *A nurse should make sure he gives his patients the best possible care.* However, we can see that speakers do make assumptions about the likely sex of certain referents. Unless otherwise stated, it is assumed, for instance, that kindergarten teachers and nurses are female because most in fact are women.

Historians have obscured the contributions of women when they discuss civilization in terms of "the family of man," "the history of mankind," "founding fathers," and so on. The cartoon in Fig. 4.2 shows how generics render the female half of the human race invisible by describing our achievements as if they were those of men alone. Stephen Jay Gould deliberately titled his historical survey of the racist and sexist bias in certain areas of science *The Mismeasure of Man* (1981) in order to draw attention to the fact that European males were taken as the standard of measurement against which other groups were unfavorably measured. When humanity is equated with being male, women become insignificant Others.

FIG. 4.2. Stoneage man.

As I noted in chapter 1, even neutral terms are often used in this gender-specific way, as in this example: "To make love, a dinosaur had to get his leg over. Even if he happened to be a 160 ton brontosaurus, the female could bear his weight" (*Guardian*, August 29, 1987). Where gender-differentiated pairs of words exist, such as *dog* and *bitch*, the male term can generally be taken to include the female. As I show in the next chapter, names marked with endings such as *-ess*, such as *lioness* and *actress*, and other suffixes like *-ette* can only be female. The unmarked forms are used either generically or for males specifically.

Grammarians' arguments about the inclusiveness of words like *man* and *mankind* have been applied to pronouns too. The assumption that the average person is male is reinforced by the use of the male pronoun. Robert Louis Stevenson, for example, wrote that "an intelligent person, looking out of his eyes and hearkening in his ears, with a smile on his face all the time, will get more true education than many another in a life of heroic vigils." How do we know when generics include or exclude women?

When Thomas Jefferson wrote that "all men are created equal," it probably did not occur to him to question whether anyone would think he intended the word *men* generically or gender-specifically. Women at that time were not allowed to vote. By the middle of the 19th century most people in Britain and the United States evidently agreed with him that *man* was equivalent to male, at least with respect to its legal interpretation. As I showed in chapter 1, male suffrage in fact really meant White male suffrage at that time.

Charlotte Stopes demonstrated that 19th-century lawyers were willing to admit *man* as a gender-neutral term only under conditions that were favorable to men. In Britain it took an Act of Parliament in 1850 to clarify the generic *man* and *he* so that "words importing the Masculine Gender shall be deemed and taken to include Females." In the following year, however, John Stuart argued for the repeal of Parliament's Abbreviation Act for fear that it might inadvertently give women rights they should not have, such as the right to vote. My own college at Oxford recently inserted in its by-laws a statement similar to the Abbreviation Act to avoid a more complete reform of its sexist language. Yet declaring women's inclusion in this way does about as much to combat sexism as a sign saying "Negroes admitted" would do to combat racism (see Miller & Swift, 1991).

The case of Susan B. Anthony, in the vanguard of the first wave of feminism and instrumental in obtaining the vote for women in the United States, showed how the male pronoun has been used both specifically and generically to discriminate against women. In 1872 she cast a vote to test the use of generic *he* in U.S. laws defining citizenship and the right to vote. She was convicted and fined $100 on the grounds that women were excluded from voting by a statute that read, "if any person shall knowingly vote without his having a lawful right." Anthony then argued (cited in Hill 1986):

> The use of the masculine pronouns *he, his* and *him* in all the constitutions and laws, is proof that only men were meant to be included in their provisions. If you insist on this version of the letter of the law, we shall insist you be consistent and accept the other horn of the dilemma, which would compel you to exempt women from taxation for the support of the government and from penalties for the violations of laws. There is no *she* or *her* in the tax laws and this is equally true of all the criminal laws. (p. 61)

Noting that the law that was being used against her as well as the marshall's warrant served on her referred to *his* and not *her*, she said the clerk of the court prefixed an *s-* to the *he* and made *her* out of *his* and *him*. She insisted that "if government officials may thus manipulate the pronouns to tax, fine, imprison and hang women, it is their duty to thus change them in order to protect us in our right to vote." In another such instance, Lavinia Goodell was denied admission to the bar due to a statute that referred to attorneys as "he." In her appeal she drew attention to the fact that an earlier section of the law contained a rider about the masculine gender extending to and including females, but the court denied her petition.

PRONOUNS AND PICTURES

Linguists call male terms used to include females *androcentric generics*. Grammarians have long insisted that *everyone should get his hat when he leaves the room* is supposed to refer to both men and women, despite the use of the masculine pronoun *his*. In informal English, of course, the alternative that uses the plural forms of the pronouns, which are not gender-specific, *everybody should get their hat when they leave the room*, exists, even though it has been condemned for some time as nonstandard. Grammarians argue that the plural is ungrammatical because a singular referent or antecedent such as *everyone* or *someone* requires a singular pronoun to agree with it. However, many English speakers have seen the plural forms as more elegant replacements for masculine pronouns than using both *he/him/his* and *she/her/hers*, that is, *everyone should get his or her coat when he or she leaves the room*. This solution is more cumbersome for languages with grammatical gender, because both singular and plural pronouns as well as a range of nouns and other forms would have to be repeated in both masculine and feminine forms. Consider, for instance, Spanish: *Ella/el es bastante buena/bueno al tennis*, She/he is quite good at tennis.

In a study of contemporary American English discourse from television interviews and talk shows, Michael Newman (1996) found that speakers used the plural forms *they/them* 60% of the time to refer to singular antecedents of indeterminate sex like *person, everyone*, and *anyone*. The male pronominal forms *he/him* were used in only 25% of such cases. The use of *he/him* occurs with items that are stereotypically associated with males, such as *lawyer* and *plumber*. Newman also found, however, that reference to women in any fashion was much less frequent than reference to males, confirming a trend that other investigators have found: Women are not often the subjects of discourse.

Some feminists have suggested new gender-neutral singular pronouns such as *tey* to replace *she* and *he*, or combining them as *s/he*. French feminist Hélène Cixous has used in her writing a new plural pronoun *illes* (they) fused from the French masculine *ils* and feminine *elles* plural forms, but it has not been widely adopted. Others such as Cameron want to practice positive discrimination and use *she/her* generically. I will look at some more of these innovative usages in women's speculative fiction in chapter 11. According to one count, at least 80 proposals have been made for replacement singular pronouns in English, but none has caught on (see Baron, 1986, pp. 205–209 for a chronology of some of these). This should not be surprising in view of the fact that the plural forms are already well established. Moreover, few languages of the world have such a pronoun, although the Zande language of Africa is apparently one such and has a separate pronoun distinct from the normal personal pronouns used when no specific individual is intended or the person is unknown. At the moment English usage is very much in flux, with alternatives such as *he/she*, *(s)he*, and *he or she* being symbolic of different values and attitudes (see chap. 10).

But do androcentric generics actually influence the way we conceive of the entities they refer to? Linguists such as Indo-Europeanist Calvert Watkins claimed that women suffered from "pronoun envy" needlessly because generics were simply a feature of grammar—moreover, a "natural" one, too. At the time Watkins made the pronouncement he was head of Harvard's Linguistics Department. He and his colleagues wrote a letter to the student magazine in response to a protest in 1971 led by women at the Divinity School, who objected to the use of masculine pronouns specifically in reference to God as well as generically to human beings. Watkins and his fellow linguists dismissed the debate because it was simply a matter of markedness that the masculine forms had generic uses. His use of the term *pronoun envy* is, as Brawn (1995, p. 2) pointed out, "wonderfully dismissive" because it tries to put an end to the debate by declaring the premise ludicrous. To envy the generic use of the masculine pronoun is as foolish and pointless as to envy a man his penis. This attempt to defuse the debate overlooks entirely the ideological dimension of markedness, in particular its dependence on unequal power relations for its maintenance (see also chap. 5).

Even in languages with grammatical gender, masculine forms are used generically. For example, in Russian in cases where the person referred to must be one of a group of women (e.g., *who did this?*), masculine forms of pronouns and agreement markers are still used. The problem disappears in the plural, however, because genders are neutralized in the plural, as they are in English too with the pronoun form *they*. In related Slavic languages such as Serbo-Croat there are male and female plural forms, and the male ones are used generically for referring to mixed groups.

Still, we must exercise caution because there are some Aboriginal Australian languages in which the unmarked gender is female. Unfortunately, we do not have adequate information about the social groups in which these languages are spoken. In the Maasai language of Africa the masculine form of the pronoun is used only when it is certain a male is involved. The feminine is used either when a female is involved or when the sex of the person involved is unknown. In the Native American language Seneca and other Iroquoian languages the feminine is used for indefinite reference to people in general. There are a few other reported cases of this type in non-Western languages.

For example, in Nauruan, a Micronesian language spoken on the island of Nauru, even when only one woman is among a group of men, the feminine is used, although the language does not have grammatical gender. Thus, as Alois Kayser, a Christian missionary who wrote a grammar of the language, commented (1936/1993, p. 200), "even one little girl amongst a great gathering of men (public meeting, large congregation in the Church) will cause them all to be referred to in the same way: i.e., women." Strictly speaking, this means that certain utterances will be ambiguous in Nauruan because a statement such as *these two women are in the church* can refer to two women or to a man and woman who are in the church. It is even possible to say *these two women are married* when referring to husband and wife. Kayser (1936/1993, p. 200) concluded his observations on the subject by noting that "This way of speaking is strictly and correctly for women only and used as to include men it must be considered as a pure Nauruism." I am not sure what this comment means, but the language deserves further examination. In Nauruan the female member of a pair takes precedence in order, leading to expressions such as *Eve and Adam* and *Mary and Joseph*.

There are also other languages where a mixed group of people is referred to with a feminine plural pronoun, but in at least one of them, the feminine form is used because the presence of even one woman in a male group is enough to contaminate it, and therefore a marked pronoun must be used. From all these examples we can conclude that grammatical categories may lead us to perceive things in certain ways, so that women are in effect contaminated by their association with fire and dangerous things in Dyirbal, as well as in English, where terms marked as female may be used to express or create negative views of women.

Despite the insistence of some grammarians on the genericness of the masculine, experiments have shown that women feel excluded when they read texts with generic *he* and *man*. When we read sentences such as *Man has the capacity to adapt to his environment*, we think of men, not men and women. When people are asked to make drawings to go with such texts, they tend to draw men. One study involved more than 500 high-school students who were asked to make drawings of prehistoric people based on statements that described them. One group received statements with generic nouns and pronouns, such as *Prehistoric man left behind images of himself in his artwork*. Another group was given gender-specific and gender-neutral statements such as *Prehistoric people left behind images of themselves in their artwork* and *Prehistoric men and women left behind images of themselves in their artwork*. A higher proportion of students confronted with the generic statements drew male images.

Mira Ariel (1988) reported that when Israeli schoolchildren are asked to give a name to a character referred to generically as *adam* (Hebrew for human), they tend to give a man's name. Only one child gave a female name. Similarly, Ole Togeby found that when he asked Danish people to make drawings of a teacher, a social worker, and a worker, roughly half of the men and women drew figures that were clearly male. Only 27% were female and 25% unisex. Men, however, drew mostly male figures (69%) and few unisex figures (6%). Women drew more unisex figures (32%), even though they too drew mostly male figures (49%).

At least two things are striking about such experiments. One is that we do not seem to have strong mental images of androgyny to match gender-neutral terms. Another is the fact that even though most teachers and social workers are in fact female, the terms themselves, even though not formally marked for gender, evoke primarily male images. It is less surprising that apparently gender-neutral terms such as *surgeon* should evoke male mental images. I can remember hearing a number of years ago a popular story that presented a paradox for many listeners. A father and son were involved in a car crash in which the father died. The son was taken to the hospital, where a surgeon exclaims, "I can't operate on this boy because he's my son." It would be interesting to see if there are still listeners who cannot imagine the surgeon as a woman.

An even more telling experiment modeled on a 1973 court case involved a woman accused of killing a man. The defense argued that she had shot him in self-defense because she suspected him of trying to molest her young son. In the original case, defense attorney Elizabeth Schneider successfully argued to the Supreme Court in the state of Washington that the jury may have been unable to consider adequately the defendant's plea of self-defense due in part to the masculine generics used in the judge's instructions to the jury about self-defense. The judge asked the jury to consider whether "he [the person claiming self-defense] has a right to stand his ground." Schneider claimed that the male generics prevented the jury from seeing the circumstances from the defendant's point of view.

In the experiment, a group of students were given the facts of the case along with the judge's instructions and asked to make a decision about whether the defendant had acted in self-defense. Three versions of the judge's instructions were used: the original in the masculine generic, another in which *he/she*, *his/her* were used, and a third in which feminine pronouns were used. The results showed that when people were given the masculine version of the instructions, they were less likely to accept the defendant's claim of self-defense. Those who had been given the instructions with both masculine and feminine pronouns were much more likely to decide in favor of self-defense. The same result was obtained when only the feminine pronoun was used, although the effect was not as strong as when both pronouns were used.

Results such as these show that the structure of language can affect thought processes. They point to the psychological cost many women experience at being nonpersons in their own language and the damage they may suffer when they are compared to a male standard on the legal system. Women are at the margins of the category of *human beings*. Just as when we think of a prototypical bird, the chicken does not readily come to mind. It is somehow less of a bird than a robin or sparrow.

One reason why male images come to mind more readily can be seen in linguistic practice. Men and their activities are more often talked about than are women and theirs. What is more frequently used, is more easily and readily accessible. A very simple indication of this imbalance in reference to women and men can be found by doing a word search for the pronouns *he/she* in the many computer corpora available for English and other languages. One such count in the Brown corpus of American English containing just over 1 million words yielded a total of 9,543 occurrences of *he* compared to 2,859 of *she*. Generic usages do not account for the great discrepancy. Men are referred to three times as often as women (see the next chapter for frequencies on *man, woman,* and other words). There were some interesting differences among the different text types included in the corpus. Romance and love stories, for instance, include a greater number of occurrences of female pronouns than does science fiction. Not surprisingly, women are seldom referred to in texts with religious subject matter.

One of the newest corpora, the British National Corpus, may provide evidence of women getting more discourse time. I did a search of *he* and *she* in a 3-million-word subcorpus, which revealed a total of 352,239 occurrences of *she* and 652,547 of *he*. If these rather gross statistics are indicative of changing usage over the past 30 years, it appears that men are referred to only twice as much rather than three times as much as women! Donald MacKay has estimated that Americans are exposed to generic *he* a million times in a lifetime.

Similar evidence of a lessening gap between reference to men and women has emerged from Robert Cooper's survey of American English usage between 1971 and 1979 (see Cooper, 1984). The frequency of reference to *he* and *man* fell from around 12 occurrences per 5,000 words to about 4. Women's magazines showed the steepest decline, followed by science magazines, with newspapers further behind, and the U.S. Congressional Record last of all. As I show in chapter 10, however, such statistics reveal only a superficial view of language reform.

MALE SUBJECTS/FEMALE OBJECTS

Until quite recently, grammar books reflected the view that the male was the species and female, a subspecies. In this fashion, women are defined as the negative opposites of men instead of as different but equal. Such ways of talking also seem to equate what is universal with maleness. This bias is at the crux of French feminists' claims that women as subjects need to change their place in discourse, as I observed in chapter 2 (see also chaps. 10 and 11).

Although linguists have generally insisted on the basic arbitrariness of grammar, it is not just words that may be used as rhetorical resources for creating a social reality in which women are subordinate. Grammatical forms are also powerful tools in which linguistic subjects become constituted as social agents. Until quite recently when linguists cite examples to illustrate their theories, more often it is male subjects who do things and women who get things done to them. Thus, it is usually John who kicks the ball, kisses Mary, and so on. Marie-Odile Junker (1992) has noted how formal grammatical analysis has made use of predominantly masculine imagery with terms such as *dominance, government, command*, and so on, to describe syntactic patterns, relations, and constructions. In addition, Julia Stanley and Susan Robbins (1976) have discussed the way in which the so-called passive voice is used to suppress the identity of the agent responsible for an action, for example, *Many women are battered*. Here the agent is deleted to downplay the fact that men are generally the ones who batter women. Similarly, as I show in chapter 8, the passive voice is used in discussions of rape and sexual coercion, thus making the persons who are responsible invisible.

Anomalous forms in Japanese arise from the fact that certain things can be said of women, but not men. For example, it is possible to say *Taroo bought a woman last night*, where Taroo is a male name and the subject of the sentence. It means that Taroo paid a prostitute for sex. It is not possible to substitute a female name such as *Hanako* into the same slot as the subject of the sentence, with *man* as object, for example, **Hanako bought a man*. Similarly, one can say *There is a daughter for sale in that house/Their daughter remained unsold*, but not **There is a son for sale in that house/Their son remained unsold*. These asymmetries reflect the male view of women as saleable commodities and indicate the subordinate position women occupy in Japanese culture in relation to men (see also chap. 9 for discussion of how advertising's presentation of women as sexual objects makes use of some of these grammatical constructions in slogans).

In French the verb *baiser* ('to kiss') used colloquially to refer to sexual intercourse enters into a different type of grammatical construction when the subject is male, for example, 'a man has sex with a woman' (*un homme baise une femme*) than when the subject is female, for example, 'a woman is had sex with' (*une femme se fait baiser*). Technically speaking, the grammatical difference is one of transitivity; a transitive verb requires an object to complete its meaning. The verb *baiser* behaves transitively when the subject is male. When the subject is female, there is no object. Yet when the subject is male, the object is woman. This suggests the woman is passive and the male, active. Intercourse is something done to women rather than something they actively participate in (see chap. 2, and Stanley & Robbins, 1978). Something similar can be seen in English in the way we speak of a man *taking* a wife, but a woman being *given* in marriage.

Psycholinguists have known for some time that we interpret certain verb types in accordance with different patterns of causality. In a sentence containing a verb such as *like* which describes an emotional state, for example,

Jim likes Paul, people tend to see the object of the sentence, *Paul*, as being responsible. In other words, the reason why Jim likes Paul is that there is something about Paul which makes Jim like him. With other verbs describing interpersonal actions such as *compliment*, people tend to attribute causality to the subject. In a sentence such as *Jane compliments Alice*, people see *Jane* as the reason for the compliment to Alice.

In a study examining the interaction of gender with verb type, researchers found that when the object of the sentence was female, for example, *Jim likes Helen*, people were more likely to attribute the cause to the subject *Jim*, despite the verb type. Thus, a sentence subject is perceived to be more causal when the sentence object is female rather than male. The tendency for women to be discounted was especially noticeable in sentences where a female subject behaved toward a male object, for example, *Helen compliments Jim*, where we would have expected the verb type to bias causality towards the subject *Helen*. When a male is on the receiving end of the verb's action, he draws attention away from the female subject. When a woman acts or feels toward a man, people perceived the action as being brought about because of the man. Even when the woman is the subject, the man is the one who gets noticed. This is the disappearing agent effect. As Virginia Woolf (1928) noted, "anonymous was a woman."

Alessandro Duranti (1994, p. 142) has observed how grammar is closely tied to politics. In his study of language in Western Samoa, he found that the frequency of certain types of grammatical patterns was correlated with the nature of the event and the political roles of its participants. Transitive utterances in Samoan typically contain a verb and an object rather than a verb and an agent. Those who used transitive utterances with agents as subjects most often were politically powerful persons, usually men with senior status in the community. Even women at home, for instance, when using transitive sentences tended to express the agent much less than men did in more formal public settings (see chap. 7 for discussion of images of women as passive in children's books).

SEXISM: A DELIBERATE MASTER PLAN
FOR LANGUAGE?

When the first allegedly nonsexist Bible published in Britain was launched, a press release said that "the revisers have systematically changed expressions such as *any man* to *anyone*, but have kept the masculine, especially for God, on the grounds that this is faithful to the original" (*Guardian*, October 4, 1985). This comment draws attention to the way in which our mental imagery associated with God is, by cultural convention, masculine, at least within the Judeo-Christian world view. As I noted in chapter 2, the belief that the universe is created by a male God has an impact on how we see the creativity of men and women. No wonder there are few female pronouns in religious discourse. After all, we say God made man in HIS own image! Or was it men who created God in a masculine image? Male grammarians such as James Beattie writing in the 18th century tried to argue for the inherent logic behind this.

> Beings superiour to man, although we conceive them to be of no sex, are spoken of as masculine in most of the modern tongues of Europe, on account of their own dignity; the male being, according to our ideas, the nobler sex. But idolatrous nations acknowledge both male and female deities; and some of them have given even to the Supreme Being a name of the feminine gender.

In chapter 3, I showed how some grammarians had argued for the natural logic behind gender classification in languages with grammatical gender.

For millennia in other cultures, deities were depicted as female. Today most Western religions insist that God has no gender but still rely nevertheless, quite heavily on male imagery and symbols. As one theologian convinced of the gender-nuetrality of God put it when asked if she thought God was male or female, "Neither, I see him as an absolute Supreme Being." There have been some reported cases of clashes between indigenous feminine conceptions of deities and that of the conventionally masculine Christian God in attempts to translate the Bible into non-Western languages. Feminists such as Mary Daly (1973) urged us to move beyond our notion of "God the Father," the brotherhood of man, and so on, but some religions still refuse to admit women to the priesthood and reject language reform. The Atlanta Presbytery made news in 1996 when it very narrowly upheld the ordination of minister Eric Swenson after he underwent male-to-female transsexual surgery (see chap. 2).

Generations of women have been expected to accept the use of *brother* in terms that served as symbols of universal human kinship. Even Germaine Greer (1971) urged woman to cooperate with one another in "the matriarchal principle of fraternity," a seeming oxymoron better served by the simple term *sisterhood*. In 1992, a group of Catholic bishops objected to changes in the English mass which they said would diminish the Fatherhood of God (Ostling, 1992). The proposed changes included eliminating *man* and male pronouns to refer to humanity as a whole, for example, Jesus Christ is the Son of Man. Oxford University Press subtitled its 1995 edition of the *New Testament and Psalms* "an inclusive version." This version replaces God the Father with "Father–Mother" and the Son of Man with "the Human One."

Because it is men who make the dictionaries and define meanings, they persistently reserve the positive semantic space for themselves and relegate women to a negative one. Feminists such as Julia Penelope (1990) argue that English is a language founded in elitism and White male ethnocentricity. It promotes and maintains a misogynist view of women. Ever since Eve was blamed for the loss of Paradise, men have feared and hated women.

The fact that the grammarians who created standard English and set forth its rights and wrongs were male has not gone unnoticed by women such as Dale Spender and Julia Penelope. From the beginning, grammars were written primarily by men for men. A much earlier male commentator, Elias Molee, repelled by linguistic snobbery, remarked in 1888: "It looks to me as if the English language were constructed by some eccentric, rich and learned bachelors who had nothing else to do but hunt up the meanings of words in dictionaries and to spell." Bailey (1991, p. 274), who cites this remark, notes parenthetically that this description applied aptly to Molee's successors, the Fowler brothers.

Penelope, in particular, draws our attention to the expression "mother tongue" and suggests that men have held up purity as an ideal state for language as well as women. For Penelope, the connection between "proper" English and "proper" women is not a historical accident. It is one of the crucial connections in what she terms a *patriarchal universe of discourse* (PUD). In George Bernard Shaw's *Pygmalion* (and *My Fair Lady*, the popular musical based on it), phonetician Henry Higgins teaches Cockney flower seller, Eliza Doolittle, to speak "properly" so that she can be a "real lady." Although the plot is conventionally interpreted to be about the British class system and its connection with accent, it is also very much about gender. Higgins makes a bet that once he has "improved" her accent, he can pass her off in the best of society.

Like many other women both before and after her, Doolittle submits to remodeling her social and linguistic persona according to male standards. Just as the fashion and advertising industries tell women what they must look like, advice books tell women how they should speak, or indeed whether they should speak at all (see chap. 6). Women have long been targets for elocution lessons. Deborah Cameron (1995) points out that "tinkering with your speech through such practices as elocution is seen as a 'feminine' activity precisely because it is superficial, merely cosmetic" (p. 170). Correctness in speech has been associated with both femininity and upper social status.

These links between linguistic purity and a person's social standing have their origins in the rise of standard English and the dissemination of an accent which did not betray the social or regional origin of the speaker. In 18th- and 19th-century England, elocution became a public and private pursuit. Mugglestone (1995, p. 4) says that five times as many works on elocution appeared between 1760 and 1800 than had done so in the years before 1760. Sixpenny manuals with titles such as *P's and Q's: Grammatical*

Hints for the Million and *Poor Letter H: Its Use and Abuse* under the name of the Hon. Henry H. sold thousands of copies. Phonetician Henry Sweet (1890), who supposedly provided the basis for Shaw's character Henry Higgins, described all too well the anxiety bound up with validating one's social place through accent when he said:

> The Cockney dialect seems very ugly to an educated Englishman or woman because he—and still more—she—lives in a perpetual terror of being taken for a Cockney, and a perpetual struggle to preserve that h which has now been lost in most of the local dialects of England, both North and South. (pp. vi–vii)

While Sweet suggests that h-dropping was social suicide for anyone aspiring to be a gentleman or a lady, he also makes it clear how essential it was for a woman's speech to be above reproach. Figure 4.3 shows the title page of the Hon. Henry H.'s book, where a woman is caught in the act of dropping an /h/, thereby losing her claims to respectable social status.

The need for elocution in present-day Britain is evidently still felt, as I observed when a local newspaper in Oxford carried a story about a woman named Mrs. Fairlady who had opened the School of Speech and Social Skills (Hunter, n.d.). Although the article did not say that the school was restricted to or aimed specifically at women, it is implied when the article states that Fairlady, who is described as a "modern-day Professor 'Iggins," "is getting to grips with Eliza Doolittles of the eighties and turning them into proper little madams." Noting that she teaches "deportment, elocution and all-round image improvement," the article claims there is "surprising demand" for her services. The comedic nature of these services is also commented on when the author refers to people being a "little rough at the edges" and in need of "polishing off." Fairlady herself is quoted as saying "In a sense what I do is rather like plastic surgery . . . I like to think I am providing a necessary social service." More often than not, Fairlady says that elocution involves teaching people to mind their h's.

John Willensky's (1994) examination of a century's worth of citations in the Oxford English Dictionary (OED) from 1884 to 1989 provides additional understanding of the male sources of linguistic authority that have shaped the English language from Victorian to modern times. The editors of the OED invested a select group of writers with the power to define the history and scope of the English language. James Murray's tenure as editor of the OED coincided roughly with the period that historian Eric Hobsbawm has called the Age of Empire (1875–1914). The OED was, in effect, the last gasp of British Imperialism. At the center of this process of national and cultural self-definition is the act of citation. The OED's creators

POOR LETTER H

ITS USE AND ABUSE.

" Please, Ma'am, you've dropped something."

BY THE HON. HENRY H.

LONDON: JOHN F. SHAW AND CO.,

PATERNOSTER ROW AND SOUTHAMPTON ROW,

PRICE SIXPENCE.

FIG. 4.3. H = Dropping.

115

defined themselves as the White, male, property-owning center of a British Empire. The dictionary sets standards by deciding whose words get included, who gets to speak as part of the language, and who governs the words of others.

By looking at the persons and works most heavily cited, the male bias is evident in a number of respects. While women comprised just over a third (36%) of the readers who voluntarily collected citations, the majority were men. (Interestingly, 64% of these women were designated as *Miss.*) The Bible is at the top of the list of books cited in the OED and accounts for the placement of its translator Wyclif near the top of the authors list. Shakespeare citations amount to nearly 2% of the total and play a supporting role in roughly 14% of the dictionary's main entries. The top 20 authors cited in the OED is a list of famous male literary figures. The OED even contains 55 words for which the only documented source is James Joyce, who is seen as holding a special place in the formation of the English language.

Certainly, it was difficult for the average woman to obtain the education and skills necessary to write, let alone the time to write. Many of those who did write were not able to get their works into print—a fate that guaranteed that the OED would overlook them since it based its citations only on the printed word. Lady Mary Wortley Montagu, for example, carried on a considerable correspondence relating to her travels and public campaigning for smallpox vaccinations, but it would have been unseemly for an aristocratic lady to have sought publication. Only toward the end of the 18th century did middle-class women begin to write with the intention to publish. Even though many of these women such as George Eliot, Jane Austen, and others came to dominate and shape the development of the English novel to an extent their male contemporaries did not, they are still overshadowed by these men in terms of the number of citations they received in the OED.

It was no doubt due to the industry of one (Miss) Marghanita Laski that women authors received as much representation in the OED as they did. Thanks to her eclectic reading habits, which included not only literary classics such as the novels of Dickens, Eliot, and many other authors, but also domestic arts such as gardening, embroidery, and so on, many more citations from women authors have made their way into the OED than might have otherwise. She was also an avid reader of crime novels, including the work of Dorothy Sayers, Agatha Christie, and Ngaio Marsh.

Nineteenth-century novelist and children's writer Charlotte Mary Yonge is the only woman to be included in the list of the top 20 authors whose works are cited in the Supplement to the OED. This is due entirely to the fact that Marghanita Laski was a founding member of the Charlotte Yonge Society. Among the works of Yonge cited in the Supplement is *Womankind,* a book on improving women's education and creating a better place for single women. Yongè is responsible for the first citation of the term *home-making* and for 675 other citations.

The Supplement to the OED included entries for the taboo words *cunt* and *fuck*, establishing a long history of usage in male authors going back to the 16th century and citing in the modern period the works of D.H. Lawrence, Samuel Beckett, and Henry Miller. While many of the examples illustrate the use of the terms to denigrate women, the dictionary ignored feminist attempts at positive redefinitions such as found in Germaine Greer's essay (1986) "Lady love your cunt." At the same time, however, the editor decided to include a note after some of the citations expressing prejudice against Jews to indicate that usages such as *to jew down* ('to drive a hard bargain') indicating that these expressions were now considered offensive.

We can see then that the dictionary is hardly a neutral storehouse of words and their meanings. Meanings are shaped by usage and it is largely men's usage and meanings that are selected for inclusion. The OED managed to ignore virtually the entire body of women writers until quite recently and its definitions reflect a consistent social stereotyping of women. The dictionary derives part of its authority and power in defining the language by the process of exclusion of texts and authors. The omission of women makes women's words and meanings invisible. The exclusion of women from the dictionary has prompted a variety of feminist dictionaries, some of which I will look at in chapter 10. A new project established at Oxford University Press to help keep the dictionary current has included a few women on the list of top 20 authors whose works are cited, including Lady Bird Johnson, Alison Lurie, and Kate Millett.

As I will show in chapters 6 and 10, the predominantly male control of the codification of language in the form of grammars and dictionaries explains why feminist activism for language reform is perceived as an attack on the moral and social order. In the next chapter I turn to some more evidence for the claim that language is man-made.

EXERCISES AND DISCUSSION QUESTIONS

1. Many companies, newspapers, and publishing houses have tried to adopt guidelines for nonsexist usage. How consistent are they? Here are two examples I found while traveling.

Delta Airlines boarding card (1993)

Please do not change seats without consulting a flight attendant. No person may drink any alcoholic beverage aboard an aircraft unless the certificate holder operating the aircraft has served that beverage to him.

Egon Ronay Recommends (Winter 1993/1994, magazine distributed in London's airports with information about places to eat in the airports and related food stories) Extract from "Cooking by Proxy": "What is a chef? Is he in charge of kitchen staff? Or is he simply one of several cooks under the command of another?"

2. Is it justifiable for publishers to expect their authors not to use words such as *man, mankind, manpower, man-made,* and *he* as if they were sex-inclusive? Is this censorship?

3. Look in the library catalog and see how many books include the words *man* or *mankind* in their titles. Look at some of the books to see what they are about, whether and how they refer to women.

4. Compare the version of the creation story in a traditional Bible with one which has reformed its sexist language use.

5. If you have access to a corpus of texts, examine the collocations of the word *feminist.* You can introduce a time dimension to your study by comparing some of the early corpora compiled in the 1970s with some contemporary ones. Have there been any changes in its meanings? Examine the collocations of words such as *fetus, abortion,* and so on. What do they reveal about the connotations of these and other terms used in the pro-life/pro-choice debate? You may want to refer to the discussion in chapter 1.

ANNOTATED BIBLIOGRAPHY AND SUGGESTIONS
FOR FURTHER READING

The British National Corpus, launched in 1995, comprises 100 million words of spoken and written British English. In addition to Dale Spender's work, many other authors have discussed the masculine bias in English (see, e.g., Jenny Cheshire, 1985, and also Marlis Hellinger, 1990, and Luise Pusch, 1984, for similar discussion of German). My examples from Japanese are taken from Masako Hiraga's article, and some of the French examples are from Marina Yaguello's (1978) book. The statistics on the occurrence of *he/she* in the Brown Corpus are from Göran Kjellmer (1986; see also Yokoyama, 1986, on Russian). Casey Miller and Kate Swift's book (1988) has a good discussion of generics in chapter 1 and "the pronoun problem" in chapter 2. The example from Robert Louis Stevenson can be found in the collection *The Lantern Bearers and Other Essays* ("An Apology for Idlers," 1988, p. 38). The case of Charlotte Stopes is discussed by Dennis Baron (1986, pp. 139–140). The case of Susan B. Anthony is discussed in Alette Hill's book (1986, p. 61). Experiments relating to people's perception of androcentric generics can be found in the (1973) article by Joseph W.

Schneider and Sally L. Hacker. Studies of adolescent talk about sexuality, words for boys and girls, and so on, can be found in Susan Lees (1986) and Julian Wood (1984). On sex role stereotyping in the OED, see Hannah Fournier and Delbert W. Russell's (1992) study. Elizabeth Schneider's case is discussed in an article by Mykol C. Hamilton, Hunter, and Stuart-Smith (1994). The study of effect of verb type and causality was done by Marianne Lafrance and Eugene Hahn (1994). Caitlin Hines (1994, 1995) has looked at animal and dessert metaphors applied to women as sexual objects. For popular press accounts of some of the issues dealt with in this chapter see reports by Judith Judd (1989) and Fiona Rafferty (1994), the article in *Newsweek* (Kantrowitz, 1996), and the *Weekend Australian* (1988).

5

What's in a Name?

Naming is an act of power. In Genesis Adam's first recorded act of domination is naming, assigning the symbol, the act of a I-am-he-who-tells-you-what-or-who-you-are. It is the ultimate gesture of paternalism. The infant child is named. Similarly the first response to the other, to the outsider, is to assign a name. The one who assigns is the insider, the decider, the winner. (Judge Gary Strankman on the occasion of the naming of Ishi Court at the University of California, Berkeley, 1993; cited by Hinton, 1994, p. 155)

In this opening quotation Judge Gary Strankman was commenting on the balance of power in colonial California at a time when the indigenous Indian population became subordinated to the expanding White settlers. There is little question who were the winners, who were the namers, and who were the named. Although not addressing gender specifically, his remarks draw our attention again to the connections between race, gender, and power, and how paternalism has defined women in its own terms as others and outsiders. The names we give to things are not arbitrary. In this chapter I explore the significance of naming. I also show how the intellectual foundations of linguistics based on the principle of arbitrariness of the linguistic sign and theories of markedness have discriminated against women.

NAME CALLING

Do you remember the childhood taunt usually said by one child who has been called a bad name by another, "Sticks and stones may break my bones, but names can never hurt me"? Names do have the power to hurt and abuse, and define us as "others" in relation to some norm. As James Valentine (1995) said about name calling, "names can wrap us up with sticky labels that give us a permanent address on the other side of the tracks." A name assigns us to a group at the same time as it creates a reality in which we have to function.

It is easy to see why women have been especially sensitive to gender differences in naming practices and forms of address because these are a particularly telling indicator of our social status. To answer Shakespeare's question of "what's in a name?" we could reply, a person's social place. To be referred to as "the Mrs." or "the little woman" indicates the inferior status to which men have allocated women. When Yvette Roudy became Minister for Women's Rights in France following a 1983 law making sexual discrimination illegal, she observed that women had not yet won the political right to be titled accurately. Her new ministry's slogan became "Aujourd'hui les metiers n'ont pas du sexe" ('Today occupations have no sex'). She appointed a government commission in 1984 headed by Benoîte Groult to "feminize" the names of those jobs that conventionally were masculine in gender, such as *professeur*, *juge*, and so on, discussed in chapter 3. She herself wanted to be called *Madame la ministre*, whereas Edith Cresson during her brief period as Prime Minister used the title *Madame le premier ministre*.

When Roudy's commission for the feminization of job titles published the results of its work in 1986, it met with indifference and ridicule. One woman journalist asked, "Why create new words when no one is going to use them?" The French language academy, an institution noted for its conservatism and purism, condemned the new words in terms very similar to those expressed by Calvert Watkins in his "pronoun envy" statement (see chap. 4). The academy said that the commission had misunderstood that grammatical gender was arbitrary and largely independent of natural gender. The feminine was the marked category. For a great many men at least, feminism has been equated with what is perceived as a pointless and at times amusing or irksome insistence on the replacement of titles such as *Mrs.* and *Miss* with *Ms.*, and other gender-marked terms, such as *chairman*, with *chairperson* or *chair*, which I examined in the last chapter.

Many articles and cartoons such as the one in Fig. 5.1 appear in the press about this, and most have a jocular tone to them, suggesting that somehow the proposed gender-neutral terms are ridiculous and preposterous. One press item, for instance, had the title "Death of a salesperson," and another, from New Zealand, "Gone like the melting snowperson." When the Australian Broadcasting Corporation (ABC) decided to avoid sexist language, *The Sun* (May 7, 1984) came out with the headline, "ABC plans attack on manhood." The article related how "Aunty is killing off men . . . sportsmen, gentlemen, aldermen, the whole lot." Press releases

"Are you the house person who advertised for a cleaning person?"

FIG. 5.1. Housepersons and cleaning persons.

on the replacement of sexist religious texts were entitled "Scrubbing the scriptures" (*Newsweek*, 1983, p. 49) and "The Church of our Fathers is asked to watch its language" (Judd, 1989). Still others created terms such as *one uppersonship*. One male humorist, Ambrose Bierce, suggested *Mush* (abbreviated *Mh.*) as a title for unmarried men (see Baron, 1986, p. 166). However, I have more to say about the question of reform and the use of ridicule to undermine it in chapter 10.

IS IT MISS OR MRS.?

When I first began teaching in Britain, I was puzzled by the fact that males and females were indicated on student lists by using the initials and last names for the men, whereas women had the title *Miss* (or *Mrs*) added to their names. When I asked a colleague why this was the case, he replied that it was done so that we would know which students were male and female. He had no answer to my next questions, which were, why on a class list was it even necessary to know, or why were the women singled out to have titles indicating their marital status ("nubility titles," as one linguist has put it!). That was simply the way it had always been done, and it had never occurred to him that we should abandon this as a sexist practice. I cannot count how many times after having given my name over the phone with no title that I was immediately asked, "Is it Miss or Mrs?"

This system of marking females with nubility titles is still used at all levels of society. At the time I was appointed to my chair at Oxford in 1984, there were only 3 women holding the rank of full professor out of a total of more than 200 professors. (There are not many more women in such positions now!) In the diaries printed for academic staff, various other official lists of the university, and the different colleges, the names of men are still given in this way or with a title, followed by a list of degrees and where they were obtained, so that, for instance, a man named John Smith who is professor of modern history would be listed as "J. Smith, M.A., Ph.D. (Edinburgh), Professor of Modern History." I and my women colleagues were given a title, either *Miss* or *Mrs*, rather than simply *Professor* before our names. The term *Ms* is still not as widely used in Britain as it is in the United States (where since 1973 it has been sanctioned as an optional title), as can be seen in sporting events such as the Wimbledon tennis matches, where women players such as Chris Evert and Martina Navratilova are referred to as *Miss Evert* (or latterly *Mrs Lloyd* after she married), and *Miss Navratilova*, but men such as Boris Becker are referred to with last name only. The men are also just *men*, but the women are always *ladies*. The use of *lady* as a polite euphemism for *woman* is far more common in Britain than in the United States, for reasons I discuss later.

As I showed in the previous chapter, the many asymmetries in the ways that women are referred to or addressed reflect differences in power (see chap. 8 for discussion of their impact in rape trials). Nonreciprocity of address to women is a feature of many societies. Javanese women, for instance, use more deferential speech levels to their husbands than they receive in return. There are different Japanese pronouns for I and you, depending on the sex of the speaker. When used by women, the terms represent a greater degree of deference than when used by men. Traditionally, only men used the terms *boku, ore, wasi*, and *wagahai* to refer to themselves, whereas women used *atakusi, atai*, and *atasi*. Now some women have begun to use *boku*. The forms *watakusi* and *watasi* can be used by both men and women, particularly in formal contexts.

To take some examples from Western societies, women teachers in some schools in Italy tend to be addressed as *signora* (Mrs.) or *signorina* (Miss), but men receive a title plus their last name. Some women did not regard this as unfair because they thought of *signora* as a term of respect and valued their role as women more than the role of professional. In one school the headmaster announced a policy specifying that he would address the women by *signora* or *signorina* plus last name and the men by their first names. The male teachers could also address him by first name, but women were expected to call him *headmaster* or *Mr. Headmaster*.

Women are also more likely than men to be addressed by their first names. Women often protest that male doctors call them by their first names even on the first consultation. Men, however, are more likely to be addressed by a title plus last name. It would break the conventional rules of address if women were to call their doctors by their first names. Patients are subordinate to doctors, but it seems that female patients are even more so, according to Candace West's findings. Doctors interrupt female patients and female doctors are interrupted more by male patients than male doctors, which suggests that to be a woman is to be a subordinate, no matter what professional level she attains. I have more to say about interruption in the next chapter.

Some feminists recommend that women should begin using their male doctors' first names to draw attention to sexist practices. I recall being somewhat surprised to be addressed by first name in a letter written to me by the senior partner in an accounting firm, whom I had never met or spoken to before, even though I was a client of one of the junior female partners. So I wrote back to him and addressed him by his first name. The use of reciprocal first names in English-speaking countries and many other places too is indicative of intimacy, familiarity, and solidarity, whereas nonreciprocal use signals unequal power.

Thus, as I observed in chapter 1, it is not the linguistic forms themselves that discriminate, but the way in which they are used in particular contexts to particular persons. If I call a student by her first name but expect and insist on being called *Professor* in return, it is the asymmetry itself, not the particular forms of address, that can be considered discriminatory. In this case, however, some would argue that the greater seniority in terms of education and often age entitles certain professionals to expect those junior to them to use special address terms. In another context, say a professional meeting among colleagues, all might adopt the title *professor* in referring to one another, just as in another, we might all adopt first names. Both would be signs of solidarity and acknowledgment of equality.

LADIES FIRST?

Men have been reluctant to use the simple term *woman*, which according to some men is too blunt, too overtly sexual, too demeaning, or too common, so polite usage has called for euphemism, the most common being *girl* or *lady*. When a male colleague commented to me that he would like to see "more ladies" in our college at Oxford, he was puzzled and possibly embarrassed when I asked him if he was referring to women. The expression *ladies and gentlemen* has long been a polite convention (running counter to the prevailing trend I noted in chap. 2, whereby males come first in expressions such as *boys and girls, man and wife*, etc.), but *lady* is not simply the polite equivalent of *gentleman*, as men like to claim when women protest at being called ladies. We can see this from the fact that *lady* is used in circumstances where *gentleman* would not be. We say, for example, *cleaning lady* but not **garbage-gentlemen*.

As I was writing this chapter, a headline appeared in the *Financial Times* (May 12, 1995) declaring "Old Lady bites back." It was referring to inflation figures higher than the government had projected and action being taken by the Bank of England. What, I wondered, could be thought of as polite in referring to a bank as an "Old Lady"? The fact that the Bank of England has long been known as the Old Lady of Threadneedle Street is another example of the continuing use of the female form to symbolize abstractions, as discussed in chapter 3, as well as the general prejudice against old women, spinsters, old maids, and so on that I noted in chapter 4 (see further in chap. 10 on language as an old lady). In the previous chapter we saw too some of the pejorative associations *lady* has acquired over the course of its history as it ceased to be used exclusively in reference to a high-ranking woman. This is especially true in the United States, with the exception of the term *First Lady* to refer to the President's wife. When a woman becomes president of the United States, it will be interesting to see how her husband is referred to. I predict that he will not be called the *First Gentleman*!

American feminists have paid much more attention to the term *lady* than their British counterparts. Nessa Wolfson and Joan Manes, for instance, give examples to show why *lady* is not interchangeable with *ma'am* and is therefore not a term of respect in American English (although in South Africa it is, in interchanges between so-called "colored" and White, where it marks asymmetries of power grounded in racism). The term *lady* is often uttered sarcastically, as in this exchange they recorded on the telephone between a female caller and a male respondent (Wolfson & Manes, 1980, p. 89):

Mr. Jones?
Yes, ma'am?
I'm calling for Jim Smith, who's running in the Democratic primary next Tuesday.
Yes, ma'am.
May I ask what you think of Mr. Smith?
I'll tell you lady. I'm voting for Jim Brown.
Well, thank you very much.
Yes, ma'am.

This contrast between *lady* and *ma'am* explains why many women, myself included, do not want to be called ladies. Julia Penelope (1990, p.

36) once told a telephone caller who asked her if she was the "lady of the house" that no ladies lived in her house. The expression *lady of the house* is not matched by *gentleman of the house*, but contrasts instead with *man of the world*, another indication of the linguistic mapping of the division between the public and private spheres onto male and female, respectively. Indeed, the French equivalent of 'woman of the world' (*femme du monde*) carries the meaning of 'prostitute'. Looking at the British National Corpus, for instance, we find 25 cases of *lady of the house*, 3 of *woman of the house*, and none of *gentleman of the house*, and only 8 of *man of the house*. By contrast, there are 29 occurrences of *man of the world*, but only 12 of *woman of the world*. There are no cases of *lady/girl/gentleman/boy of the world*.

In a 1982 speech about the economy, Ronald Reagan blamed the recession on the increase in women in the workforce: "It is the great increase of the people going into the job market, and—ladies, I'm not picking on anyone but . . . because of the increase in women who are working today." By pointing the finger at "ladies," while disclaiming that he was "picking on anyone," he drew attention away from his own economic policies. His use of the term *lady* was a double whammy here. It is polite, in keeping with his claim that he's not "picking on anyone," but it's also intended to suggest that ladies should be ladies of the house and have no place in the workforce. Ladies don't work, unless of course they are doing housework, which is not "real" work, as I noted in chapter 1. Thus, there are no working ladies, only working women.

The idea that a real lady does nothing was part and parcel of the Victorian construction of ladyhood at a time when conduct books spelled out what it was proper for ladies and gentlemen to do. Gentlemen's wives were ladies of leisure, not to be engaged in baking, brewing, and tending the chickens and garden. In commenting on the considerable waste of talent and energy directed toward becoming a lady in this constrained sense, Margaretta Grey noted that "A lady, to be such, must be a mere lady, and nothing else" (Butler, 1894, p. 288). Many writers such as Sarah Ellis (1839, p. 71) observed how deficient was the education given to women with its concentration on manners rather than matter, in show rather than substance, as Lynda Mugglestone (1995, p. 177) put it. Because a woman's object in life was to please men, skills such as dancing, singing, and how to enter and leave a carriage or room were supposed to add to her attractiveness. In the Jamaican novel *Lionheart Gal* (Sistren with Honor Ford Smith, 1986, pp. 180–181) we find the contrast between the meaning of *lady* and *woman* similarly distinguished when a child relates how she used to play at being a market woman with a basket on her head. She stood under her grandmother's window calling out, "Lady, you want anything to buy, Maam?" Her grandmother told her to come inside at once, and asked what she was doing. Upon hearing that she was playing the role of market woman, her grandmother reprimanded her. The girl asked what was wrong with "market ladies." Her grandmother replied, "Ladies? They are not ladies. They are women. Go and take a seat in your room."

When the British nation as a whole became more affluent during the Victorian era, with the gap between rich and poor filled in by the middle classes, the term *gentleman* became a term of social approval and moral approbation; *ladies* were of the middle class and *women* of the working class. Female students at Owens College in Manchester, for instance, were divided between *ladies* (taking a single course, presumably for pleasure only because ladies would not need to do real work) and *women*, who were registered for examinations, which they needed for career purposes. This suggests at least one reason for the finding that there are no *ladies of the world*, but only *women of the world*, and conversely that the woman who stays at home is overwhelmingly referred to as the *lady of the house* rather than the *woman of the house*.

It was in this social and historical context that speaking properly acquired its social capital in Victorian England. In a letter to his sister Hannah in 1833, historian Thomas Macaulay (cited in Trevelyan, 1878, p. 338) wrote that "the curse of England is the obstinate determination of the middle classes to make their sons what they call gentlemen." Likewise, Sarah Ellis, a contemporary of Macaulay, commented (1839, p. 107) on the metamorphosis in the meaning of the social label *lady* brought about by modern schools:

> Amongst the changes introduced by modern taste, it is not the least striking, that all daughters of tradespeople, when sent to school, are no longer girls, but young ladies. The linen-draper whose worthy consort occupies her daily post behind the counter, receives her child from Mrs. Montagu's establishment—a young lady. At the same elegant and expensive seminary, music and Italian are taught to Hannah Smith, whose father deals in Yarmouth herrings; and there is the butcher's daughter, too, perhaps the most ladylike of them all.

What was the elite to do in a modern society when even the daughter of a herring seller could call herself a lady if her father could afford to send her to an elegant and expensive school where she would learn to read and write, and to speak like a lady? Anyone with money, ambition, and the right connections could aspire to be a gentleman or a lady. The daughters of the butcher, the herring seller, and other categories of tradespeople mentioned would all belong today to the upper working class and lower middle class, precisely those levels in the social hierarchy where modern sociolinguistics finds the greatest differentiation in male and female speech (see chap. 6).

The term *girl* was also used during the late Victorian period to refer to adult women, as is clear in the title of the "Hammersmith Sculling Club for Girls and Men," set up in 1896 and concerned only with "working girls." Without a father who could support her or a husband who could elevate her status to that of lady, working women had only domestic service, governessing, or prostitution as a livelihood.

Not surprisingly, many women feel that *lady* cannot be reclaimed. Women are so degraded and demeaned that even the polite euphemism and aristocratic title of *lady* does not confer dignity on women. The historical association of the terms *woman* and *lady* with different social classes may be partly behind the greater and more positive use of the term *lady* today in British English. Deborah Cameron (1995, p. 46), however, reported that *Today* newspaper, a down-market publication, has now banned the word *lady*, designating it as a "coy genteelism."

What then do women want to be called? Alette Hill (1986) recalled being in a restaurant where a waitress addressed her husband as "sir" and her as "dear." Nessa Wolfson and Joan Manes (1980) discussed this pattern of address in more detail. In their study of 800 service encounters, they found that women were most commonly addressed as *dear*, *ma'am*, or nothing. Terms such as *honey*, *dear*, *babe*, *doll*, and so on are often called terms of endearment and function as such between equals and intimates, but when used by strangers, they have other connotations, such as condescension and irritation, similar to the example of *lady* cited earlier. Women and children are called *dear*, *babe*, *doll*, and *hon* more often than men, indicating the connection between the use of such terms and subordination. *Babe* and *doll* when used as female address terms also equate women with children. Consider this telephone conversation initiated by a female caller to a doctor's office (Wolfson & Manes, 1980, p. 88).

Does the doctor have office hours tonight?
Yes he does. He has hours from 7 p.m.
From 7 until when?
From 7 until he's done, hon.

Shere Hite, author of a U.S. national survey on sexuality and relationships, was rumored to have punched a cab driver for calling her "dear."

Judith Martin, author of the popular U.S. newspaper column "Miss Manners," has attempted to reclaim the word *madam* as a title and term of address for women. In a column on the subject she suggested that it is a "solid-sounding word, unaffected by the office holder's marital status" and therefore appropriate as an equivalent title to *Mr.* in combination with certain job titles, such as *Mr.* or *Madam Vice President*, or for addressing a person whom one does not know (instead of *Miss*, or *Lady*). She pointed out too that its abbreviated form *ma'am* is the correct form for addressing the Queen of England. In concluding her case, she reminded men that " 'Madam,' gentlemen, is no longer funny." She added, "We are not going to lose this very proper term because of anybody's improper thoughts, the way we lost the once useful and respectable title 'Mistress.' " *Madam* is actually the most commonly used form of address for women in Britain, where it is the female equivalent to *sir*, though the first women officers admitted to the elite Sandhurst military academy were addressed as *sir* and not *madam*. The term *mistress* too, as I noted in the last chapter, has a wider usage in Britain, where it serves as a title for a female head of school (e.g., *headmistress*), or female school teacher (see chap. 10).

MARKED WOMEN

In the last chapter I looked at some "marked women" in the category of mothers. More examples show us that women are more generally marked. Consider, for instance, expressions such as *lady/woman/female doctor*. It is assumed that a doctor is a man, so a woman who is a doctor must somehow be marked as such, which conveys the idea that she is not the "real" thing. In the British National Corpus, for instance, I found the following usages: *lady doctor* (125 times), *woman doctor* (20 times), *female doctor* (10 times), compared to *male doctor* (14 times). There were no occurrences of *gentlemen doctor* and only one case of *man doctor*. The fact that housekeeping is a female occupation is explicitly marked in *char-woman* and *cleaning lady*, but implicit in *housekeeper*, and in the short form *char*, as well, which is assumed to be female. There are no *charmen* or *cleaning men/gentlemen/boys*. A "cleaning man" is a *janitor/care-taker/custodian/superintendent* (depending on your variety of English). However, the common British English usage *cleaner* is gender neutral. Likewise, we have *midwives* and *parlor girls*, but no *midhusbands*, no *parlor boys*, and so on.

When we look at data from the British National Corpus, we can see, as I noted earlier in this chapter, that the preferred term for a woman who cleans is *cleaning lady* (30 occurrences), followed by *cleaning woman* (23 occurrences), and *cleaning girl* (1 occurrence). There was also one case of *lady cleaner*. The combination *charwoman* (17 occurrences), however, is preferred over the term *charlady* (9 occurrences). There are no occurrences of *chargirl*.

Conversely, we have terms such as *male nurse* (or *male midwife*), where the male has to be marked because the norm is assumed to be female. The British National Corpus has 20 instances of *male nurse* and only 1 of *female nurse*. Compare also *widow* and *widower*, where the male member is marked with the suffix -er, presumably because women generally outlive men, thus making the man who survives his spouse less common than a woman who survives hers. It would be interesting to look at languages spoken in cultures where circumstances are different. The only other case I am aware of in English where the male term is the marked one is that of *bridegroom*, where *bride* is the basic term.

Similarly, we have the *career woman* (or even *career girl*, as I heard Sarah Ferguson, the Duchess of York, referred to on the BBC news in 1992), but not the *career man*. Men by definition have careers, but women who do so must be marked as deviant. A man can also be a *family man*, but it would be odd to call a woman a *family woman*. Women are by definition family women. We can check my intuitions against the British National Corpus, where the expression *family man* occurs 94 times, and the corresponding *family woman* 4 times. Similarly, *career woman* occurs 48 times, *career girl* 10 times, and *career lady* once, but *career man* only 6 times, and *career boy* or *career gentleman* not at all. Expressions such as *career woman/lady/girl* count as two strikes against women. On the one hand, they suggest that as women, females can't be real professionals, and on the other, they suggest that as professionals, females can't be real women, unless, of course, they are prostitutes! Not surprisingly, the term *business girl* used to be a slang term for a prostitute. When Alma Graham was called "the leading lady of lexicography," she pointed out that the label implied she was playing a role and not doing the job of a bona fide professional.

In my college at Oxford, which was formerly all male, I have often been referred to as the college's "lady professor." An American colleague once reported to me that when he had tried to reach me on the telephone, the college porter had told him he believed the "good lady" was having lunch. Even after I became the college's first woman fellow, it was and still is common for speakers at college meetings to begin their remarks by saying, "Gentlemen." I routinely received announcements about events such as the annual fellows' wives dinner (since abolished!) asking me to indicate if I would be bringing my wife. I cannot count how many times when I was present among the still primarily male gatherings at my college that it was assumed I was either someone's wife or a junior research fellow. These incidents show the effects of what Julia Penelope referred to as PUD (patriarchal universe of discourse). Not surprisingly, a lady fellow who is also a professor is marked by her presence in a context where all fellows are assumed literally to be fellows.

At times I have felt as if Beatrix Walsh were writing about the present status of women at the university when she wrote of her time there in 1932 when she matriculated at St. Hilda's College, Oxford. On the issue of the standing of women dons within the university she noted that "it was not allowed to be great." Men accorded a similar lack of status to the newly admitted women undergraduates and the newly established women's colleges. Walsh (1993, pp. 10–11) wrote that "almost all the men, senior or junior, had difficulty in concealing the curled lip which sometimes asserted itself despite the universal politeness." She then related how she received many invitations sent to her by a history student, all addressed to her at St. Hilda's Hall. When she pointed out to him that St. Hilda's had the status of college, he replied, "You're not really a college, are you? I mean, your Principal couldn't really be Vice-Chancellor, could she?" Walsh also reported that the male dons were also "exquisitely polite," although some hid behind it as a shield for their contempt and refused to take women students in their lectures and tutorials. One claimed that Greek Comedy was too obscene for "girls." As a linguist, I found it interesting that in looking back on her experience, Walsh was struck by how her treatment and that of other women had been obscured by politeness—as she put it, "the really seductive politeness. There is a lot to be said for it, both as treatment and as weapon" (see chap. 6 for further discussion of the politics of politeness).

It is also due to what Penelope calls PUD that any woman at home during the day is assumed to be a housewife or lady of the house. On occasions when I have been the only person in the English Faculty Office, people coming in have assumed I was the secretary because any female sitting in an office must be a secretary. One day a call was put through to me at Merton College from a man who wanted information about doing a degree in Teaching English as a Foreign Language at Oxford. After much discussion and my repeated insistence that we didn't have such degrees, he wanted to know if it was possible to "speak to the professor himself." I told him he was speaking "to the professor herself." He assumed that there must be some male professor of greater authority to whom he could appeal.

We have seen then in these and other examples how the prevailing world view assumes that everyone is male unless otherwise designated. The use of the nearly obsolete convention of referring to women as "the sex" in British English illustrates Monique Wittig's contention that men have appropriated the universal, while women bear the mark of gender. Because markedness is essentially an asymmetrical and hierarchical relationship between the poles of an opposition, the marked term always conveys a more narrow meaning. We can see this in the advice given by one Victorian commentator writing in 1856, who noted the different standards of behavior expected of gentlemen and ladies (whom he refers to as "the sex"):

A young man may talk recklessly of 'lots of bargains', 'lots of money', 'lots of fellows', 'lots of fun' etc., but a lady may *not*. Men may indulge in any latitude of expression within the bounds of sense and decorum, but woman has a narrower range—even her mirth must be subjected to the rules of good taste. It may be naive, but must never be grotesque. It is not that we would have *primness* in the sex, but we would have refinement. Women are the purer and the more ornamental part of life, and when *they* degenerate, the Poetry of Life is gone. (cited in Bailey, 1991, p. 259)

We can see how language was imbued with the similar sort of subtleties of social meaning, as was every item of a woman's clothing. Davidoff (1973, p. 93), for example, noted how "every cap, bow, streamer, ruffle, fringe, bustle, glove and other elaboration symbolized some status category of the female wearer." One could add to this list, her every "h." Talking properly was very much like putting on the right sort of clothing and makeup, or having gloves that fit. The process of codification of standard English by male grammarians and dictionary makers, which I discussed in the last chapter, is in effect an allegory of Pygmalion's carving of a statue of a beautiful young woman. Although grammars were made by men, they were carved in woman's image. Grammar is language tamed and made perfect. Like the idealized female form, grammar is glamorous (see further in chap. 6).

As Tannen (1994b, chap. 4) correctly observed, there is no unmarked woman today either. Everything about a woman's choice of clothing, behavior, and so on carries additional meanings. The range of style options for women is far wider than for men. Women have to choose among skirts, slacks, or dresses. Women have to choose between shoes that are comfortable and shoes that are attractive. If her clothes are tight or revealing, it sends a message of wanting to be attractive, which may be interpreted as "asking for it" (see chap. 8). If her clothes are not sexy, that too sends a message. Similarly, heavy makeup calls attention to the wearer, whereas no makeup is anything but unmarked. Some men even see it as a deliberate and hostile refusal to please. Thus, the choices open to women are generally forced choices between alternatives that send messages they may not want to send. In filling out forms that require them to give titles, men have only one choice, *Mr.*, which is unmarked for anything but maleness. Women nowadays often have a choice of three, *Mrs./Miss/Ms.*, all of which are marked and therefore say something about a woman beyond the fact that she is female. This shows how complex the issue of reform is because the adding of a term such as *Ms.* to the system means that the other terms *Miss* and *Mrs.* undergo shifts in meaning (see chap. 10).

Women's markedness is manifested not only in these various ways in language and dress, but also in models of linguistic analysis, some of which incorporate formal notions of markedness. Some analyses, such as the one offered in a widely used introductory textbook on semantics, assume maleness is the more basic and positive semantic category and that females are therefore to be described as [−male]. This is another example where people are divided into two categories, male and nonmale, with the masculine term functioning as both the positive and neutral member of the opposition. The female term denotes not just the opposite, but can only be used negatively. Thus, if we were to break down nouns such as *man* and *woman*, *boy* and *girl*, into their semantic building blocks, we would analyze them as follows. All the terms share the feature of [animacy], which distinguishes them from inanimate objects such as tables and chairs, and the words *boy* and *girl* are distinguished from *man* and *woman* in terms of both sex as well as age. We also need the feature [human] to distinguish between human beings and other animate beings such as cats and dogs, which would be marked for [−human]. Again, we see a bias expressed in the distinction [−human] and [−adult], which suggests that the adult human life form or state is more basic, and that children are in a sense regarded as deficient adults, whereas animals are not on a par with humans. One could of course argue precisely the opposite from a biological point of view because all adults were once children, and pushing the argument further, humans are evolutionarily later life forms than animals.

Although such a feature analysis shown in Table 5.1 may seem elegant because it captures a number of semantic contrasts with a minimum of binary features, it is sexist and one can easily see that the cards are stacked against women, who have one negative feature, and little girls, who have two strikes against them. Is it surprising that grown women have objected to being called "girls"? (For a male counterargument, see chap. 10.) Deborah Cameron (1985) used this example to illustrate how the practices of linguists are implicated in patriarchal ideology and oppression.

The annoyance women feel at being called *girls* was made clear in a full-page advertisement in the *Wall Street Journal* entitled "Let's get rid of 'The Girl' " (August 28–September 22, 1978). One of the important connections Erving Goffman (1976) drew attention to is how gender is displayed and portrayed in advertising with the repeated imagery of women posed as children (see chap. 9).

There are other technical problems with this analysis that arise from the subordinate status of women. The feature [adult] does not adequately distinguish the meanings of *girl* and *woman* because the term *girl* is often applied to adult females. Speakers should find this next sentence nonsen-

TABLE 5.1
Semantic Feature Analysis of *Man*, *Woman*, *Boy*, and *Girl*

Man	Woman	Boy	Girl
[+animate]	[+animate]	[+animate]	[+animate]
[+human]	[+human]	[+human]	[+human]
[+adult]	[+adult]	[−adult]	[−adult]
[+male]	[−male]	[+male]	[−male]

sical, but in fact do not: "Practically no adults were using it [a reformed number system in Norway SR], including the girls in the telephone exchange, and schoolchildren appeared to drop it when they became adults" (Haugen, 1966, p. 188). Here the author's use of *including* makes it clear that "the girls at the telephone exchange" are adult females, who are contrasted with "schoolchildren," who are not adults.

Linguist John Lyons (1977, p. 334) remarked as follows on the unequal status between the terms *girl* and *woman* with respect to *boy* and *man*, which should make a phrase such as "girls at the telephone exchange" a logical contradiction:

> By any of the most obvious criteria (sexual maturity, etc.) girls reach what would normally be described as adulthood earlier, rather than later than, boys; and yet they are described as girls far longer than boys are described as boys. The proposition "X is now a man" may well imply "X is no longer a boy"; but "X is now a woman" does not imply "X is no longer a girl."

As another linguist, Dwight Bolinger (1980, p. 100), put it more bluntly: "A female never grows up." His remark was prompted by an examination of job ads in the *Los Angeles Times*: 97 used the term *gal* or *girl*, whereas only two used *boy*. Neither education nor social status spares a woman from being called a girl. In a 1989 letter to the *Sunday Gleaner* newspaper in Jamaica, eminent jurist Morris Cargill referred to Dr. Carolyn Cooper, an academic at the University of the West Indies, as a "very clever girl." This dismissive and patronizing remark served to underline the negative force of his attack on her for having criticized an earlier letter he wrote to the newspaper. What do girls know about anything, even if they have PhDs?

Lyons's observations point to problems both with the linguist's assumption that meaning can be reduced to a few basic semantic distinctions, and with the use of binary values in a relation of markedness to characterize the nature of their opposition. The asymmetries between the male and female basic terms can again be easily revealed by looking at the collocations in which words such as *boy* and *girl* appear. From the following example from the Brown Corpus of American English we can see that *girl* is the more general term and modifiers such as *grown-up* and *baby* are used to make the age dimension clear.

> Pink, Vivian once had told him, was for baby girls, and grown-up girls who wore pink were subconsciously clinging to their infancy.

The collocation *grown-up girls* should likewise be a contradiction in terms if the preceding semantic feature analysis were correct. Similarly, we should not expect to find expressions such as *old girl*, but this is in fact common (as is of course *old boy*, as in the expression *old boy network*). The same female may be referred to as a girl or woman in the same context without any semantic oddity. This raises the question of when the word *woman* is used and what connotations it has. In the Lancaster–Oslo–Bergen (LOB) corpus of British English from the 1960s the collocations *unmarried girl* and *married woman* are common, whereas *married girl* does not occur. This suggests that marriage is one of the features speakers use in deciding whether to call a female a *girl* or *woman*. This is borne out by my findings from the more recently compiled British National Corpus. The term *married girl* occurs 4 times, while *married boy* does not occur at all. Generally speaking, the word *married* occurs more often with the word *woman* (182 times) than it does with *man* (160 times). Likewise, the term *wife* is more frequent (15,918 times) than *husband* (10,686). There are also 984 occurrences of *housewife*, but only 2 of *househusband*.

This follows more generally from the fact that women tend to be referred to in terms of their marital status, even though they are much less often referred to at all than men. Another finding reflecting this is the usage of titles. There are 30,031 cases where women are referred to with the titles *Miss* (9,123), *Ms* (1,313) or *Mrs* (19,595), compared to 14,454 cases where men are referred to as *Mr*. We can see from this that the nubility titles *Miss* and *Mrs* are still preferred over *Ms* in Britain, as I noted earlier. These findings are also in line with the fact that women are more generally referred to in terms of the roles they play, such as mothers, wives, and so on, rather than as persons in their own right. There are also more occurrences of the term *mother* (24,146) than there are of *father* (22,306). Otherwise, women are much less talked about.

This finding is in line with the results of Mira Ariel's (1988) study of how men and women in Israeli society were introduced in TV, magazines, and popular literature in the 1980s. She summarized her results in the following formulas:

F   dependency > sex > profession > name > other
M   profession > name > dependency > other > sex

This means that for men sex is given lowest priority, whereas for women reference to sex is high priority. The most frequent reference in the introductions given to men is to profession, for example, *Dr. Brown, a chemical engineer, and his wife*. Women, however, are most likely to be referred to first in a dependent capacity, as mothers or wives rather than in terms of their profession or as individuals in their own right. Describing a man as a husband is far less common than describing a woman as a wife. Women are introduced as females more often than men are introduced as males. Male authors introduce women as females 4 times more often than they introduce men as males. Even women write in the male style, although to a lesser extent. Women authors introduce women as females 1.5 times as often as they introduce men as males.

Ariel points out that the initial information we receive about a person is of primary importance in impression formation. It influences the way that we organize and evaluate the whole text. Twice as many women as men were described in terms of how they looked. The media also tended to use first names for women rather than only last names or full names. Women politicians were referred to by first name, such as Golda (Meir), Maggie (Thatcher), and Jihan (Sadat).

Contemporary media in the English-speaking world show similar patterns. In an interview with Emma Nicholson, for example, a member of Parliament who was about to lobby Margaret Thatcher for compensation for hemophiliac victims of AIDS, BBC Radio 4 introduced her by saying that she was there "in a red dress, with a handbag, so well armed" (*Today Programme*, November 11, 1989). Clare Burstall, Director of the National Foundation for Education Research, was described by the *Times Higher Educational Supplement* (March 8, 1991) as being "five foot nothing" and having "blond hair" and an "animated manner." Although these examples are slightly dated, such practices continue. In noting the first overseas visit of Madeleine Albright in her capacity as newly appointed U.S. Secretary of State, the *Financial Times* reported what she wore. Similarly, a cover story for *Newsweek* (February 10, 1997) described Albright as a "divorced mother," provided intimate details about her divorce, and noted that she had not dated seriously since. Rarely do reports about women discuss only their professional lives and qualifications.

Gunnar Persson (1990, p. 50) looked at some of the contexts in which terms such as *man, woman, boy, gentleman,* and *lady* are used in two corpora dating from the 1960s, Brown and LOB. He found that *man* was more than three times as frequent as *woman* in LOB and nearly three times as frequent in Brown. These asymmetries reflect a number of things: One is that men are more often talked about, as the statistics on the frequencies of *he/she* in the last chapter showed. The second is that most of the authors of the texts are men. However, another factor is that the overwhelming majority of the uses of *girl* refer to adult women. This is one reason why *girl* is 40% more frequent in LOB than *boy*. The data also indicate that *lady* is also a substitute for *woman* more so than *gentleman* is for *man*. Yet even with these adjustments, *man* is still much more frequent than *woman*, as can be seen in Table 5.2.

When we compare the figures I have added from a 3-million-word subsample of the more recent British National Corpus, we can see the same basic asymmetries, but the gap between references to men and women has lessened considerably in the space of roughly 30 years. For example, if we

TABLE 5.2
Frequency of Occurrence of *Man*, *Woman*, *Boy*, *Girl*,
Gentleman, and *Lady* in Three Computer Corpora

	LOB	Brown	British National
man, men	1,763	1,340	92,797
generic	130	185	?
woman, women	496	469	58,816
boy, boys	334	409	19,269
girl, girls	458	374	22,613
gentleman, gentlemen	63	49	6,235
lady, ladies	184	122	11,960

add the occurrences of *lady* to those of *women* we get 70,776, which can be compared with the total for *man* and *gentleman* 99,032. The real figure for references to women is actually higher than that since some of the instances of *girl* refer to adults. I have also not taken into account how many of the occurrences of *man* are generic. Nevertheless, it appears that in the 1960s men are referred to nearly 3 times as often as women, whereas in the mid-1990s, men are referred to only 1.4 times as often as women.

Persson also looked at collocations between adjectives and the terms *man/boy* and *woman/girl* in LOB and Brown. He grouped the adjectives according to whether they were positive (e.g., *attractive, handsome, good, rich*), neutral (e.g., *dark-haired*), or negative (e.g., *fat, ugly, silly*). This classification is rather difficult to apply because what may be positive for a woman may be negative for a man, and vice versa. No doubt the reason why we regard some adjectives as negative is their long-standing association with women. Nevertheless, Persson's results in Table 5.3 are revealing.

Among the adjectives Persson regarded as positive that occurred more than once with *girl* were *attractive, beautiful, golden, good, lovely, lucky, nice, old*, and *pretty*. Among the so-called neutral words occurring more than once were *blond(e), brown(y)-haired, dark-haired, little, naked, small, tall, unmarried*, and *young*. Among the negative ones occurring more than once were *fat, silly, strange, thin*, and *ugly*.

Both women and girls are associated with weakness and helplessness, as can be seen in collocations with adjectives such as *helpless, defenseless,*

TABLE 5.3
Collocations With *Man/Boy* and *Woman/Girl* in LOB and Brown

	Positive	Neutral	Negative
girl	39	22	24
woman	49	30	44
boy	27	21	33
man	173	110	113

fragile, poor, pathetic, and so forth. *Girl* is most frequently associated with negative attributes involving looks and intelligence. There is a huge number of very negative adjectives such as *evil, frightful, debauched, chattering, gossiping, scheming,* and so forth. The word *man,* on the other hand, is associated with many positive attributes. Although with women the positive attributes focus mainly on looks, with men there is a wider range of adjectives denoting mental properties, such as *intelligent, learned,* and *educated,* and of personality traits, such as *kind, noble,* and *brave.* However, there is also a large set of negative attributes for men, such as *violent, weak,* and *spineless.* Persson concluded that the terms *man* and *girl* tend to collocate on the whole with more positive adjectives than do *woman* and *boy.*

Here we see yet another apparent asymmetry; for the male, the adult term is positive, whereas for the female, the adult term is the one with more negative associations. This may reinforce a reluctance to use the term *woman.* The adult female is too threatening to men. She is too charged with sexuality as well as with other negative connotations—hence the euphemism *lady.* Unintentionally, Persson adopted these distinctions in his own writing. When reporting an example from a BBC television comedy in which a male character says "Interesting girl—sorry, woman, er . . . person," Persson commented (1990, p. 64), "an embarrassed young male doctor discussing a Lesbian woman with a young lady with feminist leanings." The lesbian female is referred to as a *woman,* whereas the feminist is a *lady*!

It is instructive to look at some of the collocations of *man/woman* and *boy/girl* in the more recent British National Corpus for comparison (Table 5.4). Not surprisingly, words with negative overtones are still more frequently used together with *girl/woman* than with *boy/man.* I have also included *lady,* which competes with *girl* and *woman.* The figures indicate

TABLE 5.4
Collocations With *Gentleman/Man/Woman/Lady*
and *Boy/Girl* in the British National Corpus

	woman	girl	lady	man	boy	gentleman
blonde	25	28	0	1	1	
frigid	2	0	0	0	0	
good	57	253	0	258	216	
honest	11	2	0	68	1	
hysterical	14	1	1	0	0	
intelligent	17	9	0	44	3	
loose	3	2	0	1	1	
neurotic	2	2	0	2	0	
silly	16	35	1	0	10	
ugly	6	4	0	0	0	

the number of times words such as *silly*, *hysterical*, and such are found together with the basic terms *man*, *woman/lady*, *boy*, and *girl* in a sample of 3 million words.

We can start by comparing collocations containing positive adjectives such as *good*, *honest*, and *intelligent*. Men are more likely to be referred to with these adjectives than women, although the results for *good* require a more complex interpretation. It may be due to the social stereotype of the "good girl" that the expression *good girl* is used more often than *good boy*. Another possibility may be that Persson is right in thinking that *girl* is more generally positive than *boy*. However, this is not borne out by some of the other collocations here, such as *silly girl*. Negative terms such as *frigid*, *neurotic*, and *loose*, relating to sexuality, occur predominantly with the female terms, as do terms such as *blond(e)* and *ugly*, describing appearance. Women's association with blondness may derive partly from fairy-tale images, where the heroine, overwhelmed or enchanted, is often blonde with masses of golden hair as in Goldilocks or Rapunzel. Other popular images of blonde females are found in the stereotype of the "dumb blonde" and the advertising industry's slogan used to promote hair coloring that asked, "Is it true blondes have more fun?"

The term *lady* still stands out as an anomaly, not collocating very often with any of these adjectives. The only adjective it is found frequently with is *old*; this may be due partly to the expression *old lady* to refer to one's wife.

THE LESSER MAN

Other naming practices that show the negative connotations as well as the markedness of females can be found in the many cases where female terms are formed from the male terms by adding endings such as *-ess/-ette*, such as *actor/actress* or *major/majorette*. Such usages are not arbitrary. We can compare other terms such as *salesman/saleswoman/saleslady*, and *salesgirl* (though not *salesboy*). This is found in other languages too, such as German, where *der Student* (the student) is male and *die Studentin* 'the student' is female. Another example of asymmetry of reference to men and women that takes the form of marking the female comes from Italian, where the definite article is used in front of a woman's but not a man's surname, for example, *è arrivata la Rossi/è arrivato Rossi*. Note that the argument used by my colleague about the need to mark women with titles doesn't apply here because the verb forms are already gender marked in Italian, which makes it perfectly clear whether the Rossi referred to is male or female, if anyone needs to know. The English-speaking press has also been reluctant to refer to women by last name only (see chap. 10 on how reform has affected these usages).

Women are also more likely to be addressed in adulthood with names marked with the diminutive suffix -ie/-y more so than men. An adult called *Chrissie* is more likely to be a woman named *Christina* or *Christine*, and *Chris*, a man named *Christopher*. Four-year-old *Robby* or *Bobby* insists on being called *Rob* or *Bob* when older, just as children who continue to address their mother or father as *Mommy* and *Daddy* will be regarded as babyish. Interestingly, articles of women's and children's clothing are more likely to be referred to with diminutive endings than those worn by men, such as *nappy* (American English 'diaper'), *panties/undies* ('underpants': note also British English *smalls*), *nightie* ('nightgown'), *hanky* ('handkerchief'), and *jammies* ('pajamas'). One exception I have found is male underwear referred to as *skivvies*, which is apparently U.S. Marine Corps slang dating from World War II. Names given to household pets are also often diminutive forms. Baby talk, that is, talk addressed by adults to children, often contains many diminutive forms, like *potty*, *doggy*, *beddy-bye*, and so forth. Sometimes the diminutive -ie/-y suffix is combined with other diminutive suffixes such as -kin or -s, such as *Suzykins*.

David Crystal (1995, p. 153) uncovered further gender differences in the names commonly given to men and women. Based on his analysis of 1,667 entries in a dictionary of English first names, he found that female names tended to be longer than male names. There were few female names containing only one syllable (e.g., *Ann, Joan, May*). Many more male names contained only one syllable (e.g., *John, James, Fred, Frank*). Where male names did contain more than one syllable, 95% had a strongly stressed first syllable (e.g., *Jonathan, Edward*). None of the most popular male names in Britain had a strongly stressed second syllable. Only 75% of women's names with more than one syllable had initial stressed syllables (e.g., *Catherine, Ellen*, etc.). The others had unstressed first syllables (e.g., *Elizabeth, Rebecca, Patricia*).

Crystal also found that the stressed vowels of female names also made more use of the high front vowel /i/ (e.g., *Cecilia, Lisa, Tina, Maxine*). Male names with stressed /i/ were much less common (e.g., *Steven, Keith*). Female names were also more likely to end in a vowel (e.g., *Linda, Beverley, Tracey*). If the last sound was not a vowel, it was likely to be a nasal sound (e.g., *Jean, Pam*). Male names, on the other hand, were more likely to end in so-called "hard" (or more technically "stop") consonants (e.g., *Dick, Bob, David, Pete*). Thus, a name like *Bob* is prototypically masculine by all these criteria. It has one syllable and ends in a stop consonant. By contrast, *Sabrina* is prototypically feminine. It has more than one syllable, ends in a vowel, begins with an unstressed syllable, and contains the vowel /i/ in stressed position. Similarly, *Christine* and *Christina* are highly feminine. In fact, in one U.S. survey men judged *Christine* to be the most sexy female name.

I noted in chapter 3 the folk tradition of regarding languages with more vowels as more feminine and those with more consonants as more masculine in my mention of Jespersen's views on the Hawaiian language compared with Germanic languages like English.

Some of Crystal's findings about sound symbolism may well be tied to my earlier observations about nicknames. Another reason why *Bob* does not want to be called *Bobby* when he gets older is due to the fact that /i/ is a prominent sound in many female names. In turn, there has also been independent evidence suggesting an association between words containing that sound and smallness. Some phoneticians have suggested a physiological explanation, namely, that smaller vocal tracts, typical of smaller and less threatening creatures, produce higher pitched sounds (see chap. 2). Thus, suffixes and names containing this sound indicating smallness get used in names referring to women. In languages other than English it is also common for the diminutive to be expressed by high front vowels, by consonants articulated in the front rather than back of the vocal tract (e.g., /b/ as opposed to /k/), and by vowels with high tone. Thus, there are similarities in the way the diminutive is marked, as well as in its range of meanings, as I show later.

Although more research needs to be done on other languages before we can conclude anything more from this discussion, regularities in sound symbolism are intriguing because they point to areas of language where the relationship between sound and meaning is not entirely arbitrary. Crystal raised the interesting question of whether *Kate* is more masculine sounding than *Katie* or *Kath*. Some challenges to this analysis, however, are raised by Anna Wierzbicka's discussion of Australian English naming and nicknaming practices. Australian English shows an overwhelming preference for monosyllabic nicknames ending in a consonant (particularly -*z*), which fit the masculine prototype just discussed, such as *Gaz* (*Gary*), *Baz* (*Barry*), *Marz* (*Mary*), *Al* (*Alice*), and others. Although the diminutives ending in -*i*/-*ie* found more generally in English also occur, interestingly, a child called *Suzie* is likely to become *Suz* when she becomes a teenager. Wierzbicka attributes this shift to teenagers' need to display their friendships in "tough," "non-babyish," and "non-sentimental" terms. Observers of Australian culture have noted informally its generally masculine character and emphasis on male values such as "mateship" forged through historical associations with convict settlement and bushranging.

At the same time, however, commentators on Australian speech have noted its greater tendency to diminutive forms such as *cozzie* (*swimming costume/bathing suit*), *prezzie* (*present*), *mozzie* (*mosquito*), *barbie* (*barbecue*), and so on. Other words take the suffix -*o*, such as *compo* (*workman's compensation*), *rego* (*car registration*), *preggo* (*pregnant*), *journo* (*journalist*), and *arvo* (*afternoon*). Wierzbicka argues that these forms are not really

WHAT'S IN A NAME?

equivalent in meaning to the common diminutives used in other varieties of English. One fact that supports her claim is that they are used as much by men as women. It would not be strange, for instance, for an Australian man to complain about *maggies* (*magpies*), but it would be unthinkable for him to use the term *birdies*. The meaning of the Australian usages seems to reflect informality, a desire to "knock things down to size," and not to make a big deal of things.

Other English suffixes such as *-ette* used both in women's names and occupational titles also show a complicated historical association with women and small things. *Suffragette*, for example, one of the key words of the early 20th century, appears to have been the first word in which the suffix *-ette* was used to indicate a female person. The movement to enfranchise women began in the mid 1880s when a resolution supporting suffrage for women was brought before the British Parliament. However, the *Oxford English Dictionary* records the first usage of the word in 1906 from an article in the *Daily Mail* in which the leaders of the Women's Social and Political Union (WSPU), formed in 1903 by Emmeline Pankhurst and her daughters, Christabel and Sylvia, were called *suffragettes*. The women were referred to as *martyrettes* by another newspaper. The WSPU adopted the label *suffragette*, although some women never liked it because it was a term often used by their opponents to belittle them, just as the shortened form *women's libber* is often pejorative today. Even though the American press applied the term to American women seeking the vote, many of the women prominent in the suffrage movement in the United States preferred the term *suffragist*.

In an entry published in 1915 the *Oxford English Dictionary* defined *suffragette* as "a female supporter of the cause of women's political enfranchisement, esp. one of a violent or 'militant' type." The word *militant* is placed within inverted commas because it was a new 20th century use of the term. Emmeline Pankhurst was one of the first militants in this political or trade union sense of a person who advocated the use of direct action, demonstrations, and so forth as a way of enforcing or obtaining change.

Although the suffix *-ette* was in English earlier, from the 18th century onward, it had two main functions when added to a noun: (1) It indicated something small of its kind, such as *balconette* (1876), *novelette* (1820), *kitchenette* (1910), *launderette* (1949), and others; and (2) it indicated a cheaper imitation of something, as used for example by manufacturers for materials intended as imitations of some other more expensive cloth or fabric, such as *leatherette* (1880), *flannelette* (1882), and *satinette* (1904). Coinages of the first type to indicate something small are still occurring, such as *diskette* (1973). In the 20th century other formations with *-ette* indicating a woman in a certain occupation occur, such as *usherette* (1925) and *majorette* (1941). From 1919 for about 30 years female undergraduates were called *undergraduettes*. The term *professorette* was used at Berkeley in the 1950s to refer to a teaching assistant.

Former editor of the *Oxford English Dictionary* Robert Burchfield (1989, p. 66), who cited these examples of earlier usage, also recorded an interesting case in the *Observer* (October 16, 1988, p. 52) by the journalist John Naughton, who referred to a junior member of the trade as a *hackette* (it is not clear, however, whether this junior member was female). Other journalistic usages occurred in *Private Eye* (September 16, 1988, p. 6), which referred to Polly Samson as a "dauntingly beautiful hypette," and the Chicago *Sun Times* (April 28, 1988, p. 2), which mentioned a *snoopette* (again gender indeterminate, but I suspect female). Other usages of this type that suggest a snide reference to women are *awarette, editorette, voguette,* and *whizzette*. The term *Veepette* was even applied to former U.S. Vice President Dan Quayle. We can see here some of the historical trends I discussed in the last chapter, namely, that terms associated with women become more negative over time. No endings first used to derive feminine forms are later used to derive masculine ones. In chapter 3 I showed how other languages such as the Dizi language of southwestern Ethiopia single out what is small and what is female by grouping them in the same gender class. Everything else is masculine by default.

Many other feminine occupational terms are formally derived from the male version. For example, the term *actor* is assumed to be male, and the derived form *actress* is female. (Compare also *manager/manageress* common in British English, *poet/poetess*, etc.) Another example is *hero/heroine*. Many women's names are diminutives of men's, such as *Henrietta (Henry)*, *Georgette/Georgina (George)*, and *Pauline (Paul)*. Some have noted that some names that were originally male, like *Shirley, Leslie, Beverley,* and *Jocelyn*, became popular as female names and then were no longer used for boys. This may be due to the stereotypically feminine sound patterns found in them. There are no reported cases of girls' names being appropriated for boys. Nor can male names be derived from female names; *Doreen* or *Sabrina* is not matched by *Dor* or *Sabrin*. Generally speaking, there is little overlap between male and female names in English.

When we look at languages other than English we can see some of the same trends. The Italian suffix *-essa* related to English *-ette/-ess* has similar negative, comic, and belittling connotations, as can be seen in words such as *filosofessa* 'pedantic and conceited woman'. The Chinese language has a feminine-specific root *nu* that marks ideographs associated with women in much the same way as the English suffixes *-ette* and *-ess* do. However, it also appears in words belonging to four other semantic fields (see Penelope, 1990, pp. 84–88):

1. Words that refer to an occupation, position, or state of women in society, such as *mother* or *wife*.

2. Words that include activities or actions including women, such as *to be pregnant*.
3. Words that describe attributes men believe to be desirable in women, such as *graceful* and *attractive*.
4. Words that refer to evil in general or evil characteristics of people, such as *jealousy*, *hate*, *foolish*, and *greedy*.

Daniel Jurafsky (1996) attempted to identify universal tendencies in the meanings of the so-called diminutive in order to explain the wide range in its connotations, including smallness of size, femaleness, and affection, among others. In Cantonese, for instance, the diminutive can be used to mark a small object resembling some large object, to mark female gender, and to mark socially marginalized women such as prostitutes, a dance hostess, or a frigid woman. In another variety of Chinese the diminutive marks a 'foreigner'. Compare the term *limey* to refer to an 'English-man/woman' and *Okie* (originally a diminutive of *Oklahoma*) to refer to poor migrant farm laborers. In chapter 3 I observed some of the connections between women and foreigners.

In languages such as Hebrew with grammatical gender the unmarked form without the diminutive is masculine in gender, whereas the diminutive form is marked for feminine gender. Compare *mapa* (m) 'tablecloth' with *mapit* (f) 'napkin'. In languages such as Ojibwa and Tibetan the diminutive marks a form as denoting 'young' in contrast to 'old' or 'adult', such as Ojibwa *kwe* 'woman' versus *kwezens* 'girl' and Tibetan *dom* 'bear' versus *dom-bu* 'bear cub'. As I pointed out in chapter 3, in languages like German the word itself for 'girl' (*Mädchen*) is a diminutive form (compare *Junge* 'boy'), although grammatically it is neuter in gender.

Jurafsky argued that the concepts "small" and "child" lie at the heart of the semantics of the diminutive cross-linguistically. The other senses are derived by metaphorical extension from "child" to create more evaluative meanings such as contempt, ridicule, intimacy, marginality, or affection seen in some of the terms like *hackette*, *sweetie*, and so on that I looked at earlier. I argued in chapter 3 that sex and gender are highly salient dimensions for classification. Because woman is the classic and quintessential Other, metaphors in which females are the source or target are common cross-linguistically. The metaphors that make it possible for diminutive markers to be extended from their original meanings of "child" and "small" are: Women are children. Women are small (things). Women are generally smaller than men and, like children, subordinate to men. That is why a wife is "the little woman." Interestingly, these characteristics of women as small and childlike link women metaphorically with children in quite different ways than in their capacity as mothers (see chap. 4 for a discussion of metaphorical extensions of mothers).

Certain pragmatic uses of diminutives in meaning "small" also serve to mitigate requests by making them seem less of an imposition. In Dutch, for instance, a visitor says she will stay only an *uurtje* 'a little hour'. Compare English, "Can you give me a little help?" In the next chapter I discuss the use of hedging requests as a feature of politeness associated with women.

THE INVISIBLE WOMAN: A ROSE BY ANOTHER NAME

It may at first glance seem paradoxical that language seems to single out women for special treatment by marking them as deviant and inferior at the same time as it serves to make them invisible through androcentric generics. Many feminists have pointed out that it is difficult even to trace the history of women because the history of most countries, as Virginia Woolf wrote (1928a) in talking about England, is "the history of the male line." The opening of the Gospel according to St. Matthew gives an impressive list of 30 males successively begetting one another from the Patriarch Abraham down to Christ. Only once is a woman mentioned, not because she plays the role of begetter, but because she is a non-Jewish Moabite. Men are seen as the creative force. Fathers pass their names on to both male and female children, and when women marry they have traditionally taken the names of their husbands, abandoning their "maiden names" and becoming, as Una Stannard (1977) put it, "Mrs. Man." In Greece, a married woman takes the possessive form of her husband's name, indicating that she belongs to him. In Arabic a married woman is usually not referred to by name, but by the title "wife of X." In China, adult women may have no proper names but only names which refer to them in some role, for example, "third daughter," "little sister," and so on. Susan Blum (1997, p. 363) mentions Alice Murong Pu Lin's story entitled "Grandmother Had No Name" as an example where Lin's grandmother had no name of her own, but was referred to as "wife of Li." Even Lin's mother did not know her own mother's name. There are Chinese males with no proper names but they tend, not surprisingly, to be low in social status. Upper class men often have a multitude of names. In Western culture, a woman who has remarried can pass through several name changes. *The Book of Common Prayer* pronounces a man and a woman as "man and wife." His status as a person remains the same, whereas she exchanges her person for a role. Even though some churches have changed this line in the marriage service to read "husband and wife," they have often retained the traditional order of male before female.

Only men have a right to the permanency of their names. In Western societies when there is no male heir, a family's line dies out because there is no one to carry on the name. Traditional Scandinavian naming practices call attention to the importance of the male heir line because both the female and male children in a family would carry names such as *Johansson*, literally 'Johann's son' and even in Iceland, where names such as *Johannsdottir* 'Johann's daughter' were used, the female child is still seen as a possession of the father. This is yet another way in which women become invisible.

Nothing is more personal or as closely related to our identity as our names. This explains one reason why having your name misspelled or mispronounced can be so irritating. A rose by any other name does not smell as sweet. One of the struggles in the women's movement has centered on the legal right to name or rename ourselves. The issue of naming was prominent at the 1848 convention on women's rights when women signed the Declaration of Sentiments with their own first names. When Lucy Stone tried to vote in 1879 in Massachusetts using her birth name, she was prevented from doing so, even though there was no law requiring wives to use their husbands' names. Stone proclaimed, "My name is a symbol of my identity which must not be lost."An American colleague of mine who married an Australian and wanted to keep her own name was dismayed when told by U.S. immigration officials reviewing her husband's application for a residence permit that she would have to take her husband's name to prove she was "really" married.

A common practice among some feminists has been to replace the father's last name with the name of a female friend or relative, or to drop the father's name. In this way, Julia Stanley has become Julia Penelope. Similar motivations are behind the change in designations witnessed among newly independent countries such as Vanuatu (formerly the New Hebrides) and Zimbabwe (formerly Rhodesia), and the practice among certain Black Muslims to take new names. In his autobiography Malcolm X made the point that the names of Blacks were appropriated by their White masters.

In changing their names, women and other minorities are asserting their right to be called by a name of their own choosing rather than one given by an oppressor. Names are a fundamental part of our identity. Whoever names has power, as indicated in the epigraph to this chapter. The biblical account of the world's creation tells us that God gave Adam the right to name the animals and to have dominion over them (see chap. 2).

Due to the power inherent in the naming process, subordinate groups have pressed for reforms in usage in order to promote a positive self-image. When African Americans first adopted the name *Black* to refer to themselves (in place of *Negro* or *colored*) and asserted that Black is beautiful, they were attempting to create a positive image for blackness, just as women have been trying to reclaim or revalorize derogatory names such as *crone*, *hag*, and such. The group Queer Nation is trying to achieve precisely this by adopting the abusive name for themselves as an act of defiance and gay pride.

Yet, like words referring to women, the term *black* still has negative connotations, as can be seen in terms such as *black market*, *black sheep*, *blackball*, and others. Attempts to reclaim a word may not always have the intended effect (see chap. 10 for further discussion of the "rename and reclaim" approach to reform). When the Reverend Jesse Jackson announced that Blacks should be called African Americans, some argued that this was a meaningless or arbitrary change—"onomastic restlessness." Significantly, however, the derogatory term *nigger* has not been reclaimed. Its power to degrade and abuse has even made it practically ineffable, at least, on White lips. In the O. J. Simpson trial it was referred to publicly as "the N word."

Just as many colonized peoples are writing their own histories, many women are now trying to write "herstory" or "hystery" as a way of replacing history as a story told in men's words about men by men. Under patriarchy, women's experience had no cultural or political significance. It is important to find a voice in which to talk back as the subject of one's own experience rather than be the object of someone else's. Rewriting the past at the same time provides a means of reconceptualizing the future, as I show in chapter 11. French feminists have discussed the paradox of how women are still able to express their own points of view from within what Penelope would call PUD (see chap. 4).

These challenges raise the issue of whether there is a "women's language," as many such as Robin Lakoff have claimed. If so, what distinguishes it? In the next chapter I consider this question.

EXERCISES AND DISCUSSION QUESTIONS

1. Samuel Johnson was 67 and his friend Mrs. Thrale 35. The language of Johnson and Mrs. Thrale, and that of their adult contemporaries, was the stately language of the time, polished, stylish, unordinary, even in the intimate pages of their diaries, and the regime of instruction was severe and practical. Hester Thrale wrote in her diary (see Burchfield, 1989, p. 117). Analyze the patterns of address in this passage.

2. Write down as many terms as you can think of that are used to refer to men/boys and women/girls, such as *bloke*, *bird*, *lad*, *bitch*, *bastard*, and so on. What do ways of referring to men and women demonstrate about the values and behaviors associated with the two sexes? When you evaluate the connotations associated with each word, do you find any patterns? One way of looking at the connotations is to mark each word according to whether it is associated with animals (A), objects (O), food (F), sex (S),

young (Y), old (Ol), no positive or negative connotation–neutral (N), positive connotation (P), derogatory or negative connotation (D). Each word may be characterized by more than one of these features. You can include whatever other categories you need.

3. Keep a diary for a week in which you write down all the terms of address people have used in speaking or writing to you. Include in your entries information about the context and the relationship between you and the person addressing you.

4. Janet Holmes (1995, p. 145) gave this example of an asymmetrical greeting pattern in New Zealand at a police station desk. A woman stands waiting while a male police officer finishes what he is doing before paying attention to her.

Male: Mornin' love.
Female: Good morning, officer. And it's not "love" it's sergeant.

Make observations of patterns of address in public service encounters, such as at a restaurant, post office, doctor's office, or some other public place. How are men and women referred to?

5. Does your name fit the patterns observed by David Crystal? Explain why or why not.

ANNOTATED BIBLIOGRAPHY AND SUGGESTIONS FOR FURTHER READING

Robin Lakoff's book (1990) has an extensive discussion of the semantic contrast between *woman* and *lady* (see also Julia Penelope, 1990). Geoffrey Crossick's article (1991) and K. C. Phillips's book (1984) contain a discussion of the terms *gentleman* and *lady* in the Victorian era. Suzanne Romaine's (1997b) article illustrates how the Pygmalion myth has been reworked in the construction of the concept of lady in the guise of "glamour girl." The semantic analysis of the terms *man/woman, boy/girl* can be found in Geoffrey Leech's textbook (1974, pp. 96–102). Carolyn Cooper (1995) describes the name-calling incident in her book. Kathleen Connors's article (1971) contains a discussion and useful bibliography of feminine agentive suffixes in European (particularly the Romance) languages. Further information on gender in Italian can be found in Giulio Lepschy's (1987) and Dominic Stewart's (1987) articles. Ann Cutler, James McQueen, and Ken Robinson's (1990) article contains a more detailed analysis of the sound patterns in men's and women's names.

6

Gendered Talk:
Gossip, Shop Talk,
and the Sound of Silence

What becometh a woman best, and first of all: Silence. What seconde: Silence. What third: Silence. What fourth: Silence. Yea if a man should ask me til' dowmes day, I would still cry, silence, silence. (Wilson, 1533, cited in Baron, 1986, p. 56)

I think girls just talk too much, you know, they—they—talk constantly between themselves and—about every little thing. Guys, I don't think we talk about that much. (What kind of things do you talk about?) Not much. Girls . . . , cars, or parties, you know. I think girls talk about, you know, every little relationship, every little thing that's ever happened, you know. (teenage boy interviewed by Penelope Eckert, 1993)

Admonitions about silence directed at women are many and have a long history in Western as well as non-Western cultures, as is obvious from my opening quotation. Aristotle proclaimed silence as "women's glory." The New Testament, by implication directed to a male readership, says: "Let your women keep silence in churches: for it is not permitted unto them to speak. . . . And if they will learn any thing, let them ask their husbands at home: for it is a shame for women to speak in the church" (I Cor. 14:34–35). A male audience is also implicit in the medieval handbook written in 1523 by Vives on the topic of Christian female institutions that says, "Let few see her and none at all hear her. There is nothing that so soon casts the mind of the husband from his wife as does much scolding and chiding, and her mischievous tongue" (Baron, 1986, p. 57). The Bedouins describe the ideal woman as having a soft voice and not a long tongue.

The Prophet Muhammad says that a woman's tongue is what keeps her from entering heaven. In medieval woodcuts and paintings the Virtue Prudence is portrayed as a housewife with a padlock on her mouth, and Obedience puts a finger to her lips.

Many proverbs stress the general value of silence, such as the one suggesting that children should be seen but not heard and another declaring that silence is golden. It is no accident that women, children, and also servants are singled out for this kind of advice because they have in common a subordinate status. Women used to be punished publicly for talking too much. They were strapped to ducking stools and held underwater, as well as put into the stocks with signs pinned onto them. A French print of 1660 depicts the Skull Doctor who turns women brought by their husbands into properly docile wives by hammering away at their heads on his anvil. Severed heads hang from the ceiling and the shop sign shows a headless woman with the legend "Everything about her is good," while the anvil is inscribed with the words, "Strike hard on the mouth: she has a wicked tongue."

A medieval image of The Old Wives' Mill shows a similar early instance of cosmetic surgery in which bald and toothless old women are fed into the hopper and ground on the millstone to emerge young and attractive, bright-eyed and bushy-tailed, into the arms of their husbands. In the doctor's smithy and at the mill wives are recycled when their husbands tire of their nagging, gossiping, disobedience, or simply because they grow old and unattractive, just as the fictitious Stepford wives in Ira Levin's novel are replaced with obedient and docile robots (or fembots, as Mary Daly would probably call them; see chap. 10) when they do not conform to male standards of behavior. This is yet another allegory of the Pygmalion myth to be perpetuated in our own time by the fashion and advertising industry, with the glamour of makeup and fashion replacing the crudity of the mill and hammer.

These images indicate a long-standing belief that women talk more than men. It is still with us today, as evidenced by my second quotation, which illustrates yet another belief with ancient roots, namely, that women gossip and talk more about details, emotions, and topics that men consider trivial, and potentially dangerous too, as I show when I consider the history of gossip. Women's talk about social relationships gives rise to fear because it poses a threat to male social order. Female speech can be fatal and therefore must be contained. The fact that we give labels to certain genres of talk, such as *gossip* and *shoptalk*, indicates that talk is important in our culture. Yet we stereotypically associate the former with women and the latter with men. Marina Warner (1994) documented the prejudices against women, in particular old women and their chatter, in fairy tales and myths, often dismissed as "old wives' tales" or "small talk" with their connotations of triviality, falsehood, bitchiness, and superstition.

Yet many recent studies are questioning the stereotypical association between women and gossip and men and shoptalk. In line with the trend in feminist theory toward the celebration of difference approach, scholars such as Jennifer Coates (1996) have turned their attention to documenting the nature and functions of talk among women friends. In this chapter I examine whether there is any basis to claims made about the existence of "women's language." However, as the title of this chapter indicates, I prefer to pose the question in a broader fashion, asking instead whether talk is gendered, and if so, in what way(s), and in what contexts. This means we have to deal first with some of the claims about how women and men speak. Do they reflect how women and men actually speak or how people believe they should speak?

"WOMEN'S LANGUAGE": FACT OR FICTION?

For the most part, the question of how women actually speak has just been ignored. Not until sociolinguists turned attention to urban speech in the latter half of this century were studies designed to examine differences between male and female speech. I noted in chapter 1 that anthropologists for the most part omitted women from their studies. Nevertheless, there have been some intriguing mentions in some of the early anthropological literature of cultures with so-called "male" and "female" languages. In Yana, an American Indian language formerly spoken in California, most words had distinct male and female forms. Male forms of words have a final vowel or syllable that turns up only at the ends of sentences. Compare these male forms, *yana* ('person'), *pana* ('deer'), *sawa* ('arrow'), *hi.si* ('man'), and *hacílsi-'numa* ('We will try it') with their female counterparts, *ya/yah*, *pa/pah*, *saw*, *hi.s*, and *hacílsi-'num*. The male forms were used exclusively by males speaking to other males, but the female forms were used not only by females speaking to other females, but also by females speaking to males and males speaking to females. Men's speech was also used in public speaking to a mixed audience, as well as to an all-female audience, which suggests that perhaps the underlying explanation lies in relative formality rather than gender differentiation. Interestingly, Yana had no separate third person pronouns for *he* and *she*.

Many of the so-called male and female languages described in the anthropological literature have their basis in taboo, often affecting women more than men. For example, Robert Herbert (1990a) reported that in the Nguni culture of Africa women are expected to honor their husbands' families by practicing *hlonipha*. Women have to avoid using any word containing a syllable also contained in their husbands' names (see also Finlayson, 1995). Bedouin women rarely use their husbands' names, out of deference and respect for them; instead, they call them "that one," "the old man," or "the master of my house." In traditional Aboriginal Australian culture there were strong taboos against any kind of verbal or nonverbal contact between a man and his mother-in-law. If a man did need to communicate while his mother-in-law was within earshot, he did so with a special "mother-in-law" variety of language. Where the practice existed, the special variety had the same grammar as the ordinary language in question, but it had an entirely different vocabulary.

Most 19th- and 20th-century dialectologists investigating European languages based their surveys almost entirely on the speech of men, often on the assumption that men better preserved the "real" and "purest" forms of the regional dialects they were interested in collecting. I noted in chapters 1 and 2 how stereotypes rather than systematic research underlay the views of earlier linguists such as Jespersen and Cederschiöld on the matter of how women spoke.

Although practically all linguists would regard these early accounts as sexist, even some of the early work of the 1970s prompted by the women's movement proposing the existence of a "women's language" has been recently criticized by feminists. One particularly influential book by Robin Lakoff (1975) tried to identify a number of characteristics of women's speech that made women seem as if they were tentative, hesitant, lacking in authority, and trivial. She came up with a list of nine features that she believed were characteristic of women's speech.

1. Tag questions (*That's a beautiful picture, isn't it?*)

2. Rising (i.e., question) intonation where one might expect a falling (i.e., declarative) intonation (Q: *When will dinner be ready?* A: *Around six o'clock?*).

3. "Empty" adjectives expressing speaker's feelings (e.g., *divine, adorable, charming, cute*).

4. "Women's words" relating to women's interests, such as color vocabulary. Women have more specialized terms for colors, such as *mauve, chartreuse,* and *baby blue.* Note that there is nothing particularly surprising in this. Most occupational groups have specialized terminology too. Painters and interior decorators, whether male or female, have a larger and more precise set of color terms than the average person, just as a carpenter will have a more elaborate set of names for tools of the trade. Horse breeders and traders in central Russia have around 60 color terms to describe the different bloodstocks.

5. Frequent use of emphasis (also known as "speaking in italics") as if to indicate, "Because my saying something by itself is not likely to convince you, I'd better use double force to make sure you see what I mean" (e.g., What a *beautiful* sweater!). This evokes another popular stereotype of women as more "emotional" than men (see chap. 2).

6. Intensive *so* (I like him *so* much!). Presumably this and the previous feature overlap with the differences in pitch range between men and women discussed in chapter 2.

7. Politeness devices and hypercorrect grammar (greater use of *please* and *thank you*). Women use more standard language, and have less use of swear words (see chap. 4). Greater use of mitigated syntactic structures. Consider the following series: *Open the window. Please open the window. Will you open the window, please? Won't you please open the window? Would you mind opening the window? I was wondering if you could open the window. It's warm in here, isn't it?*

8. Hedges (*well, you know, kinda, sort of, like, I guess,* etc., as in *he's sort of tired* or *she's, you know, not so interested in going to the party*). Notice all the examples of *you know* used by the teenage boy in the second epigraph to this chapter! Although the use of hedges such as these has been said to stereotype the female speaker as indecisive and inarticulate, Alice Freed (1996) found that both men and women engaged in different types of talk in same-sex friendship pairs behaved identically. That is, both males and females used *you know* most when they were asked to talk together about friendship, and least when they were engaged in the task of filling out a form.

9. Women don't tell jokes. This reflects another stereotype about women as humorless.

Many of these same features have been cited anecdotally as features of women's language for quite some time. Lexicographers such as C. E. Funk (1938) gave lists of words used mainly by women. He also said women were prone to hyperbole because they were so emotional. Secondary sources, such as how women are portrayed to speak on TV, in comic strips, and in novels, also provide interesting data for comparison with empirical research.

Upon closer examination we can identify at least four common traits underlying Lakoff's list of features comprising women's language that require explanation: indirectness, emotionality, standardness, and conservatism. Why should these particular features cluster together? Isn't there a paradox in the claim that women's speech in certain societies is closer to the standard or prestige norm than men's when in those same societies men's speech is more highly valued due to the greater power of men? Eckert and McConnell-Ginet (1992, p. 90) summed up some of the seemingly contradictory claims made about women's language, which is said to reflect women's "conservatism, prestige consciousness, upward mobility, insecurity, deference, nurture, emotional expressivity, connectedness, sensitivity to others, solidarity. And men's language is heard as evincing their toughness, lack of affect, competitiveness, independence, competence, hierarchy and control."

When we consider some of these claims in more detail, we can see a circularity in argumentation as well as a neglect of context. Take, for example, Lakoff's claim that women use more tag questions as in, *It's a nice day, isn't it*? Some of the early research claimed that women used more tag questions because women were more hesitant than men and afraid to assert things without qualification. The use of a high rising tone at the end of an utterance, especially when making statements, was also seen as an indication of women's tentativeness and lack of confidence in putting forward their views.

When said by a woman, a reply with a rising intonation is taken to be a sign of her insecurity, hesitancy to assert herself, and inferior status. Imagine, however, that the roles are reversed: A woman asks *When are we leaving for the party*? and a man replies, *Six o'clock*? with a high rising intonation, making it appear he is asking a question. Most likely the man would be thought of as considerate rather than as someone unable to make up his own mind without checking with someone else first.

We can see the same kind of circularity being used in these arguments as in the ones I discussed in chapter 2. Women are labeled as lacking in confidence because they are believed to use more tag questions. Tag questions are thought to indicate a lack of confidence because they are believed to be used by women. Unfortunately, a great deal of the early research on language and gender suffered from this kind of circularity and was anecdotal or flawed in other respects. Even Lakoff was relying on her intuitions rather than real data. When empirical studies were actually conducted to test some of these claims, some found that men actually used more tag questions than women. Nevertheless, this discovery was not accompanied by any suggestion that men might be lacking in confidence!

In fact, out of a number of studies done between 1976 and 1980 on tag questions, six found that women used more tag questions than men, and five found that men used more than women. One study found no differences between men and women. Many researchers simply counted the number of tags used by men and women without paying attention either to the function or context in which they were used. When a tag question is added onto a sentence, it may have a number of meanings. It is in the communicative functions of linguistic features that we should seek out explanations for gender differences. A speaker can make an assertion without appearing to be dogmatic by leaving open the possibility that others may not agree. This can also be used to check whether one's ideas are accepted, or to put forward a suggestion without making it sound like a command. Some tags facilitate contributions from hearers, as in, from one friend to another, *you've bought a new house, haven't you*?, whereas others more aggressively force replies or challenge the hearer, as with police officer to a teenager caught shoplifting, saying *You're not ever going to do that again, are you*?

Indeed, much of the empirical research directed at the question of whether there was such a thing as women's language has, not surprisingly, produced ambiguous results. The many studies on tag questions and interruptions (which I examine later) are good examples. This shows that the way in which research questions are formed has a bearing on the findings, as I pointed out in chapter 2. If men's speech is taken to the yardstick for comparison, then women's speech becomes secondary or a deviation that has to be explained. Those in a position of authority define the world from their perspective, so it is not surprising that academic disciplines are not only androcentric but Eurocentric too, because European males have defined the world's civilization in their own terms. Because males have been in power, they have enforced the myth of male superiority. Women and their speech have been measured against male standards and found to be deficient and deviant, just as not too long ago there was a widespread consensus that something was "wrong" with working-class speech, Black speech, bilingualism, and so forth (see chap. 1).

GETTING A WORD IN EDGEWISE

Another unresolved question in language and gender research is that of whether men interrupt women more than women interrupt men. Different studies have found different results. As with the research on tag questions, the result depends very much on the people involved, the situations in which they interact, and what they are doing. Pamela Fishman (1978), for example, found that most of women's talk in mixed-sex groups was supportive of men and encouraged them to talk. Interestingly, Janet Holmes (1986) found that women used more tags than men in a way that facilitated conversation. Once the men did begin to talk, Fishman found that they took over the conversation. They interrupted women three times as often as they were interrupted by women. As she put it, women did the "shit-work" of conversation. In mixed groups then, women run the risk of being silenced. In a series of articles, Don West and Candace Zimmerman claimed that men interrupt women more than women interrupt men, that men interrupt women more than men interrupt men, and that men interrupt women more even when women are in relatively more powerful positions (i.e., a female physician with a male patient).

The results of such investigations also depend very much on research design and how basic concepts such as interruption are defined. I remember when one of my students came to me in the early 1980s to discuss a research paper she wanted to do on possible gender differences in classroom interaction. One of the features she intended to keep track of in her observations was interruption, so I asked her how she was going to decide when someone was being interrupted. She hadn't thought of this. She took it for granted, as many untrained observers do, that it is easy to tell when someone is being interrupted. All you need to do is see when another person starts talking at the same time that another person is already talking. Yet it is far more complicated than that, and some of the differences in the findings reported by the many studies of interruptions may reflect the fact that the investigators defined interruptions in different ways. In one study, for example, an interruption was defined as cases where one speaker cut off more than one word of another speaker's talk.

Deborah Tannen (1994a) examined the ways in which different ethnic interactional styles might need to be factored into discussions of interruptions. A key issue is how to interpret the intentions of those who overlap with the ongoing talk of another and how those whose talk is overlapped perceive the overlap. As she and others have pointed out, *overlap* is a more neutral term, whereas *interruption* suggests that someone is to be blamed for being a conversational bully. Consider a person giving a dinner party who "interrupts" the table talk to announce that he or she is putting desert on the table for anyone who wants it.

The notion of interruption also assumes an idealized model of conversation in which one person should talk at a time, and one person should finish a turn before another person begins. Yet when we start analyzing recordings of actual conversations, we can see there are often many overlaps in turns. Some of the overlap may be intentional and may be part of a conversational strategy used to show solidarity and agreement. In some cases the talk that is overlapped repeats some of what the other person is saying, or anticipates how that person will finish what they are saying. Some people don't stop talking when their talk is overlapped, whereas others do, rather than to try to take over the conversation or dominate the person who is speaking.

In this example from Coates's (1996, p. 64) study of talk among women friends, Anna, Jen, Liz, and Sue are in balance and work together to arrive at a collaborative account that satisfies them all. As some of the women put it, women "meld" or "blesh" (a compound of *blend* and *mesh*) when they talk. As they discuss what they value about female friendships, they overlap, repeat each other's words such as *expect, accept, ok*, and agree with other by saying *yes, yeah*, and so forth. The group takes priority over the individual in constructing a shared story, like a jam session between musicians. The collaborative floor that emerges creates a shared conversational space where no one individual dominates. The conventions I have used here in representing the exchange are used by discourse analysts to represent where overlaps occur (i.e., extended square brackets), where there is no gap between one speaker's utterance and the next (i.e., =), and the end of a chunk of talk (i.e., /).

Liz: I know that these two don't expect anything from me/ same as
I don't

Anna: yeah/   we're
accepted
Liz: ex pect anything from them/ they're just them and that's it=

Anna: for what we are/ each of us/
Liz: and we're ok/ and you're accepted
Jen: =and you're ok?

Anna: yeah/
Liz: as being ok just by being you=   =yes/ yes/
<laughs>
Sue: =just by turning up

In other cases, however, such overlaps may be a result of mistiming if the speakers come from different cultures with different conventions and signals marking the ends of turns. Different cultures have different habits with regard to the pacing of conversation. For most American speakers a pause of more than a few seconds is an uncomfortable silence; people leap in to fill the gap with talk. In conversations between Finns and Americans, Americans are more likely to interrupt, because Finns don't mind a longer pause between turns. The one who overlaps may not intend to take over the floor, but simply doesn't recognize whether the other person has finished. This means that counting overlaps does not necessarily lead to understanding interruption.

Speakers who come from ethnic backgrounds allowing overlap are likely to be perceived as pushy and aggressive when they engage in conversations with others who do not talk that way. This conversational style is often seen as a more negative feature when engaged in by women than by men, probably because aggression and violence are tolerated more from men than from women.

Cooperative overlapping of the type Coates found is a feature of many casual conversations. According to several studies, it is even more characteristic of women's casual conversation than it is of men's. Carole Edelsky's (1981) study of faculty committee meetings found differences between men's and women's contributions to talk. In some cases one person, more often male than female, spoke and the others listened. In other cases, however, a number of people overlapped. Under these circumstances women contributed as much as men. This suggested that women felt more comfortable speaking collaboratively. This style of talking may be partly what gives rise to the stereotype of women as a group of hens clucking at the same time. This image may have a long history and be reflected in the semantic evolution of terms like *biddy* (see chap. 4). This stereotype appeared in the film version of the popular musical *The Music Man*. A group of women are talking ("gossiping") and the scene switches back and forth between the women and a view of a farmyard, where a group of hens are simultaneously clucking—a hen party (see chap. 4 on animal metaphors for men and women). However, there is a deeper significance here in the use of hens, and as I show next, and in other birds, in particular the goose, as symbolic of women's storytelling and the passing on of female experience in narratives (see chap. 11).

All this talk about interruptions and overlapping naturally brings us back to the issue of silence and the stereotype of the gossiping woman, which need reconsideration in view of some of the variables I have just looked at such as context, culture, power, and solidarity.

IS SILENCE GOLDEN?

Despite the image of the overly talkative woman, actual studies have shown that men talk more than women in a variety of situations. Hattie Caraway, the first woman elected to the U.S. Senate, made only 15 speeches on the floor in her 13 years in office. After listening to the more numerous orations of many of her male colleagues, she wrote in her diary, "and they say women talk all the time." Susan Herring's studies (1995, 1996a, 1996b) of men's and women's contributions to professional Internet discussions also revealed that men "talked" more than women, even on woman-oriented discussion lists where female subscribers were in the majority. On a list started in late 1996 where only 6% of the subscribers were men, Herring found that nearly half the men (45%) had posted messages, compared to only 28% of the women. Men's messages were also longer than women's. Moreover, women received fewer responses to their messages than did men. Among highly active members, those posting five or more messages, males also communicated disproportionately relative to number of subscribers.

Her results question the alleged democracy of Internet communication and reveal a transfer from the spoken to the electronic medium of deeply entrenched perceptions of male entitlement to speak in public space. Women may also be discouraged by the medium itself, because men heavily dominate the computer and related "high tech" industries, where few women have advanced beyond the ranks of middle management. Industry leader

Microsoft Corporation, for example, appointed a woman to its Board of Directors only in 1996.

Perhaps it just seems that women talk more because men expect women to be silent. When silence is your yardstick, any woman who talks at all seems to be talking too much. Spender (1980b) found that people perceive women as talking more even when they contribute only a third as much as men do to a discussion. Thus, we have the myth of the loquacious woman juxtaposed with the ideal of the silent one. Even more modern advice and conduct books contain warnings similar to those of medieval handbooks about the woman who talks too much. Writing in the 1950s as Mrs. Dale Carnegie, Dorothy Carnegie (1957) provided tips to women who wanted to help their husbands get ahead. According to her, a woman who had a "receptive ear" was a great comfort and release to her husband. A "quiet, unpretentious" woman who is "fascinated" by another's conversation and acts as if she is "digesting every word" is the "girl" most likely to succeed socially with both men and women.

Many languages have proverbs or sayings linking an excessive amount of talk or gossip to women in an unflattering way. In Bedouin culture there is a saying that men's talk is full, but women's is empty; whenever two women talk, the devil is there between them. Compare also German *klatschen wie ein Waschweib* 'to chatter like a washerwoman', Italian *È pettegola/o come una serva* 'He/She gossips like a servant girl', and Japanese *onna sannin yoreba kasimasii* 'Three women together mean din'. A dictionary published by the Swedish Academy contained 16 compound nouns whose structure paired a word meaning talk with a word for a woman, such as *skvallerkäring* 'gossip hag'.

Gossip was originally a *god sib*, that is, a god parent, but its meaning narrowed to refer primarily to female friends at a child's christening. The related term *gossiping* was originally the christening feast at which family and friends gathered to congratulate the mother. Jan Steen's painting dating from 1664 carried the title "Gossiping" and depicted such a domestic scene with the new mother lying in bed attended by two women while others surround the kitchen table and heat water by the hearth, gesturing to one another as they engage in conversation. As was the case with other terms connected with women that I examined in chapter 4, *gossip* underwent pejoration and came to mean 'idle or malicious talk', or a newsmonger, usually a woman, engaged in such chatter.

The terms for 'godmother' in French (*commère*) and Italian (*commare*) also took a negative semantic turn, unlike the terms for 'godfather'. The feminine version came to refer to a midwife, but in modern Italian a *commare* is a gossip or crony, and the connections to midwifery were lost. The French term too came to mean a gossip-monger, whereas a related English word (now obsolete) *cummer* also meant 'godmother', an intimate friend and gossip as well as midwife and wise woman. In Haitian Creole French it carries an additional negative meaning of 'effeminate man' or 'sissy'.

In her work among the Tchambuli people of Papua New Guinea, Margaret Mead (1935, p. 257) observed what she called a reversal of the Western notions of masculinity and femininity. Although she provided very little information on speech styles, one of her comments is interesting in connection with the gossiping and bickering stereotype associated with women.

> Whereas the lives of the men are one mass of petty bickering, misunderstanding, reconciliation, avowals, disclaimers, and protestations accompanied by gifts, the lives of the women are singularly unclouded with personalities or quarreling. Solid, preoccupied, powerful, with shaven unadorned heads, they sit in groups and laugh together. . . . Here again the solidarity of women, the unessentialness of men is demonstrated.

Although Mead's conclusions have been challenged, they do point clearly to the necessity of taking culture into account in discussions of silence and gossip. Many cultures value silence more than others. In Japan talk is likely to be avoided in a confrontational situation. Japanese speakers allow longer pauses between their turns at talk than do most speakers of American English. The stereotype of the silent Finn I noted earlier comes partly from the fact that a higher value is placed on silence in Finnish culture than in many other Western cultures. Silence is thus ambiguous. It can be used as a weapon by those in power. Among the Burundi people of Africa, the powerful are silent, and those who ask favors of them must act like bumbling peasants. Similarly, among the Wolof of Senegal the nobles speak as little as possible, whereas the underclass of griots bears the responsibility of talk. The ability to get people to do things without asking them directly is often a sign of great power. A Wolof village chief almost never speaks aloud in a public gathering; he will ask an intermediary to speak for him.

In Western culture we too encounter the stereotype of the silent man, who keeps his feelings to himself. We are all familiar with cartoons depicting the silent husband behind his newspaper at the breakfast table. In fact, lack of communication is one of the most frequently given reasons for breakdown of marital relations leading to divorce in the United States. Wives commonly complain to their husbands, "Why don't you ask me how my day was?" or "Why don't you listen to me?" Other studies have found that when tension arises in marital relationships, men tend to distance themselves from conflict whereas women pursue intimacy. The dominant partner has less to lose by withdrawing. In her survey of sexuality and relationships in the United States, Shere Hite reported that women's number one grievance about their partners was that they didn't listen. So who's doing the talking and who the listening? And why has women's talk long aroused such fear?

Gossipy gatherings of women were the focus of much male anxiety about the power of female tongues during the Reformation, as can be seen in conduct books, engravings, and paintings, some of which I mentioned at the outset of this chapter. In their roles as midwives and housewives, women dominated the informal and domestic webs of information and power, hearths, spinning rooms, washing places, wells, and markets in the villages and towns. In many parts of the world women still control these public and private meeting places, where they pass on information. Even in modern industrialized societies we can find counterparts to these unofficial, but nevertheless socially influential, conduits of news, ranging from women's volunteer groups of various kinds to bridge groups who meet at members' homes to play cards and gossip. At one university in Britain the familiar institution of the wives' club, a gathering intended to bring together the wives of new faculty members to help them integrate into the community, is called "Stitch and Chat," carrying on the traditional associations of women with spinning, sewing, and weaving, and, of course, the gossip accompanying the working of textile.

Marina Warner (1994, chaps. 3 and 4) pointed out how the changes in the meaning of the word *gossip* illustrate the influential role of women in communicating and storytelling through informal and unofficial networks. Gossip poses a threat to the social order because it may give rise to slander and intrigue and expose illicit and secret liaisons. Professions such as midwifery allowed women passage between households, largely free of male control, to exchange mother wit—knowledge of intimate matters such as contraception and abortion. In 17th-century England, broadsheets denounced women's gossip and its dangerous powers, among them curses and spells. Contraptions like dog muzzles were used to gag women who had been found guilty of blasphemy and defamation. One broadsheet entitled "Title-tattle; or the several branches of Gossiping" shows the places where women gathered unsupervised to talk—at the baker's, the childbed, the well, the alehouse, the riverbank where they did laundry, and so forth. The industrial revolution confined women increasingly to their homes, where they were isolated from one another.

The undesirability and evil of gossip are also strongly emphasized through its association with old women, hags, and crones, another allegorical representation of the female body in terms of speech. The association between face, figure, and tongue means that looking fair and speaking fair are feminine virtues, as I showed in chapters 4 and 5. Ugly talk comes from ugly women, unwomanly women beyond the age of childbearing, and therefore is unnatural. The woman who is no longer fertile outlives her purpose. Childbearing is redemption for woman's sin, for her sexuality, and by implication for her speaking. The New Testament tells us that "A woman ought not to speak. . . . Nevertheless, she will be saved by child-bearing" (1 Tim. 2:15). The tongue is associated with lust because talk is a tool of seduction, ever since the Devil spoke to Eve to tempt her to eat the forbidden fruit (see chap. 2).

The 17th century also saw the appearance and spread of Mother Goose tales in print form. Old women, either as godmothers, stepmothers, or wicked witches, exercised their influence in fairy tales. Their power in fairy tale is primarily verbal; they riddle, cast spells, conjure, and perform other magic deeds. Speech works strong magic. Women are associated with birds like the goose, which was sacred to Aphrodite, the Greek goddess of love, who used it as a means of travel. A Mother Goose tale tells how old Mother Goose "when she wanted to wander would fly through the air on a very fine gander." Geese are also emblems of gossip, as in the 15th-century English proverb "Many women, many words, many geese, many turds." One of La Fontaine's fables, "The Women and the Secret," relates how a husband tests his wife's discretion by telling her that he has laid an egg. She immediately rushes to tell her neighbor and the egg increases in size, and in number when that neighbor tells another, until the whole town marvels that the man has laid more than a hundred eggs. The metaphor of laying an egg stands for the storytelling goose who passes on a whopper.

The hen's cackle and the goose's honk are also associated with women's talk. In French the word *caquet* means 'women's talk' as well as the 'cry of a goose'. In Dutch the word for the sound of stork bill's clattering (*klepperen*) also refers to women's talk (*clapperij*). French *canard* means both 'duck' and 'tall tale'. The Sirens in Homer's *Odyssey* are femmes fatales with webbed feet and the bodies of birds, who lure sailors onto the reefs with their sweet songs. Their names are connected with speech, such as Shrill (Ligeia), Lovely Voice (Aglaophonos), and Spellbinding Words (Thelxepeia). Like the three classical fates representing past, present, and future as they sit spinning, the Sirens who tempt Odysseus and his men hold out the promise of knowledge, as did the Serpent to Eve in the Garden of Eden in the form of the forbidden fruit.

The stork of course is said to be the one who brings babies. In Hans Christian Andersen's fairy tale of the Bog King's daughter we are told that storks tell their offspring many stories and fairy tales. The image of the storytelling goose or stork appears on many Victorian children's books. The well-behaved, cozy and domestic version of the goose or stork becomes the respectable vehicle for children's tales, the wise old grandmother, god-mother, or Old Mother Hubbard who passes on nonsense rhymes and songs, tales of foolishness and fantasy to her young charges, both to en-tertain them and to instill morality and knowledge. Although male writers and collectors have dominated the production and dissemination of popular tales, what they have passed on is women's oral stories from the domestic milieu.

Distribution of talk in fairy tales also falls into stereotypical patterns, as Ruth Bottigheimer has shown in her analysis of the Grimms' stories. The equation of silence with female virtue results in virtuous characters speaking less than villainous ones. The more she speaks, the more she is likely to be up to no good (see also chap. 11 on silence as punishment, and feminist rehabilitation of fairy tales).

WAIT TILL YOU HEAR WHAT HAPPENED TO *ME*!

We have seen some evidence that men and women have different conversational styles in certain contexts, but are there differences in what men and woman talk about? Phil Donahue, who hosted a popular TV talk show, explained once to Gloria Steinem why he prefers to talk to women on his program rather than men. He implied that if men talked more, it would be a "boast" show and not a "talk" show (cited in Hill, 1986, p. 132).

> If you're in a social situation and women are talking to each other, and one woman says, "I was hit by a car today," all the other women will say, "You're kidding! What happened? Where? Are you all right?" In the same situation with males, one male says, "I was hit by a car today," I guarantee you there will be another male in the group who will say, "Wait till I tell you what happened to me."

Some discourse analysts have found that stories told by men and women differ in theme and structure. Women talk more about relationships and feelings than men. This, however, may reflect the fact that one of the most frequent settings for all female talk is domestic rather than public. Jennifer Coates (1996), for instance, found that the women whose talk she studied tended to meet in each other's kitchens (a primarily female space) and living rooms rather than, say, in restaurants. Barbara Johnstone (1993) found differences in the plots of stories told by men and women. She claimed that women's stories tend to be about community whereas men's tend to be about contest. The men talked about physical contests such as fights, as well as social contests in which they used verbal and/or intellectual skill to defend their honor. Stories about contests with people or animals can take the form of tall tales, which are themselves a kind of contrast between tellers and their audience. When a male storyteller was not the protagonist in his story, the protagonist was a man; men rarely told stories involving women. The women's stories, on the other hand, revolved around the norms of the community, and joint action by groups of people. The women told about incidents in which they violated social norms and were scared or embarrassed as a result—for example, about people helping other people out of scrapes, about sightings of apparent ghosts that are then explained by others, about meeting their partners and acquiring their cats. The women told about peculiar people, dramatizing their abnormal behavior and setting it implicitly in contrast with social norms. They told stories about themselves, about other women, and about men. The men's stories tended to be about male characters acting alone and being successful, whereas the women's stories stressed the importance of community. I show in the next chapter that some of these tendencies can already be found in children's storytelling and writing at school. In chapter 11 I discuss women's attempts to write themselves back into stories.

Susan Kalcik (1975) believed that there is a distinctive way of telling stories that characterizes all-women groups, especially feminist all-women groups. She cited a cooperative interactional style, with no story being told before another is finished, and frequent attempts to solicit the opinions and comments of those present as the story is progressing, particularly from those who have not been actively participating up until that point. In addition, stories are often begun with apologies (e.g., for the content of a story or its length) as a way of recognizing others' desires and face. She also described a phenomenon she called story-chaining, in which the telling of a story suggests a story to another member who then tells a story. She believed story-chaining works as a way of showing support by sharing a similar experience rather than, say, as an attempt to top the previous narrator's story (as Johnstone found in men's stories). When it comes to telling stories, men choose the self and women choose others. Likewise, Kerstin Nordenstam (1992) found in her study of male and female conversational styles in Sweden that all-female groups mentioned names of acquaintances and kin almost twice as often as men did in single-sex groups. She also noted a greater number and higher variety of back-channeling signals in the all female groups. These are expressions that indicate that the listener is paying attention to and is in sympathy with what is being said, such as *yes, ok, that's right, yeah, you don't say, really, exactly, uh-huh*, and so on. Moreover, all of the expressions of surprise, which might be thought of as expressing greater emotionality and involvement, were uttered by women talking to other women. Interestingly, Nordenstam found the fewest backchannels in conversations involving husbands and wives! Moreover, only men yawned! Although male groups tended not to engage in talk about people of the type usually defined as gossip, she did find that one group of young men talked about human relationships, unlike the other all-male groups, who spoke about more stereotypically male topics such as sports, cars, and so forth. Nordenstam also observed that the women were much more amenable to having their conversations investigated and more cooperative in giving her access to their talk. More research needs to be done to investigate the extent to which the findings on male and female conversational style reflect our lack of access to a full range of data covering talk of different types in different settings.

From the perspective of the feminist approach that celebrates female difference and anything traditionally associated with women, some of these features of women's storytelling and behavior are accentuated as skills and positive assets, as evidence of women's greater interpersonal skills. Feminist analyses of women's talk about relationships and involvement with others have observed how such conversations are about problems in women's lives that are often suppressed from public discourse. When male difference is valorized, women's emotionality is considered a liability that dooms their talk to idle chatter. Moreover, just as playing within all-girl groups may be a strategy for girls to avoid male domination (see chap. 7), talk within female friendships may provide an oasis from as well as a form of resistance to the heterosexual script that dictates that in male/female relations, the woman is usually subordinate. Coates (1996, p. 41), however, drew attention to another strand of research claiming that female friendship in fact helps to prop up the heterosexual hierarchy by serving as an emotional outlet for women frustrated in their relationships with men. Nevertheless, numerous reports indicate the centrality of female friendship in women's lives, such as Hite's finding that 87% of married women and 95% of single women reported they had their deepest emotional relationship with another woman.

The centrality of talk as a means of sustaining female friendship emerges clearly in Coates's research as well as in other studies. When she asked women what they did with their women friends, many balked at the word *do*, despite the fact that talk was the one thing they all emphasized. One said, "what I remember about the relationship is *not* like what we *did* together, but just you know the amount of time we just spent sitting around and talking" (Coates, 1996, p. 67). Another replied, "We talk, primarily we talk, we never stop" (Coates, 1996, p. 44). As I have stressed throughout this book, however, talk is a form of doing, of doing things with words. As Coates put it, what these women friends are doing with their talk is friendship. In the next chapter I discuss how talk becomes central to girls' activities.

Yet women's conversations are routinely trivialized with the labels *gossip, girl talk, bitching*, and so on, whereas similar conversations among men are called *shop talk*. It is unimaginable that a meeting between the President of the United States and a foreign head of state would be billed in the press as "gossip" or "boy talk." Yet a British newspaper used the headline "girl talk" to describe a meeting between Margaret Thatcher and Indira Gandhi when the two were Prime Ministers in their respective countries.

Similarly, an American newscast carried a story about a "disagreement" between Arab and Israeli heads of state, and another on women "bickering" at a conference on the ordination of women to the priesthood. These judgments reflecting the differing social values we have of men and women, as well as of the settings where they usually speak, define what men do as more important. We expect men's talk to be serious and women's talk to be trivial. Pamela Kipers (1987) found that women did not in fact talk more about topics that were independently rated as trivial by both men and women. Actually, nearly half of all the discussions undertaken by all-male, all-female, and mixed-sex groups were on topics that had been independently judged as trivial! Coates found that some women were aware of some of these negative stereotypes and were therefore eager to stress to her that they did not talk about "domesticky" or "girly" things.

Male and female politicians in Sweden believe that men and women talk about different topics, but Kerstin Thelander's (1986) research on parliamentary language in Sweden shows that this is not in fact always the case, although men spoke more about finance. The men also talked longer than the women. Men and women described each other's language in different terms. Women, for instance, said that men's speech was more authoritative, solemn, impersonal, repetitive, pompous, and abstract. They described their own speech as softer, more sensitive, spontaneous, concrete, brief, simple, and understandable. The men described women's speech as soft, sensitive, friendly, simple, engaged, and inexperienced, and their own speech as prestigious, aggressive, difficult, formal, bureaucratic, and too wordy. Interestingly, both men and women ascribe many of the negative characteristics of political language to men. In fact, however, women used longer sentences than men, even though their contributions take up less time than men's and have not increased much over the past few decades, and in spite of the fact that they profess nervousness about speaking.

WOMEN ARE MORE POLITE, AREN'T THEY?

People generally think that women are more polite than men. This makes intuitive sense when we consider that the onus is on the subordinate person in an encounter to be polite, for example, employees vis-à-vis their employers, students vis-à-vis their teachers, sales personnel vis-à-vis their customers, and so on. What is universal about politeness is acting deferentially to the person perceived as higher in status or power. As Pierre Bourdieu (1977, p. 662) remarked, "politeness contains a politics, a practical and immediate recognition of social classifications and hierarchies." Indeed, some of the differences between male and female behavior we have just looked at, such as amount of talk, distribution of talk, interruptions, questions, and backchanneling, may be better handled as differences in politeness.

Yet there are a number of ways to be polite. What differs cross-culturally or even from group to group within the same culture is the matter of when to be polite and how to show it. Janet Holmes (1994) defines politeness as behavior that either actively expresses positive concern for others or expresses distance and the desire not to impose. Japanese women, for instance, generally avoid *kango*, forms of speech characterized as "rough." Female speakers tend much more so than males to avoid the second person pronouns of direct address entirely. There are also many special particles used only by women, such as *wa*, associated with young women in particular, and honorific forms in Japanese to indicate politeness. Where a male speaker would say *sizuka da* 'it is quiet', a woman would say *sizuka da wa*. Nobuko Yotsuya, the first woman elected to serve as Vice Chairman of the Metropolitan Assembly in Japan, could not bring herself to address the other members with the honorific suffix -*kun*, used only by men. Other particles are used mainly by men, such as *yo*, one of whose uses is to command compliance from an addressee. In order to do so, the speaker must outrank the addressee. A Japanese woman would rarely use *yo* because she would not want to violate explicitly the conventionally subordinate position of women.

In her studies of male and female conversational patterns in New Zealand, Holmes (1994) took the amount of talk depending on the context as a measure of politeness and cooperation. She found a striking contrast between the amount of talk produced by men and women depending on their role as interviewer or interviewee. Males acting as interviewers on TV programs appropriated half of the speaking time, whereas women interviewers made much briefer contributions and allowed their interviewees more time to speak. Young male interviewees, on the other hand, when interviewed by other young men as part of Holmes's project on New Zealand English, produced very little talk, answering each question as briefly as possible. Most of the women interviewees, however, were willing to talk at length. This has implications for the use of interviews as a standard elicitation technique in sociolinguistics. Members of each sex speak the least in situations they find least comfortable.

Holmes also looked at the forms and functions of compliments and apologies used by men and women. She found remarkably similar patterns for both speech acts. Women give and receive more compliments and apologies than men. The similarity may have to do with the function that both features share of showing and maintaining concern for personal relationships. A person who apologizes shows concern over the possibility that a relationship might be damaged by some careless act or oversight, whereas a person who compliments shows solidarity. Most compliments and apologies occur between equals, but women apologized more frequently to those who were more powerful. Even men, however, offered more of their apologies to more powerful people. Interestingly, men apologized more for time offenses, such as keeping someone waiting, or offenses involving possessions, such as damaging something, whereas women were more likely to apologize for offenses of space, such as bumping into someone, and talk, such as interrupting or talking more than others. Male concern for time may be a reflection of the ethics of the business place in which time is money, and therefore a valuable possession. Women also apologized more for less serious offenses than men. Women offer both apologies and compliments to show solidarity, and hence give more of both to others who are their equals.

However, the fact that women also receive more compliments from men than men give to other men is indicative of women's subordinate status. Women's behavior and appearance is open to social judgment. Most compliments occur between persons of equal social status, but even lower status men offered compliments to higher status women. Holmes also found that compliments on appearance accounted for more than half of the compliments given to women. Men appear to compliment other men on their possessions rather than appearance. Compliments given to women function in the same way as praise given to children, as reinforcement to continue with some behavior that meets with approval. They can also function as power plays by putting the person who compliments in a one-up position, just as apologies can put the one who apologizes in a one-down position.

For Lakoff, indirectness was yet another way in which women appeared hesitant, unassertive, and unsure of themselves, particularly when making requests of other people. Because saying no to a direct request can be very difficult in many cultures, being indirect or hedging is one way of being more polite. Both indirectness and hedging have been seen as typical and expected of women, but at the same time, in some respects, as undesirable features of female speech.

Some of the recent advice and assertiveness training courses aimed at teaching women to express their needs and wants directly are based on the "women as problem" view of gender differences, and the assumption that it is women who do not fit into the public sphere and therefore have to change. Indeed, the popular press has cited "women's language" as one reason for women's ineffectiveness in the business world. Communicative styles perceived as feminine make women seem less serious. One newspaper article entitled "Job-hunting advice for women: Talk like a man" (Knotts, in the *Baltimore Evening Sun*, 1991) said, "Women's language is not the language that business people want applicants to speak. Even women don't want to hear it. They want a woman to talk like a man."

In the broadway musical *My Fair Lady* Professor Henry Higgins wondered why a woman couldn't be more like a man. Requiring women to be "one of the boys," by talking like men, as suggested in the quote from the newspaper article, treats symptoms of women's inequality rather than its causes. French feminists such as Luce Irigaray have been critical of Anglo-American feminism for its preoccupation with equality because this forces women to be like men in order to be treated as equals. At the moment, there is still a great deal of tension involved when women try to combine femininity and power.

Many of the first women to be successful in achieving powerful positions, like politicians Margaret Thatcher or Geraldine Ferraro, have tried to sound and act like one of the boys. Margaret Thatcher's voice was considered a liability to the public image of her the media wanted to project. In fact, one source noted that "the selling" of Margaret Thatcher as a politician had been set back years by the mass broadcasting of Prime Minister's question time because she had to be at her "shrillest" to be heard over the din. She undertook training both to lower her average pitch and to reduce her pitch range and was advised to try to maintain a steady pitch to carry her voice through rather than over the noise (see chap. 2 on sex differences in pitch, and J. M. Atkinson, 1984, pp. 113–115 for further discussion).

If men's greater success in business lies not in the way they act and speak, but is due instead to their gender and society's endorsement of male behavior as "normal," then the advice being given to women is self-defeating. The cosmetic nature of such makeovers offered in elocution and other forms of self-improvement is evidence of their futility. Women are still women at the end of it. Quite often, women who make such extreme attempts to accommodate to male norms are then made fun of or criticized for trying to be one of the boys! When Geraldine Ferraro tried to talk in the way accepted by men, it prompted then First Lady Barbara Bush to refer to her as "the word that rhymes with rich." When Ferraro was announced as presidential candidate Walter Mondale's running partner, John McLaughlin, host of the news talk show "The McLaughlin Group," announced, "It's a girl."

Yet, like all of the other features I have examined, the meaning of indirectness and the role it plays in politeness depend on who uses it, as well as the context and culture in which it occurs. In some cultures directness can be offensive. In Madagascar Elinor Keenan found that it is in fact women who haggle most loudly and directly in the marketplace, whereas the men silently weigh the vegetables and hand them over to the buyers. If a man and woman are walking along trying to hitch a ride into town, it is the woman who will hail cars passing by. Women are the ones who blurt out directly what they have to say. Directness, however, is rude according to traditional Malagasy speaking culture, and women's ways of speaking are not valued there either. In Malaysian society compliments tend to be rejected rather than accepted, especially by women. The pressure to be modest and avoid self-praise affects both men and women, but is strongest for women. In other cultures to compliment someone on something functions as a indirect request for that item.

Holmes (1994) also looked at the implications of differences in politeness between men and women in two professional settings, education and the workplace. Although her results tend to support the "different cultures" approach popularized by Tannen (1990a), Holmes went beyond Tannen's conclusion that mutual respect and tolerance for differences in conversational style will resolve communicational difficulties. Holmes saw power as the key issue. It is power differences that sanction men's norms and give them the right to ignore the contributions made by others, to interrupt others, and to not apologize. When they want to, men can and do engage in the kind of talk women value, such as when they are trying to begin a romantic relationship with a woman. There is also evidence that married men accommodate more to the female style of talking as long as the conversation is not conflictual (see Fitzpatrick & Mulac, 1995).

Holmes argued that many of women's strategies and norms for politeness have the potential for improving communication in public and formal contexts, where male ways of speaking have tended to prevail. This too is welcome because the opposite approach has been far more common, namely, to teach women to be more like men. Coates too observed how hedging allowed women to negotiate sensitive and controversial topics and thus to encourage open discussion. The reason why some researchers have found hedging to be more typical of female conversation is that it reflects women's choice of more personal topics than men and their greater sensitivity to personal relationships. Hedging may also be grounded in the experience of being subordinate. In order to survive, less powerful groups in society pay more attention to the face needs of the powerful. Coates also suggests that women's friendships can be seen as a model of the way human relationships should be.

WHY LADIES ARE SUPPOSED TO TALK PROPERLY

Another dimension of the alleged politeness and greater indirectness of women's speech is the question of standard versus nonstandard speech. One of the well-established sociolinguistic patterns to emerge from quantitative research on urban social dialects is that women, regardless of other social characteristics such as class, age, and so forth, use more standard forms of language than men. In fact, one sociolinguist has gone so far as to say that this pattern of sex differentiation is so ubiquitous in Western societies today that one could look at women's speech to determine which forms carry prestige in a community, and, conversely, at men's to find out which are stigmatized. Similarly, Trudgill (1983, p. 162) emphasized the same point when he claimed that the association between women and standard speech was "the single most consistent finding to have emerged from social dialect studies over the past twenty years." Certainly, the popular view on the matter is in substantial agreement. Most people believe that women speak better than men and, as I showed in the last chapter, that if they don't talk properly, they aren't real "ladies" to begin with!

Table 6.1 shows a typical example from sociolinguistic research, in this case, the results for multiple negation, such as *I don't have no money*, for male and female speakers in Detroit. Women in each social class use the more standard variants more often than men of the same group. The variable is more sharply stratifying for women than for men, and the biggest gaps occur in the lower middle class and lower working class, where, as I noted in the last chapter, a high number of young women aspiring to the status of lady were to be found in Victorian England. Sociolinguists have noted too that women tend to hypercorrect more than men, especially in the lower middle class. This means that for some variables lower middle class women use even more standard forms than the middle class. Similar results have been found in other places, such as Sweden, Britain, and the Netherlands.

Although many reasons have been put forward to try to explain these results, they have never been satisfactorily accounted for, partly due to a failure to distinguish adequately between sex and gender. Sociolinguists such as Peter Trudgill (1972) claimed that one reason why women's speech in Western industrialized societies was closer to the standard was that women were more status conscious. He proposed a related hypothesis that using nonstandard forms of speech carries connotations of masculinity. One piece of evidence taken to support this is that when asked to say which forms they use themselves, women tend to "overreport" their usage and claim they use more standard forms than they actually do. Men, however, are likely to underreport their use of standard forms, and to claim that they speak more nonstandardly than they really do. From these findings Trudgill suggested that for men, speaking nonstandardly has "covert" prestige, while the "overt prestige" associated with speaking the standard variety is more important to women.

TABLE 6.1
Multiple Negation in Detroit

Social Class	Men	Women
Upper middle class	6.3	0
Lower middle class	32.4	1.4
Upper working class	40.0	35.6
Lower working class	90.1	58.9

Penelope Eckert (1993) thinks it is more accurate to speak of women in the home as being status-bound. Women may be using linguistic means as a way to achieve status that is denied to them through other outlets such as occupation. The marketplace establishes the value of men in economic terms, but the only kind of capital a women could accumulate was symbolic. She could be a "good" housewife, a "good" mother, a "good" wife, and so on, with respect to the community's norms for appropriate behavior.

The fact that women are now entering the workforce in large numbers has not fundamentally altered this distinction in the way men and women are accorded social status. According to one woman U.S. senator, politics is more complicated for women because they have to demonstrate to the public that they are good wives and mothers first. If you're married, then you are neglecting your husband and children. If you're divorced, this proves that you couldn't keep your husband. If you're a widow, you must have killed him. If you're single, you couldn't get a man to begin with.

In attempting to account for the sociolinguistic findings on women's greater use of the standard in many Western societies, there are many questions that need to be asked about women's position in society. If men and women do not really have equal status, then comparisons drawn between the classes do not have equal validity for men and women. It is only within the last few decades since the modern feminist movement that government departments and academic disciplines such as sociology have come to see women's relationship to social classes as a political issue and a technical problem for official statistics. Censuses and other surveys rely on a patriarchal concept of social class, where the family is the basic unit of analysis, the man is regarded as the head of a household, and his occupation determines the family's social class. Women disappear in the analysis because their own achievements are not taken into account and their status is defined by their husbands' jobs.

In a large-scale survey of around 200 married couples from the upper working and lower middle class in the Netherlands, Dédé Brouwer and Roeland van Hout (1992) found that most of the women in the sample were better educated than their husbands. Because level of education correlates well with degree of use of standard language, if there were similar discrepancies in the other surveys I mentioned, then this could easily account for the finding that women are closer to the standard than men. Moreover, more of these Dutch women who worked were in lower status part-time jobs. After Ireland, the Netherlands has the lowest percentage (35%) of women in employment in the European Union, where on average half the women work.

Many sociolinguistic surveys of urban dialects have simply adopted traditional notions of social status uncritically. Based on the 1971 British census, however, it is actually the case that more than half of all couples had discrepant social classes. The concept of the traditional nuclear family of man, woman, and children is also outdated. Studies in both the United Kingdom and the United States have shown that already by the late 1960s the majority of families were not of this type in both countries, even though advertising and textbooks still present this view as typical (see chap. 9). Over the past few years government inquiries have been mounted expressing concern that the breakup of this family structure has serious consequences for society. Is it that the family had suddenly changed radically or were families really never that way to begin with (see Coontz, 1992)?

Another factor seldom considered is the effect of children, with respect to both employment patterns and language use in families. The Dutch study found that when a couple had children, both parents used more standard language. As I show later, one of the reasons why women may adopt a more prestigious variety of language is to increase their children's social and educational prospects.

Most of the early sociolinguistic studies were in fact done by men, and many of the questions asked of both men and women reflected a masculine bias. For example, in his study of New York City speech, William Labov (1966) asked both men and women to read a passage ending with a very unflattering comparison between dogs and a boy's first girlfriend, namely, "I suppose it's the same thing with most of us: your first dog is like your first girl. She's more trouble than she's worth, but you can't seem to forget her." In other parts of the interview he asked men and women about their words for different things. He asked women about childhood games, whereas he asked men, among other things, about terms for girls and even, on occasion, terms for female sex organs. Naturally, researchers have since questioned the nature of the relationship established between male sociolinguists and the women they have interviewed. It is not likely that a discussion of hopscotch would establish the same kind of rapport between a male interviewer and a female interviewee as talk about obscene language would between two men!

In fact, reanalysis of some of these early classic findings has shown that some patterns of social class stratification are actually better accounted for as gender differences. In a study James and Lesley Milroy did in Belfast there was even one group of working-class women who used more nonstandard forms than men. There is also a paradox in a related sociolinguistic finding that although women have less social prestige than men generally, they appear to set the prestige norms by leading the introduction of certain types of linguistic change. This too seems to have been elevated to the status of an axiom. Consider, for instance, Trudgill's (1974, p. 95) statement that we can expect men to be in the vanguard of change from below, whereas changes from above are more likely to be led by women: "Only a reversal of this pattern, or a large increase in the normal type of male/female differentiation can be considered to be significantly unusual in any way."

James and Lesley Milroy and Sue Hartley (1994) found, for example, that glottalization, a long stigmatized feature of urban varieties of British English, is on the increase in middle-class speech in Cardiff. They believed that the greater presence of glottal stops in female speech has led to a reversal of the stigma attached to it. Holmes's (1995) study of New Zealand English revealed that young working-class speakers are leading the introduction of glottalized variants of word final /t/, such as *pat*. They use more of these variants than do middle-class speakers, but young women in both the working and middle classes are ahead of men. Here we have a case where a once vernacular feature has changed its status, first by losing stigma, then gaining prestige as a feature of the new variety. There is little doubt that glottalization originated in working-class London speech. Milroy (1992) suggested that it is the fact that women adopt a variant that gives it prestige, rather than the fact that females favor prestige forms. In other words, women create prestige norms rather than follow them. Thus, they are norm makers, whatever social connotations the forms may originally have had.

The part played by women or men per se in linguistic innovation as well as their relation to the standard seems, however, to depend very much on roles of men and women in the community concerned. This suggests that some of the findings of these studies have misinterpreted gender differences as sex differences. A critical variable is whether women have access to education, or other institutions and contexts, where standard or prestigious forms of speech can be acquired. Edith Raidt (1995), for instance, found that early settler women in colonial South Africa preserved many more conservative forms of Dutch dialects than did men. At the same time, however, typically local forms (subsequently to become part of standard Afrikaans) appeared 70 to 100 years earlier in their letters, including some forms that were highly stigmatized at the time.

In many non-Western cultures women are further away from the prestige norms of society. This is true, for example, in parts of the Middle East and Africa and, as we have seen, in Madagascar, where women's directness is regarded as rude by traditional standards. It was also true historically in Britain, where even high-ranking women did not often have as much education as men and were therefore further away from the norms of the written language. In a study I did of letters written by men and women to Mary Queen of Scots, I found a higher incidence among women of nonstandard features of the kinds that in other texts were associated with persons of low social status (Romaine, 1982). Cicero, however, believed his mother-in-law preserved conservative Roman speech because she did not mix widely and therefore was not exposed to some of the nonstandard forms in male speech.

In a study Tove Bull conducted (1991) in a formerly Sami area of Northern Norway called Furuflaten (about 120 km from the city of Tromsø), women appear innovative in some respects, although conservative in others, like the early Dutch pioneer women in South Africa. This part of Norway was originally Sami speaking until the turn of the last century, even though there were some Finnish immigrants. Most of the bi- and trilinguals were probably males, while women and children were monolingual in Sami.

Today, however, all the village children are monolingual in Norwegian, although the older generations are still bi- or trilingual. Knowledge of Finnish is declining, but most middle-aged people have passive knowledge of Sami. The reasons for the men's greater bilingualism in earlier days was connected with the division of labor. The main sources of income were fishing and farming, and most adult men went away to the fisheries in Lofoten and Finnmark twice a year. Although the mothers had no such contacts outside the home and therefore did not need Norwegian, they tried to bring their children up as Norwegian speakers. All education was in Norwegian, and children who were already Norwegianized when they entered stood to gain more from their schooling.

Nevertheless, at the same time as the women were innovative, they were conservative in other ways. The men had fewer features characteristic of Sami carried over into Norwegian than did women. These features are widely recognized and stigmatized stereotypes of the Norwegian spoken by Sami speakers, yet they occur more in the speech of women than that of men. Thus, although women led in the introduction of the dominant, more prestigious language, Norwegian, they speak a more localized and stigmatized variety of it than men. One reason for this was probably simply time. Sami women went from monolingualism in Sami to monolingualism in Norwegian in a very short period of time without much of a period of transitional bilingualism, whereas for men, the shift was not as rapid or dramatic.

Marjut Aikio (1992) concluded from her study of Sami language shift in Finland that some women initially were hostile to the Finnish language and did not want to learn it. By resisting the encroachment of Finnish into their homes, they sought to protect themselves from the invading culture around them. Traditionally, Sami women had higher status in their own community than did the Finnish women in the surrounding area. Both sexes among the Sami took care of the children, did handicrafts, and took part in reindeer herding chores. Even though Sami women did not travel as much as men, they were still much more mobile than Finnish women, as well as economically more independent. Sami women had their own brands to mark their own reindeer, the power to decide how their reindeer were to be cared for, and the right to divide their own estates at death. Thus, one cannot conclude, as Susan Gal did in her study of peasant women in Austria who were leading the shift from Hungarian to German, that the Sami women shifted to Finnish more rapidly than men to escape from their low status. This explanation is essentially the same one that has been offered to account for the sociolinguistic finding that women use the standard language more often than men as a way of improving their own social status. When women's status is high in their own culture, there is no reason for them to reject their own language.

The Sami women did, however, shift to Finnish, and once they did the shift was relatively rapid. The key factor in this case was concern for their children and pressure to assimilate. The schools sent messages to Sami homes indicating their desire for parents to speak Finnish to the children. Speaking Sami at school was also forbidden.

We might reinterpret the findings of urban sociolinguistics in a different light by assuming that middle-class women are simply being conservative in their adherence to the standard, while lower class women's aspirations toward the standard would be innovative. Age, of course, makes a difference too. In Pat Nichols's (1983) study of the Gullah Creole spoken in parts of the southeastern United States, older women were the heaviest users of Gullah because they worked in domestic and agricultural positions. Older men worked mostly in construction. Younger people of both sexes had more access to white-collar jobs and service positions, which brought them into contact with standard English. Younger women were ahead of the younger men in their adoption of a more standard form of English. Given the findings of the Dutch study I mentioned earlier, it would be interesting to know if there were differences between the speech of younger and older women depending on the presence of children. Older women with no responsibilities for children may also not be concerned with using prestige varieties. Interactions between gender, age, and taking care of children require more detailed study.

Although Trudgill's explanation has been much criticized, as I mentioned earlier, subsequent research has shown that the use of the standard may also function differently for men and women. This has influenced the thinking of scholars such as Eckert (1989), who elaborated what is fundamentally Trudgill's insight when she brought in the notion of how standard speech functions as "social capital" for women. The marketplace establishes the value of men in economic terms, but the only kind of capital a women can accumulate is symbolic. Women use standard speech to gain respect and exert influence on others. Larson's (1982) study of two villages in Norway revealed that although women's speech was on the whole more standard than that of men, women produced more features of standard speech when they were trying to get someone to do something or to persuade someone to believe something. Men rarely used speech in this way.

A more sophisticated understanding of the different functions speech plays for men and women in different contexts has likewise illuminated our understanding of language change, as well as the connections between race, class, and sex in the distribution of linguistic variables. Holmes (1994), for instance, made at least one intriguing suggestion about the overlap between culture and gender with respect to two New Zealand linguistic features, namely, the use of the tag *eh* by Maori speakers and the use of high rising intonation by White women. Because both features have the function of seeking agreement and increased involvement from listeners, the reason for their overlapping distribution may be that Maori culture (like other Pacific island cultures) and also middle-class women place a high value on consensus achieved through talk.

Eckert (1989, p. 245) reminds us however, that "the correlations of sex with linguistic variables are only a reflection of the effects on linguistic behavior of gender—the complex social construction of sex—and it is in this construction that one must seek explanations for such correlations." I believe Elizabeth Gordon is right in suggesting that women are more con- cerned with avoiding the stigma of nonstandard speech than they are with promoting the standard. I have already argued in chapters 4 and 5 that the cultural construction of femininity in the Victorian era equated talking properly with both the upper class as well as with being female.

Gordon (1994) conducted an experiment in which she asked school pupils between the ages of 16 and 19 years and teacher trainees to match up samples of female speech representing three distinct social groups with photographs of models dressed in different ways. A home economics class chose the clothing used in the photographs to be typical of what girls representing three social classes might wear when accompanying their moth- ers on a visit to town. Listeners identified the girl who spoke with a broad New Zealand accent with the photograph showing a girl dressed like a member of the working class. Listeners also had to offer various other social judgments. Most thought the working-class girl's parents had the lowest income and that she was the least intelligent of the girls. They also thought she was the most likely to be "sleeping around." Gordon's experi- ment shows how the clothes and accent associated with working-class females elicited stereotypical judgments about their morality.

As I noted in chapter 4, the connection between "proper" English and "proper" women is not a historical accident. This is why some women have engaged in deliberate action to reclaim language in order to liberate them- selves from men's linguistic standards (see further in chaps. 10 and 11).

Here we have one reason why some men are so resistant to some of the linguistic reforms that have accompanied the struggle from women's liberation. I look at more examples of such rhetoric in chapter 10. I noted in chapters 1 and 4 that the making of standard English was largely a male enterprise. In Britain the idea of a Standard English pronunciation was clearly conceived of as a male norm by both H. C. Wyld and Daniel Jones. In commenting on the characteristics of what he called "Received Standard," Wyld (1934, p. 614) noted that it was heard most consistently at its best among officers of the British Regular Army. "The utterance of these men is at once clear-cut and precise, yet free from affectation; at once downright and manly, yet in the highest degree refined and urbane." Such men had confidence in their speech without reflection on it. Fundamentally hereditary (at least in the male line), it sufficed simply that "their fathers have told them." Departures from this standard were so distasteful to Wyld that 60 years after his departure from the University of Liverpool to take up the Merton Chair of English Language at the University of Oxford (which he held from 1920 to 1945), he was remembered for having reduced women students to tears by his fierce comments on their northern pronunciation. Similarly, Daniel Jones (1917, p. 170), in circumscribing the norms of standard English pronunciation so narrowly that they were synonymous with the speech of the best educated southern English families, reminded his readers that these were families "whose men-folk have been educated at the great public boarding schools."

Again, we have another example of how women can't win games played by male rules. To alter language is to undermine male control of it. When women are believed to be innovative in other respects, they are also criticized for it. If they refine their speech too much, women get blamed for weakening the language.

Jespersen, for instance, claimed women had a debilitating effect on language. He believed there was a danger of language becoming languid and insipid if women's ways of speaking prevailed. If women try to reform sexist usage, they are being politically correct. Jespersen claimed (1922, p. 214) that women were responsible for the loss of tongue-trilled /r/ in English and other languages. Women were to blame because tongue-trilled /r/ is "natural and justified when life is chiefly carried on out-of-doors, but indoor life prefers, on the whole, less noisy speech habits, and the more refined this domestic life is, the more all kinds of noises and even speech sounds will be toned down." French women were blamed for the loss of /r/ in the word for chair because it was a domestic object, which belonged more naturally to the speech of women. Thus, whether she stays at home and keeps quiet or goes out into the workaday world, "Mrs. Interior" runs the risk of being blamed for the degeneration of language.

In a similar fashion, some have blamed female speakers of minority languages such as Scottish Gaelic, Welsh, Sami, and Breton (to name only a few) for "killing" these languages by not speaking them to their children.

Yet as I showed in chapter 3, one reason why such languages were not transmitted to children is that they became symbolic of a despised female identity and thus were tainted with the stigma of conquest by more powerful peoples and their languages. Languages such as Norwegian, German, and French, by contrast, became symbols of modernity, urbanity, finery, and higher social status. Those aspiring to be ladies had to escape both literally and figuratively from their status as rural peasants by leaving the land and their language behind (see Romaine, forthcoming). Maryon McDonald (1994, p. 91), for example, related how some rural Breton-speaking women asked the parish priest not to deliver his sermons in Breton. His response was, "It is almost as if Breton smells of cow-shit to them. They think they are ladies." Indeed, McDonald (1994, p. 103) observed how one woman spoke French to her two teenage daughters, Breton to the cows, hens, and sows, but French to the animals' young offspring.

At the same time, however, a number of young women involved in the Breton militant movement have gone back to the countryside in search of Breton grassroots authenticity, and have learned Breton as an act of liberation from French oppression. Although the militants reject French finery in their aspirations to the rugged naturalness associated with the land, the peasant women, now their neighbors, look to femininity, the towns, and French. Thus, the same language is a symbol of both oppression and liberation, depending on the beliefs of those who use it. As far as the peasant women are concerned, there is a paradox in the fact that "First they [i.e., the French SR] wanted us to speak French, now they want us to speak Breton" (McDonald, 1994, p. 102). In chapter 10 I show that some of the language forms resulting from feminist activism have also taken on different meanings in the context of opposing value systems.

Although most grammarians disapproved of whatever they branded as "slang," some even accused women of not contributing to it! Flexner and Wentworth (1975, p. xii), for instance, claimed that American slang was created and used by men to such an extent that the majority of entries in their dictionary could have been labeled "primarily masculine use." Although they named a few female subgroups who provided input to slang, among them airline stewardesses, beauty parlor operators, chorus girls, nurses, waitresses, and prostitutes, I noted in chapter 4 some of the constraints on observing slang, taboo, and nonstandard language use among women, including studies that do not support these stereotypes. Another authority on the language of the underworld, however, believed that prostitutes were not capable of the same kinds of innovative thought and lacked the technical vocabulary found among the predominantly male criminal element, thieves, pickpockets, and so on. He attributed the absence of prostitute slang to a combination of low intelligence and adverse working conditions. "Her vocabulary for discussing technique is no more adequate than that of the average semiliterate farm wife" (Maurer, 1981, pp. 114–115).

Dennis Baron (1986, p. 88) pointed out that women are accused of lexical conservatism and the inability to produce new vocabulary, yet at the same time their speech is criticized for containing an innovative use of words that "real" men would never use. Women are encouraged to develop a passion for correctness that would supposedly represent a rejection of their own natural feminine dialect, but in adopting the male version of standard English they are asked to learn an alien tongue. This leads to a situation of self-hatred felt by any subordinate group when forced to adopt the norms of a dominant group. The obliteration of one group's language by another more powerful group is one way in which the latter exerts its hegemony.

Judith Irvine (1990) reported that among the Wolof of Senegal, kings and high-ranking nobles were expected to make mistakes in minor points of grammar because correctness would be seen as an unnecessary concern with frills or performance for the sake of performance.

NO LAUGHING MATTER

Question: How many feminists does it take to change a light bulb?
Answer: That's not funny.

The genre of light-bulb jokes that spawned this example is well known. The butt of the joke is perhaps more often an ethnic group, a nationality, or an occupational group the joker wants to poke fun at. Interestingly, there is no real male counterpart to the genre of jokes based on familiar stereotypes such as the mother-in-law or woman driver. Again it is the behavior of those marked as others who are subjected to ridicule.

The reply to this joke about feminists, however, points to a stereotype of female humorlessness, well exemplified by the schoolmarm stereotype. Interestingly, this reaction is at odds with the way in which some critics have treated the issue of language reform. As I showed in chapter 4, a common reaction is to dismiss changes proposed by women as humorous (see also chap. 10). Yet making others laugh is also a way of gaining power over them. This may be one reason why women are expected to be the audience for jokes, but less commonly the tellers of jokes (see chap. 9 for discussion of male and female differences in humor).

Within the entertainment field woman have found it difficult to overcome being cast in stereotypical comic roles. Lucille Ball, for instance, made her career by playing the zany housewife. One popular response to the more recent Supermom or Superwoman image of the working woman/mother/

housewife has been to make fun of her. One joke book advises that "the first step in a good relationship with your children is memorizing their names." One mug shows a woman with briefcase in one hand and a broom or wailing child in the other. The caption reads, "I'm a working mother. I'm nuts." The phrase "I'm nuts" is ambiguous. It could be suggesting that she's crazy to try to juggle both child and career, or that she's being driven crazy by the demands of both. Either way she is being made fun of, as are her choices and lifestyle.

Erma Bombeck, author of a number of books and a popular newspaper column, was well known for her attempt to turn the problem that has no name into a farce, but not everyone laughed with her. Betty Friedan for one thought it was no laughing matter. On one occasion Bombeck said to her, "God, lady, you can't make it better tonight. What more do you want from us? . . . First we had to laugh, the crying had to come later." Note the irritation in Bombeck's use of *lady* (cited in Hill, 1986, p. 22).

Deborah Tannen (1993a) remarked on how she has seen herself transformed into characters in films, plays, and so on. In all of these she said she was stripped of her sense of humor. On one occasion a joke she told a newspaper reporter in an interview was transformed into a scene in a play. The funny story Tannen told the reporter came from a conversation she and her husband had at the dinner table in their home one evening. She commented that she was thirsty. He made a move to get up to get her a glass of water, but stopped himself. Looking at her with exaggerated sympathy, he said, "I know what it's like to be thirsty. I was thirsty once." They both laughed because the husband was satirizing one of the points Tannen makes in her best-selling book about the differences between men's and women's conversational styles. When a woman describes a problem, she would like sympathy and empathy as a response, not a solution offered summarily.

In the film version, however, the scene moved from the dining table to the bedroom. A wife wakes up her husband to tell him she's thirsty. He gets out of bed to get her a glass of water. Instead of thanking him, she gives him a lecture about how he should have told her he understands what it's like to be thirsty instead of solving the problem by bringing a glass of water. He throws the water in her face, which gets a good laugh from the audience.

Tannen pointed out that in the film version her real-life story was transformed, from a woman who had seen the point of the joke and had laughed with her husband at the parody he had performed, to a humorless woman who is the butt of the joke. In the film version she is the humorless woman who takes herself too seriously.

On other occasions Tannen has seen herself on stage in her role as a linguist who analyzes conversations. There again she was portrayed as a humorless academic who used long and pompous-sounding words. In another play she was cast into the role of the linguist who irritates her friends by placing a tape recorder on the dinner table and stringing from the ceiling a microphone, which dangles in front of their faces, so she can record their conversations. In the play the linguist has tricked them to coming to a Thanksgiving dinner when she doesn't actually have the turkey in the oven they all are expecting to eat.

On at least two other occasions Tannen found herself fictionalized. One was in a novel where a linguist moves into the home of a couple to diagnose their conversational disorders. The other was in the popular U.S. situation comedy called *Home Improvement*, whose main character is a man who hosts a TV show about fixing things. In reality, however, he is not very handy at all, either in fixing things or in communicating with his wife. The man who lives next door acts as a confidant and dispenses advice about how to patch things up at home with his wife. The neighbor's commentary on the differences between men and women often comes out of one of Tannen's books.

After seeing herself transformed into a male role in both these instances, Tannen suggested that perhaps what is humorous from a male point of view is the very idea of a woman speaking as an authority. An authority needs to be serious to gain respect, a role often associated with men rather than woman. Any woman who tries to speak authoritatively runs the risk of being seen as humorless and taking herself too seriously, as a kind of schoolmarm, a nitpicking Miss Fidditch.

These differences should not be surprising given the basic indeterminacy of language and meaning. This suggests that the efforts to locate the existence of women's language and to define it in terms of specific linguistic features is misguided. It suffers from some of the same problems as the essentialist approach to male and female identity and experience I discussed in chapter 2. As Tannen (1993b) pointed out, the potential ambiguity of linguistic strategies, in particular their ability to signal both solidarity and power, can make mischief of language and gender research at the same time as it causes problems in cross-cultural and cross-gender communication. This is another dimension to the problem noted in chapter 2, namely, that whatever it is that is associated with women will be devalued. The same trait when used by men will be valued.

EXERCISES AND DISCUSSION QUESTIONS

1. Here are two sample dialogues between men and women taken from Suzette Haden Elgin's (1993) book. Discuss how these dialogues illustrate stereotypes of the different styles used by male and female in cross-gender communication.

A. Good morning, darling. Did you sleep well?
B. I guess so. Sure.
A. [long pause] Well?
B. Well, what?

A. Are we going to your mother's for Easter?
B. Do we have a choice?
A. How would *I* know? She's *your mother*!
B. Well, you don't have to get *nasty* about it!

2. Deborah Tannen related a joke about a woman who tells the judge she is suing her husband for divorce because he hasn't spoken to her for 2 years. When the judge asks the husband why, he replies that he didn't want to interrupt her. Discuss the stereotypes that make this joke funny.

3. Consider the following dialogue reported by Janet Holmes (1994, p. 85), which took place between two students talking about Robin Lakoff's claims.

A: But it's true. Women are always using tag questions aren't they?
B: Well, it depends what you mean by "women." Do you mean "all women" or "most women" or "some women"? And what sort of tag questions do you have in mind? Some are quite aggressive aren't they? Others are much gentler. And what about the context? In my opinion people use tags to get people talking so I bet you hear more from good teachers and facilitators than you do in boardrooms!

Make a record of the tag questions that occur in two different situations, such as the classroom, conversation between friends, a TV talk show, or a formal meeting. Analyze the functions of the different tags you find.

4. Marina Warner (1994) observed that Mother Goose began to appear on stage in British pantomime from around 1800, when the part was played by a man dressed as a woman. Since then and up to the present the character has been performed by men in drag. Discuss the significance of the drag role for Mother Goose.

5. Compare the story of Cupid and Psyche (you can find a version in Edith Hamilton's book *Mythology*, 1940) with a fairy-tale version of "Beauty and the Beast." You can also include in your comparison the television version of the tale and Walt Disney's cartoon version. Or compare Hans Christian Andersen's version of the Little Mermaid with the Disney cartoon version. What transformations have taken place and of what significance are they? Pay attention also to the illustrations and images. What messages about gender do they display?

6. Conduct interviews with women who have achieved high-level positions in male-dominated fields such as university teaching, administration,

or business to find out whether gender makes a difference to them in their jobs. What pressures have they experienced? How have their male colleagues reacted to them? Do they try to talk and act like their male colleagues or in ways they think reflect their gender? Do they think there is a glass ceiling?

ANNOTATED BIBLIOGRAPHY AND SUGGESTIONS FOR FURTHER READING

Diane Bornstein's article (1978) contains many example of advice given to women during the Middle Ages. Alexander Rysman's article deals with the history of the word *gossip* (see also Kerstin Nordenstam's 1994 article). Cheris Kramer's article discusses stereotypes of women's speech in cartoons. The anthologies by Thorne, Kramarae, and Henley (1983) and by Thorne and Henley (1974) are good sources for studies of some of Lakoff's features of women's language; see also the articles by Betty Lou Dubois and Isabel Crouch (1975, 1987), Penelope Eckert (1989, 1993), and Janet Holmes (1986, 1995). Chapter 13 of Leanne Hinton's (1994) book contains a brief discussion of male/female differences in Yana. R. M. W. Dixon's book (1972) contains a discussion of "mother-in-law" language in Dyirbal. Deborah Tannen's 1993 and 1994 collections provide critical evaluations of the research on interruptions, amount of talk, and other gender differences (see in particular the contributions by Penelope Eckert, 1993; Deborah James & Sandra Clarke, 1993; Deborah James & Janice Drakich, 1993b, 1993c; and Deborah Tannen, 1994a). See also chapter 7 on interruptions in Deborah Tannen (1990a), Stephen Murray's article (1985), and his article together with Lucille Covelli (1988). The Detroit data in Table 6.1 are taken from the Detroit dialect survey by Walt Wolfram (1974). See Deborah Cameron (1994) for a discussion of "assertiveness" training courses aimed at women. Deborah Tannen and Muriel Saville-Troike's (1985) collection deals with cross-cultural perspectives on silence (see especially the paper by Jaako Lehtonen & Kari Sajavaara, 1985). Discussion of Henry James's article can be found in Dennis Baron's book (1986, pp. 74–76). Penelope Brown and Stephen Levinson (1987) and Janet Holmes (1994) treat politeness. Ann Oakley's (1982) book contains a critique of social stratification theories applied to women. Robin Lakoff's (1990) book deals more specifically with power (see especially chap. 11, "Why Can't a Woman be Less Like a Man?"). O'Barr and Atkins (1980) connect some of the features attributed to women's language to lack of power. Gerry Philipsen's article (1975) discusses the value of silence in male culture, and the collection of papers in Sally Johnson and Ulrike Meinhof's book (1996) examines male ways of speaking. Jennifer Coates (1996) discusses the functions of talk among female friends, and Kerstin Nordenstam (1996) examines gossip in male and female friendships. Senta Troemel-Plöetz (1991), Aki Uchida (1992), and Alice Freed (1993) present critical reviews of Deborah Tannen's "different cultures" approach to male/female communication (see also Deborah Tannen's 1992 reply to Troemel-Plöetz). A good overview of Kerstin Thelander's findings can be found in Toril Swan's (1992) article. Janet Shibamoto's (1985) book discusses some of the features of Japanese women's language. Deborah James's (1996) article is a useful overview of the conflicting findings on women and prestige forms.

CHAPTER

7

Learning How to
Talk Like a Lady

You always try to be the same as everyone else. You don't sort of want to be made fun of . . . sort of posher than everybody else. Then you get sort of picked on. But then if you use a lot of slang and that, people don't think very much of you. (teenage girl in Birmingham, cited by Cullum, 1981, p. 108)

In chapter 5 I showed how girls must tread a fine line in their behavior or they risk being called slags and whores. It is the same with their talk, which serves as an index of their conduct, as can be seen in my epigraph to this chapter taken from Cullum's study of girls' peer groups in England. How do girls learn to talk like ladies? And how do boys learn to talk like men?

Recall from the last chapter Robin Lakoff's (1975) speculation that both boys and girls learn "women's language" first because that is the language children are exposed to at home, where mothers are usually the primary caretakers, at least in most Western societies. Both male and female children develop initial close bonds with their mothers. We might expect this pattern of exposure to predominantly female speech to continue into the early school years because elementary schools generally have more female than male teachers. Researchers have commented on the more feminine aspects of the early school years, with their concentration on female values such as quietness, order, neatness, and so on.

Teachers often pay more attention, both positive and negative, to boys. At school, girls have to balance the competing images of females as passive and docile and of successful learners who are active, independent, and willing to take risks. When their teacher is female, girls are confronted with a contradiction between what the teacher says she values and what she actually does. As Marina Warner (1994, p. 394) pointed out, the paradox in women's education is that the very women who pass on the legacy as they speak and teach transgress against the burden of its lessons, namely, that good girls are silent. Some girls react with hostility, helplessness, or silence. Girls learn to get along, while boys learn to get ahead.

In this chapter I consider three major influences on children's socialization in which language plays a crucial part: family, peer group, and school. Each of these worlds has its own organization and messages about gender. Family and school are two major social institutions whose influence few of us escape. The family usually provides the most important speech model for young children; it is where most of us learn our ideas about gender as well as race and class. As I pointed out in chapter 2, gender identity is a basic concept of maleness or femaleness that children develop early in life. As they mature, children acquire increasing knowledge of their society's gender stereotypes and the expectations associated with male and female roles from interacting with parents, siblings, and peers, as well as through playing with certain types of toys, dressing or being dressed in ways typical of their sex, and through images in children's books, television, and so on.

I also observed in chapter 2 that the family is generally seen as a central site where children construct their sense of self. Many families are still traditional in terms of their division of labor by sex. Chores given to children or performed by parents provide clues about what adults consider appropriate for each sex. At a young age children are already practicing for adult roles of male and female.

Schools too show patterns of gender separation, some of which continue patterns already learned at home, whereas others are introduced in the school setting. Studies show that children who are heavy television viewers tend to give more sex-typed responses when asked about their preferences for toys and appropriate gender roles. Most of the personal things children bring to school already divide along gender lines, for instance. Girls bring makeup, little stuffed animals, and jewelry, but boys bring little toy trucks, plastic dinosaurs, and such. Such findings have led some researchers to argue that boys and girls live in different worlds in which separate cultures are developed and transmitted, each with quite different patterns of verbal interaction. This has been proposed as one explanation for some of the differences in men's and women's ways of speaking discussed in the last chapter.

Although women predominate in both the home and the early school years as the primary caretakers and teachers of children, their presence diminishes in the higher levels of education and practically disappears by the time students are in universities. Only 2% of professors are women in Australia, and only 3% in the United Kingdom. In the United States, women account for only about 10% of tenured faculty at 4-year institutions. Men also outnumber women at all professional teaching and administrative ranks. The higher the position, the more dramatic the gap between the number of men and women. The absence of women from the highest levels of specialized knowledge and prestige professions communicates a clear message that what women do is not important, or that they are not suited to these positions. This is part of what some have called the "hidden curriculum" (or as a similar phenomenon in the workplace is known, the "glass ceiling"), an agenda made explicit in languages like French where le professeur is masculine in gender (see chap. 3). It is also reinforced by the stereotypical gender images in many textbooks. Dick has a lot more adventures than Jane, and he talks more, too, both in books and in the classroom itself.

Yet the influences of school and home are counterbalanced by the effect of peers. As the girl points out in my epigraph to this chapter, "You always try to be the same as everyone else." You do not need to be a sociolinguist to know that children come to speak more like their peers than their parents. Dramatic instances of this can be observed in cases where families have moved from one place to another; the children acquire the language or dialect of their new peers. For example, the British-born children of West Indian immigrants who have settled in London soon sound indistinguishable from their White London peers.

DOING GENDER AT HOME

From the time their children are born, mothers and fathers treat males and females differently. In chapter 2 I considered some of the ways in which we have different expectations of boys and girls. Boys learn that they shouldn't cry. "Real men" keep their emotions to themselves. To express feelings openly in front of others is to risk embarrassment and to be vulnerable, a sign of weakness for men. Girls, on the other hand, are expected not to engage in rough-and-tumble play. They are supposed to be little ladies, to be quiet and nice. A little boy who cries after fighting with a girl is likely to be told "Don't cry," but the girl who cries after the fight is more likely to be told "Don't fight." The Bedouins, for example, believe that girls should be treated with less indulgence than boys so that they will not be willful. Boys should not be disciplined as harshly lest they become fearful and not gain a sense of power.

Many researchers have also shown that boys tend to have a somewhat higher activity level than girls. This may be partly a result of different patterns of interaction mothers and fathers adopt with boys and girls. Jean Berko Gleason's (1987) research in the United States (see also Gleason & Greif,

1983) revealed different parental patterns of verbal interaction with children. Girls may get more physical and verbal attention than boys at home before they begin school. Mothers appear to be more in tune with their children's linguistic development than fathers. This is reflected in the finding that mothers were better able to understand what their children said. One study showed that fathers used rarer and more complex vocabulary with children. For example, when playing with a toy car they used the names of car parts with both boys and girls and asked the children to produce them.

American fathers interrupted their children more than mothers did, and both parents interrupted female children more than male. Fathers also used more direct commands and threats with their children, such as *Don't do that*, or *Don't go in there or I'll break your head*. Many studies have found boys to be more physically aggressive than girls, so it should not be surprising to find adults making more negative commands and threats to boys. Women, however, tended to do this in a more indirect or polite way, such as *I wish you would stop that*, or *Please don't do that*.

I showed in the previous chapter that one of the features often said to be part of women's language is politeness. One study found that 4-year-olds were indeed modeling the behavior of their same-sex parent. Little girls were using more indirect commands just like their mothers, and little boys were using more direct ones like their fathers.

Even 6-year-olds I worked with in Edinburgh were aware of stereotypical differences between girls' and boys' speech. They said that girls spoke more politely and boys roughly, and that boys used more slang and swear words. There is also some explicit coaching by mothers and schoolteachers (and even neighbors!), who tell children what is polite speech. One woman vividly recalled being corrected as a child for using a local dialect word, *ken*, meaning "you know": Her mother slapped her in the face so hard that she lost a tooth as a result. This is perhaps an extreme example of the pressure young children can be put under to conform to adult ways of speaking.

One 10-year-old girl told me in answer to the question of whether her mother ever told her to speak politely:

Girl: If there's somebody polite in. Like see, some people come in. There's new people in the stair we've moved up to and they come in and I'm always saying "doon" [the local way of pronouncing *down*] Shep, cause it's my wee dog, so I say "doon." My mum says, "That's not what you say." She says, "It's sit down." Ken, cause she doesn't like me speaking rough.

SR: Why do you think she doesn't like it?

Girl: Well, if I speak rough, she doesn't like it when other people are in because they think that we're rough tatties in the stair.

SR: Does your Mum ever speak polite?

Girl: She doesnae really speak polite, but she corrects all her words.
SR: How about your teachers, do they ever say anything to you about the way you speak?
Girl: I've never actually said "doon" to the teacher.

It is clear from this passage that this girl knows a lot about the social significance of the options open to her, that is, using the local Scots form of speech, as opposed to speaking in a more standard English. She evaluates these ways of speaking in the same terms that local adults use, namely, speaking local Edinburgh Scots is "rough," whereas more standard speech is "polite." Moreover, she is aware that the way one speaks is an important part of the impression one conveys to others, and that others make judgments about social character on the basis of speech. She has also learned that there are at least two contexts for polite speech, that is, in front of strangers and the teacher in the classroom. She can also identify the local pronunciation "doon" as an inappropriate one for contexts requiring polite speech. This is the form she would most likely use consistently at home among family members, and, as she says, when addressing her dog. When used in the home and with in-group members, speaking this way is the normal unmarked way of talking, but outside this domain it becomes "speaking rough."

Similarly, in Hawaii, where a variety of creole English locally called "pidgin" coexists with Standard English, a male university student told me he had been "grossed out" by hearing female classmates use "pidgin" so openly. Their behavior appeared to him to flout the expectation that women should be polite by speaking more standardly, particularly in public.

Boys are corrected for their linguistic behavior too, however, as was evident from this story told to me by a Scottish boy whose neighbors corrected him for nonstandard grammar:

My next door neighbors [correct me SR], cause see they've got a boy four called Andrew and they don't want him to learn the bad habits and they're always checking me for saying it [*done* instead of *did* SR] cause I usually go there for my dinner in the holidays and they're always correcting me for that sort of thing. When I say—I don't know if it's right or wrong—I say like, if "I done something today," they go, "you *did*," and they do like that all the time.

Although many preschool children have consistent notions of what is "correct" and "incorrect," it is not clear how early they associate "correctness" and "politeness" specifically with female speech. Carole Edelsky (1977) tried to investigate how early children learn gender appropriate speech by showing them pictures together with sentences such as "Damn, the TV's broken." She asked the children whether they thought a man or a woman would be more likely to say such a thing. Adults were also shown the pictures and their responses were compared with those of the children, who were between the ages of 6 and 11 years. However, the results were difficult to interpret because children and adults were being asked to perform different tasks. Although the adults were offering their own intuitions about adult speech, children were being asked to make inferences about adults' speech behavior. The responses given by the younger children appeared to indicate that they linked sex with topic. Thus, they seemed to think that a man was more likely to say "Damn, the TV's broken" because it was Daddy who watches TV or Daddy who fixes the TV, and so on. The oldest children's judgments, however, matched those of adults.

GENDERED PLAY

Researchers have observed gender differences in both talk and behavior in the early years when children play in same-sex peer groups. Boys tend to talk about being buddies and being tough, whereas girls tend to talk about being "best friends" and being nice. Boys tend to have a larger network than girls, who usually have one or two girlfriends with whom they play regularly. To some extent the size of these groups may be determined by the different types of activities they engage in. It takes only three girls to skip rope or two to play house, whereas more boys are needed for team sports such as football. To some degree the kinds of activities chosen may also determine the nature of the verbal interaction in them. Traditional girls' games such as hopscotch and jump rope rely on turn-taking more than some of the team sports played by boys, which depend on rules. As I pointed out in chapter 2, it was not all that long ago that girls were not even given the opportunity to engage in traditional male team sports. More traditional ways of dressing girls in more restrictive clothing than boys ruled out some of the rough-and-tumble play associated with boys.

However, much less attention has been paid to girls' networks than those of boys, leading one researcher to comment that we have a clearer picture of what girls do *not* do than what they do. Before the 1970s research on youth culture tended either to exclude or devalue the experiences of girls. Girls' play was described as "immature" by comparison with that of boys. Betty Harragan, for instance, suggested (1977) that girls' games like playing house are less complex than those of boys and teach "meaningless mumbo-jumbo" rather than rules. Thus, the kinds of play activities girls engage in do not lead to the development of the kind of skills such as performing under competitive stress, which will be potentially useful later in life. Boys' games, on the other hand, have been seen as adaptive to the demands of corporate life, with its emphasis on hierarchy and competition.

Some researchers have claimed that girls use language to create and maintain cohesiveness, and their activities are generally more cooperative and noncompetitive. Differentiation between girls is not made in terms of power. When conflicts arise, the group breaks up. Bossiness tends not to be tolerated, and girls use forms such as *let's*, *we're gonna*, and *we could* to get others to do things instead of appealing to their personal power or issuing direct commands. When they argue, girls tend to phrase their arguments in terms of group needs rather than in personal terms. They also stroke or comb their friends' hair, express interest in each other's clothing and haircuts, and so on. Best friends share secrets with one another. By early adolescence some girls spend their playground time talking rather than playing. Stories may also provide a substitute for fighting. One study showed that inner city junior-high-school girls spent more time telling stories about past or possible fights than they spent fighting.

Boys, on the other hand, tend to have more hierarchically organized groups than girls, and status in the hierarchy is paramount. They also tend to play more outdoors and with higher levels of physical activity, often involving rough-and-tumble play as well as fighting, but rarely any touching that could be termed affectionate. In boys' groups speech is used to assert dominance, to attract and maintain an audience when others have the floor. Boys issue commands to other boys rather than suggest what should be done. Certain kinds of stylized speech events, such as joking and storytelling, are valued in boys' groups, and are turned into competitions. A boy has to learn how to get the floor to perform so that he can acquire prestige. Some of the most extensive sociolinguistic work on the verbal skills of male peer groups has been done in Black communities in the United States, where there are a number of competitive speech events such as "sounding" or "playing the dozens" in which insults (usually about mothers!) are exchanged. Some of these are in the form of rhymed couplets and some are more like taunts or challenges, such as *Your mother wears high-heeled sneakers to church*. The winner in these contests is the boy with the largest store of sounds and the best delivery. High value is placed on obscene language and swearing (see chap. 4).

Some of these differences can be found in the following examples of talk recorded by Marjorie Harness Goodwin (1980) in single-sex peer groups among Black working-class children between the ages of 8 and 13 years. In the first extract the boys are making slingshots from coat hangers, and in the second the girls are making rings from old bottle tops.

Michael: Gimme the pliers
           All right. Give me your hanger Tokay.
Huey: Get off my steps.
           Get away from here Gitty.

Michael: Get out of here Huey.
Huey: I'm not gettin out of nowhere. (Goodwin, 1980, pp. 158–159)

Sharon: Let's go around Subs and Suds.
Pam: We could go around looking for more bottles.
Terry: Maybe we can slice them like that.
Pam: We gotta find some more bottles. (Goodwin, 1980, pp. 165–166)

Studies emphasizing the "separate cultures" view of boys and girls conclude that boys stress hierarchy and competition in their play, whereas girls focus on cooperation and intimacy. Deborah Tannen (1990b), for example, looked at gender differences in videotaped conversations of pairs of same-sex friends at each of four age groups, second graders, sixth graders, tenth graders, and young adults. At every age there were differences in physical alignment of the partners and in the way they introduced topics and talked to one another. The pairs of girls and women looked into each other's faces, had little trouble in finding topics of conversation, and talked at length on a small number of subjects. The boys and men sat at angles to one another, rarely looked one another in the eye, and had difficulty settling on topics. The younger boys produced small amounts of talk on many topics, whereas the older males talked about a few topics at length, but more abstractly and impersonally than the females. Tannen concluded from these interactions that males and females had different ways of showing involvement. Some of the differences may also be due to the fact that girls more often than boys can be found talking to one another. The boys may have felt more uncomfortable in this kind of experimental situation where there was nothing else to do but talk.

As I showed in the previous chapter, women friends often spend time together talking at each other's homes, or while doing "recreational" shopping (i.e., with no intent to buy), whereas male gatherings are more often the result of a focal activity such as watching a game on TV, playing poker, or working on some task such as car repair. Although talk is the central component of many female friendships, it is indeed quite striking to find that most American men in Shere Hite's study (1987) said they had no friends. For girls, talk may be a form of play itself, which carries into adulthood. Coates (1996) speculated that knowledge of the collaborative style of communication that characterized the close female friendship networks she studied may not emerge until adolescence. Girls have to learn not to talk too much as well as not to talk too little, because both extremes violate norms of the cooperative style.

Extensive interaction in single-sex peer groups is probably a crucial source of gender differentiation, but it is all too easy to focus on the differences and lose sight of similarities, and of within-group variation. For one thing, most of the studies have concentrated on popular and dominant children, most of whom are White and middle-class, rather than on children of other social classes and ethnicities. Subsequent work by Marjorie Harness Goodwin (in press) on Latina girls in Los Angeles showed that girls do fight and compete with one another over games of hopscotch. She found that the girls fiercely scrutinized virtually every move within the game for possible evidence of a foul or rule violation. The girls also competed to be first to have a turn, boasted when they did well at the game, teased other players, and argued with one another about the rules.

Studies of African American girls and working-class British teenage girls have shown that both these groups are also skilled in verbal conflict. Some researchers have also found less gender separation among African American children. In many of the studies emphasizing differences, the behavior of boys and girls actually overlapped. Studies reporting differences are also more likely to be published and popularized in the media than those that find none. All these findings point to the importance of examining the different nature of talk used for different purposes in different contexts.

Boys, for example, have been observed to play more cooperatively when playing in dyads rather than in larger groups. Girls who cooperate with one another when engaged in the shared task of making rings out of bottle tops become bossy and hierarchical when playing house, where they tell others what to do. The one playing the role of mother uses commands to direct others what to do and how to play. Whalen (1995) showed that fantasy play requires a great deal of planning on the part of participants as they negotiate who will be who and who does what before the actual play activity can proceed. In overlooking the work of planning, the allocation of roles and tasks to particular characters, researchers have underestimated the complexity of fantasy play in comparison with competitive games.

There is an extensive literature on bonded groups of boys, who are aggressive and often resistant to the school culture, probably because their dominance overshadows the activities of others around them. One such study is that of Paul Willis (1977) with a working-class group of boys in a vocational secondary school in England, who called themselves simply "the lads." In an Australian study by R. W. Connell (1989), so-called "cool guys" opposed the school's authority and labeled those who did well in school as "swots" and "wimps." Teenage slang is usually full of terms of abuse for those who do not fit in, such as *nerds, dweebs, jerks, squares,* and *lames.*

Marcyliena Morgan (1993) illustrated how the voices of African American women have been marginalized in the sociolinguistic research on Black English, much of which has focused on the street language of poor urban male adolescents. It is this variety that has been thought of as constituting core Black culture. Those outside, that is, virtually all women, are "lames."

In addition to its exclusion of women, Morgan pointed out that this de-piction of African American speech reinforces racial stereotypes about young unemployed men with nothing to do but talk "bad" language. Many of the speech genres that sociolinguists such as Labov (1972b) have de-scribed as typical of this group include insults directed at mothers and recounting of sexual exploits and misogynistic boasts (see chap. 4).

BEST FRIENDS

There are many competing pressures on children from their peers. Boys, in particular, feel they have to talk "rough" with other boys in order not to be ridiculed. Although girls are under the same pressure to fit in with a group, they have to be careful not to go too far or people will judge them negatively. These conflicting patterns were expressed by the girl I quoted in my epigraph to this chapter.

In a French study done by Claudine Dannequin (1977), girls put pressure on each other to use standard speech, as can be seen in this extract:

Girl 1:   Moi, j'ai un oncle qui s'appelle Gérard.
          'I've got an uncle called Gerard.'
Girl 2:   Ah, bon.
          'Oh really'.
Girl 1:   Ouais.
          Yes (with nonstandard pronunciation)
Girl 3:   On dit pas "ouais." On dit "oui."
          'One doesn't say "ouais." One says "oui" (with standard pronun-ciation)'
Girl 1:   Moi, j'sais dire les deux.
          'But I know how to say both.'
Girl 3:   Ici, on dit "oui."
          'Here we say "oui".'

Similarly, Jenny Cheshire (1982) found in her study of teenagers in Reading that both boys and girls had specific in-group markers of identity, but in this case, they consisted of features of nonstandard English. The boys used *ain't* much more so than the girls, although both groups swore. The girls took part in similar kinds of delinquent activities as the boys, such as setting fire to the playground, and stealing from shops and from their mothers' purses. Both boys and girls hated school and anyone who spoke with a "posh" accent.

These sorts of peer groups exert powerful pressure on their members to conform to norms that are at odds with those approved by the family and school. The groups' influence can even extend to levels of acceptable aca-demic achievement and reading ability. In one school in Edinburgh where

I interviewed some children, a group of boys operated a system of fines that they levied against those who were seen to cooperate too much with the teachers. What made a boy successful in school was irrelevant to prestige in the peer group. Some boys were less well integrated into the group's activities than others and were "lames" because they did not know the rules for these events. It was these boys who used more standard forms of speech. Those who were most integrated rejected the ethic of the school and spoke more nonstandardly.

In her study of high-school students in a suburb of Detroit, Penelope Eckert (1988) found that two groups of students, calling themselves Jocks and Burnouts, reacted in quite different ways to peer-group pressures. The Jocks were mainly middle-class youths who oriented themselves primarily to the school and its culture, whereas the Burnouts were working class and rebelled against the school and its values. Their different orientations and projections of self were reflected in their language choices. The Burnouts went to the city to attend parties and to "hang out." Their contact with peers from Detroit brought them into closer touch with its urban speech-ways, which they adopted as symbolic of their knowledge and endorsement of the urban environment. The Burnouts were ahead of the Jocks in certain sounds changes taking place in the adult urban population.

These examples show that socialization is not simply a passive process. Children often resist, although they do it in different ways according to gender, ethnicity, and social class. In a low-income school observed by Peggy Orenstein (1994) one African American girl told her, "You got to have something that blends in: the way you talk, the way you dress, if you have something to talk about, something like that. If you talk white, you a schoolgirl, you a nerd" (1994, p. 157). This girl sanctioned another African American girl, an honor-roll student, for acting White and not speaking according to Black norms. One day when the girl greeted her with "Hi, LaRhonda," she corrected her by saying, "It's L! You call me L and it's 'Yo, wahddup!' Not 'Hi' " (1994, p. 156).

Interestingly, the American Association of University Women (1991) report on how girls gets shortchanged in U.S. educational systems concluded that African American girls had higher self-esteem than did White girls. They were more satisfied with their appearance and felt more entitled to speak out. They spoke out more and demanded more attention from teachers in the schools Orenstein visited than did White or Latina girls. Although their self-confidence decreased as they entered adolescence, their decline was only 7%, compared to a 33% plunge for White girls, and 38% for Latina girls. Yet Black girls overall still do less well in school than Whites. One reason can be found in the fact that even though African American girls challenged the teachers and sought attention, they were more likely to be refused than White children. Another explanation for their relative lack of success, however, may come less from a loss of self-esteem and more from an active rejection of school values that they label "acting White." In order to be successful in a White male dominated world and still have self-esteem in their peer group, these girls have to assimilate just enough to satisfy the demands of the school system, but not enough to subject themselves to ridicule.

hooks (1995) claimed that this spirit of resistance to White racism has been a fundamental component of Black identity in the United States. Moreover, she noted that most Black females were not socialized into being women in the traditional sense of being subordinate and weak. Since the days of slavery, African American women have had to develop strategies of survival against oppression by Whites as well as by Black men, and we may be seeing something of this in the girls' behavior.

In her autobiography, Audre Lorde (1982) related that her mother told her not to run for class president. When Lorde ran anyway and lost to a White classmate, she came home crying, unable to understand how this could have happened when the teachers had said the election would be won on the basis of merit, effort, and grades, and she was the smartest student in sixth grade. She was even more astonished when her mother gave her a whipping and told her she had no business trying to compete with the other students in such foolishness.

According to Orenstein's study, however, the Latina girls suffer most from silence and marginalization. They less often have the self-esteem of African American girls or the academic opportunities of White girls. Teachers are less likely to call on them in class than any other group of children. These students too may resist teachers' efforts, as revealed in Brenda Weikel and Suzanne Yerian's (1995) discussion of "Tough Anna," a Mexican American girl who was an excellent student but also had a reputation for being one of the high school's toughest female gang members. Anna did not want the other students to know that she was receiving good grades, so she made a big show of flunking. When her history teacher handed back an A paper, Anna ripped it up and said loudly "Damn, another F!" In order to keep up her tough image, Anna felt she had to conceal her academic talents, so she never spoke in class either.

As classrooms become increasingly diverse, there is a need for greater understanding of how culture and class in combination with gender influence school achievement in complex ways. Most teachers are still White, middle-class females with little exposure to the different value systems and backgrounds of their students. They may also exercise authority in ways that are unfamiliar to minority children. Indirect and polite appeals, such as *Would you like me to send you to the principal's office?*, may be less effective with a child who is used to more direct disciplining strategies at home, like *Don't do that or I'll . . . .*

GENDERED CLASSROOMS

Schools have their own distinctive patterns of organization, which can be quite different from those found in peer groups outside the school. In a working-class area of London with a mix of White children and Black children from the Caribbean, Helena Wulff (1988) found that girls and boys interacted on a neighborhood street corner in a group mixed by both age and ethnicity. In school, however, the same children divided into groups separated primarily by gender, and to a lesser extent by race or ethnicity. At home and in the neighborhood, interaction is more individual, whereas in school, children are generally organized in much larger groups based primarily on age, supervised by one or only a small number of adults. Although children have no choice over who their classmates are because this is determined largely by age, they do usually get to choose whom to eat lunch with and whom to play with. Nearly all studies of children in school from kindergarten to high school show a pattern of self-chosen gender segregation, with many finding an increase in gender separation peaking in early adolescence.

Researchers have observed in a number of cultures as diverse as the Philippines, Japan, India, Kenya, Mexico, and the United States that children are more likely to separate by gender where they are grouped in the same age category. The fact that school provides a context for socializing with agemates increases the significance of the same-sex peer group. In countries such as Britain there are also strong traditions of same-sex schooling. Because most studies have taken place in the school setting rather than at home and in neighborhoods, the tendency for gender separation has probably been exaggerated. When researchers have looked at children outside school, they have found more evidence of gender mixing. In such circumstances, children are also more likely to play in mixed age groups too, no doubt due to the fewer choices of exact agemates in a particular neighborhood. Some children observed by Barrie Thorne (1994) commented that they had friends of the opposite gender outside school, but they either ignored them or were ignored by them at school in order to avoid being teased. In the neighborhood setting more girls were likely to play games such as football, which they rarely played at school.

The more crowded atmosphere of the school makes keeping down noise and maintaining order a constant preoccupation of teachers. Children have to line up to go from the classroom to the cafeteria, or to use the toilets, or to get drinks of water. It is often a punishable offense to talk while waiting in these lines, and the lines are usually divided by sex. The separate-sex lines for toilets of course have a basis in the fact that there are generally separate facilities for males and females. This too marks school as part of a different domain for children, because in the home both sexes use the same facilities.

One teacher commented to Thorne that even on the first day of school she had come outside to find boys and girls already standing in separate lines to come into the classroom. Some children had been doing this before in kindergarten, either by choice or teacher's instructions. Nevertheless, even when teachers told children simply to line up, more often than not, the children themselves formed two lines, one a boys' line and the other a girls' line. In one class Thorne observed, where the teacher allowed children to sit where they wanted, boys and girls chose to sit on opposite sides. This led teachers and students to talk of the girls' side of the room and the boys' side, and on occasion for the teacher to reinforce this division by organizing competitions according to gender with boys "against" the girls in spelling or math. One teacher put up on the blackboard the headings "Gossipy girls" and "Beastly boys" as the names of the two teams, setting up a confrontational situation in which the sexes were negatively stereotyped and pitted against each other. Sometimes this division was reinforced in other ways, such as when a teacher assigned a particular class its own portion of the cafeteria or playground or specific times for using these common areas.

These practices were the subject of discussion for teachers at one school Thorne observed. After the passage in 1972 of Title IX of the Education Amendments in the United States, mandating equal access to all school activities without regard for gender in programs receiving federal funding, one kindergarten teacher told another she ought to stop grouping her children according to gender and should not make the boys' name tags blue and the girls' pink because it was sexist.

In the classroom children have to learn to raise their hands before speaking and to speak one at a time. Teachers often put children into smaller groups for reading or other activities, sometimes based on performance or ability, but sometimes also according to gender. Barrie Thorne (1994), who observed a school in California and another in Michigan, found that in both schools the public address systems always addressed the students with "boys and girls." Unlike the male generic for adults, the age-marked terms are used only specifically. In some varieties of English, however, *guys*, especially *you guys*, can be generic and refer to either mixed groups or single-sex groups of males or females. Often when teachers singled out students who were disruptive or not doing what they were supposed to be doing, they said things such as "You boys be quiet" or "Ladies, this isn't a tea party."

The tendency for children to separate more by gender in the same age group may be to avoid teasing, because children of the same age are more likely to be seen as potential girlfriends and boyfriends. Here we have the beginning of a pattern that carries through to adult cross-sex friendships, where there is often an undercurrent making such friendships potentially fraught with sexual tension. It is difficult to be "just friends." When boys and girls did mix, they ran the risk of being teased for liking or acting like a member of the opposite sex. This contributes to the desire to increase distance. Girls sometimes threatened to smear boys with lipstick kisses. Boys, in particular, acted at times as if they would be contaminated if they touched the girls or allowed themselves to be touched. In the schools Thorne visited either boys or girls could be defined as having "cooties" or "girlstain," but girls were more often talked about as giving their cooties to the boys. There were also "Cootie Queens," but no "Cootie Kings." The persons believed to carry cooties generally had some other stigmatizing feature, such as being overweight. This is highly reminiscent of non-Western cultures that have pollution rituals associated with women, who are seen as a source of contamination. In many traditional societies of the island Pacific men eat and live separately from women to avoid being polluted by them. These beliefs are quite often tied to women's reproductive abilities, as they are among the Bedouin Arabs I discussed in chapter 2. Pollution rituals, whether in playground teasing or in the broader context of an entire culture, express larger patterns of inequality, and fear of female sexuality, as I show in the next chapter. According to some psychological theories I looked at in chapter 2, boys try to dissociate themselves from women and to devalue behaviors and activities linked with women as a way of separating from their mothers. The development of boys is thus marked by discontinuity with what is feminine.

Girls too may have their own reasons for preferring to play by themselves in order to avoid being dominated. Researchers have noted a tendency for boys to be disruptive to girls' activities and for boys to dominate in mixed-gender play. Thus, boys and girls may separate from the other in order to avoid something.

On the playground, where teachers exert much less control than in the classroom, researchers have reported even more extensive separation by gender than in the classroom. Activities, space, and equipment divide up by gender, leading one observer to speak of the "geography of gender" on the playground. The boys and girls tend to play largely in single- rather than mixed-gender groups, with certain activities such as hopscotch and jumping rope being mainly for girls, and others, such as football, for boys. There were, however, some games that both played together, such as tag, chasing, kickball, and dodgeball. Interestingly, Thorne and others observed children who crossed the traditional gender lines and played, or tried to gain access to, games usually played only by the opposite sex, such as a boy jumping rope with the girls. However, this was generally more often the case for younger children. By adolescence it was much more difficult and less likely for a boy to join in a girls' game.

The boys also tended to have a larger area of the playground for their games. In one case, as much as 10 times more space was available for boys.

Playgrounds are in another sense largely a male space, because boys tend to invade the girls' space periodically to disrupt their games far more than girls try to break up male games (see chap. 9 for further discussion of how the use of space reflects dominance). In some cases this tendency leads teachers supervising the playground to increase the separation between boys and girls as a way of maintaining order. However, such strategies are likely to lead to more hostility and emphasize the dichotomous nature of gender.

Boys and girls chase in both mixed- and single-sex groups. Games such as girls chasing boys or boys chasing girls are gender plays that contain messages about sexuality and aggression. Generally when boys chase one another, however, the game ends in wrestling or a fight, whereas the girls are less physically aggressive with one another. There are cases, though, where girls fight boys. I observed some in Edinburgh schools. Younger children and girls of all ages are more likely to be called "tattletales" for complaining to adults about the behavior of other children. Girls may also have to resort to tattling more because they have less power and control over boys' activities. Appealing to an adult who has more power is a way of resolving conflicts.

THE HIDDEN CURRICULUM: HOW BOYS GET AHEAD, WHILE GIRLS LEARN TO GET ALONG

The transition into puberty brings changes for both sexes, but research tends to emphasize the female disadvantage. Girls between the ages of 12 and 14 years are more likely to be depressed than boys, more likely to have lower self-esteem, more likely to have more negative images of their bodies, and more likely to show declining academic performance in math and science. Boys also tend to be better with computers. The attention of many girls shifts away from academic achievement to their physical appearance and to romantic relationships with boys.

Because sex education usually focuses first on the bodily changes leading to the maturation of girls' reproductive systems, in particular the menstrual cycle, it reinforces the definition of females in terms of sexuality. Girls also tend to develop 2 years earlier than boys. Their height peaks at age 12 years, whereas boys' height peaks at 14 years. This means that in one class grouped by age, there can be an enormous span of variation ranging from those who haven't yet gone through puberty to those who are sexually mature. In the classrooms observed by Peggy Orenstein the obvious signs of physical development tended to be more often the subject of teasing for girls than for boys. Girls who were big breasted were called "cows," and those who wore bras had their bra straps snapped. Boys "barraged" girls with sexually explicit insults. Orenstein saw boys grab girls' thighs, rears, and breasts. This happened more often to African American than to other girls.

Such cases of verbal and physical "teasing" are increasingly the subject of complaints to the Office of Civil Rights in the Department of Education and have resulted in lawsuits (see further in the next chapter on sexual harassment). The Title IX legislation I referred to earlier is now being interpreted to protect students from a "sexually hostile environment" that may impair their ability to learn. To call attention to a girl's body size by calling her "fatty" may be just as, if not more, upsetting as calling her a "slut."

Studies have shown that dissatisfaction with their body image is part of the loss of self-esteem many adolescent girls experience. Although boys tend to become more satisfied with their bodies during the course of their sexual development, girls become less so. In males the observable signs of physical development are less tied to sexuality—for example, having a deep voice, being muscular and tall, or growing facial hair—and are regarded more positively. A boy is more likely to be teased for being a late developer. Tall girls, on the other hand, or girls with too much body fat for their height are likely to be ridiculed, as are flat-chested girls (see chap. 9 for discussion of advertising's influences on women's images of their bodies).

Silence may reflect girls' loss of self-confidence. Many researchers have noted that from the very outset of schooling through to university level male students talk more than females. Studies of women graduate students have claimed that women tended to speak in class more to support other students' statements or to offer their personal experience to the discussion. When asked about which students speak more, teachers often do not realize there is a bias in favor of males, both in terms of who they speak to the most and who speaks more often. Even when subsequent analysis of videotaped classroom interaction patterns revealed that a teacher asked three times as many questions of males and gave four times as much praise to males, most people had rated the teacher as fair. In other classrooms researchers found that teachers gravitated toward areas of the classroom where boys sat and concentrated their activities there. The girls who receive less attention from their predominantly female teachers in the early school years become the women who receive less attention from mainly male college professors.

Studies show how gender bias in schooling results in lower levels of achievement and self-esteem for girls. Although they achieve at higher levels than boys in the early years, girls leave school at a lower level. Boys outperform girls on the Scholastic Aptitude Test and the American College Test. At the graduate level, men outperform women on the Medical College Admissions Test (MCAT), the Graduate Record Exam (GRE), and the Graduate Management Admissions Test (GMAT). Women still receive less than men in grants and loans, too, and are more likely to drop out for financial reasons.

In an eighth-grade U.S. classroom observed by Peggy Orenstein the teacher asked the students to imagine what their lives would be like if they had been born as members of the opposite sex. The boys made statements about things they'd "have to" do, like "help my Mom cook," "spend lots of time in the bathroom on my hair and stuff," and so on, while the girls thought of the opportunities that would be available to them, such as "I could stay out later," "I'd get to play a lot more sports," and so forth. Both girls and boys appeared to equate being female with constraints and being male with opportunity. In chapter 9 I discuss research that shows that sex stereotyping in television advertising is a major source of influence on children's perceptions of sex roles. When Orenstein asked girls what they thought was lucky about being a girl, she got pauses, silence, and answers such as "nothing really. All kinds of bad things happen to girls, like getting your period. Or getting pregnant." Regardless of race or class, girls saw boys as freer, with fewer concerns and more power.

These constraints continue throughout adult life, as is evident in the advice on how to succeed in business given by one female executive, who said, "Don't be attractive. Don't be too smart. Don't be assertive. Pretend you're not a woman. Don't be single. Don't be a mom. Don't be a divorcée" (Carlson, 1996). To be female is to be defined in terms of what you cannot and should not do in order to fit into the male world.

Eckert (1989, p. 256) pointed out that girls experience greater pressure than boys to be "popular" but have fewer outlets for achieving this status. High-school social activities often cast girls in supporting rather than in primary roles, for example, as cheerleaders rather than athletes. There are no school accomplishments for girls that have the same status as athletics does for boys. A boy who is a star athlete can enjoy considerable status, regardless of his character or appearance, but there is virtually nothing a girl can do but be the right sort of person, that is, dress, act, and speak nicely, in accordance with expectations about how girls are supposed to behave. Because the status of Jock girls depends almost entirely on their social networks, they are concerned with presenting themselves as nice. Burnout girls, however, reject this as a phony putting on of airs, just as Burnout boys avoid school athletics as a way of gaining recognition. The imperative to be nice is so strongly ingrained in female socialization that Margaret Atwood argued both in her novels and in interviews that women will only be liberated when they assert the right *not* to be nice! Her novel *Cat's Eye* (1989) attracted criticism for its portrayal of the emotional cruelty within girls' friendships. However, as indicated in the research I discussed in the last chapter on female friendships, talk among women friends may provide a crucial outlet for not being nice without facing male sanction.

Parents and teachers generally place more restrictions on adolescent girls to try to protect them. Rebellious girls may become sexually active as a way of resisting adult pressure, but this only serves to subordinate them to men because girls face the risk of pregnancy. Here we see double standards at work. The parents of a quiet son who does not go out much or have dates with girls may be more worried than they would be about a son who behaves in a sexually aggressive fashion, because this is more in line with "normal" views of masculinity. As feminists have pointed out, however, at both ends of the spectrum of masculinity, from the sissy to the aggressive, dominant male, lies a devaluing of women. There is no real equivalent of this for women. Girls may have more leeway to begin with to cross the gender divide, but by the time they are adolescents their options are tightly constrained. Girls come to define themselves in terms of their positions in the heterosexual marketplace. Girls compete with other girls for boyfriends as in the plots of fairy tales such as Snow White and Cinderella, where ugly old women and beautiful young women are played off against one another for the attention of the prince. Fairy tales connect youth and beauty with good girls and ugliness and old age with bad girls.

Magazines such as *Seventeen*, with their emphasis on fashion, educate girls into consumerism and teach them to orient their appearance and sexuality to men. Their message, like those of similar magazines aimed at women, implies that female identity lies in their bodies and popularity with men (see further in chap. 9 on the role of advertising in the construction of standards for female beauty). Girls who refuse to talk and act like ladies are made fun of. Yet when they behave according to male norms of femininity, they are dismissed as trivial and frivolous. According to Robin Lakoff, the choices a girl has are to be less than a woman or less than a person. These different beliefs about girls, how they should be brought up and how they should behave, correspond to their future positions in the gender hierarchy. As I have noted in previous chapters, these beliefs have been enshrined in the stereotypical representations of women in fairy tales, myths, pop music, and so on, and have been given religious legitimacy in the New Testament with its injunction, "Let the woman learn in silence with all subjection" (I Tim. 2:11).

In the Victorian era most girls were educated at home. Those who went to day or boarding schools learned reading, writing, arts, and languages, things that would prepare them for careers as governesses or wives. Their brothers were sent to boarding schools where they received an elite classics-based curriculum. Some women who look back on this experience recall how their education consisted mainly of hard domestic labor, whereas their brothers when home from boarding school were free to play or read books. Cross-cultural studies in places as diverse as the Philippines, Japan, India, Kenya, Mexico, and the United States have shown that even today girls do more unpaid household work than boys, with some suggesting that girls work while boys play, a phenomenon sometimes called the "leisure gap."

For a long time, girls have learned to become second-class citizens, to be more accommodating, to be silent, and not to take risks. Boys, on the other hand, learn to prove they are men by exhibiting antisocial behavior and lack of consideration for others. Television comedies such as "Men Behaving Badly" reinforce this traditional condoning of male insensitivity to women. In 1993 there was widespread publicity about a group of male high-school students calling themselves the Spur Posse and coercing female classmates into sexual activity. An article in *People Weekly* (April 12, 1993, pp. 35–36) appeared to endorse the "boys will be boys" view of male sexuality I discussed in chapter 2, when it referred to the boys' sexual activities as "exploits." The author reported that "Parents . . . as well as [students] . . . take the position that boys will be boys, arguing that the youths have been persecuted for doing only what comes naturally." One parent added that "nothing my boy did was anything that any red-blooded American boy wouldn't do at his age." As in the rape cases I discuss in the next chapter, sexual coercion is either referred to euphemistically (e.g., "doing what comes naturally") or made invisible by shifting the blame to the victims, who are said to have "asked for it" rather than to have been coerced into unwanted sexual activity.

As far as their sexuality is concerned, girls learn to be silent because there is no acceptable outlet for their sexual desire, or indeed even an adequate vocabulary for talking about it in a positive way (see chap. 4). Boys learn that they can interpret female passivity and silence as consent to sexual activity if they exert enough pressure. Girls meanwhile have to be silent or risk ruining their reputations. I show in the next chapter that these definitions of appropriate heterosexual activity sanction male sexual aggression against women as "natural" expressions of an uncontrollable male sex drive.

According to the conventional stereotypes, girls are supposed not to have the same sexual needs as boys, nor are they supposed to initiate sex, whereas male sexuality is portrayed as an unavoidable biological urge. The female role becomes one of gatekeeper. Girls become responsible for setting limits on the extent of sexual intimacy by resisting male advances. Traditional expectations about males being the active ones who initiate sex leave to a woman only the power of veto, which she is expected to use, but not be believed when she does, particularly if her behavior and clothing communicate otherwise. It is in this context that nonverbal behavior comes powerfully into play both to express and be interpreted as sexual desire that is not acceptable to express in words. Although fashion magazines and ads tell girls to be glamorous, girls learn that dressing attractively can also be grounds for provocation of male sexual desire. Elizabeth Gordon (1994,

p. 244) provided an example from a reply given by Dr. Miriam Stoppard, an advice columnist, to a reader who wrote about the "provocative" clothing worn by girls between 9 and 12 years of age. Stoppard replied:

Women of all ages have to beware of the effect they cause when they wear provocative clothes. "Pretty" in the 1990s can mean "provocative." And "provocative" can mean "dangerous." Every woman has the right to make herself look attractive without endangering her safety, but it's a right she has to be careful about exercising, even if it means her freedom to dress how she likes is curtailed.

Here Stoppard was really endorsing a chain of reasoning linking attractive clothing with risk and danger. Her recognition of a woman's "right" to wear what she wants was thus undermined by her logic because she ultimately accepted that a woman is not really free to exercise her right after all. Men will judge her by her clothing; if they find it/her attractive, she is in danger because she has provoked their attention (see the next chapter for a rape case involving a victim deemed to have worn provocative clothing). Terms used to describe attractive women, such as *striking* or *knockout*, suggest that female sexuality is a physical force impelling men to sexual activity. As I showed in chapter 5, everything about a woman's choice of clothing carries additional meanings. There is no such thing as an unmarked woman.

Advice columnist Ann Landers also endorsed this view of women as gatekeepers of male sexuality in her reply to a reader about how women "lead men on" with both their clothing and language (cited in Reinholtz, Muehlenhard, Phelps, & Satterfield, 1995, p. 153):

Women should be aware of the ways they invite trouble. Here are just a few: Telling raw jokes and street language. Bouncing around (no bra) in low-cut sweaters and see-through blouses. Wearing skirts slit to the city limits up the sides, back or front. Most males will be as sexually aggressive as their partners allow them to be. . . . It's the female who calls the signals and decides whether she wants to hold that line.

Yet, as I show in chapter 9, images in advertising and TV display girls and women in precisely this sort of provocative clothing, thus reinforcing opposing views on male and female sexuality as they teach boy and girls to value females for their sexual appeal. Pop music portrays the male sex drive as inevitable and uncontrollable; once unleashed, it must culminate in intercourse. Songs such as Lou Christie's "Lightnin' Strikes" and Billy Idol's "Cradle of Love" offer metaphors of male sexuality as an unstoppable tide, a lightning bolt, a speeding train, and so on. Rap music tells its listeners that girls and women are sluts and bitches. Popular rap artist Ice-T commented in a television interview that the only way to stop sexism would be to "castrate every boy at birth. We can't help it" (Reinholtz et al., 1995, p. 148).

Popular magazines and advice columns aimed at women and teenage girls routinely feature articles and letters from readers concerned about "giving in" to a boyfriend or partner's requests to have sex before marriage. Statistics are often provided about female virginity, but less often about male virginity. The way in which male sexuality is portrayed makes it natural to assume that men will not be virgins, but it also suggests erroneously that men always want sex and therefore are not ever the victims of sexual coercion.

The assumption is that one thing will lead to another and engaging in any sexual activity can be dangerous because the male won't be able to stop. Because having sex is equated with penetration, consent to other forms of sexual activity such as kissing is regarded as "foreplay" to the act of intercourse itself, a step in a progression to the "real" thing. As I show in the next chapter in my discussion of the metaphors used in talking about rape, images from the domain of combat and war pervade male understandings of sexuality. A related metaphor of sport as war also comes into play, and can be seen in the way having intercourse is referred to as "scoring," and other sexual activities are spoken of as if they were moves in a baseball game, such as getting to first base. In a letter to a female reader who preferred to engage in sexual activities other than intercourse, columnist Ann Landers used this gaming metaphor in her warning that "it is foolish to take such chances. Going to bat with the intention of stopping at third base may prove hazardous to a woman's health" (Reinholtz et al., 1995, p. 154).

Consistent with the gatekeeping role assigned to girls and women, as well as the fact that only women get pregnant, contraception is also seen primarily as a female responsibility. Ads for birth control products such as the one used by Today vaginal sponge suggest to women that "interruptions spoil mood. Prevent the pregnancy, preserve the mood. All you'll turn off is the light." The message to women is that they are responsible for using contraception, as well as using an unobtrusive method that requires no discussion or acknowledgment, but most of all no interruption of foreplay and sex that might turn off their male partners. Synthetic devices like the sponge and diaphragm can be inserted beforehand and are invisible, unlike the male condom. Most of the research on contraception has focused on limiting female rather than male fertility. Until recently, women have not had the option of a contraceptive method that matches the male condom in terms of its easy availability (particularly where teenage girls are concerned) and effectiveness both in preventing pregnancy and transmission of venereal disease and AIDS.

Teens who do not conform to expected gender stereotypes are often the subject of heavy peer ridicule. The terms *tomboy* and *sissy* show many of the asymmetries associated with pairs of gender-differentiated terms like *witch* and *wizard* that I discussed in chapter 4. The words *tomboyism* and *sissy-boy syndrome* were once used as medical terms by clinical psychologists to describe what was regarded as deviant gender identity requiring therapy (see chap. 2 for more examples). It is a much greater insult to call a boy a sissy than to call a girl a tomboy. It is easy to see why. A girl who is a tomboy has appropriated some of the more masculine qualities that are on the whole positive. The word was used as far back as the 16th century to refer to a "wild, romping girl" who behaves like a "spirited or boisterous boy." The character Jo March in Louisa May Alcott's *Little Women* (1871/1946) is a good example from children's literature.

These fictional tomboys, like their real-life counterparts, resist having restrictions imposed on them because they are girls. They dislike dresses and dolls and would rather play outdoors. Like their fictional models, many real-life tomboys became more conformist once they were no longer children and were not free to cross gender boundaries. Quite often it is the mother who tries to bring her daughter more in line with conventional female behavior. The term *tomboy* may be less common now than it was previously. The term *jock* now seems to be used by today's younger generation, at least in the United States, to refer to a girl with some of the qualities of a tomboy. It may have replaced *tomboy* due to a lessening of gender stereotypes.

The term *sissy* (from *sister*) has its origins in a term of address for girls. It shares some common ground with other insults associated with childishness and immaturity, such as *crybaby*, *scaredy-cat*, and other terms linked with sexual deviance, such as *wimp*, *fag*, and *nerd*. And of course, boys are often simply called *girl* in the same derogatory tone with the same effect. It is far less stigmatizing to be called a tomboy than a sissy. There are women who reminisce positively about having been tomboys, but few men feel that way about having been called sissies. A boy who is called a sissy has taken on feminine qualities that have a taint of pollution. Both terms, however, are sexist and perpetuate gender stereotypes, suggesting that maleness and femaleness are rigidly defined and should not be deviated from. Why should a girl be called a tomboy just because she likes to play sports? Why should a boy be called a sissy if he does not like to?

GENDERED TEXTS

I have pointed out already that gender images in children's books also need consideration, and so do children's television programs. Traditional books portray few girls and women engaged in science. Joan Swann (1992) reported that while reading a book to her 4-year-old daughter about a male bear who travels to the moon, she substituted *she* for *he*. But her daughter corrected her: "It's a he, look, he's got a space helmet." Females appear less often in books, talk less, do less, and have more stereotyped roles. Books tend to show males more in active roles. They have more adventures. Livia Polanyi and Diana Strassmann's (1996) content analysis of college-level economics textbooks revealed sex stereotyping in the way they presented the traditional family as an economic unit with male breadwinner (see chap. 6).

Mackay and Konishi (1980, p. 149) looked at personification in children's books and found that the persons, animals, and so on referred to as *he* tended to be strong, brave, wise, clever, and active, while those referred to as *she* tended to be weak, passive, and foolish. As I showed in the last chapter, these patterns reflect a long tradition in children's stories going back to fairy tales in which femininity is equated with silence and forbearance. Marina Warner (1994, p. 395) suggested that perfection in a woman entailed exemplary silence and self-effacement to the point where she simply disappeared from the text altogether. There are, however, new versions of children's traditional fairy tales and nursery rhymes, such as *Father Gander's Nursery Rhymes for the Nineteen Nineties* (Gander, 1989; see chap. 2).

Marlis Hellinger (1980) looked at the English-language books used in German schools. She found that women were not agents in clauses involving personal achievement, creative activity, or professional activity. Men also spoke more than four times as much as women. Children's cartoons are also very much male dominated, and science toys (e.g., chemistry sets) and video games are still marketed almost exclusively to boys, as I show in chapter 9.

Research done even in the late 1980s shows a persistence of these trends. A study of the beginning reading books used in Australia revealed that the words *boy* and *boys* appeared more frequently than the words *girl* and *girls*. The books more frequently described girls as *young, little*, and *pretty*, whereas boys were more likely to be described as *kind, brave*, or *naughty*. Similarly, Gupta and Yin (1990), who looked at the English textbooks used in Singapore schools, found the same trends. There was a male bias in amount of talk, ratio of male to female characters, and in role presentation, which increased as the level of the texts rose. Women and girls appeared primarily in the roles of nurturers and service providers, that is, nurses, mothers, teachers, and waitresses. Books described them in terms of their relations to men. Linguistically speaking, Gupta and Yin noted that possessive forms where a female is the possessor (e.g., *Jill's father*) rather than the one possessed (e.g., *Andy's mother*) are rare.

Television is an early window on the world for children, who begin to watch regularly around the age of 2 years or even earlier. According to

Levinson (1975), even in the mid 1970s more American homes had television than indoor plumbing. By the time children reach the age of 18 years, they will have spent more time in front of a television set than in school or in any other activity except sleeping. Heavy television viewing among children is correlated with a high tendency to express sex-stereotypical career choices. Even among preschoolers there is a high consciousness about sex roles and limitations. Researchers in one study asked children what they would like to be if they were members of the opposite sex. Girls had thought about the question and had answers, although they saw their sex as a limitation on their capabilities. Boys, however, regarded the question with suspicion and mystification. One boy said, "Oh, if I were a girl I'd have to grow up to be nothing" (Courtney & Whipple, 1983, p. 49). These findings are in line with those of Orenstein that I discussed earlier, as well as with those of other researchers who have found boys much more reluctant to take the role of the opposite sex in play activities.

Cartoons as well as commercial advertising to children, which I discuss in chapter 9, reinforce these gender stereotypes. In one study of Saturday morning cartoons, males outnumbered females 3 to 1 (and 4 to 1 where adult characters were concerned). That applied to animal as well as human characters. Males have a greater variety of roles. Jane Jetson, Wilma Flintstone, and Betty Rubble are all housewives, whereas George Jetson works at the Spacely Sprockets factory and Fred Flintstone and Barney Rubble work at the stone quarry. Although the Jetsons are a space-age family and have a robot that organizes all the household chores, it has a female voice. Women in cartoons are housewives, teachers, or secretaries. In terms of the cartoon roles they perform, women are rarely superheroes or archvillains (the Bionic Woman and Wonder Woman are exceptions, although the stereotypical Amazon woman is a familiar character in science fiction, as I show in chap. 11). Women rarely drive vehicles either. More often than not, they portray the sweet faithful girlfriend like Olive Oyl in Popeye, or Lois Lane in Superman, or Daisy Duck and Minnie Mouse in cartoons that go by the name of the main male characters, Donald Duck and Mickey Mouse.

Textbook companies and cartoon producers often try to rationalize the male bias by saying that boys are less willing to read books or watch programs about girls than vice versa. Cartoon producers claim that both boys and girls prefer to see male characters in more prominent roles in children's books. They also point out that boys usually lag behind girls in the acquisition of language skills, so that more effort must be made to engage boys' interest. Others say that their books and programs merely reflect reality. I do not find these arguments convincing (see chap. 9 for further discussion of advertising). Certainly the textbooks used in Singapore do not reflect reality there, where women already perform many more job types than the books indicate. Some textbook producers are not even aware of the male bias in their books, as Gupta and Yin found when they wrote to ask if the producers had any policies regarding gender.

Another indication of the asymmetry in the terms *tomboy* and *sissy* can also be seen in traditional children's literature, where sissies are not treated in the same way as tomboys. There were some exceptions to this in the 1970s, when, as a result of the women's movement, some books tried to challenge gender stereotypes. In *William's Doll*, a young boy begs his parents for a doll to hug and cuddle. His father disapproves at first and gives him a basketball and train. A neighbor boy calls him "sissy." In the end William's grandmother buys him a doll, arguing that it will help him practice being a father. A study done in Australia, however, has shown that some young children may not get the feminist message in such books and are puzzled when traditional gender boundaries are crossed. Teachers who have removed sexist books from the library have been accused of censorship.

Many studies also report that girls seem to enjoy reading and writing more than boys and often perform better than boys on these activities. One explanation may be that these are less active pastimes and therefore girls are given more encouragement to pursue them. In Victorian England reading aloud was regarded as an activity well suited to the domestic role of girls and as a skill that would enhance a woman's home.

Despite the fact that these are subjects in which girls do well, there are fewer women engaged professionally as writers, for example, as novelists, journalists, and advertisers. Historically, men have controlled public forms of literacy. Few women have made it to positions of power based on their skills as writers, although in Western societies women generally have more training in basic "scribal" skills, such as typing and shorthand. Where men perform scribal functions or work as secretaries, they are usually paid at a higher level than women. The secretary to a university, or a secretary of state, for instance, is more likely to be a man than a woman, although a woman in a more junior position is probably doing the actual work generally thought of as secretarial, such as typing letters, taking dictation, and answering the phone (see chap. 10 for further discussion). The association of women with positions requiring routine scribal skills has in effect devalued the acquisition of literacy more generally in the popular mind. Thus, as with teaching, although males come to dominate in literacy activities, the territory itself may be seen as female. This is true for reading more so than for writing. The responsibility for literacy rests largely with females both in the home and in the early school years, because it is mothers and female teachers who most often teach a child to read and write.

The fact that literacy learning is embedded in society's perceptions of it as a female activity may create tension for both girls and boys. If becoming literate represents a choice in favor of female identity, a child in a family where gender divisions are sharp may risk loss of emotional connection with the father or valued aspects of self that are tied to the male world. The threat of disconnection may be too daunting. Reading and writing are for some girls a way of connecting with and being like their mothers. Being good at literacy becomes a way of engaging the mother's attention and praise, and of learning how to be female through relating to their mothers. Yet girls too have to deal with separation. They may have greater difficulty in establishing their independence because they have to reject as well as accept aspects of their mother's behavior.

Judith Solsken's work (1993) showed that a lot depends on how the mother regards literacy and how she plays her role as "teacher." In cases where the mother treats reading and writing as play, the transition to school literacy with adult standards of competence may be difficult for her daughter. Some girls are afraid to risk making mistakes. This may result in choosing to stick with books they know they can read, rather than more challenging books. Mothers' reading to their children may serve in some cases similar functions as reading romance novels. Reading by oneself or to children is an escape from the demands of other less pleasurable household chores. Reading to one's children, however, is more likely to be accepted as time spent legitimately on women's work than is reading by oneself. In Janice Radway's study (1991) of women's reading of romance novels, only when women actually engaged also in the writing of them for potential publication did their husbands value the time spent reading. This is another indication that writing is more likely to be more highly valued than reading due to its association with the world of men, where business interests dictate that time is money.

When mothers and teachers treat literacy as work, boys often resist. The tension surrounding literacy for boys may be reduced if the mother treats it as play. There is some evidence that exposure to male teaching models at school may help boys want to engage in reading and writing. When women are solely responsible for literacy-related activities, the act of reading and writing may be implicated in the child's formation of gender identity.

Some of these gender-related tensions in the acquisition of literacy may help to explain why girls are more likely to read boys' books than vice versa. Boys can only lose status by reading girls' books. Although children may read stories with main characters of the opposite gender, they give the leading roles in their own stories to a person of the same gender. Boys almost never write about female main characters. There are also major differences between the favorite themes of boys and girls as readers and writers. Girls more often choose fairy stories and boys adventure tales. When boys write fantasy stories, they generally involve combat and competition, just as the stories told by men do (see chap. 6).

In higher levels of education a major problem is the almost exclusive concentration on literature texts written by male authors. In the late 1980s in Britain the GSE (General Standard of Education) examination paper on English literature had few questions focusing on female characters. Poetry, in particular, seems to carry the stigma of being seen as female. Nevertheless, English literature is actually one of the subjects in which girls have traditionally excelled, despite the content of the courses, the authors studied, and the perspectives taken. One study showed, however, that students have difficulty understanding the point of view of the opposite gender. Women have as much trouble empathizing with the point of view of a male story character as men do with that of a female character. When asked to read Sherwood Anderson's short story "Nobody Knows," most males read the story as one of a male coming of age, whereas women looked for some relationship between the two people. In the story the male character has his first sexual encounter with a "loose" woman who is the source of much gossip in a small Midwestern town.

DEGENDERING SCHOOLING/ENGENDERING LEARNING

What goes on in school is important because it is one environment in which more egalitarian behavior is possible. Young boys lack many of the things that give men greater power over women, such as higher income or control of political power. It is thus critical to promote egalitarian behavior while children are still young, even though this will not initially be easy. Peggy Orenstein (1994) observed one classroom where a history teacher required her students to perform brief dramatic monologues in which they took on the role of a male or female historical figure. Each student had to do two, one from the point of view of a male and the other from that of a female character. She adopted this strategy after finding that when she let the children choose freely, the boys never chose to adopt the roles of women. Students told Orenstein that the boys resented the teachers' attempts to be fair to women. They perceived equality as a loss.

Because talk is crucial to learning, boys and girls should have equal time. Donna Lillian (1996) offered personal testament to her own unsuccessful efforts to give equal time to male and female students in her eighth-grade French class. On a "good" day if she "used every scrap of energy and determination," she might manage to give the girls the floor 40% of the time, but on such days the class was "absolute pandemonium" with the boys calling out, banging their feet and desks, and even verbally abusing her. In order not to have bedlam, she estimated she could allow the girls no more than about 25 to 30% of the talk time. In spite of what she perceived as her own failure to give equal time to the girls, she was regularly accused of favoring the girls and giving them all of the attention. One father even came to her classroom to complain that she was a "man hater" just like his ex-wife!

Children's textbooks, games, toys, and television programs should not be gender biased. More socially responsible television programming is needed in order to promote gender equality by altering our images, and thus our beliefs, about women. Studies show that extensive television viewing can affect our beliefs about appropriate behavior (see Rodgers, Hirata, Chandran, & Robinson, 1995). However, the power of television to reform is closely tied to the commercial interests of advertisers in countries like the United States, where broadcasting systems are not government owned and the government exerts little or no control over the content of programs. Nevertheless, programs such as "Sesame Street," designed for children, have shown that education can be effectively combined with entertainment and still be popular.

Educators know that playing games provides an important context in which children learn how to use computers, an increasingly necessary skill for school and employment. The computer software industry is finally paying attention to girls now that it realizes the sales potential to be derived from designing multimedia games specifically for them. Most products have been aimed at boys because men dominate the computer industry. One reason why girls' usage of computers drops after age 10 years is lack of appealing software. Research done by the Mattel Company showed that for every four software programs parents buy for boys, they buy only one for girls, even though both boys and girls between the ages of 6 and 10 years spend the same amount of time at the computer.

Unfortunately, some software manufacturers still have conventional gender stereotypes and are producing titles such as "The Babysitters Club" and "Let's Talk About Me," in which girls can keep a diary, take personality quizzes, and get advice on their bodies. This sounds all too much like an interactive women's magazine with its emphasis on appearance and personality. A game called "Barbie Fashion Designer" lets girls design clothes for Barbie dolls (see chap. 9 for more on Barbie). Although some claim this is what girls want, others have dubbed such games "pink software" and have been trying to develop titles such as "Oregon Trail," which appeal to both boys and girls.

The fact that girls tend to talk less and get less attention from teachers in mixed-sex groups has been one important argument in favor of single-sex schooling. Women who attended all-female institutions have tended to perform better academically than those attending coeducational schools. The one-to-one tutorial favored in Oxbridge colleges is essentially a male form of pedagogy that emphasizes hierarchical relations between teacher (usually male) and student. Collaborative learning in groups is more consistent with female modes of interaction. Similarly, girls and women may take fewer risks on examination and tutorial tasks involving essay writing, or be reluctant to engage in competitive argument with their tutors. This has been suggested as one factor behind women's poorer performance at Oxford in certain subjects such as history, where examiners and tutors have traditionally put higher value on essays and tutorial sessions in which the student is willing to go out on a limb, advance a bold thesis, or engage in a cut-and-thrust argument with a tutor. We need to question how and why we have been conditioned to think that the argumentative debating style associated with the male-dominated academic world is more appropriate and conducive to learning than the collaborative talk associated with female groups.

Women's difficulty in accommodating to the expectations of male standards of behavior that govern academic life may be responsible for the greater dropout rates for women entering graduate study. A women who behaves and talks like a woman in an academic setting runs the risk of not being taken seriously. On the other hand, when she does not behave like a woman, she may suffer sanctions from her peers and be almost forced to apologize for her success. Victoria Bergvall (1996) showed that when female engineering students were assertive active participants, they were criticized for not facilitating the work of others. When the women did behave in a more traditional way, their contributions tended to be taken for granted and not acknowledged.

The increasing visibility of women in important public positions will also help reform our mental imagery. At the United Nations Fourth World Conference on Women in Beijing in 1995, Gro Harlem Brundtland, who had been the Norwegian Prime Minister over the past decade, told how 15 years ago it was difficult for Norwegians to get used to having a female Prime Minister. Now it appears that the gender image associated with the office is reversed: A 4-year-old child asked her if a man could be Prime Minister.

In this chapter and the preceding one I have examined some of the ways in which males and females behave differently due to varying patterns of socialization. In some cases they talk differently as well as talk about different things, reflecting their different worlds of concern and their unequal positioning in the social structure, which exposes them to different daily experiences. An extreme view of the "difference position" such as that of John Gray (1992) has it that we even behave as if we live on different planets: Men are from Mars and women from Venus. Perhaps even more interesting, however, are cases such as those I discuss in the next chapter, where men and women have different understandings of the *same* key words and concepts in everyday use. These can be thought of as different representations of reality.

EXERCISES AND DISCUSSION QUESTIONS

1. Examine some traditional popular books aimed at the adolescent market, such as the Nancy Drew or Hardy Boys series. Make a list of the adjectives used to describe the activities and appearance of the main characters.

2. Examine television advertising of children's toys for evidence of gender stereotyping. You can extend your study by visiting a retailer that sells children's toys and games and looking at the packaging of these products and how they are displayed in the store.

3. Observe patterns of interaction in a classroom. Keep a record of which students raise their hands to speak, and which ones are called on. Make a note of any interruptions. You will have to decide how you are going to define an interruption. Do you find any gender-related patterns?

4. Should teachers try to get male and female students to use talk in the same way? Should they try to change gender-based styles of talk or support them?

5. Consider the case of women who have filed discrimination lawsuits to enter formerly male-only academic institutions such as South Carolina's military academy The Citadel. Are separate educational institutions for males and females desirable? On what grounds?

6. Some school districts now give adolescent girls the opportunity to enroll in all-female science and math classes in order to increase their skills in these subjects. What are the advantages and disadvantages of such segregated courses?

7. Discuss some of the ethical issues in proactive television programming for children. Who decides what goals programming should have? Is it possible to give fair treatment and equal time to all social and cultural groups?

ANNOTATED BIBLIOGRAPHY AND SUGGESTIONS
FOR FURTHER READING

In my discussion of U.S. classrooms I have drawn heavily on research done by Barrie Thorne and Peggy Orenstein. The early work done by Iona and Peter Opie (1959) on the language of childhood games, rhymes, and so on remains a classic reference, but there is now a great variety of research on school-age children and adolescents, as can be seen in the work of Bronwyn Davies (1982), Valerie Hey (1996), Linda Hughes (1993), Susan Lees (1986), Janet Lever (1978), Medrich, Roizen, Rubin, and Buckley (1982),

Stephen Richert (1990), and Beatrice Whiting and Carolyn Edwards (1988). Works focusing more specifically on language and gender differences include those by Elaine Andersen (1992), Penelope Eckert (1988), Daniel Maltz and Ruth Borker (1982), Suzanne Romaine (1984), Amy Sheldon (1993), and Amy Shuman (1986). On gender and schooling, see Susan Gabriel (1990), Phyllis Rosser (1989), Dale Spender (1980b, 1982), and Carol Stanger (1987). There have been many studies of gender bias in children's literature; see, for example, the books by Carolyn Baker and Peter Freebody (1989) and by Bronwyn Davies (1989). Joan Newman (1982) and Denise Wilms and Ilene Cooper (1987) provided guides to some of the available nonsexist children's books. Andre Michel's book (1986) provided some guidelines for eliminating stereotypes from children's books. Mary Douglas's book (1966) offered a cross-cultural perspective on taboo and pollution, and Marilyn Strathern (1988) offered an analysis of similar phenomena in Papua New Guinea. The American Association of University Women (1993) report discussed the problem of sexual harassment in schools (see also discussion question 3 in the next chapter). The collection of case studies in Judith Kleinfeld and Suzanne Yerian's book (1995) raised many useful questions about gender equity in educational systems, some of which I have adapted in some of the discussion questions at the end of this chapter. For media discussion of girls' loss of self-esteem, see Suzanne Daley's article (1991), and on gender differences in the use of computers, see Deborah Tannen's (1994c) and Jennifer Tanaka's (1996) articles.

8

Different Words, Different Worlds?

[My aunts] told about the wild-looking town in Northern Ontario where Aunt Iris wouldn't stop the car even to let them buy a Coke. She took one look at the lumberjacks and cried, "We'd all be raped!"

"What is raped?" said my little sister.
"Oh-oh," said Iris. "It means get your pocketbook stolen."
Pocketbook: an American word. My sister and I didn't know what it meant either but we were not equal to two questions in a row. And I knew that wasn't what rape meant anyway; it meant something dirty.
"Purse. Purse stolen," said my mother in a festive but cautioning tone. Talk in our house was genteel.

(Munro, 1983, p.)

In the last chapter I looked at how girls are brought up to talk and act like ladies, while boys are expected to talk and act "rough." The epigraph to this chapter reinforces the discussion in that chapter about how girls are taught to avoid putting themselves into situations where they might be raped, and how even the very mention of the word is shameful and dirty. Just by being at the wrong place at the wrong time a woman "is asking for it." Saying "no" is never enough within a discourse world where male sexuality appears uncontrollable and inevitable. Metaphors linking male sexuality to violence and predation of the type I wrote about in chapter 4 sanction male aggression and female acquiescence as normal, making it easy to overlook the misogynistic elements of a variety of crimes ranging from sexual harassment to murder that men commit against women. Official statistics underestimate to an unknown degree the incidence of such crimes, in part because behaviors we talk about as normal and natural are generally not regarded as criminal or socially unacceptable.

When male verbal and physical coercion are taken for granted, women are gatekeepers who must keep a man from going too far, and rapes just "happen" as part of normal sexual relationships between men and women. Researchers have noted a tendency for the passive voice to be used in discussions of rape and sexual coercion, such as 24% *of women have been raped*. Here the victim is made prominent, while the persons responsible are invisible. The use of the passive voice reinforces blaming the victim (see chap. 4 on missing agents).

Many raped and sexually harassed women remain silent rather than face the ambiguous status of being both the victims of crime as well as the ones judged responsible for it. The media cast female victims into two extremes, good girls or bad girls, virgins or vamps, Snow White or the Wicked Witch. This too suggests a sexual double standard behind official statistics, because the assignment of crimes to categories such as rape or date rape, as well as murder, manslaughter, and so on, is based not on the incident itself, but on the outcome of the juridical process, where competing views about sexual activity and violence are contested through discourse in the courtroom.

In this chapter, I look at evidence indicating that men and women do indeed have different conceptions of many terms relating to sexuality and sexual behavior, such as *rape, date rape, sexual harassment,* and others. Champion boxer Mike Tyson, for example, when convicted of raping Desirée Washington, insisted he hadn't hurt her because no bones had been broken. This suggests a fundamental difference in male and female understandings of force, violence, and pain, and the extent to which they impact on women's experience of male sexual behavior. Male and female views may differ sharply on the matter of rape, but due to male power, legitimate sexual practices are defined primarily from a male point of view and protected within an androcentric legal system.

The ultimate act of violence one person can commit against another is to take that person's life deliberately. Although women commit murders, it appears that only men are driven by the lust to kill, to commit womanslaughter, or femicide. Very few women are killers. Women who are husband killers almost always act in self-defense. Moreover, there has never been a female counterpart to so-called sex murderers, men such as Jack the Ripper, the Yorkshire Ripper, and the Boston Strangler, who systematically stalk, murder, and mutilate a series of female victims. Yet most of the investigative emphasis of such killings has aimed at individual psychology, rather than at the gender bias and the reasons for it. Insofar as gender does become prominent, it is usually not to ask why men rape and kill, but what women do to provoke male lust.

LANGUAGE AT WORK: SEXUAL HARASSMENT

Many problems arise in the application of laws concerning sexual harassment, and even rape, due to differences in interpretation of what constitutes harmful and violent action to others. A researcher investigating the attitudes of American men toward violence asked a thousand men from various backgrounds to classify certain acts as violent or nonviolent and to rank them on a scale indicating their degree of violence. She was surprised when most of the men classified the burning of draft cards as violent but the shooting of looters by police as nonviolent. Further research was needed to clarify the nature of violence. Although men and women seemed to agree that violent acts were negative, intense, and deliberate, and that they involved force, for men they were also avoidable. For most women, violent acts were also harmful. This goes some, but not all, the way to explaining why most men would perceive the act of police shooting looters as nonviolent. The police cannot avoid such actions if they are to carry out their duties. Burning a draft card, on the other hand, is thought of as a violent act because it can be avoided.

Most people will agree that if a boss asks an employee to have sex or lose a job, this is sexual harassment. Most cases are rarely this straightforward. A woman who lost her job as a Piedmont Airlines pilot in 1992 said it was the result of a "sexually hostile" environment. She was one of 20 women in a crew of 200 pilots. She claimed she did not receive as much training as the men. A chief pilot told her she wore her "hat like a bonnet." A captain called her a "space cadet" and a "little blonde thing." When she showed up in a crew room before a flight, a first officer said, "I've never flown with a girl before." Similar resistance to the air perceived as a male space can be seen in the reluctance to allow women to become astronauts, and in the limited presence of women in science fiction novels. Because men have traditionally regarded the air as no place for a woman, the claiming of outer space through the writing of feminist science fiction is a highly symbolic act, as I show in chapter 11.

A large number of professional women, myself included, endure remarks such as those directed at the pilot, in addition to numerous "pranks." A woman who, after much persistence, got a job as a "road maintenance man" discovered that her coworkers put many obstacles in her way. The men kept the women's toilet locked, and while on the road they wouldn't stop to let her use the restroom. Her supervisor told her, "You wanted a man's job, you learn to pee like a man." He would not issue her a pair of coveralls until she filed a formal grievance to get them. The men put obscene graffiti about her on the sides of the trucks and told her they didn't want her there. In another instance a woman ordered to clean a transit bus by her supervisor found that her coworkers had smeared excrement across the seats. Women workers at American Cyanamid found signs on their lockers calling them "whores" and fended off sexual assaults in the showers.

These incidents are part and parcel of a wide range of male behaviors often dismissed as minor nuisances, such as wolf whistles, flashing, name calling, and obscene phone calls, which (re)assert male power over women and establish male sexuality as predatory and aggressive. Men feel entitled to unrestricted access to women, even against their will. All these acts function to restrict women's autonomy at the same time as they reassure men of their ability to frighten and humiliate women.

These incidents occur not just when women are in subordinate positions, but also when woman are in positions equal to those of their male co-workers, as well as when women are in much higher level positions. When a female assistant professor at Fleming Graduate School of Business and Public Management in Toronto took off her blazer in class due to a heating system malfunction that caused the temperature to rise to near 90 degrees, one of the male students let out a long loud wolf whistle. Although most of her male colleagues began their classes by removing their jackets and rolling up their shirtsleeves, a woman cannot do this without risking being perceived as a striptease artist. As I showed in the last chapter as well as in chapter 5, women have to worry more about their wardrobe. If a woman wears something too frilly, she will be dismissed as provocative or lacking seriousness, but if she wears something too severe, she is branded a hu-morless schoolmarm, or a man-hater. A woman's appearance is always available for public scrutiny and comment. Female colleagues have often told me that they routinely receive teaching evaluations containing remarks or comments about their appearance and clothing, even though the evaluation does not cover these topics.

A survey conducted for the magazine *Working Women* reported that 63% of the 9,000 women in corporate management positions who were questioned had experienced some form of harassment. General complaints include the feeling that women are not taken seriously as colleagues, or are expected to perform more subordinate tasks (e.g., making the coffee), or do not get enough information about what is going on. One woman who was vice-president of a computer company said that her male cowork-ers slotted her into a mother role. When they greeted her, they asked how her kids were. She did not notice anyone greeting men in this way. Writing about the problems posed to conventional "office etiquette" by pregnant women, journalist Lucy Kellaway commented that her male colleagues referred to her upcoming maternity leave as "holiday." She was irritated when business contacts she scarcely knew would ask her whether the child she was expecting was her first, and then proceed to tell her about their own families. She also noted the way in which a business seminar was advertised. It promised to teach managers about "energy and aggression, lust and libido."

In cases of sexual harassment, as in rape, the onus is on the person so harassed to prove the claim, and most often there are no witnesses. Many women do not report harassment or rape because they do not want to undergo the ordeal of questioning they must face in order to prove they were not "asking for it" by dressing or acting in a way that would have invited unwelcome sexual advances. A complainant risks losing not just her credibility, but her job too.

The charges made by law professor Anita Hill against Supreme Court nominee Clarence Thomas represent one of the highly publicized instances where the person claiming harassment was afraid to speak out—in this particular case, for many years. It was also Hill's word against that of Thomas because there were no witnesses to the events she said took place in the early 1980s, when she had worked for Thomas in Washington, DC, while he was head of the Equal Employment Opportunity Commission (EEOC). Although an all-male, all-White, 14-member Senate Judiciary Committee subjected both Thomas and Hill to intense public scrutiny and questioning, the onus was on Hill to prove her case. The Judiciary Committee focused the issue more on why Hill had come forward after so long rather than on the charges themselves. She took a lie-detector test and passed. Then her opponents began to argue that she was mentally unbalanced and delusional, had concocted a fantasy, or was trying to get back at Thomas because he had rejected her own romantic interests in him. Hill was typecast as the sex-starved "hysterical woman" prone to exaggerate, hallucinate, and therefore not credible. Senator Orrin Hatch drew vivid parallels between Hill's harassment charges and a passage from the fictitious but sensationalist book *The Exorcist*. Some commentators noted that Hill had fallen victim to a similar kind of dilemma faced by rape victims. She had reported the harassment in too calm a fashion and been too matter-of-fact about it.

Although naming a process that women have experienced for years has brought it into our consciousness, and facilitates its identification for legal purposes, we can also begin to see in this example how the meaning of *harassment* is constructed in different ways by men and women. The EEOC's legal definition of sexual harassment specifies it as "unwelcome sexual advances, requests for sexual favors and other verbal or physical contact of a sexual nature" that are connected to decisions about employment or that create an intimidating, hostile, or offensive work environment. There is nothing in the EEOC statement on harassment that makes reporting it part of its definition. Yet the press seems to imply that sexual harassment that goes unreported cannot really have been harassment. In Australia, researchers such as Ramsay and Stefanou-Haag (1991) noted resistance in the form of anger and ridicule to the very term *sexual harassment*, as evident in the comment made by one man who said, "The only problem about sexual harassment is that there's not enough of it around here" (p. 36).

Another case where a woman spoke out after enduring sexual harassment for many years while she was professor of neurosurgery at Stanford University was that of Frances Conley. She told of how she was tired of being called "honey" by male colleagues, having her legs fondled under the table at meetings, being invited to have sex, and so on. When asked why she had put up with it all for 23 years, she said that it had been crucial to go along with it in order to achieve her position. She was prompted to speak out when a male colleague who was one of the worst offenders was going to be promoted to the position of head of the department, where he would determine policy.

A book designed to help readers identify behavior that counts as sexual harassment offered case studies such as these:

1. You and your boss are single and like each other a lot. You invite him to dinner, and one thing leads to another. Was someone sexually harassed? (No—although it wasn't very smart.)

2. Your boss invites you to a restaurant for dinner and—much to your surprise—spends the evening flirting with you. Just before inviting you to her house for a nightcap, she mentions that promotion you are hoping to get. (You are being sexually harassed. Whether or not you welcome her interest in you, she has implied a connection between the promotion and your response.)

Interestingly, in both cases, it is the woman who initiates a sexual advance. In the first case, which does not count as harassment, the woman is subordinate, while in the second, which does, she is the boss. Susan Ehrlich and Ruth King (1994) commented on the improbability of the second scenario and the political significance of its use in a book designed as a guide to sexual harassment. What is presented as a prototypical case of sexual harassment, where a female boss makes a sexual advance to a subordinate male employee, flies in the face of the majority of such cases, where it is men in superior positions who harass women. By using such an atypical case, the book serves to redefine harassment as something women do to men. Yet, in its review of the book, Castro (1992, p. 37) described it as "refreshingly free of ideology and reproach."

A best-selling novel, *Disclosure* (1994), by Michael Crichton, made into a movie in 1994 starring Michael Douglas and Demi Moore, prompted much media discussion of the topic of sexual harassment. It too portrayed a role-reversal case in which a female boss proposed sex to a male executive. Many women are annoyed that the first major film to give prominent attention to the subject should treat the atypical case of a man being the victim of harassment. According to the EEOC, men filed 10% of the 14,400 charges of sexual harassment in 1994. This represents an increase of 2% from 1990, when men filed 8% of the 6,100 cases. Although men are very much in the minority as victims of sexual harassment, the cases that they do file receive a lot of media attention, such as the so-called "Boston Eight," who sued weight-loss company Jenny Craig for denying them promotions or firing them. In Britain the case of a male academic who claimed discrimination because he was not able to obtain a teaching job in gender studies departments prompted a number of letters from men to the *Times Higher Educational Supplement* (February 18, 1994). One wrote that departments of gender studies "exist to give the dogmas of feminism a veneer of scholarly respectability, and to provide well-paid jobs for man-haters to propagate their doctrine at the expense of public funds."

Another way in which women's charges of sexual harassment are defused is through framing them within sexist discourse. Mary Talbot (1995) examined how a popular British tabloid, *The Sun*, reported to its readers a 1989 case where an industrial tribunal decided that a boss had sexually harassed two female employees and awarded them £6,000 (ca. $10,000). The headline said "£6,000 bill puts randy fish boss in his plaice," and the report told of how boss Mike Alway tried to "net" the two women, who were described as "pretty," "young," "lovely," "attractive," and "buxom." The style of reporting, with its puns on the theme of fish and overall playfulness, set a tone for readers to interpret the charge of harassment as trivial, just a bit of "boys will be boys" office fun that got carried too far but didn't harm anyone. To titillate readers, the reporter quoted some of the "chat-up" lines the boss used to try to seduce the women, but suggested that they weren't good enough and hence the women refused his advances.

The story itself was featured as a "Sun News Special" alongside the customary pinup photograph of the "Page Three Girl," which legitimizes nude women as objects for male gaze. This too framed the case of sexual harassment as being within the bounds of normal male behavior toward women, and undermined the significance of the court's decision. Talbot also examined how the paper referred to the boss and the two employees. The story most often called the two women by their first names and described their appearance, whereas it referred to the boss most often as Mr. Alway, or with his full name.

An incident dubbed as "virtual rape" occurring on the Internet in 1993 straddled the boundary between sexual harassment and rape at the same time as it raised questions about freedom of speech. A male character in a recreational real-time forum posted graphic descriptions of a violent rape of a female character in the forum. The man responsible for the actions of the male character claimed afterward that he had not intended his words to describe what the man was doing to the woman to be taken seriously.

He argued that he was experimenting with the freedom to construct different textual characters in the new medium. Other members of the group, however, voted to deny the man future access to the forum because his behavior had constituted harmful actions and the women whose character was raped felt considerable distress.

WHEN IS SEX RAPE?

Issues of definition are also at stake in cases of rape. If a man is fully aroused and pressures a woman for sex despite her wishes, is this an avoidable act? If he proceeds without her explicit consent or in spite of her denial to participate, is this rape? Can a husband be convicted of raping his wife, or does marriage in and of itself guarantee her unqualified consent to all forms of sexual activity? Whether unwanted sex counts as rape, date rape, or rape at all depends largely on the relationship between the victim and attacker. The legal status of women as subordinate to fathers and husbands meant that until recently a woman could not charge her husband with rape.

Gregory Matoesian (1993) discussed the prevailing patriarchal assumptions in the courtroom, which narrowly define rape from the male point of view as a violent, random assault on a woman by an unknown assailant. Other forms of sexual assault and coercion resulting in intercourse generally do not count as rape, and therefore are either not called rape at all, or they go by a special kind of name like "date" or "acquaintance" rape. Official statistics distort the amount of rape as well as the profile of the typical rapist.

Where societies use violence as a normal and sanctioned means of controlling and dominating women, rape and fear of it keep women in their place and function as a means of legitimized social control. A woman knows it is *her* responsibility to *avoid* rape. By blaming the victim for provoking their sexual aggression, men control as well as define acceptable female behavior. Masculinity often gets confused with abuse and degradation of women, and in some cases leads to murder. In this sense, Matoesian concludes that rape is not a violation of the social order, but a reinforcement of it. The state fails to intervene against violent male behavior perpetrated against women and thus condones and reproduces it. Even when rape is reported and prosecuted, the rate of conviction is much lower than for other forms of crime such as burglary, aggravated assault, and manslaughter. Cases are more likely to be prosecuted and result in conviction if the rapist is a stranger, assaults his victim violently, and the victim is a "good girl." In court, issues about the relationship between victim and assailant are relevant in determining whether sex was consensual, and a woman is questioned about her past sexual practices in order that the court may judge whether she is a "good girl." In this way rape is decriminalized, forced sex becomes acceptable, and a woman's "no" does not really mean "no." The female version of the reality of rape is suppressed.

These differences in viewpoint are one reason why rape is very much underreported. Many studies have found that although as many as 50% or more women had experienced some form of male aggression, ranging from rape, to attempted rape, to some unwanted form of sexual contact, fewer than 10% reported these incidents to the police. Although some forms of forced sexual contact such as anal penetration and oral-genital contact are included within the legal category of sodomy and hence are criminal offenses, other sexual acts such as fondling of breasts or genitals, whether they occur between heterosexual or same-sex partners, do not count as rape even if they take place without consent. This reflects a more general view that sex involves penile–vaginal penetration.

Despite the prevailing narrow definition of rape as sexual activity involving penetration, most rapes are committed by men known to the victims rather than by strangers. A large proportion of them occur on dates. The majority of reported rapes, however, are of the violent assault type, so-called "aggravated rape" committed by strangers using a weapon. An alternative feminist point of view, however, is based on the belief that rape in the wider sense, that is, any sexual act without consent, is an extension of normative male sexual behavior.

The legal definition of rape is based primarily on consent. Valid consent to an act or contract cannot be obtained if a person is coerced. Coercion need not be the result of force or violence, although many men believe rape takes place only when force or threat of force is involved. If a woman is incapable of consent, for example, by reason of unconsciousness, intoxication, or mental deficiency, any sexual activity with her is legally classified as rape. Yet men are more likely to interpret routine encounters with women as sexual in nature and to interpret sexual interactions as consensual even if they involve force or coercion. Because women do not generally report such incidents to the police as rape, they are not prosecuted and rapists are not convicted.

One study done by Jacqueline Goodchilds (1991) with adolescents in Los Angeles indicated considerable discrepancies between male and female points of view concerning the circumstances when male sexual force against females would be justified. For example, in response to the statement, "he spends a lot of money on her," only 12% of females, but 39% of males, said forced sex would be legitimate. Nearly a third of the females and over half the males said force would be legitimate if the woman has "led him on." The answers to the statements reveal men's expectations that spending money on a date, or being aroused by her, entitles them to sex.

A study of college students revealed that men and women with traditional gender-role attitudes considered a woman more responsible for rape if she "led him on," for example, by asking him out, letting him pay for a date, going to his apartment, and so forth (Reinholtz et al., 1995, pp. 152–153). Other studies indicated that many men would consider raping a woman if they thought they could get away with it.

George Lakoff (1987) showed that sex and violence are linked via metaphors whereby sexual desire is understood in terms of physical force and combat metaphors. I showed how in chapter 3 sexual conquest is linked with the territorial conquest of war. Lakoff also illustrated that our metaphorical understanding of lust shares a great deal with our understanding of anger. Sexuality is conceptualized as a physical force and lust is a reaction to that force (see the last chapter for discussion of this metaphor in pop music, and the next chapter on its use in advertising). Historically, the word *lust* once expressed a desire or wish, but its meaning has narrowed to apply primarily to sexual desire and violence (e.g., blood-lust).

WHEN "NO" DOESN'T MEAN "NO": FORCING A "YES" OUT

Language plays a crucial role in the definition and construction of rape, in everyday life as well as in the media and in the legal system. When rape cases come to trial, the issue is less about truth and falsehood than about presenting evidence in a persuasive way. The outcome depends largely on how language is manipulated in the courtroom. The court does not determine so much whether a woman has consented or been forced to engage in sex, but whether she has conformed to patriarchal standards of female sexuality. These dictate that whether she has said "no" matters little as long as it appears reasonable for her attacker to have understood consent. Through cross-examination of the victim the defense attorney tries to transform a woman's experience of rape into consensual sex. In this war of words the odds are stacked against women because the male standpoint is the basis for the legal system. It thus passes for objectivity. It sanctions rape as part of normal male sexual behavior, making no distinction between rape and normal sexual intercourse as long as the woman knows her attacker and force is not aggravated with a weapon. The prosecuting attorney and the defense attorney must make what is in effect the same act of intercourse appear in a different light to the jury. The prosecuting attorney portrays it as a criminal assault, whereas the defense attorney shows it as consensual sex. Studies have also shown that women jurors tend to identify with rape victims more than men do, so cases involving a majority of male jurors are more likely to be decided against women.

Defense attorneys attempt to construct the victim's moral character by controlling the talk to their own advantage. They rephrase and summarize the testimony in their own words. The asking of questions requiring yes/no answers leaves the victim little scope and disempowers her. She is dependent on the attorneys and police to speak for her and present her testimony in their words to the judge and jury.

In this example from a trial, Matoesian (1993) studied how the defense attorney constructs through cross-examination a definition of the term *partying* that implies that the victim was deliberately seeking sexual activity. The victim met her attacker outside the parking lot of a bar after closing time and left with him in his car. By leading the victim through a series of questions, the attorney gets her to collaborate in a definition of "partying" that starts out as involving things "some" people do to things "many" people do, such as taking drugs, drinking, and having sex. Thus, the definition the defense attorney constructs becomes the normative one.

D[efense] A[ttorney]:   So one of the objectives, when you left that party at the parking lot was to go out and party, is that correct?

DA: What's meant among youthful people, people your age, Brian's [the defendant] age by partying?

V[ictim]:   Some take it just to go and with some friends, people, and have a few drinks and do some smoke some do take th— pills.

DA: Partying.

V: (Drugs)

DA: Is it not true partying among people your age does not mean go to a party?

V: That's true.

DA: It implies to many people that implies sexual activity, doesn't it?

P[rosecuting] A[ttorney]: Objection Your Honor.

J[udge]:   Overruled.

DA: To many people your age that means sexual activity, does it not?

V: To some yes, I guess.

DA: At the very least it means the use of intoxicants.

V: Yes.

Later in the same trial the defense attorney paints a picture of the victim as a "loose woman" who was willing to take risks by getting into the car of a man about whom she knew very little. He elicits this information by asking a series of questions, "Did you know his last name?," "Did you know where he was from?," "Did you know where he worked?" After she answers "no" to all of these, the defense attorney summarizes, "You didn't know a thing about him, did you?" This suggests she was willing to engage in a casual relationship possibly leading to casual sex. In his closing arguments directed at the judge and jury, the defense attorney states:

She was willing to go along with him in the beginning without knowing his last name, where he was from, where he was employed, what he was about, except that he was good looking. . . . Linda Sims without knowing him. Just concerned about his looks gets into an automobile with him, takes off with him. Obviously has an objective, she knows they're going partying. We've heard from her own mouth on the witness stand what partying means.

He manipulates her testimony in such a way as to make the jury believe that the definition of partying constructed through cross-examination is the victim's own. He also links together answers to a whole range of questions in order to undercut her accusation, which allows him to suggest she was "asking for it" by the way she acted. The woman never actually used the words *good-looking* or *attractive* in relation to the defendant; nor did she ever say she was attracted to him. These words were literally put into her mouth in the cross-examination process. The defense attorney wanted to set up a causal chain of events that implied that if a man is attractive looking, she must have been attracted to him and therefore willing to have sex with him. Here we have an example of the metaphorical understanding of sexual desire as a physical force compelling a person to engage in sexual activity. Contrary to what the defense attorney claims she said, what she actually said is that he appeared *nice* and was *clean-looking,* a more neutral statement with no sexual overtones.

DA: You were attracted to Brian, weren't you?
V: I thought he was a nice clean-looking man.
DA: He was attractive looking, correct?
V: Yeah.
DA: And basically when you left that parking lot all you knew about him
     was that he was a good looking man, isn't that true?
V: Yeah.

The victim is at a disadvantage in her attempt to present her own experience and point of view to the jury because she is allowed only to respond to the questions she is asked. Who gets to say what and when in the courtroom is carefully governed by legal practices. Power is balanced heavily in favor of the attorneys and judge, who decide who gets to say what and when. From a male point of view the victim implied her consent to whatever else might happen to her once she got into Brian's car. The court does not address the question of whether she consented to sex, but only whether she consented to male sexual standards. A woman who is too independent runs the risk of getting into trouble and is asking for it. As the defense attorney put it in his closing arguments, "She calmly entered the car. There can't be any question I don't think in anybody's mind that at the very least she was willing to engage in some sort of sexual activity. There couldn't be any question in the defendant's mind at that point in time that she'd be willing to." In this statement the defense attorney transformed the act of getting into the car into an agreement to sex. The defendant's act of forced sex was made to appear reasonable by comparing what was in his mind with what would be in "anybody's mind." The use of the generic *anybody* is a powerful ploy to legitimize as universally valid what is in effect the male point of view (see chap. 4 on generics). The court did not convict the defendant of rape.

Lois Forer (cited in Sanday, 1990), a judge who has presided over gang-rape cases, pointed out an underlying similarity in the behavior, language, and attitudes of young men belonging to some fraternities on U.S. college campuses and young men from poor and underprivileged backgrounds tried in court for gang rape. Both groups engaged in sexual behavior they referred to as "gang bang" or "playing or pulling train," where a series of men line up like cars in a train to have sexual intercourse with the same woman. Both groups consider it a form of male bonding within the bounds of acceptable and normal conduct. Indeed, sexual exploitation of women is seen as a prerequisite to manhood. The use of alcohol and drugs often precedes or accompanies intercourse. The big difference between the two groups is that the fraternity brothers are rarely, if ever, prosecuted for rape. These young men represent an elite and largely homogeneous group of males, constituting one of the last bastions of male exclusivity and privilege on campus. Their behavior is often excused as an instance of "boys will be boys." This phrase becomes part of a cultural discourse of the type I discussed in chapter 2 that rationalizes male sexual aggression against women by excusing it as part of normal and natural male biological urges. It therefore becomes a woman's responsibility to protect herself. A man is not held responsible for his sexual desire. Again, we have an example of the metaphorical understanding of sexual desire as a force compelling sexual activity.

In one case Forer tried, the victim was 14 years old and lived in a public housing project. She was on her first date with a classmate who also lived in her neighborhood. She thought they were going to a party, but she was gang-raped. The judge learned during the trial that the young woman's date was a member of a gang whose members were obligated to bring women to an old shed they used as a clubhouse, where each of the members would have sex with them. Peggy Reeves Sanday (1990) found that some fraternities on U.S. college campuses required women whom they admitted as "little sisters" to have sex with the members. In this and other similar cases where the victim reported the incident and the men were brought to trial, the defendants admitted what they had done, but insisted they had not committed a crime because they hadn't harmed their victims. Instead, they blamed the victim for "asking for it" and had bragged about getting laid.

Sanday studied some cases of rapes that took place in fraternity houses, where the victim was generally a woman attending a party in the house. In some instances the woman had agreed to have sex with one man and then found herself forced into having sex with more than one man. In the eyes of the men involved this kind of sexual behavior was not classified as rape. If a woman has agreed to some sexual activity, then she agreed to all sexual activity, whether she was conscious and capable of giving consent or not. The members believed that rape involved forcing a woman to have sex against her will, whether or not she was drunk or high on drugs. As long as she did not resist advances, a woman had consented even if she was unconscious and unable to resist. The members also believed that while drunk they were not responsible for their actions.

In fact, the purpose of the parties was to lure women into the fraternity house so that they could be seduced. Some of the posters advertising the frat parties announced that women could attend without paying. One poster showed a woman's legs as a bowling lane with a frat brother as a bowling ball ready to roll down the lane. At one house advertising "Loss of Innocence" as its party theme, the centerpiece was a model of a bride clothed in white stretched out on a pool table with her legs open.

At the parties the men "scope" for likely sexual partners. "Hitting on women" and "riffing" (pressuring them for sex in exchange for alcohol or by talking nicely to them) are part of the ethos of such fraternities. At one fraternity the men stuck colored dots on the women's clothing to indicate how easy they thought the women were to pick up. They provide drinks and in some cases drugs at their parties to weaken women's resistance to their requests for sex—a practice called "working a yes out." The brothers see nothing wrong with this practice because they restrict rape to sex involving physical force. Yet even after a woman has said no and shown physical resistance, the men don't accept no for an answer. They keep trying, often by using alcohol. As Sanday pointed out, however, there is a thin line separating rape and working a yes out. The main difference between a rapist who uses violent force and the fraternity brothers is primarily in the latitude given to the victim to escape. The assumption is that people attending the fraternity parties are there of their own free will to get drunk and have sex. Women who attend therefore risk being riffed, hit on, and even raped. From the male point of view women have given unspoken consent to all of these things just by attending the party and drinking. They have asked for it without saying anything. Yet no woman consents to a gang rape.

If a brother "scores," he generally goes upstairs with a woman to a bedroom to have sex. Sanday described the discourse used by fraternity brothers in talking about the women they have intercourse with as demeaning. The women were called *gashes, hosebags, heifers, scum, scumbags, scumbuckets, scumdoggies, trolls, bitches, beasts, swatches, cracks, wenches,* and *queens.* Terms such as *corpse riff* and *unconscious riff* indicated that the men did not care if a woman was unconscious or incapacitated by alcohol or drugs. By talking about the women in this way the brothers degraded them at the same time as they denied the dependency that sexual desire aroused in them. They separated sex from emotional involvement. Some fraternities even posted minutes from in-house meetings referring to the sexual exploits of the members. One mentioned that various brothers had applied new riffing techniques named as "let's make a deal riff," "Negress riff," and "black hole riff," with the latter two referring in racist fashion to Black women the men had coerced into sex.

Sanday observed a deep-seated fear of homosexuality underlying the behavior and discourse of some of the fraternity members. The men gained status through sexual encounters with women, and there was considerable peer pressure for men to participate to demonstrate their virility. In one house the men frequently watched pornography together. In one film a number of men had sex with the same woman, who was described as having been "fucked unconscious." The film equated the unconsciousness of the woman as female sexual desire aroused by "rough sex." In initiation rituals at some fraternities the prospective new members are verbally and physically abused. According to Sanday the initiations were similar to male initiation rites documented by anthropologists in other cultures, where the objective is to separate boys from the psychological and social bonding with their mothers and to forge new bonds with men. In some fraternities the new pledges (men seeking admission as members) are treated as polluted and despised women. They are called *faggots*, *pansies*, and *wimps*. At one fraternity the pledges had to wear diapers and expose their genitals, for which they were then ridiculed. Brotherhood in the fraternity was achieved by killing the supposed inner woman.

These rituals can be compared with similar behaviors among the Sambia people of Papua New Guinea described by Gilbert Herdt (1993), where men have secret cults and activities that take place in a special all-male house. Boys are initiated into the male cults between the ages of 7 and 10 years, when they are taken from their mothers and forbidden to interact with women and children, from whom the initiation ceremonies are kept secret. These activities involve painful ordeals and purification rituals presided over by adult men, the revelation of secret knowledge, and training in warrior skills. The initiates' noses are made to bleed and they are forced to vomit to rid themselves of pollution. In Sambia culture men always stand or sit above women to avoid contamination. The men's house is situated at a high point in the village, and the whole village is partitioned into men's and women's areas, complete with separate paths for men and women. Sambia men assault their wives both verbally and physically. Traditional Burmese culture also associates women with pollution. It is dangerous for a man to use a toilet or bathroom used by a woman or even to walk underneath a clothesline on which a woman's sarong is hanging. Avoidance rituals provide a way of reducing the threat a woman's sexuality poses. In all these instances female subordination goes hand in hand with a belief in the power of women. Male aggression against women, in some cases in the form of gang rape, wife beating, and murder, is prompted by fear of female power. As I observed in the last chapter, boys are already acting out aggression against girls in playground-chasing and name-calling rituals.

GOOD GIRLS, BAD GIRLS, VIRGINS, AND VAMPS

In her critique of the way in which the press covers sex crimes, Helen Benedict (1992) demonstrated the pervasiveness of certain myths about rape and negative public attitudes about women. Sex crimes touch on deep-seated beliefs and stereotypes about gender. Because the press both reflects and shapes public opinion, and most reporters and top media personnel are men, the male perspective on rape predominates and defines what counts as rape. Similarly, in the courtroom most judges and lawyers are male and the legal system treats women as men treat them. Benedict examined four sex-crime cases that figured prominently in the media in the 1980s, paying particular attention to language. Most cases were covered by men, reflecting in part the fact that men still outnumber women in media jobs. This means that one of the most violent crimes against women, rape, is reported to the public by men. This may explain why the press has been slow to change its views. Men still determine what counts as news. Women are pushed into conventional images as mothers, wives, or sensationally as crime victims. Crime stories are also popular with the public. Readers pay most attention to violent crime, and second most attention to sex crimes. As one editor put it, what sells is "sex," "scandal," "pretty girls," and "classy people doing things they aren't supposed to." The print media should be more properly thought of as advertisers because their aim is to sell newspapers and magazines. Like advertisers, they use language to construct a particular view of the world in which sex sells products, as I show in chapter 9.

Ordinary events thus receive less coverage. Women hardly figure in the news at all. When they do, they are often trivialized. World leaders who are women find that the press more often reports what they wore rather than what they were doing or what they said. This means that violent crimes against poor women, Black women, and so on are likely to be passed over in favor of more unusual and bizarre cases. The fact that the alleged rape of a young White woman in Florida by William Kennedy Smith got so much attention can be attributed to the Kennedy name. In general, crimes against non-White minorities get less coverage. Rapes by Black men against White women, however, have always received and continue to receive more attention than rapes of Black or Latina women.

The FBI released statistics in 1990 that showed that rape is the fastest rising crime in the United States. Victims are still widely blamed for rape. Because rape involves sex, there is a myth that it does not "hurt" the victim any more than ordinary sexual intercourse, and that a man who commits rape must be hot-blooded, oversexed, or even provoked into the act by seeing a woman dressed in an alluring way. This ignores the fact that rape constitutes a physical, aggressive, and often extremely violent assault, in some cases preceded or followed by mutilation and murder. Rapists are not motivated exclusively by sexual lust or desire but seek to dominate, degrade, and humiliate their victims. They are angry. Anger, in turn, is linked with the perceived power and force of female sexuality. Interviews with rapists indicate that they barely notice how their victims look.

The use of rape to dominate the victim also provides the motivation for prison rape, where new male inmates often find themselves attacked. The act of rape establishes the position of new prisoners in the jail hierarchy. A rapist owns his victim. The raped prisoners are seen as female and called *wives* or *old ladies*. Angela Davis (1981) showed that White masters systematically used rape to terrorize and humiliate Black women rather than to satisfy their sexual lust. Abolitionist discussions of the sexual exploitation of Black women seldom used the term *rape* for fear of offending their audiences, but spoke instead of *prostitution*, lending further credibility that Black women were responsible for provoking White male desire.

The sexual aspect of rape also leads to the myth that only "slutty" and "loose" women are raped. They invite it by the way they look and act. The media, public, and court scrutinize the behavior of victims. Whenever a woman "takes a risk," such as by jogging late at night, going to a bar alone, or going home with a man after a party, and a rape takes place, she is blamed. This is part of a larger belief that bad things do not happen to good people. This myth also leads women to blame themselves for attacks, or to feel that they must have done something to deserve being raped. The scenario is reminiscent of Little Red Riding Hood, who disobeys her mother's instructions not to talk to strangers or stray from the path through the woods to her grandmother's house. Instead, she stops to pick flowers and speaks to the wolf.

Rape victims are seen as dirty or spoiled, a stigma often carried on by children conceived from rape. In some cultures women who have been raped are disowned by their family for having brought shame. This is due to the fact that a woman's sexuality is still seen as male property, belonging either to her husband or father. Rape is thus conceptualized as a crime of property rather than one against persons. This is one reason why systematic and widespread rape of women is often part and parcel of war: Physical conquest of a territory is metaphorically linked with sexual conquest. What you have conquered in war, you now own. Women's bodies are among the objects the new male property owners take possession of (see the next chapter for discussion of how women's bodies are objectified).

The media have brought two recent instances of this to our attention in connection with the wars in Bosnia and Rwanda. An article in *Newsweek* (September 23, 1996, p. 49) observed that "rape wasn't just a byproduct of ethnic cleansing in Bosnia and Rwanda. It was a devastating weapon." Although the United Nations Tribunal has ruled it a war crime, no one expects many rapists to be brought to justice. The European Union estimates the number of rapes at 20,000, while the Bosnian Interior Minister says it is closer to 50,000. In both countries many of the woman abandoned their children or gave them up for adoption because the child reminded them of the violent and painful act of rape—in some cases women were gang-raped, or held as sexual slaves in refugee camps. Some saw their husbands and children murdered and could not bear the thought of giving birth to a child whose father had killed her family. Sixty percent of the 300 to 400 raped and pregnant women who were admitted to one Rwandan hospital had been mutilated by their attackers with machetes, scissors, and even acid. One Bosnian woman related how her neighbor raped her repeatedly after her town was taken by Bosnian Serb forces. He slashed her with a knife, beat her, and threatened to kill her if she told anyone.

As I noted in chapter 3, it is this metaphor connecting sexual and territorial conquest that is partly responsible for the fact that we refer to countries and landscape with feminine pronouns and imagery. Taking of the land is accompanied by taking of the women with ties to that land. It is also why in many countries a woman cannot legally charge her husband with rape; it is assumed he is entitled to her sexual services. Just as the Western powers have been slow to act in the war on Bosnia, the police have generally been reluctant to intervene in so-called "domestic violence" cases, a common form of which involves a husband physically assaulting his wife and possibly raping her. In Britain it was not until 1991 that a British Court of Appeal invalidated the "marital rape exemption law" and recognized that a rapist is a rapist regardless of his relation to the victim. The state of California made "spousal rape" a felony only in 1993.

When a woman in Oregon accused her husband of rape in 1978, the media were very much interested in the story because the case centered on women's legal rights within domestic relationships. The *Chicago Tribune* covered the story with a front-page headline: "Landmark rape case: man vs. wife." The juxtaposition of the unequal terms *man* versus *wife* drew attention to the very crux of the matter: Is a woman's sexuality her husband's property? Although the press referred to her husband with his last name, she was referred to as *Mrs. X*.

This is also why the press pays so much attention to cases where a Black man rapes a White woman. White women are the ultimate symbol of White men's status and power. Very little attention was paid to the systematic rape of Black women by White male plantation owners. For Black activist Eldridge Cleaver (1968), raping White women was "an insurrectionary act," an "act of revenge" on Whites for their racism. "It delighted me that I was defying and trampling upon the white man's law, upon his system of values, and that I was defiling his women" (p. 79). Yet the privileged position of White men has resulted in almost no attention being paid to cases where White slave masters raped Black women. The Black man was cast into the role of sex beast, whereas the Black woman was condemned as morally debased.

These popular myths about women provoking male aggression are among the most important reasons why many women do not report rape at all. The woman will be forced into the press image of the "vamp," a "bad" woman who tempted a man with her sexuality. She deserves what she gets for daring to display her sexuality. In some cases where the crime is particularly violent, such as gang rape, rape accompanied by substantial beating, disfiguration, or even murder, use of a weapon, or, notably, where the victim is White and the rapist Black, the woman can be cast into an opposite role, that of the "virgin." Thus, "decent" women can be raped too, even if they happen to be in the wrong place at the wrong time through no fault of their own. In such cases, the media reworks a kind of "Beauty and the Beast" scenario in which the rapist is portrayed as a depraved and perverted monster who damaged the reputation of a good woman. Extreme battering is also important evidence of physical coercion and struggle. In order to be a credible victim, a woman has to be able to demonstrate that she resisted. This was probably what saved the investment banker who was savagely beaten and gang-raped in 1989 from being victimized by the press for tempting fate by daring to jog at night in New York's Central Park. She was portrayed in the press as an innocent victim and not described in terms of her sexual appeal. Although she was still called a "girl," "attractive," and "bright," she was also turned into a heroine.

Whether a woman gets cast as a virgin or a vamp depends on all these factors as well as others, such as whether she is young, knows her assailant, is of a lower social class or different ethnic group from her assailant, and so on. These images of raped women are in line with more general stereotypical condescending and infantilizing images of women found elsewhere in media, particularly advertising (see chap. 9), where women are more often than not sex objects or "glamour girls." When women who took part in the Gulf War in 1991 were shown in the newspapers and on television, they were hardly ever shown performing their duties or holding weapons. They were almost always portrayed as mothers.

The myths about women and rape are supported by existing gender stereotypes in our culture as well as by gender bias in language. Women are already categorized into "good girls" and "bad girls." I showed in chapter 4 that there are more positive words for men than women, and more words for women have sexual overtones than words for men. Moreover, there are many more words for a sexually promiscuous female than there are for a male. According to the double standard, a man who is popular with women is admired—he is a "ladies' man"—but a woman popular with men is a "slut" or a "prostitute" (and not a "gentlemen's woman," which suggests a high-class prostitute or mistress). Because the press generally describes women and their physical appearance in greater detail than it does men, reporters single out the victim for attention by their choice of words to describe her.

Jennifer Levin, raped and murdered in 1986, was "tall," "beautiful," "bright," and "bubbly," a "little girl" rather than a young woman. She was called "Jenny," whereas her murderer was referred to by his last name. When the press revealed the name of the woman who accused William Kennedy Smith of rape in 1991, one newspaper carried the headline "Kennedy Rape Gal Exposed." Here the informality and colloquial nature of the term *gal* to refer to the victim attempts to diminish the alleged crime and cast the woman reporting it into the role of someone not to be taken seriously, either as a flirt who got what she deserved or someone who was lying. Contrast the communicative effect of substituting *lady* or *woman* for *gal*. The words commonly describing women in rape reports, such as *pretty*, *pert*, *prudish*, *hysterical*, *vivacious*, and *flirtatious*, would never or seldom be used to describe men. As I showed in chapter 4, these words are already charged because of their stereotypically female collocations. The press draws attention to the sexual attractiveness of the victim, and sometimes even to the good looks of a female detective or policewoman on the case. Women are also defined in terms of their relations to men rather than as individuals. Males are never called *coeds* if they are students or *divorcés* if they are divorced. Male crime victims are almost never called *boys* (unless they were Black), and only rarely *bachelors*, if unmarried. Middle-aged women were called *spinsters*. The *Boston Globe* described a woman who was gang-raped in a bar in Massachusetts in 1983 as "bubbly," "hysterical," and "an unwed mother of two."

Interestingly, in the much-sensationalized rape of a White woman by a Black man in the 1950s, *Time* magazine talked about the man in the same terms as the press spoke about women. He was referred to by his first name, "Willie." The victim was portrayed as "Mrs. Hawkins," emphasizing her subordinate but respectable status as a married woman, property of White Mr. Hawkins. It is also instructive, however, that nowadays the press does not routinely refer to Blacks with demeaning labels such as "boy" or in an insulting way, but it still treats women in an unflattering way. In the case of the Oregon woman who accused her husband of rape, a local newspaper reported after the trial that resulted in his acquittal that the husband had been lucky. Had be been convicted and sent to prison, he "surely would have suffered the humiliation of other prisoners pointing at him and teasing: 'He raped his wife; he raped his wife, the sissy . . .' "

As I have shown, a woman's testimony in court is also crucial in the image the press projects of her. For many women giving evidence in court is a terrifying and humiliating experience. The woman is on trial as much as, if not even more than, the rapist. Moreover, she is on trial according to patriarchal ideas about how women should behave as legitimate victims. A woman has to describe in detail what was done to her and to answer many questions about her previous sexual history. If a victim is calm in court, she is seen as not having suffered enough. She is not a genuine victim. On the other hand, if she is sobbing and frightened, she is "hysterical" and therefore her testimony unreliable. If possible, the defense tries to discredit her testimony by casting a shadow on her reputation as a "decent" woman.

In one trial the defense attorney commented on the fact that the woman who had been raped was wearing a T-shirt with the words "Don't touch" on it. In his closing arguments he explicitly linked this behavior with indecency when he said, "No decent young woman is going to walk around with that kind of thing emblazoned across their breast." Here we have another example of how without saying anything, a woman is presumed to have communicated her sexual availability through her choice of clothing. Sexual coercion then occurs not against her will, but as a response to her clothing and behavior (see chap. 7).

The press tried to portray the woman who was gang raped in a bar as a bad mother and a slut because she had left her children at home in bed while she went out to the bar for cigarettes. Despite the fact that her boyfriend was at home, she was cast into the role of an unwed mother, a woman who would abandon her children. The assumption here seems to be that a woman who is not a good mother has no real womanhood to be violated, just as a woman who would solicit sex by wearing provocative clothing loses credibility as a decent woman. By appearing to initiate the sexual encounter, a right many men still reserve for themselves, a woman is presumed guilty on two counts: She gets what she deserves because she has asked for it and she does not behave as a proper woman should. In a paradoxical role reversal, the woman is cast as the aggressor, and the man as the one who simply complies by following his natural responses.

Various newspaper stories said that the rape would not have happened if she had stayed home with her children where she belonged. Despite the fact that the men were convicted, one local woman explicitly blamed her by saying, "I'm also a woman but you don't see me getting raped. They did nothing to her. Her rights are to be home with her two kids and to be a good mother. A Portuguese woman should be at home with her kids and that's it." Here again we see the larger myth evoked of how bad things don't happen to good people. Yet even "good women" at home are victims of violent crime. In fact, the U.S. Surgeon General observed in 1991 that "the home is actually a more dangerous place for American women than the city streets." This is due to domestic violence (see Coontz, 1992, p. 290). The special label *domestic violence*, however, protects those who commit such crimes more vigorously than if the same crime had taken place in the public domain between unknown persons.

Meanwhile, there were stories in the press portraying the accused men sympathetically. After the men were sentenced, the question of deportation was brought up because not all of them were U.S. citizens. One story focused on one of the men about whom his lawyer had said that he was the "father of a U.S. citizen." The child in question was actually his illegitimate son, born to him and a woman to whom he was not married. Although the press made much of the victim's status as "unwed mother" and used it as a synonym for "bad mother," the fact that one of the rapists was an "unwed father" was put in a positive light by an effort to depict him as a "family man" and good citizen (see chap. 4 for a discussion of the asymmetries between the terms *mother* and *father*). Her sexuality was a liability, while his became an achievement. Although the press wrote about the possibility of his deportation, it virtually ignored the fact that the victim had fled the town three days after the trial because she was hounded by threats to her home and family.

In another case, where the victim was obviously pregnant and the defendant not the father, the woman's status as an unmarried mother was made prominent through the defense attorney's use of the address term *Miss*. This was done despite the fact that during pretrial motions it had been agreed that the defense was not allowed to broach the subject of her marital status. Here the address term functioned as a convenient and acceptable symbol to mark the woman in a way that would not have been possible if the defendant had been a man (see chap. 5 for discussion of the titles *Miss* and *Mrs.*).

The women's movement has tried to inform the public about the violence against women that lies at the heart of rape. Rape is not about sex, and a woman would no more "ask for it" than she would for murder. Some such as Susan Brownmiller (1975) draw an analogy between rape and the lynching of Blacks as punishment for being uppity and failing to recognize one's place. A woman who disregards her place, who dares to leave her home and children where she belongs, who flaunts her sexual freedom as an unwed mother, deserves punishment.

A study of male and female reactions to Ernest Hemingway's (1968) short story "Up in Michigan" provides further support for men's and women's differing interpretations of rape. In the story a woman who works in a boardinghouse is approached by one of the men who takes his meals there. Coming home from a deer-hunting expedition one night, he drinks a lot of whiskey and approaches her. Although she has admired him from afar and is pleased to have him paying attention to her, his advances become too insistent and she is unable to stop him. She tells him "no," but he doesn't listen. Students were asked to write journal entries from the point of view of the female character. None of the 44 males wrote journal entries that in any way conveyed the sense of being overpowered or raped. All of them ignored the fact that she had said "no" when he began to put his hand up her leg. Many said that she didn't like it but had asked for it. The women, however, wrote most often about being overpowered and hurt.

In fact, however, the force of the woman's "no" is undermined in the story itself, because Hemingway wrote, "She was frightened but she wanted it. She had to have it but it frightened her" (1968, p. 82). This reinforces what young men have been brought up to believe: that women say no even when they really mean yes, and that women like rough sex. A similar example can be found in Albert Wendt's (1978) novel *Leaves of the Banyan Tree* in which a man and woman have been having an illicit love affair. On the occasion of what is to be their last meeting when she tells him the affair is over, he rapes her violently and repeatedly. Then the narrator writes that the woman "gasped when he turned her over on to her belly, knowing this was the final humiliation she had always feared but wanted. The pain was excruciating" (1978, p. 147). Nevertheless, he also tells us that she has two orgasms while undergoing this painful assault.

In today's terms what happened to these women would probably be described as "date rape." As is the case with sexual harassment, this term is interpreted in different ways and has become politicized in the context of the women's movement. For some men both are creations of the feminist imagination. Thus, men can challenge or deny their existence and continue to subvert women's interpretations and meanings (see further in chap. 10).

The term *date rape* arose out of women's concerns to expand the notion of sexual assault and rape so that mutual consent would become the criterion for deciding whether sexual intercourse is rape or nonrape. However, if a woman's no is routinely interpreted as yes by men, how is it possible to define mutual consent? In an article in which he attempted to demolish the notion of date rape as a form of "political correctness," John Taylor (1991) complained that feminists were stretching the word *rape* to encompass any type of sexual interaction. He quoted extensively from an article by journalist Stephanie Gutman of *Reason* magazine, who said that there was a significant increase in rape on college campuses. In Taylor's view, the reason why statistics on rape showed an increase was due to the fact that "ordinary bungled sex—the kind you regret in the morning or even during—is being classified as rape" (p. 39). Taylor went on to link women's

CHAPTER 8

attention to date rape with "hysteria" and all the negative stereotypes associated with it.

As for the woman who says no and has her denial transformed into assent, the media portray women's resistance to sexism and sexist practices as divisive, and even discriminatory against men. Women who publicize date rape are accused of stirring up trouble where none exists, or creating friction between men and women. Men like Taylor confuse the issue by trying to redefine *date rape* as "bungled sex" (see Ehrlich & King, 1994, 1996, for discussion).

Another gender difference is at work here too, namely, the assumption that because women are more emotional, emotions are women's work, a form of social labor. Like all subordinate groups, women are much better at "reading" men than men are at reading women. The onus is always on those with less power to be more familiar with the ways of the more powerful, an extra burden they bear. Similarly, women have been expected to learn men's language, to become bilingual, as I pointed out in chapters 1 and 6. Women have long been trained to anticipate male needs, and to keep male sexuality in check. A man will go as far as a woman will let him. As I showed in the last chapter, girls have learned at school they are not allowed to say "yes" unless they want to risk their reputations. A fundamental issue in sexual harassment cases is men's denial of responsibility to read and understand the signals women send out. Although some men are genuinely confused about what is acceptable behavior, others continue to assume that anything they can get away with goes and to ignore women when they say no.

As further evidence of fundamental differences in the way in which men and women talk about the role of force and violence in sexual experience, we can consider Deborah Cameron's (1992b) study of the terms for penis used by a male and female group of American college students between the ages of 18 and 21 years. A male group of four roommates (all White middle-class) produced 144 terms in 30 minutes, whereas the female group, consisting of eight White middle-class women in the same dormitory, produced only 50. The men's terms were more easily classified into semantic categories than the women's, and some categories used in male classification schemas were not used by the women.

The men's terms fell into five semantic groupings indicative of how men view the penis metaphorically: personal names, animal names, tools, weapons, and food. The personification metaphor suggests that the penis leads a life of its own. It has been popularized in Britain in the form of the *Wicked Willie* books, where Willie is referred to as "man's best friend." Other names were in some cases titles, such as *the mayor, judge, his Excellency, The Hulk,* and *Mac the Knife,* whereas others were more ordinary everyday names such as *Peter, Dick, John Thomas,* and so on.

The second category of animal names included *snake*, *King Kong* (which could also be considered a title), and others. This metaphor suggests that men's sexual desires are like animal desires, powerful and uncontrollable. The tool metaphor emphasizes the active role of the penis in intercourse as well as the urinary function, for example, *tool*, *pipe*, *hose*, *drill*, and others. The category of weapons links sex with violence, power, and force, as in *squirt gun*, *meatspear*, and *sword*. The use of food terms such as *wienie*, *whopper*, and *noodle* links sex with eating, suggesting oral intercourse. Most of the male terms are positively valued, with the exception of *wienie* and *noodle*, which could be considered insults. All but 20 of the men's terms fit into these categories. A few, such as *wife's best friend*, made reference to women.

The women's terms showed some overlap, but not only were they much fewer in number (only about one third as many as the men), they were also less clearly definable in terms of categories. Like the men, the women listed names such as *John Thomas*, *Peter*, and *Dick*, but no chiefs, excellencies, and no names of characters or animals of heroic or mythic status. There were only two animal references: *visions of horses* and *animal length*. There were only three terms relating to weaponry and war.

Strikingly, the categories that did not appear at all or were infrequent were those that feminists critical of male sexual aggression would indict most severely, such as authority symbols, beasts, tools, and weapons. If we analyze the metaphors more closely, we can see that their origin lies partly in biology and partly in culture. Some of the categories used by the men have a physiological basis. Male erections are uncontrollable, and the nature of male orgasm and penetration creates imagery associated with hoses, tools, wild animals, and so on. However, the war metaphors and mythic names are culturally derived from a male view of sex as conquest and sport, the expression of sexual desire as violence, and an image of masculinity founded on dominance over women. It would be interesting to repeat Cameron's experiment cross-culturally to see how much the content of male sexuality and its connections to aggression vary.

MISOGYNY, MURDER, AND WOMANSLAUGHTER

From a linguistic point of view it is ironic that many cases of husbands murdering their wives and sexual killings of girls and women are classified as *manslaughter*. Yet this linguistic irony should not disguise the fact that from a legal perspective manslaughter counts as a lesser crime, a killing that occurs accidentally, as a result of provocation, or under circumstances when the murderer can be shown to have diminished responsibility for the crime, usually by virtue of mental abnormality. In their study of sexual murder,

Deborah Cameron and Elizabeth Frazer (1987) referred to cases in England and Wales where husbands successfully claimed provocation after killing wives who had allegedly nagged, been unfaithful, or been unorthodox in sexual behavior.

As with rape, crime reporting is very uneven and not comparable across countries, making large-scale comparisons difficult, particularly outside North America, Western Europe, Australia, New Zealand, and South Africa. Even more disturbing is the fact that statistics often obscure gender patterns by failing to report the relationship between murderers and their victims. There are no statistics in England and Wales, for instance, to reveal how many women are killed by men, even though figures are available on sex of offender and sex of victim. Gender-neutral category labels such as *spouse* and *parent* hide gender differences in marital and family killings. In this way police, criminologists, and the media can ignore the crime of husbands killing wives under the generic heading of "domestic crime."

Official statistics in England and Wales conceal the fact that in those two countries (unlike in the United States) murder is overwhelmingly a domestic crime, with 70% of the victims female: Nearly half are women killed by their husbands and a quarter killed by lovers or other male relations. Yet atypical cases in which women commit murder, such as the South Carolina woman, Susan Smith, who killed her children, receive a disproportional amount of media attention compared to the much larger number of women who are victims, often of husbands and lovers. The media also enacts a double standard when it frames women who kill as "sadists" or "bad mothers."

Likewise, the legal systems of many countries enact a sexual double standard, either explicitly or implicitly in their different treatment of male and female killings. Late 18th-century English law, for example, classified the crime of murdering one's husband as "petty treason," for which the penalty was burning at the stake. It was legal until recently in Italy for a husband to kill his wife and lover if he found them together.

In their study Cameron and Frazer defined sexual murder not simply as the killing of women, but as killings where the victim was a sexual object for the killer. Even in cases where a woman attacked a man and mutilated his genitals, as in the sensationalized Bobbitt case, in which a wife cut off her husband's penis with a kitchen knife, women's motives are different from men's. Women acted out of jealousy or revenge against specific individuals rather than for sexual gratification.

One prominent theory about the motives of sexual murderers is that they act out of gross hatred against their desired sexual object, and ultimately against their mothers. This explanation is grounded in theories of sexual identity I discussed in chapter 2, where boys must sever their original identification with their mothers in order to become men. Because they feel rage at the loss of this pleasurable state and fear that they will never accomplish separation, they seek revenge on the mother for putting them in this situation. This may be one reason why so many sex murderers mutilate the breasts and genitalia of their victims.

The hallmark of Jack the Ripper, for instance, whose identity was never established, was extensive mutilation of the bodies of his victims, who were women living in poverty and engaged in prostitution. In a letter to the police he described himself as being "down on whores." Similarly, Peter Sutcliffe, the Yorkshire Ripper, who between 1975 and 1981 killed 13 women, most of them prostitutes, said about his murders and mutilation of the women that he was just "cleaning up the streets." At Sutcliffe's trial lawyers presented two competing images, of Sutcliffe as deviant and Sutcliffe as hero. The prosecution argued that Sutcliffe was a sexual sadist who killed for his own pleasure, whereas the defense claimed the killings were not sexual, but part of a moral crusade prompted by God telling Sutcliffe to rid the world of prostitutes. The street-cleaning defense denied a sexual motive and significance behind the murders, despite the fact that Sutcliffe raped one victim as she died and mutilated the genitalia of others. The hatred-for-prostitutes explanation also turned the spotlight on the victims and the morality of their behavior. It also overlooked the fact that once Sutcliffe murdered a "respectable" young woman, police and public concern escalated dramatically.

As Cameron and Frazer (1987, p. 106) pointed out, however, we don't have to assume that men hate women because women remind them of their mothers. It would be equally true to say that men learn to hate their mothers because their mothers are women and powerless Others. In the case of the Sutcliffe murders, Cameron and Frazer wrote that the prostitute functions as an archetype representing the sexual aspect of all women. The prostitute thus evokes the ambivalent feelings we have learned about sexuality, the pleasure and danger, desire and disgust of sex. Tim Beneke (1982, p. 16) went so far as to say that "every man who grows up in America and learns American English learns all too much to think like a rapist, to structure his experience of women and sex in terms of status, hostility, control, and dominance." As I show in the next chapter, the female figure has in general been portrayed as an object of contempt at the same time as she is an object of desire. In chapter 2, I discussed how this view of women and the equation of sexuality with sin provides the cornerstone for Judeo-Christian tradition and Western intellectual disciplines of philosophy, psychology, and so forth.

Other factors are relevant to the Sutcliffe case, such as Sutcliffe's upbringing in a working-class community, which valued an exaggerated form of masculinity of the type Beneke wrote about—in Sutcliffe's case, one based on petty crime, casual sex, hard drinking, fighting, and body building. Within this milieu Sutcliffe's father described him as a "right mother's boy from the word go" (Cameron & Frazer, 1987, p. 137). Like the fraternity brothers Sanday investigated, Sutcliffe appears to have suffered from an extreme form of anxiety about his masculinity, which led to hatred of women in general.

It is in the cultural construction of masculinity that Cameron and Frazer found the answer to the question of why only men are sex murderers. Because the male sees himself as engaged in a struggle to master and subdue his object, whether nature, knowledge, or woman, and to act upon it, his subjectivity is at the heart of his existence. Being treated as an object is a threat to the male sense of self in a way it can never be a threat to females, whose subjectivity has constantly been negated and never been supported publicly. In the final analysis, murder is the ultimate negation of a person's autonomy, right to exist, and sense of self. To turn others into objects is to kill them, to silence them forever. In the next chapter I examine the way in which advertising is still killing us softly, by turning female sexuality and female bodies into objects.

EXERCISES AND DISCUSSION QUESTIONS

1. Try repeating the experiment done by Blumenthal and her colleagues with a group of males and females by making a list of actions (including words such as *rape* and *date rape*) and asking them to classify them into violent and nonviolent.

2. Make a list of the essential features you use in defining some key words such as *jealousy*, *sexual harassment*, and a few others of your own choosing. Compare your list with one produced by someone of the opposite sex to see if there are any differences.

3. Seven-year-old Cheltzie Heintz made world headlines when she became the youngest child ever to bring a charge of sexual harassment to the U.S. Office of Civil Rights. Her mother charged the school district with failing to stop sexual harassment on the school bus when 6- and 9-year-old boys called her daughter a "bitch" and told her and other girls they had "stinky vaginas." One day a first-grade boy chased her and a girl friend off the bus in tears as he shouted sexual names at them. In 1996 when a 6-year-old school boy kissed a female classmate and was charged with sexual harassment, the media sensationalized that case too. Is age a factor in deciding whether sexual harassment has occurred? Do children have to know the meanings of the term *sexual harassment* before they can be charged with it? Is there a distinction between teasing or flirting of a sexual nature and sexual harassment, or between bad language, name calling, and sexual harassment? Are issues concerning freedom of speech involved in such cases?

4. Examine media reports involving cases of rape, domestic violence, and sexual harassment. In what way do the reporters use language to influence how we think about the persons involved? Include in your discussion the ways in which the persons are referred to and described, as well as the offenses themselves. If you have access to a corpus of texts you can also look at the collocations of these terms.

ANNOTATED BIBLIOGRAPHY AND SUGGESTIONS FOR FURTHER READING

The study of competing definitions of violence was done by M. D. Blumenthal and her colleagues (1972). I have altered somewhat the transcription of the trial scenes from Gregory Matoesian's (1993) book. Readers should consult his book for a more detailed analysis, as well as the work of Jill Radford and Diana Russell (1992), and of Robin Warshaw (1988). Susan Brownmiller (1975) viewed the story of Little Red Riding Hood as a parable of rape (see also Jack Zipes's, 1986b, analysis of different versions of the tale and their accompanying illustrations). Judith Kleinfeld's article (1995) discusses the case of Cheltzie Heintz. Marilyn Strathern's book (1988) provides an analysis of gender relations in Papua New Guinean cultures. Media coverage of some of the rape cases discussed here can be found in Mike Royko's article in *The Oregonian* (January 17, 1979), the *Standard-Times* (March 24, 1984), John Taylor's article in *New York* (January 21, 1991), and *Time* (May 23, 1959), and *Newsweek* (1996). Julian Dibbell (1993) and Susan Herring (1996a) discuss the case of virtual rape on the Internet.

9

Advertising Gender

It seems that man has always seen the "sense" in advertising his goods. (from a teaching kit designed to introduce lower secondary-school, that is, junior-high-school, students to the topic of advertising, 1978)

Advertising is one of the most important areas of public life in which gender is displayed in images as well as in language. Every day goods change hands, both as commodities and ideas. As suggested in the teaching kit from which I just quoted, advertisers see advertising their goods as a way of making money. Although the use of "man" in this epigraph is, I believe, intended to be generic, it draws attention to the fact that men have controlled both the advertising industry and the process of manufacturing marketable products. In this world of manufacturing and advertising, women's bodies, and female sexuality in particular, become marketable commodities, even though advertisers exploit male bodies and male sexuality too. Marina Warner (1985) suggested that the reason why female bodies are chosen to convey such messages is that they are convincing. For years they have lured, delighted, and pleased. Thus, women's bodies confer the power to persuade (unlike women's talk, however, which does not). I noted in chapter 2 that until recently female voices were considered unsuitable for media broadcasting.

Advertising is indeed *big* business. In industrialized societies such as in the United States and western Europe people may be exposed to as many as 1,500 ads per day through television, radio, magazines, newspapers, and billboards. Although most of these display products the advertisers want us to buy, ads sell more than products. They sell values and concepts. They present images of sexuality, popularity, success, and normalcy. They tell us who we are and who we should be.

The language of advertising also relies heavily on special effects to catch our attention. The names given to products such as L'eggs pantyhose often introduce an innovative spelling—in this case one suggesting a French connection, thereby evoking associations between the product and designer fashions. Convinced that sex sells, advertisers often exploit metaphor, puns, double entendre, and ambiguity in their slogans. For example, an ad selling subscriptions to *Penthouse* magazine used the phrase "If you're not getting it regularly," thus suggesting a link between having sex and subscribing to the magazine. By trading on the double meaning in the phrase "getting it," the statement achieved the intended effect of linking the magazine to sexual satisfaction.

As an industry, advertising concentrates primarily on women because they are the chief consumers. In the United States, for instance, women wield 75% of the buying power. This is because most of the products sold are household and other consumer items such as clothing for which women are the major buyers. More recreational shoppers are also women. Indeed, shopping itself is seen as a feminine (and therefore also frivolous, low-status) activity because women do the shopping for the vast majority of goods such as food, clothing, and gifts. Shopping is part of "women's work." Not surprisingly, one survey revealed that 75% of all consumer advertising budgets in the United States is spent on ads that will appeal to women.

One would think this would give women considerable power to influence advertising. Yet it was the exploitation of female sexuality in advertising that prompted Betty Friedan to devote a chapter of her book, *The Feminine Mystique* (1963), to what she called the "sexual sell." Instead of finding women influencing advertisers to their own advantage, Friedan told of women's exploitation by both advertisers, as well as the manufacturers of household products and the firms who conduct marketing surveys to advise product makers and advertisers on what their potential buyers think. For a long time advertisers seemed to believe that women were more easily persuaded and influenced than men and that because they were also more moody and neurotic, emotional appeals would be most effective in getting women to buy products.

Others, such as Jean Kilbourne (1987), have shown how women themselves become products for sale in ads. Her analysis documented advertisers' use of images of women in harmful and offensive ways from the 1930s to the present. The display and positioning of male and female bodies in ads communicates messages about gender roles and relationships without saying anything, although captions and voice-overs often reinforce the visual images. In his book *Gender Advertisements* (1976), sociologist Erving Goffman demonstrated some of the ways in which differences in power and authority between men and women are represented and constructed in advertising photographs. He drew attention, for example, to the imagery of women posed as children. Similarly, Nancy Henley (1977) discussed what she called the "body politics" of space and how dominance is displayed through body language. Body language, facial expression, setting, clothing, and language combine to present an image of women as sex objects, housewives, and dependent on men.

As in other areas of public life where gender is an issue, the disciplinary perspectives brought to bear on advertising must be diverse. In the decades after Friedan's pioneering work, researchers in the fields of marketing, advertising, sociology, mass communication, women's studies, and psychiatry, among others, have produced many studies on gender stereotyping in advertising and its effects on adults and children. In this chapter I show how language and body language both consciously and unconsciously contribute to the sexual sell. I also suggest some ways in which change can be brought about by research and consumer activism.

THE WORLD OF ADVERTISING: IS THIS YOUR LIFE?

The images presented in advertising reflect a stereotypical, and one could even say mythological, world, where men (predominantly White and heterosexual) outnumber women by two to one. In a review of over 100 studies devoted to analyzing sex roles in the media, particularly in advertising, one researcher found that 90% of doctors in ads were male, whereas more than half of women were housewives. Advertising emphasizes the traditional view that women's place is in the home (most often in the kitchen and bathroom) as wife and mother. The predominant image for women portrayed outside the home was not that of the business executive or in the many other roles that women actually perform today but that of secretary or the young and beautiful fashion model who looks like a Barbie doll, combining large breasts with slim waist and hips—"beautaceous babes," as one article about supermodels called them (*Voyager*, 1995). Walsh-Childers (1996) observed that the current standard for attractiveness presents a slimmer ideal for women than for men.

Advertising's general overrepresentation of the young and beautiful ("the Pepsi generation") is a symbolic statement about the value our society attaches to youth and beauty. Older men and women tend to figure less frequently in ads, although they wander back occasionally to look for laxatives, denture cleaners, and hair dyes, to discuss the advantages of different pain relievers for arthritis, or to sell treatments for hemorrhoids. In the past decade advertisers have had to come to terms with the fact that the so-called Baby Boomer generation has become middle-aged. One recent U.S. television ad for the laxative Metamucil displayed a rather youngish, but nevertheless middle-aged, couple expressing excitement about finding the product at a lower price.

Families shown in ads are more often than not nuclear, with the wife staying home and the husband going out to work. Women are more likely to be portrayed as purchasers of household products and cosmetics, and men as buyers of large items like cars. Appliance commercials often show men demonstrating the products, or advising women to buy them, but not actually using them in normal everyday circumstances. Women are generally portrayed serving men and children food. Rarely, if ever, is the single mother displayed preparing a meal for her fatherless children. The men shown in ads appear in stereotypical roles too. Men are seldom shown at all in the kitchen or with children. When a man is portrayed as father or husband, he is more likely to be shown as stupid and emasculated. Outside the home, however, he is knowledgeable, athletic, sexy, and aggressive.

The real world is of course not like the world of advertising. Only 12% of families in the United States are of the nuclear type depicted in ads. Linguistically, advertising is a mythological world too: People talk only about products, how useful and wonderful they are, but most of all, how necessary they are, and how they will transform our lives.

Because we are bombarded with thousands of incoming stimuli per second, we cannot pay attention to all of them. To avoid a processing overload, our brains must reduce this incoming information to a manageable level by paying attention selectively only to some stimuli and ignoring others. Each of us filters out messages and images in accordance with our interests, values, and so forth. Advertisers know that their ads must grab our attention quickly and hold it, particularly if the ad is shown on television, where a typical commercial runs for only 30 seconds. Because stereotypes evoke familiar images and associations, they are very effective in communicating more than can be said or shown in a few seconds.

A good ad from an advertiser's point of view sells us on the product in more than one way. Psychological theories underlying advertising derive much from Freud's distinction between the working of the conscious and unconscious mind. Advertisers know that if they want to appeal subtly but persuasively to consumers' unconscious thought processes, they must use visual images rather than verbal messages. Psychological research shows that visual stimuli facilitate superior memory performance for processed information. This is one reason why television is a more powerful medium than radio. Television conveys more complex visual and audio information and requires less prior knowledge or education than radio or print media. It is able to sustain viewer interest and attention over an extended period of time.

Ads for tobacco products provide a good example of a case where contradictory messages are conveyed in print and visual media. Printed ads must now carry warnings about the dangers of smoking, which usually appear in a small box at the bottom of the page. The glamorous visual images and catchy slogans often say good-sounding things that don't tell us anything at all and work to mitigate the impact of the blunt written warning. Here advertisers rely on actions and images to speak louder than words.

Advertisers tailor their messages according to the medium being used and the group they are targeting. Women's magazines such as *Good House-keeping* have a larger proportion of ads for household appliances and products than do magazines such as *Cosmopolitan* and *Vogue*, which focus more on clothing and cosmetics. Even magazines such as *Working Woman* are filled with these stereotypical staples of household products, cosmetics, and such. Ads for alcohol, tobacco, cars, and electronic equipment are usually more frequent in magazines aimed primarily at a male audience, like *Playboy* and *Penthouse*. Sweetened breakfast cereals, on the other hand, are marketed almost exclusively to children through television commercials.

Although there has always been an abundance of popular women's magazines, until recently the majority of publications aimed at men were either related to specific trades and business (e.g., *The Economist* or *Forbes*), special interests (*Sports Illustrated*), or pornographic. Now, however, there is an increasing number of male lifestyle magazines such as *Loaded, Maxim, Esquire*, and so on, and cosmetic products aimed at men, which suggest that the norms of masculinity are changing. The advertising and the feature content of magazines (e.g., fashion, beauty, food, problems with the opposite sex) construct representations of femininity and masculinity for their readers.

MARKETING FEMININE GENDER

Advertisers spend large amounts of money on marketing research in order to gauge the reactions of consumers to various tactics, including their responses to the use of certain words such as *life, natural,* and *choice,* which evoke very strong positive feelings. Through using catchy slogans, advertisers can create the illusion of choice among a variety of products we don't really need.

A large proportion of the money spent on advertising is actually devoted to promoting products that respond to no real need. Hence, need has to be created by manipulating the consumer's desire, along with convincing reasons to choose one product among several competing ones that may be more or less identical. The more mundane the product, such as toilet tissue or coffee, and the more choices available, the harder advertisers must work to persuade us to buy a particular brand name. Although items like cars are sold primarily on the basis of how they look, other products such as perfume, cigarettes, and deodorants have little or no intrinsic visual appeal. Simply showing or demonstrating the product does little to promote it. This is also true for products such as cosmetics that satisfy no material needs. If consumption were motivated purely by material necessity, no one would buy eyeliner or nail polish.

Where advertisers cannot sell the product by appealing to our material needs, they appeal to our social needs by turning the product into a symbol. Through displaying their product in attractive surroundings and in sexually provocative ways, advertisers delude us into thinking that by purchasing the right products we can buy the very things that money cannot buy— youth, beauty, happiness, loving relationships with family, partners, and so forth. Different brand names become symbolic of different lifestyles and aspirations of the groups we belong to or wish we belonged to. Advertisers want us to attach the desired identity to a specific commodity so that our longing for a particular identity is transformed into a need for a product.

As a good example of advertising tactics used to sell products for which there is no real need, we can look at ads for cosmetics, which typically present the ideal female beauty as someone inhuman in her flawlessness. Here the ideology of the dominant discourse about what women *should* look like is at odds with the reality that few of us have perfect bodies. Thus, the highly desirable so-called "natural" look shown in the ads can only be created artificially by buying the products. Ads encourage us to "improve ourselves." In everyday language we think of natural as what is normal and not artificial. Something unnatural is abnormal. Through slogans and brand names using the word *natural*, advertisers have transformed its meaning to "artificial." In an ad for Formfit Rogers bras with a caption that said "The natural look is busting out all over," the double meaning of *bust* is displayed in the visual image of three women wearing only underwear. Clairol markets a brand of hair coloring called "Natural Instinct." As redefined by advertisers, the "natural" look in fact rejects the actual appearance of women's bodies.

Women have to disguise themselves and spend a lot of time, money, and effort in order to look the way the ads claim is "natural." Being born a woman is not sufficient to be a "natural" woman: One has to work at it. The paradox in the exercise of applying makeup so carefully that it does not show provides the punchline in the Blondie and Dagwood comic in Fig. 9.1. The same sentiment underlies a once popular feminist poster that read, "If being a woman is natural, stop telling me how to do it." Likewise, an ad for Max Factor foundation showing a life-size model's face asks, "Is her skin really

FIG. 9.1. The "natural" woman. Reprinted with permission of Kings Features Syndicate.

this beautiful?" The text replies, "Not without a little help, it isn't. . . . Don't you love being a woman? Max Factor." Here the answer to the question is intended to be self-evident. By offering the product name instead of "yes" as the reply, the ad implies that wanting to be a beautiful woman is the same as putting on Max Factor makeup. Looking at the face in the ad is like looking into a mirror at a glamorous version of yourself as you would like to be. The image makes you envious of how you might look.

As I pointed out in chapters 3 and 6, woman in her natural state is wild and needs taming. Cosmetics and fashion provide endless new ways of remaking women at women's expense according to men's images of the "glamour girl." Deborah Cameron (1995) commented on the continuing popularity of the "makeover" feature in women's magazines, where an ordinary reader is transformed in Cinderella-like fashion through professional advice and the right cosmetics, hairdo, and fashions. Such "New You" features appeal to a fantasy that superficial alterations can transform a woman's personality and even her whole life. A huge variety of magazines aimed at women hold out the prospect of being a better mother, wife, lover, and so on through following the right advice and, of course, by buying the right products. In today's world, cosmetic surgery remakes the female image through breast implants, face lifts, and a variety of other procedures accurately dubbed "cosmetic." Women who do not conform to traditional definitions of femininity are branded as unnatural and abnormal.

Yet paradoxically the so-called "natural look" can actually be damaging to your skin, hair, and so on. While the logically "natural" remedy to the damage done by products would be simply to stop using them, the situation creates a market for yet more products to undo the bad effects of using too much makeup or of washing, coloring or perming your hair too frequently. The natural woman is encouraged instead to buy makeup remover, skin cleansers, and hair conditioners, and so on, to undo the damage she did in trying to transform herself artificially into a natural woman in the first place. In this way, advertisers obscure the cause of the problem at the same time as they suggest the remedy lies in treating the problem's symptoms with a new set of products.

In her study of Japanese advertising Keiko Tanaka observes how frequently the words *chiteki* ('intelligent') and *chisei* ('intelligence') appear in ads for cosmetics and clothing aimed at young women. Yves St. Laurent perfume, for instance, is marketed with the slogan "intelligence and wildness." As I said in chapter 5, collocations between the word *intelligent* and words for females are much less frequent than between *intelligent* and words for males. By collocating *intelligence* with beauty products, advertisers are suggesting that women should express their intelligence by choosing the right clothing, fashion accessories, and makeup. Thus, like naturalness, female intelligence is deemed to be superficial.

Ads turn the body into an object to package and display. These "spare parts" ads, such as the Kentucky Fried Chicken slogan, claiming it had "the best legs in town" objectify parts of the body by showing or talking about only the feet, the legs, the face, or the hands. Ads often direct readers' gaze to a woman's breasts or hips. In using body parts in this way, advertisers suggest that female bodies are collections of sexual features on display for male approval. Many shoe manufacturers display only a woman's legs and feet in their ads. An ad in *Glamour* magazine showed a woman's body from the torso down with the caption, "For feet that turn heads." Here the woman's feet turn heads, causing men to look. It is as if the woman's feet cause a reaction in men for which they are not responsible. Turning someone into a thing is dehumanizing and can lead to a justification of treating people inhumanely and violently, as I showed in the last chapter. Sexual coercion and rape become appropriate uses of an object. Once sex is commodified as a marketable product, it is but a small step to take it by force. Calling a woman "cheap" means she is too easily available. The marketing metaphor used here suggests that sex as well as women can be bought, but the more you spend, the better the product.

Contempt is the flip side of objectification of women as sex objects. As I noted in chapter 4, feminists have discussed the connection between women as sexual objects and the grammatical category of *object*. The depiction of women goes hand-in-hand with talking about them as objects, as in the ad for National Airlines from the early 1970s with the attractive female flight attendant saying "I'm Cheryl. Fly me." Flight attendants were required to wear badges saying "Fly me" and "We make you feel good all over." Although members of NOW (National Organization of Women) as well as flight attendant unions protested and the ads disappeared, only a few years later, Continental Airlines promoted its services with the "spare part" slogan "We really move our tail for you."

Singapore Airlines, evidently unaware of or unconcerned with the sexism in such ads, came out with an ad in the early 1980s in which a female flight attendant was shown reclining in exotic surroundings as she replied to a letter poem she has received from an infatuated passenger praising her as a "gentle hostess in your sarong kebaya you care for me as only you know how . . . Singapore girl you're a great way to fly." The reader is supposed to think of beautiful women as part of Singapore Airlines "inflight service even other airlines talk about." In another of their ads, a prominent picture of a cocktail has figures of two naked women silhouetted into the ice cubes. What such ads attempt to do by innuendo, other magazines aimed at men, such as those concerned with typical male interests in motorbikes or trucks, do more blatantly with nude or near-nude models.

Sometimes it can be difficult to figure out *what* the product is because the ad puts more emphasis on the values and lifestyle associated with it and may not actually identify the product by brand name. A leading luggage manufacturer alluded to the possibility of a weekend getaway involving a sexual encounter between a man and a woman who uses a particular brand of luggage. The text coyly asks "What turns heads, makes friends easily & often gets carried away?" Although the answer is "A bag named X ... ," the absence of the brand name and the prominence given to a couple admiring one another suggest the equally possible answer that it is the woman who turns heads and is an easy pick-up waiting for a man to carry her (and her suitcase) away. The ad shows a female figure in full and only the man's head protrudes from a window. The grammatical form of the slogan is a question requiring the viewer to name an object. I have used X instead of the name the advertisers give the bag in order not to give readers any clues to the manufacturer's identity. I have also decided not to show the ad. When contacted by the publisher for permission to reprint the ad here, the company granted permission on condition that it "can only be referred to in a positive manner."

In a Macy's ad for Red Door perfume products, a blonde model who appears to be wearing nothing more than a string of pearls is seated among a collection of Christmas presents in red and gold boxes. The ad urges the reader to "Have a Red Door holiday. Open it!" Here the woman is treated as a Christmas present for someone to open.

Women are made to feel disgusting if they are not ideal. If they don't conform to male ideals of beauty and femininity, they are accused of "letting themselves go." Feminine hygiene ads in particular suggest a loathing for a woman's body as it actually and naturally exists. But do women accept advertising's definitions of the ideal woman and femininity? Susan Douglas (1994) has described well how the mass media has created cultural schizophrenia in women, who simultaneously rebel and submit to prevailing images about what a desirable worthwhile woman should be. She writes of her own reactions on opening *Vogue* magazine:

> I am simultaneously infuriated and seduced, grateful to escape temporarily into a narcissistic paradise where I'm the center of the universe, outraged that completely unattainable standards of wealth and beauty exclude me and most women I know from the promised land. I adore the materialism; I despise the materialism. I yearn for self-indulgence; I think the self-indulgence is repellent. I want to look beautiful; I think wanting to look beautiful is about the most dumb-ass goal you could have. The magazine stokes my desire; the magazine triggers my bile. . . . Special K ads make most of us hide our thighs in shame. (p. 9)

These contradictory feelings about what it means to be a woman have created a cultural identity crisis and a fear of being sexually inadequate when measured against the standards set by product advertisers.

The media has drawn much attention to eating disorders, which affect women with much greater severity than they do men. Anorexia nervosa and bulimia, for example, are largely women's illnesses. Although not all women who have these disorders were ever actually overweight by medical standards, they generally say they are too heavy and are obsessed with dieting to the point of starvation. One study found that around 80% of women think they are overweight; another reported that 20% of college women have anorexia. Even pre-teen girls are preoccupied with their weight. In 1963 the popular Barbie doll ensemble called "Barbie Baby Sits" included three books, one of which was entitled *How to Lose Weight* and offered the extreme advice "Don't eat."

As Susie Orbach has pointed out, fat is a feminist issue. Women's preoccupation with their weight presupposes some standard of comparison, which is at odds with conventional medical opinion. Women are comparing themselves to fashion models and other images of women in advertising. The ideal body type presented in ads is not attainable without near starvation. Modern fashion models such as Kate Moss with her "Twiggy-like" figure are typical. Women of normal weight for their height are hardly ever chosen as fashion models and models routinely complain about how little they are able to eat and still keep their bodies small enough to hang onto their jobs. Many women wouldn't dream of going out without wearing a girdle, and it was not all that long ago that teenage girls were laced into corsets to minimize their waist size and emphasize their bust and hip curves. Nineteenth-century women even had their lowest ribs removed in order to be able to lace their corsets tighter. These and other fashions such as high-heeled shoes put unnatural stress on the spine, thighs, and pelvis and restrict women's natural movement. Women are confined in space, which in an androcentric world belongs to men.

Similarly, women are shown more than men in ads for tranquilizers and mood-altering drugs appearing in medical journals. Such bias reinforces conventional views about women as "naturally" more emotional and unstable than men (Courtney & Whipple, 1983, pp. 13–14). I observed in chapter 2 how male-biased definitions of mental health have prevailed in the medical profession. Advertisers try to boost sales by widening the indications of their drugs from mental illness to include the stress and problems of everyday life. Rather than deal with the causes of the problem, advertisers suggest that doctors recommend tranquilizers as the solution to relieving the tedium and stress of housework, or to calm a female patient disturbing her family with her neurotic behavior.

In ads, women position or move their bodies in ways that are accommodating to men or reveal their vulnerability. Adult women are sometimes presented as children or childlike, which suggests that they should stay passive, dependent, and powerless. In their equation of children with women, ads make it acceptable to look at children as sex objects too, and some come dangerously close to child pornography. Both girls and women become sex objects when women are portrayed as girls, and girls as women. Some of the ads in Revlon's "most unforgettable women" included girls of 5 to 7 years old. In his discussion of the "ritualization of subordination," Goffman (1976) shows the regularity with which men are portrayed as larger, bigger, higher or taller than women. Women are also portrayed as physically prostrating themselves before men. They are more often shown lying down on the floor on or beds or sofas, suggesting their availability as sex objects. Often their heads are lowered or tilted at an angle or their eyes downcast.

All of these postures turn up crossculturally as symbols of submission and deference to others who are more powerful either by virtue of age, sex, or social status. In Samoa, for instance, one's head cannot be higher than the chief's. In Britain, women curtsey and men bow before royalty. In Japan, bowing is governed by status hierarchies. On Pulap atoll in Chuuk State in Micronesia, junior siblings must keep themselves lower than senior siblings and avoid touching their upper bodies. Women stoop before their brothers and crawl on their knees as a sign of respect if brothers are seated. When the head or eye of a man is averted in an ad, it tends to be in relation to another man who is socially or politically superior, rather than to a woman. Women, social subordinates, and children are held by or around the shoulders in a way that precludes reciprocal shoulder-holding. Women lose control of their emotions. Often they are portrayed as if their minds were elsewhere, gazing off into space dreamily, or looking like a bashful or playful child. A woman's hands are rarely seen grasping something. They generally just touch or caress something. The different positioning of male and female bodies in advertising eroticizes sexual inequality and defines female sexuality from a male point of view.

Likewise, Nancy Henley (1995b) has observed the ways in which the use of space reflects dominance. I noted in chapter 7 how school boys tend to occupy a larger portion of the playground than girls, and how they tend to invade the girls' smaller space to disrupt their games. This is in line with Henley's finding that dominants control greater territory as well as move more freely in the territory of others. Subordinates also tend to have less personal body space and they yield space to approaching dominants. Studies show, for instance, that men had a much greater tendency to use the common armrest between airplane seats. Dominants also occupy positions associated with or controlling desired resources. The fact that women's space is smaller than men's reflects a dominance hierarchy, as does the fact that women are touched more than men (see chap. 7). Women also smile more, which is another gesture of appeasement or submission found among human as well as certain animal groups such as chimpanzees.

Ads also equate women's liberation with addiction. A good example is the ad for Virginia Slims cigarettes with the slogan "You've come a long way baby." This suggests that smoking is a symbol of women's new-found freedom. Note, however, how the use of the address term *baby* still marks even the liberated woman as subordinate and infantile. Such ads trivialize women's struggle for equality by connecting it with the right to smoke in public. What was a minor side-effect of the woman's movement becomes transformed into a major achievement and symbol of liberation. The product name is also aimed at women because Virginia Slims suggests that smoking is a way to control your weight. Another cigarette aimed at women, Capri 100's, bills itself as "the slimmest cigarette known to woman," and its Superslims Lights variety glamorizes the act of smoking with its text that reads "She's gone to Capri and she's not coming back," suggesting that smoking allows women to escape into a fantasy world. The brand name Misty similarly uses a slogan that describes its product called Misty Menthol Lights Slims as "light 'n sassy." At a time when the connections between cancer and smoking have become increasingly clear and many smokers are trying to give up the habit, the largest increase in smoking has been found among young women, strikingly so in Asia. Lung cancer is now the most common form of cancer in women.

THE SEXUAL SELL

Ads such as these demonstrate how advertising has a considerable literal and figurative investment in the appropriation and display of female bodies. They often make gratuitous use of women's bodies to get people's attention and to suggest that sexual access is the reward for buying the product. By "gratuitous," I mean that the body is displayed primarily for decorative purposes and has nothing to do with the product. It is certainly not hard to find products that are sold mainly through an appeal to female or male sexuality. Over the years, researchers have documented increasing use of women as decorations in a wide range of advertisements from beverages to airlines.

For many years Betty Friedan wrote for *McCall's* magazine and was able to observe how women were portrayed for years through the content and images of magazine advertising. She also interviewed some of the top advertising executives in the United States and was able to obtain access to marketing surveys conducted with housewives in the late 1940s and 1950s, a time when the U.S. economy was booming. She noted how one survey told advertisers they should put "the libido back into advertising" (Friedan, 1963, p. 198).

An ad for underwear showed a woman wearing only underwear standing on top of a canyon with a caption that read "Help Keep America Beautiful." A similar ad advertised swimsuits by showing a woman in a bikini on a beach with the statement "Keep our beaches beautiful." Here the ad implies that the main purpose of the product is to improve the landscape by making it more appealing to men. Other items of feminine apparel such as Hanes panty hose with its slogan "Gentlemen prefer Hanes" also send the message that men's preferences dictate women's fashion choices. The main benefit of buying the product is to give men pleasure. "Just wear a smile and a Jantzen," as one ad for women's swimwear put it.

Until recently, cars were one of the few items men tended to purchase more than women and advertisers have typically appealed to male sexuality, especially in selling sports cars. Now many car manufacturers emphasize features such as safety rather than speed in order to make the vehicles more appealing to women drivers. Examples of sexist advertising can nevertheless still be easily found. Fiat certainly misjudged the extent to which one of its recent ads in the United Kingdom would be regarded as sexist and had to withdraw its billboards, which said about one of its cars, "If it was a lady it would get its bottom pinched." Here we see again the equation between a woman and the object being marketed. In the United States, one Chevrolet dealer advertised its sporty Corvette model with the slogan "If your date's a dog, then you should get a vet" (i.e., a Corvette). The implication is that the male owner of such a car will be able to attract beautiful women. Daihatsu made an even more explicit statement to that effect in its 1996 ad that claimed of its van: "Picks up more women than a Lamborghini." The ad shows the Daihatsu van with a man in the driver's seat with his thumb up; the rest of the van is filled with women passengers.

Hyundai conceived of a campaign based on a reversal of this sex stereotyping, where two women ridicule a man getting out of a fancy sports car, but exclaim "I wonder what he's got under his hood" when a handsome man gets out of the not-very-flashy Hyundai Elantra. The creator of the ad, however, says it was borne of "desperation" because Hyundai was not known for making the "sexiest cars in the world" (Patterson, 1996, p. 92).

The complaints about the Fiat ad show that advertisers must be careful when using humor in their ads. Research shows significant differences in what men and women find amusing. As I showed in chapter 6, many women do not find the stereotypes of the zany and frazzled housewife and the liberated Supermom funny. Some studies have shown that men find sexual and hostile humor funnier than do women, who see more humor arising out of incongruous or nonsensical situations. Although no one likes to see himself or herself made fun of, research has also indicated that both males and females found funnier situations in which a woman was ridiculed (see chap. 6). Women also considered self-disparaging humor more appealing than men, though they did not like humor they considered sexist and neither did men with nontraditional attitudes (Courtney & Whipple, 1983, pp. 132–133).

Ads for perfumes, chocolate, and flowers usually rely on female sexuality. Naked bodies are often shown in ads for men's aftershave or women's perfume, and the product names are often sexually provocative too, for example, Allure (by Chanel), Escape and Obsession (by Calvin Klein), and so on. These names invoke stereotypical views of the power of female sexuality to attract men and arouse their uncontrollable sex drive. Sex appears as a natural but inevitable and irresistible force, which carries you away and sweeps you off your feet. The ads imply that men and women under the spell of sexual attraction and romance are not responsible for their actions and reactions (see chaps. 7 and 8 for discussion of these metaphors). An ad for Narcisse perfume by Chloe showed a man and a woman kissing with a caption reading, "Then I was in his arms and reality faded away." An ad for men's cologne called Gravity featured a man and woman in swimsuits embracing passionately on a rocky coast. The text says, "More than a fragrance, it's a force of nature . . . you couldn't resist it, even if you tried." An ad for a woman's perfume called Spellbound displayed only the word *Spellbound* together with a couple looking closely at each other. An ad for Aviance perfume showed a housewife greeting her husband at the door with a striptease act. The announcement that "it's going to be an Aviance night" promises a sexual adventure.

Ads for Jean Paul Gaultier cologne often show the bottle in which it is packaged. The bottle is in the shape of a woman's figure from the neck to the hips, but the head is replaced by the spray nozzle. This is also an example of the use of body parts in the objectification of women, which I referred to earlier in this chapter. In the Fidji perfume ad, a nude woman kneels on a deserted beach, oblivious to the rest of the world. One of the ads for Calvin Klein's Obsession shows a naked woman lying face down on a sofa. In Britain two of his television commercials were considered too sexually titillating and promptly banned. Yves Saint Laurent's perfume called Opium promises "sensuality to the extreme." Chanel No. 19 is "witty, confident. Devastatingly feminine." Vanilla Musk proclaims "what innocence does for sensuality."

Figure 9.2 provides an example of how colognes and aftershave lotions aimed at men also rely on sexuality, such as Raw Vanilla, which displays an embracing couple slightly more than waist deep in water. The man is bare-chested, and the text reads "In the raw vanilla . . . It's like meeting in the rainforest." The ad displays the bottle, which also features text saying that the cologne creates "pure masculinity." English Leather marketed its Musk brand of products with an illustration of a face, half-lion and half-man, together with a caption reading "the civilized way to roar." The

FIG. 9.2. Raw Vanilla men's cologne ad. Reprinted with permission from Coty, US, Inc.

aftershave, cologne, soap, and shaving cream are described as "earthy," "primitive," and "fiercely masculine." These words and images capture the metaphorical associations between men and male sexuality and powerful predatory animals, as I noted in the last chapter as well as in chapter 4.

Here we have a case where the cosmetics industry has been trying to increase sales of beauty products to men. Because the words *perfume* and *makeup* as well as the very notion of being concerned about one's appearance are associated with femininity, product names such as *aftershave* and brand names such as Brut redefine masculinity by trying to establish a connection between masculinity, wearing fragrances, and sex appeal. An ad for English Leather cologne, for instance, shows a woman saying "I want my men to wear English Leather or nothing at all."

The fashion industry also relies heavily on sexuality. Blue jeans manufacturers such as Levis have advertised their clothing by showing models putting them on and taking them off rather than simply showing them on a store rack or shelf. In one popular ad a young man enters a laundromat and strips down to his underwear. Some shocked women look on as he throws the jeans into the washing machine. Ads for Calvin Klein jeans caused controversy because they displayed partially clad teenagers of both sexes in pornographic poses. In 1980, when model Brooke Shields was 15 years old, she appeared in an ad for Klein jeans squatting on the floor with her legs spread wider than the edges of the television screen. She asked: "You know what comes between me and my Calvins?" Her reply was "nothing." A recent ad for Lee jeans showed a woman throwing dandelion seeds into her male neighbor's yard in order to see him take off his shirt to deal with the weeds that spring up. Di Carlo Couture Jeans used a provocative ad featuring a bare-chested man wearing the jeans with the button opened. He is flanked by two women, each of whom has a finger inserted in the waistband. An ad for Request Jeans pictured a woman in a bra and short skirt together with the caption "Request jeans." The ad implies that the woman is making a sexual request merely by wearing Request clothing at the same time as it treats her and the jeans as an object for men to request. Such ads reflect some of the assumptions about male and female sexuality I discussed in the previous two chapters, namely that a woman's appearance, and even her scent, send messages about her sexual availability. As another perfume ad put it, she "make[s] a statement without saying a word." A woman need not communicate her desire or her consent explicitly. Even if her words say "no," she cannot be coerced into sex against her will when her clothes say "yes." The Nuance ad with its slogan "Nuance always says yes. You can always say no" sends a similar mixed message about a verbal "no" being undermined by a nonverbal "yes." A woman in a black evening dress stands in front of a mirror apparently dressing for a date with the man who stands behind her with his hand resting on her back.

But even seemingly more mundane products such as toothpaste, fountain pens, and coffee increasingly rely on the sexual sell. An ad for Ultrabrite toothpaste told prospective buyers that "Ultrabrite gives your mouth sex appeal." A series of television commercials for Nescafe instant coffee adopted a soap opera or mini-drama format of linked episodes following the relationship of a man and woman who are neighbors in the same apartment building. In one episode, he borrows some Nescafe from her, and the implication is that this encounter of sharing Nescafe will lead to romantic involvement. The ad in Fig. 9.3 for Waterman fountain pens likewise suggests the possibility of a glamorous affair with the user of the pen. Two pens provide a black tie on a man's white dress shirt and the caption reads "Moments after making his acquaintance, she sensed this would be no ordinary affair." The slogan invites buyers to "Express Your Self." By using a Waterman pen writers can express their "own extraordinary style."

An ad with pictures of six Clairol beauty products such as curling irons, skin machine, and so on, displayed them together with a picture of a woman. The slogan read, "six ways to turn her on." An ad for a Tricity microwave oven used a slogan that said "beauty as well as brains," with the covert gender message that these two qualities are usually not found together, evoking the stereotype of the dumb blonde. No naked women are shown in either of these ads, but there are overtones of sexuality in the slogan. Similarly, Toshiba advertised one of its telephones with the slogan, "We look great topless." The telephone is shown with part of its

FIG. 9.3. Waterman fountain pen ad. Reprinted with permission of *The Gilette Company*.

cover removed so that the viewer can see the wiring inside. Again, there is no overt sexuality, but when the word *topless* is used, it is generally in reference not to machinery or appliances but with respect to women dancers or striptease artists. Advertisers expect viewers to tune into the word *topless*, thereby catching their attention to make them want to read the ad to see what is on offer. I noted in chapter 3 Toshiba's ad for laptop computer referring to the machine as "she," inviting potential buyers to "Open 'er up." This ad is in a sense the flip side of the Red Door perfume one I described earlier, where the woman is portrayed as a package to open. The Toshiba ad shows the open computer with text on the screen about "high performance motors" with two sports cars displayed on it. The accompanying text about the machine speaks about the computer as if it were a race car or space rocket when it mentions features such as the machine's "incredible speed," "computing in high gear," the "thrust of an integrated graphics accelerator," "bumper-to-bumper protection," and so on. Other computer companies appear to be relying on more overt sexuality, displaying women's bodies in a provocative way when there is no obvious rationale for their presence. The magazine ad in Fig. 9.4 for Samsung laptop computers covering two pages shows a woman in a low-cut black evening dress and high heels bending over with the computer held out for display hanging on her arm as if it were a handbag or fashion accessory. With her exaggerated smile and her hand directing our gaze to her breast, she appears to be offering her body as well as the machine. NEC has recently used a similar full-page ad with a glitzy model to promote one of its laptop computers.

Computer manufacturers are well aware that men still comprise the majority of computer users, but such ads run the risk of offending and alienating the growing number of women computer users. Why not show a woman dressed in a way appropriate for the office at her desk using the machine? Even though professional women are now being depicted in ads, they are often trivialized by appearing in outlandish fashions, which women would never wear to the office, at the same time as they are holding a briefcase. This suggests that the liberated women is also sexually available and not really serious about her career.

Although there has been much less research on male sex stereotyping and the gratuitous display of male bodies, the image of men and male sexuality in ads are exploited and distorted too. According to stereotypes about how men should behave, they should be invulnerable, in power and in control. Feminine values are not good for men; they must repress them. Kleenex advertises one of its large tissues as "man-sized." The Hewlett Packard ad for laserjet toner cartridges suggests a reversal of this stereotype with its large slogan reading "Why looks are everything: A surface observation" and a photo of a good-looking man, who is himself an ad for Lee's Hair Salon. Indeed, readers have to look below the surface to the fine print at the bottom

SAMSUNG notebooks

270

FIG. 9.4. Samsung computer ad. Reprinted with permission of the Samsung Corporation.

of the page to find out that the ad is really for the Hewlett Packard product, or at the top right-hand corner, where the brand name appears. Here the product, which is not particularly attractive or glamorous in and of itself, is portrayed only in its box, and the emphasis is on the results users are supposed to be able to achieve if they buy this brand.

As I observed earlier, cigarettes are often advertised with a "sexual sell," with different brand names marketed to men and women. "Marlboro country," for instance, is largely male terrain, as can be seen in the slogan "wherever men smoke for flavor." Marlboro smokers have a cowboy image and often appear riding horseback in western-style dress. Rothmans uses racing cars in some of its ads, while in others it uses the slogan "king-size flavor." Ads for beer, wine, and other alcoholic drinks are generally marketed by appealing to sexuality. An ad for Dewar's whiskey suggests that drinking and liking women are acquired tastes. "You thought girls were yucky once too," but a mature adult male will appreciate drinking just as he now appreciates "girls." Colt 45 malt liquor's slogan punned that the beverage had "six appeal." Iced tea makers have traded on the connection between alcohol and sexuality by packaging their drinks in bottles which look like liquor bottles.

Even ads on buses exhorting riders to make use of special commuters' park-and-ride services are permeated with sexual sell. At the time I was writing this book, I often took the morning bus to work in Oxford. On one occasion, I noticed a poster in the bus depicting a well-proportioned woman clad in a tight-fitting sleeveless red dress with red gloves up to her elbows and a red hat (a highly improbable get-up for riding a bus to begin with, especially during the winter when I first noticed the ad!). A caption in large letters urged riders to "Catch Gloria," who was later described as the bus company's new "lady chauffeur." It went on to detail her outfit as follows:

> At over 7 foot tall and dressed from head to toe in stunning scarlet, complete with long red gloves, diamanté bracelet, her height and sense of style are not the only things that will cause heads to turn around Oxford.

It was necessary to read on before finding out that Gloria Glide, "as she is affectionately known to all at Thames Transit, is not a real live person but an incredibly life-like painting." Subsequently, I saw one of the company's buses with the portrait of Gloria emblazoned on its side. The whole approach was highly reminiscent of the "Fly Me" campaign I mentioned earlier.

SELLING THE HAPPY HOMEMAKER

As I noted before, Betty Friedan was among the first to point out the important role that women played in advertising by virtue of being the main purchasers of household items. She documented a conspiracy to keep

American women in their homes as housewives in order to create and maintain a market for particular products. Obviously, if women were out at work all day, they would not have the same amount of time to devote to shopping and homemaking, even though they still did most of the housework.

Friedan reached the depressing conclusion that the only way in which the young housewife was supposed to express herself and not feel guilty about it was to buy products for the home and family. The stereotypical woman in ads is ashamed when she discovers ring around the collar or that her laundry isn't as white and bright as that of her neighbor. Her self-esteem resides in how clean her home is and how well she takes care of husband and children. As Procter and Gamble put it in an ad for dishwashing liquid: "Dishes so shiny you can see yourself in them . . . and that's a nice reflection on you." At the same time she still has to keep up her own appearance. An ad for Radox herbal bath in the United Kingdom pictured a worn-out looking woman surrounded by toys with a slogan promising her that "we could make you a joy to come home to."

The marketing surveys had tapped the secret frustrations of American housewives. If their needs could be identified and manipulated through guilt, housewives could be induced to buy more and more things, especially if they feel others are going to judge them by the appearance of their houses. This underlying psychology was made evident in a survey done in 1945 for a leading women's magazine, which analyzed women's attitudes toward electrical appliances (see Friedan, 1963, pp. 182–188 for discussion). On the basis of a national sample of 4,500 (middle-class, high-school or college-educated) married women, the surveyors divided the respondents into three categories, whose labels are highly suggestive of the thinking behind advertising campaigns: the *True Housewife*, the *Career Woman*, and the *Balanced Homemaker*. In 1945 just over half the women (51%) fitted the True Housewife type, whose major preoccupation was housekeeping. Advertisers identified this group as the largest market for appliances because housework was their justification for existence. The third type, the Balanced Homemaker, was also seen as a good target for advertising efforts. This kind of woman had some outside interests or had held a job before turning to housework. She readily accepted, even more so than the True Housewife, the help that appliances could offer. The Balanced Homemaker took pride in doing the work herself, but most crucially, had time to do it herself.

The second type, however, the Career Woman, although a minority, was on the increase and posed a threat to manufacturers. Advertisers were warned that it would be to their advantage not to let this group get any larger. These women, who were not necessarily jobholders, did not believe that a woman's place was in the home. Many in this group thought housework was a waste of time. The career or would-be career woman disliked cleaning, ironing, and so on, and was therefore less interested in new soap powders, waxes, and so on. The Career Woman preferred, if able, to hire someone else to do the work. While they bought modern appliances, Career Women were too critical, and therefore not the ideal type of customers from the marketer's point of view.

The moral of the study was quite explicit. Because the Balanced Home-maker represented the greatest future potential for marketing, it would be to the advantage of appliance manufacturers to make more and more women aware of the desirability of belonging to this group. They had to be "educated" through advertising that it was possible to have outside interests and become alert to wider intellectual influences (without becoming a Career Woman). "The art of good-homemaking should be the goal of every *normal* woman" (emphasis added; cited in Friedan, 1963, p. 184).

In later surveys, marketers no longer interviewed professional women. They were not at home anyway! The interviewees were deliberately chosen from among the new suburban housewives in the belief that it was this group who could be most easily persuaded. In particular, the advertisers recognized the need for women to feel creative and have a sense of purpose. Their problem was how to get women to achieve these things at home and not as career women at work. Their aim was to design and market products, which would all convince women they could be creative at home.

One advertiser revealed a perverted sense of logic akin to that of the Virginia Slims slogan when he explained to Friedan that in order to develop the need for new products, the industry had "to liberate women to desire these new products" (Friedan, 1963, p. 199). "Liberation," in this case, is understood as being caught up in the cycle of buying more and more products for the home. This advertiser's aim was to "help" women "re-discover" that homemaking is more "creative" than competing with men. Thus, he wanted to sell them what they "ought" to want. The big problem, as he saw it, was again one of liberation, in this case to liberate the woman not to be afraid of what was going to happen to her, if she didn't have to spend so much time cooking, cleaning, and so on. Friedan then asked him why the cake mix ad didn't tell the woman she could use the time saved to be an astronomer. He said that although advertising could make it glamorous for women to be astronomers, for example, the image of the astronomer getting her man, there was no point because if the woman was told to be an astronomer, she might go too far from the kitchen.

Similarly, Alice Courtney wrote of the reluctance of a male executive from a major detergent company to talk with her about sex stereotyping in ads for laundry products. He informed her that her views were of no interest because she was a working, professional woman. He was interested in women who did four or more washes a week and had nothing more to say to her, even after she protested that she did do that many washes weekly (Courtney & Whipple, 1983, p. 197).

One report Friedan examined warned against the tendency for some women to be too independent, make up their own minds, and not to be concerned about keeping up with the Joneses. Because yearning for new things is a major motivation for buying, advertisers must convince women that they are adding more enjoyment to their lives. One manufacturer of a cleaning device was advised that house cleaning should be fun. The appliance should make the woman feel like a professional who is an expert in determining which cleaning tools to use for which purposes in the home. The difficulty though is how to give the housewife a sense of achievement and status in tasks for which society hires the least trained individuals and pays low wages. The advertiser argued that when the woman could be persuaded to use different products for different tasks, a special cleaner for windows, walls, floors, and so on, she could be made to feel more like a skilled than unskilled laborer.

One report said that advertising must help her to justify her "menial task" by building up her role as the protector of the family, the killer of microbes and germs. Housework has to be made a matter of knowledge and skill with machinery and specialized products rather than of brawn. They had to convince women that they are participating in science by trying out a new appliance and to continually seek new developments in home technology.

Although Friedan conducted her research on marketing in the 1940s and 1950s, we need only look at television and magazines today to see that the advertisers' strategies are little changed in many respects. Marketing experts and advertisers still continue to focus on identifying groups of women whom they believe can be persuaded to buy their products. Whether housewives or employed outside the home, women are urged to save time by using packaged products such as Baxters soup, which is advertised in the United Kingdom as "the soup that mother makes," or Campbell's "Home Cookin'" line of soups. Advertising's images of the appreciative family eating the soup stay in our minds long after we have forgotten the claims made for the product, or even its brand name.

Many ads currently emphasize the modern view of the housewife as technician in charge of home and family welfare. They portray women in the role of protector. A slogan for Scott toilet paper declared that "Love is said in many ways. It's giving and accepting. It's protecting and selecting . . . knowing what's safest for those you love. Their bathroom tissue is Scott tissue always . . . Now in four colors and white." A similar motif of protection was used by the United Kingdom manufacturers of Flora margarine in an ad that asked, "Is your man a Flora man?" The accompanying text discussed how women should be concerned about their partners' health by looking after their diet (see chap. 2). There are far fewer ads in which the man is portrayed as being responsible for his wife's physical well-being, though occasionally, men are cast in the role of family protector in ads for life-insurance policies or investment products. The man protects through his money and earning power and the woman, by buying the right kind of toilet paper and cleaning products for her family. An ad for Robitussin's cough syrup says that the product is recommended by "Dr. Mom," which casts the woman in the traditional role of nurturer and the one in charge of her family's welfare.

The slogan for Jif peanut butter "Choosy mothers choose Jif" implies that if a mother does not buy this brand name, she is not a good mother because it takes as its premise that a good mother is choosy. This too is a common tactic advertisers use. The phrase *choosy mothers* is misleading because it presupposes the truth of another proposition (namely, *good mothers are choosy*), which the ad has not independently established as true.

The modern Happy Homemaker becomes the proud domestic engineer if she buys a Zanussi appliance. The company advertised its washing machines in the United Kingdom in the 1980s as "the appliance of science." In the United States, a contemporary television commercial for Whirlpool appliances portrays a harried and bewildered woman at home trying to do a number of things at once. The male voiceover speaks to her asking if she wishes there were more than one of her so that she could more easily do the number of things that need to be done at the same time. Then the voice tells her authoritatively, "Together you and Whirlpool know how to run a home," as the camera spotlights her Whirlpool refrigerator, washer, and dryer. Here we have another contradiction between the portrayal of a woman as an expert in household affairs, but in need of male advice and technical assistance from appliances. She cannot do the job by herself. Note too, that the ad doesn't suggest another way out of her dilemma—namely, that her husband should help with the chores.

Some ads for cleaning products carry stereotypical male images and names such as Brawny brand paper towels advertised with a lumberjack on its wrapper as "the big, tough towel." Other household products, such as Mr. Clean, also invoke the idea that the work involved in cleaning a house is of such proportions that it requires heavy-duty cleaning products, and hence the image of a tough man, even though it is women who buy the products and do most of the work involved in cleaning the house. Other products like Dove dishwashing liquid emphasize instead the stereotypical image of women as soft and gentle, by implying that the product is easy on the hands and skin.

Appliance ads such as those used by Whirlpool are in tune with the many magazines and advice books aimed at "working mothers" and "supermoms" suggesting ways of coping with pressure and organizing time when getting everything done is a complex juggling act. Here the liberated woman in the guise of working mother is no less stereotypical than the stay-at-home housewife she replaces. Just as tranquilizers treat symptoms rather than underlying causes of distress, ads for pain-relieving medications offer no solutions to the problems women face in the workplace. An ad for a headache remedy shows a woman at the office sitting at a desk. The text tells her that "Life seems tougher when you're raising a family and working, too. Sometimes the pressure can give you a terrible headache."

Science, however, should not relieve women of too much of the drudg-ery—at least from the advertiser's point of view. It must concentrate instead on creating an illusion of achievement. This conclusion was demonstrated in one study discussed by Friedan (1963, pp. 190–191) where women were asked to choose among four imaginary methods of cleaning. The first was completely automatic and operated continuously like a heating system. The second required pressing a button to start it. The third was portable and had to be carried to a particular spot and pointed at it in order for it to work. The fourth was a brand-new device for sweeping dirt away. Most women surveyed preferred the fourth. The marketers took this to be an indication that women wanted to be participants, not button pushers.

This same study also revealed that one modern cleaning device actually made housekeeping more difficult. Once a woman got the appliance going, she felt compelled to do cleaning that wasn't really necessary. Miele ad-vertises its vacuum cleaners in the United Kingdom as "too good to put away." It advises the prospective buyer that when you use it you "could get carried away" with its "vacuum cleaner technology." "You'll want to try all the attachments to see how they work with the ceramic tiles in the hall, the velvet curtains in the bedroom," in addition to simply cleaning the floor. The endless nature of housework is of course a major advantage for the advertiser and seller. The house is never clean enough and once it is clean, it doesn't stay that way for very long. As long as a woman's work is never done, there will always be a market for new products.

Paradoxically, some women seemed to find escape from their endless fate by accepting it. One woman told Friedan (1963, p. 192): "I don't like housework at all. I'm a lousy houseworker. But once in a while I get really pepped up and I'll really go to town. . . . When I have some new cleaning material—like when Glass Wax first came out or those silicone furniture polishes—I got a real kick out of it, and I went through the house shining everything. I like to see the things shine. I feel so good when I see the bathroom just glistening." The marketers recognized this and constantly bombard the market with new products, which they hope women will try just to alleviate the sameness of doing boring household tasks over and over. Yet, studies show that the lack of realism in ads such as the Miele one praising the rewards and delights of housework is irritating to con-sumers (Courtney & Whipple, 1983, p. 199).

SELLING THE CAREER WOMAN
AND THE HOUSEHUSBAND

As the number of Career Women grows, advertisers also realize they cannot afford to neglect this category of consumers, not least because such women bring increased buying power to families with their earnings. Yet, at the same time, studies show that women, with their own financial resources, are also among the most resistant to being persuaded to buy products through advertising. Still, working outside the home does not free a woman from housework, caring for children, and shopping, even if employment does affect her choice of products and the time she spends on household matters. Marketing research shows that both the Career Woman and the Housewife value variety in meals as well as low prices, but the Career Woman is more likely to value ease of preparation and cleaning. The Career Woman is also more likely to buy and use a microwave oven and meals prepared in advance that can be microwaved. This presents advertisers with a dilemma—how to make the same product appeal to groups of women with different goals, values, and resources? Commercials showing women buying investment products or cars, or using American Express cards appeal more to women with careers than to women at home with little or no income of their own. After years of aiming its ads at men urging them to buy jewelry as gifts for wives and girlfriends, a Diamond Club International advertising campaign in 1996 targeted instead high-earning women with its slogan, "Who needs a husband when you can buy yourself two studs for the price of one?" These are part of a new wave of reverse stereotyping such as the jeans ads I previously mentioned where men are on display for female gaze and men become sex objects. In another such example, three women take their Diet Coke break at precisely the moment a good-looking construction worker takes off his shirt.

Rena Bartos's book on the new woman consumer indicates that advertisers still have a lot to learn about women's changing lifestyles and how they affect purchasing patterns. In her study of "stay-at-home" housewives, "plan-to-work" housewives, "just a job" working women, and "career-oriented" women, she found they all reacted most negatively to traditional images of women in advertising. Whether they lived conventional lives as housewives or as career women, they expressed a preference for ads reflecting a diversity of roles for women. The commercials they disliked most were those implying that laundry, cooking, and housework were women's work, or that men or women were incompetent, childish, or stupid, or those that treated women as sex objects. All women responded most negatively to commercials judged as sexist in tone, for example, because they used terms such as *girl* or referred to women in a disparaging way. Interestingly, the most negative reactions to sexy commercials came from women who stayed at home. Women also objected to commercials dealing with women's intimate personal care and hygiene products. Similar studies in Britain revealed that modern portrayals of women resulted in substantially higher effectiveness of the ads as measured in terms of intention to buy the product (Courtney & Whipple, 1983, p. 171).

Much less research has been done on men's shopping activities, partly because men do not shop as much as women, and partly in the mistaken belief that men are less easily persuaded than women. In their study, Cody, Seiter, and Montagne-Miller (1995) reported that men actually spent more money in less time than women, and were more compliant with salesclerks' suggestions and tactics. Both of these patterns run counter to the prevailing stereotype of women as being more easily influenced than men. Women, however, spent longer amounts of time making their purchases, even though they spent less money and were better informed about the products for which they were shopping, largely as a result of exposure to magazine advertising. Although many more women than men were recreational shoppers, women in general were more focused, that is, had a better idea of what they were seeking such as a particular type of shirt or brand name product. The study's findings reflected the fact that men have not been socialized into shopping for basic and necessary goods. Nor do they spend time planning their purchases. As more men do household chores and shop, advertising directed to men becomes more appropriate and even necessary, at least from the advertisers' point of view. These results also suggest that advertisers may stand to make more profit by waging a campaign to make men the major purchasers of household items and clothing!

The more male and female roles change, stereotypes such as the frazzled Supermom, the women's libber, the bumbling "help-out" husband risk alienating potential buyers. As I noted earlier, studies show that men particularly do not like self-disparaging humor. This means that advertisers who want to increase their sales among men must show men as competent and intelligent users of household products and appliances.

Although men sometimes figure in such ads, it is often done so as to make the role reversal stereotypical, obvious, and amusing. Generally, a man makes a mess like the fairy tale husband left to mind the house. Such ads imply that men really shouldn't have to wash their own clothes or cook a meal, so the appliance does it all for them. This leaves stereotypes intact, as does a commercial for disposable diapers showing a father diapering the baby while his daughter advises him on child care and the merits of the product. She tells him he would make a "good mother" as the commercial ends with a male voiceover. On the surface the image of the father suggests that it is appropriate for fathers to diaper babies, but the words indicate that it is still the mother's role, and that he needs female advice to do the job correctly.

HOW TELEVISION MAKES UP CHILDREN'S MINDS

I noted in chapter 7 how television is a particularly powerful medium for the display of gender images to children because it combines, in a complex way, both visual and verbal messages in its programs and advertising. The cumulative effect of television and books, as well as influences from home, school, and peer group reinforce stereotypes. It was again Betty Friedan who drew attention to young children's exposure to sexist advertising at the time they are being socialized into sex roles and their gender identity is being shaped. Television is the main vehicle of advertising for children. Michael Geis (1982, p. 163) calculated, for instance, that the average American child spent an amount of time equivalent to one sixth of the school year's class time watching only commercials.

In the first major content study of television advertising, the National Organization of Women (NOW) examined over 1,200 TV commercials to look at how gender roles were displayed. Females were cast in passive rather than active roles. Women were almost exclusively portrayed in the home: 43% of the time they were involved in household tasks, 38% of the time they were portrayed as domestic adjuncts to men, and 17% of the time as sex objects. Less than 1% of the time did they appear as subjects in their own right with independent lives. Is it any wonder that 4-year-olds believe the primary female role is housekeeping? Women in commercials never told men what to do, but men were constantly advising women. Only 6% of the voiceovers featured female voices.

The toys advertised during Saturday morning children's television time reinforce gender stereotypes too. Commercials aimed at boys have loud soundtracks and aggressive activity. Boys play with cars and Nintendo games, while girls play with dolls (see chap. 7). Mel McCombie (1996, p. 15) explains how the Barbie doll was introduced at the end of a decade in which marketers and advertisers had literally invented "the teenager" as a new market for consumer products. When the Mattel company first introduced the Barbie doll in 1959 at the New York Toy Fair, the doll was billed as "a shapely teenage fashion model." She was the first American doll to display a flamboyantly adult figure. McCombie (1996, p. 17) estimates that if Barbie were life-size she would be about 5 feet 7 inches tall with measurements of 39–18–33. Note too the diminutive form of her name rather than the full form *Barbara*, while her male partner is called *Ken*, not *Kenny* (see chap. 5 for discussion of naming patterns). Some buyers were upset at first because they feared that the well-proportioned dolls were too sexy and would be repellent to children. They were, however, wrong in their fears; the initial shipment of a half million dolls and a million costumes sold out almost instantly. Sales of Barbie dolls continue to provide great profits to Mattel, with sales of the doll and related products topping 1 billion dollars in 1992. Now Barbie has 100% brand name recognition among American girls between the ages of 3 and 10, 96% of whom own at least one of the dolls. Few other children's toys can claim such success. GI-Joe, a doll manufactured by Hasbro and aimed at boys, emphasized stereotypical images of aggression and combat, but has not been nearly so popular as Barbie.

Barbie's preoccupation with her endless wardrobe and her boyfriend Ken socialized millions of young girls into being fashion-conscious teenagers, who aspired to the doll's idealized image of female beauty. Barbie taught these girls how to be female consumers, who both consumed goods as well as existed for male visual and sexual consumption. Much of Mattel's profits came not from sales of the doll itself, but from her numerous outfits, which were given fanciful names such as Gay Parisienne, Roman Holiday, Plantation Belle, and so on, suggesting the elite circles of French *haute couture*, high society, and fantasy adventures. Although Barbie's outfits kitted the doll out for a wide variety of activities such as shopping, sailing, traveling, and so on, studies done by Mattel showed that most girls "played" with the doll by dressing and undressing her. The emphasis on the doll's appearance thus worked to construct female gender images of a different type than those of traditional motherhood, which girls might be expected to form from playing with a more conventional baby doll.

Of course, the obviously affluent, White, and blonde Barbie with her slender, yet big-breasted, female figure, did not look like the typical teenager. As McCombie points out, however, it is precisely because she did not that she offered such a huge marketing opportunity. The gap between a woman or girl's own image of herself and what she might aspire to is what manufacturers and advertisers exploit for their own economic gain. "Good" advertising, that is, that which is effective from the advertisers' point of view, succeeds not by mirroring reality, but by creating alternative versions of it. As the doll grew more popular, Mattel created more accessories to go with it, such as sports cars, a beauty salon, a dream town house with (not surprisingly!) a large closet. Barbie's persona is defined in terms of her wardrobe and her other material possessions. More recent versions of the doll appeal to particular segments of the market, such as ethnic versions of Barbie and even Dr. Barbie!

DECLARING WAR ON SEXIST ADVERTISING

The advertising industry exerts enormous power over the interpretation of male and female sexuality throughout our culture, and not surprisingly, it has resisted reform, despite increasing complaints and pressure from groups such as NOW and WAP (Women Against Pornography). It is time for consumers to declare war. As Courtney and Whipple (1983, p. 157) have observed, the war metaphor is appropriate because advertisers themselves refer to ad "campaigns," "tactics," "strategies," and so on, as if they were engaged in a war with consumers as well as marketing competitors. However, research too can be used to educate advertisers that sexism does not sell.

Advertisers generally deny claims that their ads are sexist despite the fact that media polls conducted as early as 1971 have found that consumers agree with critics who complain of sex stereotyping. They also dismiss criticism by suggesting that it comes primarily from an atypical and radical feminist fringe not representative of the wider public. Although it is true that some of the strongest criticism has come from women-oriented groups such as NOW and WAP, there is broader support in society at large. In Britain, the Advertising Standards Authority, which rules on matters concerning public decency, revealed that in 1982, 40% of its more than 6,500 complaints concerned the portrayal of women in ads. In 1971, a survey of readers of *Good Housekeeping* magazine in the United States reported that 40% of respondents agreed that television commercials were insulting to women. Three quarters of the respondents to a similar survey conducted by *Redbook* magazine felt that the media downgraded women by portraying them as sex objects. Generally speaking, women are more critical than men about sex role stereotyping, especially younger, better educated, more affluent women who have rejected traditional female values and roles (Courtney & Whipple, 1983, p. 32). Nevertheless, interviews conducted with seven women advertising executives revealed that none saw anything offensive about advertising campaigns that had been severely criticized by feminists, despite the fact that these women supported basic feminist goals such as equal pay for equal work.

In view of this, it is depressing, but not surprising, to find companies still promoting stereotypes about women through the images displayed and associated with their products. I noted in chapter 4 how olive oil companies often use young women as emblems for the purity of their product. Similarly, the image of the Vermont Maid vouches for the purity of maple syrup. The founder of the company that makes Miller's Damsel wheat wafers sold in England explained to Marina Warner (1994, p. 31) that the significance of the company's name and logo is derived from a three-tongued rod used in the milling process. Over the years, the rod became referred to affectionately as Miller's Damsel because "it has three chattering tongues and our symbol is a representation of it."

Another argument advertisers use to defend the sexual sell is freedom of speech. Most Western democratic governments have strong free-speech traditions and are reluctant to intervene in issues where judgments appear to be based on personal taste and opinion. In 1981, the Advertising Standards Authority in Britain ruled that a computer advertisement showing a woman with her underpants around her knees and a suggestive slogan was unlikely to cause offense, but at the same time they upheld a complaint about a nude female model shown in an ad for a boat appearing in a family magazine.

As I argued in chapter 7, once books, television programs, and advertising depict women in more positive and less stereotypical roles, attitudes will change. *Ms.* magazine features a page called "One Step Forward," which provides positive advertising images. One study showed, for instance, that girls who were exposed to innovative commercials in which women had roles such as judge or computer programmer, were more likely to select those occupations as suitable for women than girls who had not seen the commercials or had seen only commercials with women in traditional roles. Just over half the children exposed to the nontraditional commercials chose judge as an occupation suitable for women, while only 27% of those who had not seen them (Courtney & Whipple, 1983, pp. 50–51). When exposure to even one commercial can affect attitudes, at least over the short term, the potential power of television advertising to educate children away from sex stereotyping is obvious.

Producers of children's cartoons and commercials have instead argued in favor of maintaining the status quo by claiming that television merely reflects society (see chaps. 1 and 10 for further discussion). Yet, in real life, 90% of American women work at some stage of their lives and are not "just housewives." As I said earlier, the world of advertising is a mythological world in many respects. It is in the business of creating dreams and satisfying fantasies, not in mirroring reality. The point of advertising is to create an imaginary world in which consumers can be persuaded that buying products will satisfy desires, which in real life are unsatisfied. In this way, advertising both plays on and convinces us of our dissatisfactions with everyday life. No one wants to be unhappy, ugly, or old.

The best arguments, however, for persuading producers and advertisers to change their tactics are economic. When it is in their economic interests, advertisers will also exploit a kind of reverse-gender stereotyping or try to reform our images of masculinity and femininity and their associations with particular products, as seen in my discussion of the Hewlett Packard, aftershave, jeans, and diaper ads. Other examples of the power of media are the British brewing industry's mounting of a special ad campaign to overcome the association of lager with femininity and in the United States, the National Fluid Milk Processor Promotion's currently ongoing and hugely successful campaign to create a macho image for milk. A special advertising section of *Newsweek* magazine (Nov. 4, 1996) entitled "Of Milk and Men," showed a series of photos of men, including prominent male public figures, dressed in business suits as well as others engaged in sport. The men all have "milk moustaches," that is, the traces of milk on their upper lips. In the ad shown in Fig. 9.5, professional baseball player Cal Ripken asks "Where's your moustache?" and adds that "with all the milk I drink, my

With all the milk I drink, my name might as well be Calcium Ripken, Jr. Really, I'm a huge milk fan. Besides being loaded with calcium, there's nothing like it when it's ice cold. Which is why I drink the recommended 3 glasses a day. And as you'd probably guess, I'm not one to miss a day.

MILK
Where's *your* mustache?™

FIG. 9.5. Milk is macho. Reprinted with permission of *The Milk Council.*

name might as well be Calcium Ripken, Jr." An accompanying article entitled "Milk is macho" tries to dispel popular male belief that milk is only for women and children.

A related campaign to promote milk drinking among women stresses that milk won't make you fat and the accompanying ad shown in Fig. 9.6 depicts a scantily clad model with a good figure and a milk moustache. Note, however, the terms *girl* and *baby* used in the text. I suspect that

FIG. 9.6. Milk won't make you fat. Reprinted with permission of *The Milk Council.*

more women will be turned off by that ad than men will be by the ads aimed at them. It would be interesting to know whether the marketers have conducted extensive research to gauge consumer reaction in advance of their campaign.

Advertisers sometimes offer as proof that sex sells the fact that women do buy their products. What they ought to ask, however, is whether they can sell products even more successfully if they abandon sex stereotyping. Research shows that responses to products are tied to the credibility of advertising. Both men and women prefer advertising which makes use of less traditional sex role stereotypes. Research findings concerning the effectiveness of male versus female voiceovers show that advertisers are out of touch with consumers in this respect too. In defense of their choice of predominantly male voiceovers and announcers, advertisers have traditionally claimed that male voices are more authoritative and therefore more effective. Sometimes they also point to the shortage of trained women announcers. Certainly, it is true that, until recently, women have had limited access to this lucrative field, where top announcers may earn half a million or more dollars a year. Yet, Courtney and Whipple (1983, pp. 134–141) claim that research does not verify superior effectiveness of male voices. Consumers rate as more effective commercials containing female voiceovers, working housewives, men participating in household cleaning and cooking when compared to more traditional ones (Courtney & Whipple, 1983, pp. 88–89).

Other research findings provide information that can be used to convince advertisers that the sexual sell does not necessarily lead to greater profits. One study found that the presence of a decorative female model had no significant effect on viewers' recall of product brand names. Even though she does get viewers (especially males) to pay attention to the ad, the model does so at the expense of attention to the product. Men were much more likely to evaluate an ad positively when an attractive female model appeared in it. Ads which were not sexually suggestive were more likely to get viewers to remember the product brand name (Courtney & Whipple, 1983, pp. 114–115). Another study showed that where the gender image of a product did not match that of a model depicted with it, consumers were less favorably disposed to the product. Consumers still think cars, for instance, are more masculine, sofas more feminine, whereas televisions are neither masculine or feminine. This indicates that marketers need to gauge how consumers conceive of a product before deciding whether to use male or female models (Courtney & Whipple, 1983, pp. 74–75).

At the same time, more direct consumer action is needed. WAP (Women Against Pornography) initiated annual "awards" for sexist ads. Among the recipients were Calvin Klein jeans (for the ad I mentioned earlier) and Maidenform Bras. All mass media are, to a certain extent, dependent on consumer support for their success. Boycotts of products marketed with offensive ad campaigns can also be effective. If consumers threaten not to buy a product, they can influence manufacturers and advertisers. When one of the new talking Barbie dolls was programmed to say that math homework was difficult, critics complained that this gave girls the idea that they weren't suited for math and science, traditionally seen as male subjects (see chap. 7). Mattel withdrew the doll from the market. Now that the company's chief executive officer is a woman, it will be interesting to see if the company will pay more attention to gender bias in its toys and games.

Consumers can also write to companies whose products are advertised in offensive and sexist ways as well as to the magazines and other media which display them. The *Standard Directory of Advertisers Tradename Index* can supply the name and address of a company marketing products having a trade name. Once the company's name is known, the *Standard Directory of Advertisers* can provide information about a company's advertising policies and agencies. Then you can write directly to the people who make the ads. Most industrialized countries have regulatory bodies which hear cases concerning false and misleading advertising. The National Advertising Review Board published a report in 1975 with guidelines about the portrayal of women in advertising in the United States. Similar agencies exist in Britain and Canada, a country which has taken a very strong stance about sex stereotyping in advertising. The Scandinavian countries and the Netherlands also have very strict controls on gratuitous use of women as attention-getting devices in ads. Television viewers can complain to the National Association of Broadcasters.

However, ads are not the only factors consumers take into account when deciding what to purchase. Price, availability in local stores, and existence of similar products are also relevant. If all products in a certain category use sex-stereotypical advertising, consumers have no choice. Although I may find Singapore Airlines ads offensive, if I have to fly between London and Singapore, there may be few other options. It is easier for me to decide that I will not buy Toshiba products, such as a laptop computer, when there are many other models on the market.

There are limitations too on the likelihood of media reform in countries such as the United States, where television is controlled privately, and run for commercial profit. Advertising is used to fund programs, and sponsors compete for the opportunity of access to large audiences. For this reason, some are skeptical about the extent to which television can be used to provide positive influences, particularly when the effects of any programs designed to promote gender equality might be so easily undermined by advertisers. Even if some programs such as "Murphy Brown," "Dr. Quinn, Medicine Woman," and "Mary Tyler Moore" promote positive images of professional women, and programs like "Who's the Boss?" show men doing housework, the ads accompanying the program may not reinforce the program's messages if they show men and women in conventional roles. Commercial sponsors also tend to shy away from controversy and avoid programs that may upset viewers. Following the portrayal of a gay male couple on a program called "Thirty Something," various protest groups organized demonstrations against the sponsors and programmers. Subsequent programs did not treat the couple's relationship. In 1996, as I was completing this book, ABC was still contemplating whether the star of its popular program "Ellen" would "come out" as a lesbian.

While it is easier to enforce restrictions against display of nudity in individual ads, it is more difficult to legislate against more subtle aspects of sexism in advertising as a whole. We cannot simply ban male voiceovers any more than we can ban the portrayal of women preparing breakfast for their children or using washing machines. The sexism in such advertising resides in long-standing associations between women and domesticity on the one hand, and between men and the public workplace on the other. In the next chapter I take up the question of reforming sexist language, where we see a similar problem. As I noted in chapter 4, sexism arises from collocations between words which derive from the context in which they are used.

EXERCISES AND DISCUSSION QUESTIONS

1. In his book, *Gender Advertisements*, Erving Goffman (1976) shows how differences in power and authority between men and women are represented and constructed in advertising photographs. Likewise, Nancy Henley (1977) argues that the use of space reflects a dominance hierarchy. Examine a number of contemporary magazines to see to what extent the use of space is related to dominance and whether the postures and gender displays they mention are still found in advertising. You can also collect data by watching advertising on television. You can also add a time dimension to your study by examining magazines from earlier periods to see how images of women and men have changed.

2. Conduct a study of one type of product (e.g., home appliances, alcoholic beverages, perfume, etc.) and analyze the strategies used to market it. You can add a time dimension to your study by looking at older magazines and other publications. You can probably find older issues of magazines and newspapers on microfilm or microfiche in the library.

3. Studies of advertising in the 1970s and 1980s revealed that the typical female in commercials was a young housewife at home, either in the kitchen

or bathroom, subject to the male voiceover of authority giving her advice, relating to others in a service role, or concerned with her appearance. The typical male was engaged in drinking, smoking, playing sports, or working in the backyard. Is this still true today? Make a record of the television commercials shown over the period of 1 hour, noting the roles males and females play in advertising the products. Don't forget to pay attention to who speaks, as well as who says what about the products, the setting, how the products are displayed, and so on. You can extend this exercise by comparing commercials aired at different time slots, for example, daytime versus prime time evening, or for different programs, for example, a football game versus an evening movie or situation comedy.

4. An article in the *Toronto Star* (Jan. 18, 1982) entitled "Wimps" complained that the men portrayed in television advertising were becoming feminized. They no longer walked but slinked, were submissive to their wives and afraid of their children. Design a study to investigate this claim. Consider also the reverse possibility: Are women becoming more masculinized through ads such as the Diet Coke one described in this chapter? Are advertisers creating new stereotypes as they try to eliminate old ones?

5. Compare print and television ads for the same products, for example, a soft drink, shampoo, car, and so on. Consider whether and to what extent the difference in medium constrains and influences advertisers' layout, choice of images, and text.

ANNOTATED BIBLIOGRAPHY AND SUGGESTIONS FOR FURTHER READING

In addition to the work of Betty Friedan (see in particular, chapter 9, The Sexual Sell), Erving Goffman (1976), Jean Kilbourne (1987) and Susie Orbach (1978), readers will find relevant material in Robin Lakoff and Raquel L. Scherr's (1984) book, in Josephine King and Mary Stott's (1977) book, in N. Wolf's (1990) book, and in Gabriel Thoveron's (1987) report. I have also drawn on articles by Linda Busby (1975), Dick Dabney (1982), the *Guardian* (1986), Jane Levere (1974), Rhonda Reinholtz, Muehlenhard, Phelps, & Satterfield (1995), Gloria Steinem (1990), Jennifer Tanaka (1996), and Richard Levinson (1975), who studied Saturday morning cartoons. There is an extensive literature on sex stereotyping in advertising and the media, as well as on language and advertising. With respect to the former I have drawn heavily on Alice Courtney and Thomas Whipple's (1983) book, which summarize a large number of studies of sex stereotyping in advertising (see also the chapters in Paul Martin Lester's, 1996, book on stereotypes more generally in the media). Chapter 9 of their book contains useful information on regulatory codes and agencies in a number of countries. More linguistic treatments of advertising include Torben Vestergaard and Kim Schroder's (1985) book about print media and Michael Geis's (1982) book on television advertising. A number of journals such as *Journal of Consumer Research, Journal of Marketing, Journal of Advertising, Journal of Marketing Research, Journal of Advertising Research*, and others contain research on advertising.

10

Language Reform:
A Msguided Attempt
to Change Herstory?

Doubtless women are entitled to the process of getting the rights and freedoms granted to men; once these goals are achieved, however, and even before that, they can leave the language alone. When women have full social, political, and economic parity with men, no schoolgirl will burst into tears over *himself* being used in the sense of *herself* too, or about "men and women" being a more common phrase than "women and men"—anymore than French schoolgirls, I imagine, weep over their sexual organs being, in both high and low parlance, of the masculine gender. (Simon, 1980, p. 37)

In preceding chapters, I have shown how language both reflects and constructs women's status as Other as it defines women's position as inferior in relation to men. Does this mean that society has to change before language can? Or can language change bring about a social reform? The dichotomy between what I termed in chapter 1 "the language as symptom" and "language as cause" position oversimplifies the complexity of the interface between language and society. Yet if male and female identities are largely constructed and transmitted through language as I have argued, then language change is obviously critical. Language is clearly only part of the problem, but how can we make it part of the solution to what Ardener called "the problem of women"? In this chapter I look at some of the arguments and strategies for reform with respect to English and other languages. I also examine resistance tactics and evaluate the relative success of some of the reforms underway.

SHOULD WE LEAVE LANGUAGE ALONE?

In the epigraph to this chapter from John Simon's sarcastic review of Casey Miller and Kate Swift's book *The Handbook of Nonsexist Writing* (1980/1988), Simon suggests that women shouldn't interfere with language. In a man's world, language belongs to men. Simon clearly belongs in what I called in chapter 1 the "language as symptom" camp. Once society recognizes equality between men and women, language will take care of itself. Language will come to reflect whatever changes take place in society. Once a woman can be a doctor, it doesn't matter if she's called a *lady doctor*, a *doctoress*, or a *doctor*. In an egalitarian society feminine marked forms will lose their negative connotations and androcentric generics will really be sex inclusive. Another prescriptivist, William Safire (1992, p. 6), suggested a "politics-grammar deal: let half the Senate be women and let the male pronoun embrace the female . . . as sexual equality is achieved, the need to stretch syntax will let up."

Endorsing this "leave language alone" view, sociolinguist Jenny Cheshire (1985), for instance, attributed certain changes in usage to the changing position of women rather than to feminist activism. A *New York Times* (July 28, 1991) editorial entitled "The Waitron's Knife and Fork" made essentially the same argument when it objected to such "jarring" usages as *waitron* in place of *waiter/waitress*. "Words will change, without strain or connivance, when attitudes change, in the minds of waitrons and patrons alike." In this scenario society has to change first, and that is what triggers language change.

Yet another reason is sometimes offered for leaving language alone, namely, that usage is irrelevant to the debate about sexism. In a letter to the *Times* (December 19, 1981), linguist Neil Smith observed that there are many languages that make no distinction between *he* and *she*, but they are still spoken in societies where men's and women's roles are markedly different and where women are subordinate to men. Consider as an example women's subordination to men within Islamic societies, many of which speak varieties of Arabic, a language with gender distinctions in its pronouns. Yet people in other predominantly Islamic countries such as Turkey speak languages without overt gender distinctions in their pronouns. However, the position of women in Turkey is not markedly better than it is in other Islamic countries. To Smith, such examples indicate a lack of direct relationship between language and society.

The issue of reform has divided feminists too. Women not content to leave language alone have sought to change language structure and use as a way of taking deliberate action to change their position in society. Women are appropriating the power to name as a way of defining themselves in a new way (see chap. 5). Naturally, not everyone in favor of reform agrees either on the direction it should take or on how far such reform should go. The campaign for language reform has taken place along several fronts: One is to replace sexist forms with gender-neutral or gender-equal forms (depending on the language); a second is to give names to phenomena that have gone unnamed. Another is to respell or reshape key words like *history* or *women* so that they become *herstory* or *hystery*, and *wombyn* or *wimmin*, with the masculine elements *his-* and *-men/-man* eliminated from the words and replaced with feminine ones. Yet another consists in trying to reclaim for positive use words such as *madam, lady, crone, hag, spinster*, and so on, whose original meanings have degenerated (see chap. 4).

As I showed in chapter 5, however, one of the sometimes more subtle forms of discrimination against women is that they are simply not mentioned at all! Eliminating nubility titles such as *Miss* and *Mrs.* in favor of *Ms.* or prescribing for public use neutral forms such as *flight attendant* instead of *steward* and *stewardess* does nothing to address this problem. Reform must therefore be directed at discourse as a whole rather than piecemeal at bits of the language such as titles and pronouns.

I show in this chapter that arguments about usage are really about the beliefs of different groups in society, about who has the right to prescribe to whom. As I showed in chapters 4 and 5, language is symbolic of the social and moral order. Debates about language are really about issues of race, gender, class, or culture, as can be seen in the controversy over "political correctness," which has been carried out largely on the battlefield of language. To advocate deliberate change is to threaten the political status quo. Reform will be resisted if it challenges the prevailing moral order.

FROM DICTIONARIES TO DICK-TIONARIES: WEBSTER'S OLD AND NEW

Despite lexicographers' claims that they record objective facts about the words they define, I noted in chapter 4 that male bias in the process of traditional dictionary making has excluded women from the making of meaning. Suppressing women's meanings and holding them accountable to male standards of correctness is a form of repression. In order to escape from male bondage, women must liberate themselves from men's linguistic standards. Symbolically, the first thing Becky Thatcher in Thackeray's *Vanity Fair* jettisons from the coach that takes her away from school is Dr. Samuel Johnson's dictionary! Some feminists maintain that as long as women must use a language that is not of their own making, societal change is impossible. If women controlled the naming and defining process, the world would look quite different. Women have to be taught to think like women because for years they have been taught to think like men.

Such beliefs have led some women to write feminist dictionaries, inventing new terms and redefining old ones in new ways seek to create a new place in discourse for women. Mary Daly (1987), for example, described her collection of words (*Websters' First New Intergalactic Wickedary of the English Language*) as a wickedary, a dictionary for women spun by websters. She played on the original meaning of the word *webster* as female weaver and the fact that the family name Webster is still closely associated with dictionary making in the United States, thanks to the work of Noah Webster.

Daly's wickedary, however, is a metadictionary of words with meanings woven by women. The word *spinster* fits into Daly's metaphor of women weaving webs of words. Many of her formations such as *Gyn/Ecology* represent the "(re)name and reclaim" approach. Daly's dictionary thus subverts traditional lexicography and many familiar words take on quite different meanings, such as *spelling*, which she defines as the casting of spells. Similarly, Erika Wisselinck attempted to portray the positive powers of women with her term *Hexikon*, a blending of *Hexe* (German, witch) and *Lexikon*. Thus, a hexikon is a witches' dictionary. Spelling in both its traditional and new meanings is important for Daly. By respelling familiar words in new ways, she tries to make readers aware of words at the same time as she tries to remove words from their old contexts and transform their meanings. Her respelling of *dick-tionary*, which she defines as "any patriarchal dictionary," is a good example. In this way she hopes to free words from patriarchal meanings. Breaking the traditional rules of spelling formulated by male dictionary makers is a symbolic act of resistance. This theme of flouting male authority through the act of making a feminist dictionary is played out in Monique Wittig's novel *The Female Warriors* (*Les Guérillères*, 1969), which I discuss in the next chapter.

Daly uses textual politics as sexual politics when she employs unconventional punctuation and spellings to draw attention to certain words and phrases. Such efforts, however, do raise questions about what feminist writing looks like and whether it is necessary to be a woman in order to speak/write as one (see further in the next chapter). Where feminist writing relies on techniques unique or specific to the written medium, such as page layout, or formations such as those of Mary Daly and others, these strategies will not be applicable to the spoken language. This does not of course invalidate them, but it does remind us that writing is only part of the question of linguistic reform. Moreover, written language is subject to more conscious control than speech. As I show later in this chapter, it is much more difficult to assess the impact of language reform on private usage.

The kind of approach to language reform Daly advocates has been at the heart of some of the claims of French feminist theory concerning the need to transform the relation of the subject to language (see chap. 2).

There is no way to fit women's experience of themselves into a symbolic universe that is male. To do so would be to accept male definitions of females as inferior and subordinate within it. Hélène Cixous, for instance, said (1975/1986) that she constantly feels restricted either because there are no words to say what she means or because the words are so invested with male meanings that they betray her identity as a woman when she uses them. Because men have used language to express their own concerns and preoccupations to the exclusion of those of women, women's experience has been obliterated. She urged women to invent words to fill in the spaces left empty by language. One example is the term *gyn/affection*, to refer to the close relationship between female friends. The fact that there are systematic gaps in our vocabulary to express female concepts and experience reflects trends I referred to in chapters 4 and 5 concerning asymmetries in our vocabulary for words referring to men and women.

A *cuckold*, for example, refers to the husband of an unfaithful wife, but there is no word to refer to the wife of an unfaithful husband, presumably because it is more humiliating and outrageous for men to be cuckolded. A man can never be certain whether the children he thinks are his are actually his. English has no expression corresponding to *virility* to refer to female potency, and likewise no counterpart to *emasculate*. The term *gynergy* has been proposed as the opposite of *virility*. The lack of a word to refer to the normal sexual power of women has gone hand in hand with outdated beliefs about female sexuality, in particular, the idea that women lacked sex drive, and did not (and were not supposed to) enjoy sex. Other terms such as *phallustine* and *testeria* have also been created.

Likewise, Julia Penelope (1990, p. 202) asked, "How can I write in a language I want to change? Isn't there a contradiction when I use structures I've described as patriarchal?" Some words, she argued, are beyond redemption, such as *lady, wife, feminine, whore,* and *slut.* Similarly, Ursula Le Guin (1986), a science fiction writer, whose work I discuss in the next chapter, has talked about the problem in making the transition from what she calls the father tongue to the mother tongue.

> The dialect of the father tongue . . . only lectures. Many believe this dialect— the expository and particularly scientific discourse—is the highest form of language, the true language, of which all other uses of words are primitive vestiges. . . . And it is indeed a High Language . . . Newton's Principia was written in it in Latin . . . and Kant wrote German in it, and Marx, Darwin, Freud, Boas, Foucault, all the great scientists and social thinkers wrote it. It is the language of thought that seeks objectivity.
>
> . . . The essential gesture of the father tongue is not reasoning, but distancing—making a gap, a space, between the subject or self and the object or other. . . . Everywhere now everybody speaks [this] language in laboratories and government buildings and headquarters and offices of business. . . . The

father tongue is spoken from above. It goes one way. No answer is expected, or heard.

... The mother tongue, spoken or written, expects an answer. It is conversation. . . . The mother tongue is language not as mere communication, but as relation, relationship. It connects. (p. 33)

Here Le Guin alludes to the diglossia between the language of public affairs and politics and the private domestic sphere that has served to define society as masculine (see chap. 1). In the next chapter I show that one of the focal points of feminist literary criticism has resided in challenging the traditional objectivist authority to define the meanings of words and texts. Such theories argue against the idea that a text supports only one particular meaning but not some other. This is a way of challenging the power behind the claim that one's own objectification is more authoritative than someone else's. I also examine some of the ways in which French- and English-speaking feminists have tried to write in engendered (as well as degendered) voices in response to this dilemma.

There is, however, a danger in posing the problem of reform in terms of an essentialist dichotomy between male and female language and through refusing to participate in the political and social order it has created, that women's subordinate status will be perpetuated. Betty Friedan after all showed it *is* possible to write a highly articulate and precise book about a problem that still has no name! Although certain forms of speech or even whole languages may be declared as illogical, nonstandard, uneducated, and so on, and banned from official use, no group can ever exert total control over language. No one has ever had the power to determine the meanings of words or to fix them in any absolute sense. Cameron (1990a) makes a helpful distinction between language as an instrument of communication and language as an institution. Men control the institutions that regulate language, but language itself as a means of communication can never be appropriated, nor can its meanings be absolutely determined, because it is an inalienable endowment of human beings. It is therefore language the institution that is not freely accessible to all. This is reflected in the fact that women still make up two thirds of the illiterate population of the world, and 61% of the children who have no access to primary education are girls. For example, in Papua New Guinea, as in many other developing countries, many more women than men are not literate and therefore do not have the option of expressing their views in writing. This is because many more boys than girls are given opportunities to go to school, where literacy is acquired.

If we reject any notion of absolute determinism, this means that men do not really have control over language, but it also means that women's attempts at reforming the meanings of words will never be completely successful either. Moreover, it is not simply the meanings of words in dictionaries at stake, or words themselves that discriminate, but how language is used in specific contexts to refer to and talk about women. As I showed in chapter 4, however, words referring to women have semantically deteriorated over time. Although many women have argued that all sexist words in the English language should be eliminated in order to rid language of its male bias, this is clearly not feasible. It would be necessary to oust not only most words referring to women, but also most referring to men too, because the enhanced positive image of men in relation to women would also have to be removed from the language or neutralized in order for linguistic parity to be achieved. Otherwise, how could linguistic reform deal with seemingly gender-neutral words such as *aggressive* and *professional*, which have different connotations when applied to men as opposed to women, without a change in our beliefs about men's and women's roles in society?

As I showed in chapter 4, sexism arises in the way the words are used in reference to men and women. To call a man a professional is a compliment. To be an aggressive male is acceptable and expected in society, but to be a woman and a professional is perhaps to be a prostitute, in English as well as in other languages as diverse as Japanese and French, where *une professionelle* is a euphemism for a prostitute. To be an aggressive female is undesirable because such a woman would pose a threat to men. Should these terms be eliminated too? This makes it obvious that society's perceptions of men and women and attitudes concerning sex stereotypical behavior must change in order for linguistic reform to be successful.

In any event, most of the reforms I examine next that have made inroads into mainstream public usage have been far more modest in scope, and even those have been met with considerable resistance. Such resistance raises the question of the extent to which a nonsexist ideology can be encoded in a language still controlled by a dominant group that is sexist.

RESISTING REFORM

As indicated in my subtitle for this chapter (taken from Stephan Kanfer's popular treatment of language reform in *Time*, October 23, 1972), critics have regarded some attempts to reform sexist usage as ridiculous. I noted in chapter 5 that numerous male commentators have poked fun at women's attempts to reclaim and reform the language by suggesting, for example, that women are trying to get rid of the word *man* wherever it occurs, so that words like *Manchester* would be *Personchester*, the *Isle of Man* would become the *Isle of Person*, or words such as *boycott* would be replaced with *girlcott*, and even *chairperson* really ought to be *chairperdaughter*.

According to such critics, women's issues are, like women, trivial and to be laughed at. This is a familiar strategy dominant groups use to reassert their power over minorities by continuing to define norms of behavior according to their own standards. As far as Simon (1980, p. xiv) was concerned, attempts to reform language are "nonsense" that produce "linguistic absurdities" leading to a "bastardizing" of language. He objected vehemently to terms such as *chairperson* and *chair*, as well as to efforts to do away with the use of *girl* to refer to adult women. Simon (1980, p. 26) insisted there is "something ineffably lovely about being a girl . . . instead of enjoying girlhood, the feminists want to be women the moment they leave high school, if not before. How wrongheaded!" Coinages such as *wimmin* reveal antimale fanaticism in his view.

As I argued in chapter 5, many women have other views about the use of *girl* to refer to grown women. More importantly, however, I showed how disputes about the proper names for people and things are ultimately power struggles. Who has the right to decide how a person shall be called decides how that person shall be classified and defined. Although proposals for reforming sexist language are considerably older than the political correctness controversy, they have become caught up in it, as can be seen in Simon's lumping together of a variety of groups discriminated against on grounds of class, race, sexual orientation, sex, and ethnicity. He objected (1980, p. xiv) to the "notion that in a democratic society language must accommodate itself to the whims, idiosyncrasies, dialects, and sheer ignorance of underprivileged minorities, especially if these happened to be black, Hispanic, and later on, female or homosexual."

Although it is generally considered unacceptable to use discriminatory and pejorative labels to refer to persons with disabilities or to racial/ethnic groups, there is less hesitation about public name-calling of feminists, gays, and lesbians. Valentine (1995) observed, for instance, that it is these groups whose terminology is most generally scorned as politically correct. In the debate about what people and things should be called, simplistic versions of the relationship between language and reality are often used to justify particular viewpoints. Dominic Lawson, editor of *The Spectator*, argued for "describing the world as it is" when he objected (1994) to the increasing unacceptability of terms such as *queer* and *poofter*.

Simon's rejection of feminist language reform is really a statement about keeping women (and other minority groups) accountable to White middle-class male standards by maintaining the linguistic status quo. Significantly, as Paul Scamans criticized women language reformers, he too conceptualized language as a woman, but in the guise of an "Old Lady": "Adding words and phrases to our Mother-Tongue in the natural progression of language growth is one thing, but spaying the Old Lady for the sake of change is another. Let the social-levelers keep hands off" (cited by Penelope, 1990, pp. 41–42). Here we have another instance of the general prejudice against old women I noted in chapter 4, as well as of the demeaning connotations of *lady* under the guise of politeness I discussed in chapter 5.

In addition we have another example of the use of the female form to symbolize abstractions (see chap. 3). I examined in chapters 3 and 4 some of the associations between women, rhetoric, and grammar. In such arguments we can see too how language and grammar serve as metaphors for society. This metaphorical mapping explains why feminist activism for language reform is perceived as an attack on the primarily male-defined moral and social order. Essentially the argument is an old one, but it has taken on new vigor: Women in general are out of control, and feminism in particular is to blame (see chap. 1 for discussion of the feminist backlash). Women's disobedience to male standards of authority, whether in matters of grammar or other things, violates a threat to the patriarchal moral order in which men have a natural right to dominate women.

A society or nation in control of itself is in control of its grammar—and in control of its women, Henry James would have added! What annoyed Henry James and still annoys many modern language gurus such as Simon and Safire is the passing of control over these standards of conduct and language from male hands. In an article in *Harper's Bazaar*, where he railed against the speech of American women, James (1906–1907) described a dialogue with an "interlocutress" (from his standpoint a monologue) who believed that the imposition of a standard pronunciation represented a form of sexual oppression American women would not tolerate. Innovation was for James degeneration, and it was a direct result of women's growing importance in American society. If something were not done soon, he warned that "American English, and by implication, civilization as we know it, will degenerate into the moo of the cow, the bray of the ass, and the bark of the dog" (41:113). In contrast, James praised the long-lost Puritan speech of New England, which had belonged to the "few capable of taking care of themselves, and of keeping themselves in hand—capable even of keeping their wives, their daughters, their sisters" (41:20–21). As long as women were kept in their place, the language would stay in place.

This was the guiding metaphor Dr. Samuel Johnson applied when he said in the preface to his monumental dictionary published in 1755 that languages were the "pedigree of nations." Both need rules or laws to keep their natural degenerative tendencies in check; hence the need for men to fix them once and for all. In chapter 3 I observed some of the symbolic associations between female figures and nation-states: Mother countries have mother tongues. Because the teaching of grammar was the traditional cornerstone of a classical education, grammar grinding has long been equated with the teaching of discipline. Women have long been seen as traditional guardians of morality. Grammar has been personified down through the ages variously as a "stern mistress" who holds a book in one hand and a rod or whip in the other. At the Portail Royal of the Cathedral of Chartres dating from the 12th century the female figure of Grammar is

depicted with a book in one hand and a raised birch whip in the other to
discipline two children who sit at her feet with their books. Here a moral
struggle is presented in terms of a personified abstraction.

Teaching the rules of grammar has thus become linked with teaching
children their proper civic duties as law-abiding citizens. Indeed, the traditional grammar drill evokes a mental image of a platoon of soldiers taking
part in a military drill or marching exercise! Cameron (1995) discussed the
Conservative campaign in Britain for a return to traditional grammar as
symbolic of concern over social and moral order. Thus, women's rejection
of male standards in grammar amounts to civil disobedience.

We can see how language and grammar serve as metaphors for society.
It is helpful to lay out some of the correspondences that get mapped from
the domain of society onto the domain of language.

Source Domain = Society	Target Domain = Language
Structure of society	Structure of language
Laws of society	Rules of grammar
Obeying laws	Using good grammar
Change in society	Change in language
Breakdown in law and order	Breakdown in language

Although various more specific arguments have been made against some
of the proposed changes, they are really a smokescreen for underlying issues
of control over standards. For example, some object to *Ms.* because its
pronunciation cannot be determined from the spelling, but then this is true
for *Mrs.* and *Mr.* too, and for a great many other English words and
abbreviations. The reasoning some men use against changing such male-
dominated naming practices often amounts to no more than resentment at
a change in the status quo. As one man said, it makes it "jolly difficult to
work out whether women were married these days because of the ridiculous
practice of not taking their husbands' names." This is, of course, precisely
the point! A woman's marital status is irrelevant and is marked only for
men's convenience. Practices such as taking a man's family name or using
titles such as *Mrs.* or *Miss* are symbolic of women's position as men's
property and represent their status as sex objects, whose availability or
nonavailability due to ownership by another male has to be marked in a
conspicuous way (see chap. 5). To insist on being called *Ms.* is to undermine
men's power in a visible way.

Senator Carla Ravaioli raised the issue of the different forms of address
given to men and women in the Italian senate. In the roll-call and official
documents women are referred to with both names, whereas men are referred to by last name only. Although her proposal to end this practice
was ratified, the press ridiculed her. One article warned that she would

now have to have her hair done by a barber instead of a women's hairdresser if she presumed to be equal to her male colleagues. This too is a familiar strategy of resistance—ridiculing women for attempting to be like men, demanding their assimilation to male norms of behavior at the same time as preventing it. Nineteenth century French satirist Sylvain Maréchal similarly joked that a French woman could not be an author (French *auteur*) without renouncing her sex because the word is masculine.

Another proposal to do away with the Italian title *signorina* (Miss) never got discussed due to Parliament's early dissolution. The press was nevertheless indignant that such a "trivial" topic was going to be discussed when the country was on the brink of disaster. Yet the fact that the media took the trouble to condemn the issue so vehemently is evidence that language reform is anything but a trivial issue. If "only" words were at stake, why bother to make such a fuss?

Fowler (1927) noted decades ago the "inconvenience" of not knowing whether one is dealing with a woman, in his argument in favor of the word *doctoress*: "Everyone knows the inconvenience of being uncertain whether a doctor is a man or a woman; hesitation in establishing the word *doctoress* is amazing in a people regarded as nothing if not practical" (cited in Baron, 1986, p. 131). Presumably, the seemingly gender-neutral "people" referred to here are, in fact, male. Fowler wanted to revive certain *-ess* forms that had declined in use, such as *editress* and *inspectress*, and to create new ones for words that had none, such as *lecturer* and *cyclist*. Evidently some men still feel able to revive old words ending in *-ess* when it suits their purpose of belittling a woman's achievement, as I discovered on reading a negative review of one of my books in which the male reviewer referred to me as an *authoress* (see chap. 5 for discussion of new disparaging coinages ending in *-ette*). In the early days of higher education for women some educational institutions noted the incongruity of granting bachelor's degrees to women and proposed mistresses or maids of art and doctoresses (see Baron, 1986, pp. 173–174), but most women would probably reject these terms today.

In Italian, which is similar to French in having grammatical gender and a high proportion of job titles belonging to the masculine category, women are divided over whether they prefer to be referred to with the male terms or a derived feminine form. Part of the reason for lack of agreement is the asymmetry between male and female terms. When women first began to occupy positions formerly reserved for males only, they adopted the male terms for these positions. Normally, a woman would be called by the feminine form *la segretaria*, but when she becomes the secretary of a political party or a vice-minister, she gets called by the masculine form *il segretario*. Similarly, a woman can be head of an elementary school and carry the feminine-marked title *la Direttrice*, but if she becomes a business manager, she is called *il Direttore* 'director'. As I pointed out in chapter 7, a similar bias in the distribution of male and female secretaries in English exists although it is not formally encoded, so that female secretaries tend to occupy low-paying clerical positions, whereas male secretaries are secretaries of state. In English, however, the social dimensions are not as readily apparent because they are obscured by the gender-neutral term. Nevertheless, at least one English dictionary reveals in its definition of secretary as "one who assists another with the routine organization of his business" that we still think of secretaries mainly as female assistants to male bosses.

In Italian a woman as well as a man could be *professore ordinario* 'university professor', but more recent proposals for Italian language reform have stressed the importance of using forms with the feminine marker -*a*. Now, the most widely used feminine form for professor is *professoressa*, which traditionally referred to a secondary-school teacher. Some women dislike this form so much that they abandon the title altogether and prefer simply to be called *signora* or *signorina*. One reason why women dislike *professoressa* is that other words ending in this suffix are already in use with other meanings; for example, *presidentessa*, derived from *presidente* 'president' refers to the president's wife instead of a woman who is president. Many other European languages had similar titles for women married to a man of a certain profession, such as Norwegian *bispinne* 'bishop' with the feminine suffix -*inne*. Such usages are reminders of a time when women were defined primarily as men's wives or daughters or children's mothers rather than as persons in their own right.

In German too we can see certain trends that are in line with changing ideas about feminism. As I noted earlier in chapter 3, forms of nouns referring to persons have feminine as well as masculine forms, such as *der Kollege/die Kollegin* 'male/female colleague'. Notice that the corresponding English term is already neutral, which avoids what some see as a cumbersome need to repeat male and female forms, adding to the length of a text. Although the feminine forms exist, German feminists have had to fight for their use, because the assumption until recently has been that the masculine term was generic. German feminists have also suggested some new neutral terms, such as *der/die Studierende* 'one who studies' to replace the marked *der Student/die Studentin*. However, many women have insisted on titles ending in -*in*, which is consistent with positive conceptions of "difference" in the women's movement, and on gender-inclusive job advertisements such as the following from *Die Zeit* (February 14, 1997), where the text specifically mentions both men and women as potential applicants, as in, *wir suchen Professorinnen/Professoren* 'we are looking for female professors/male professors' . . . *Berwerber/innen sollen* 'male applicants/female applicants should'. . . . Some ads retain the traditional male title, such as *Wirtschaftsdirektor* 'business manager' but follow it with m/w to indicate that male or female candidates are included.

Other common arguments against reform have been stated in terms of objections about how awkward certain changes sound, or that they violate rules of grammar. This has particularly been the case in languages with grammatical gender. Italian grammarian Giulio Lepschy, for example, says that it sounds awkward to refer to a female and male political leader such as Margaret Thatcher and Willi Brandt as simply *Thatcher e Brandt* or as *la Thatcher e il Brandt*, instead of in the usual asymmetrical way as *la Thatcher e Brandt*, with the female marked by the feminine definite article. Similarly, he finds odd the suggestion that *l'uomo della strada* 'the man in the street' should become *la personal/l'individuo della strada* 'the person/individual of the street'. He suspects that an attempt to eliminate gender-markedness is likely to be doomed to failure because it flies in the face of a deep-seated aspect of the way in which we conceive the world as divided into male and female. Yet Italian advertisers did not hesitate or argue about the grammatical awkwardness in appropriating the feminine term *la tigre* 'tiger' and changing it into a masculine in the slogan *Metti un tigre nel motore* ('Put a tiger in your tank').

As Alma Sabatini (1985, 1986) pointed out with respect to Italian, the present system is not as consistent and logical as grammarians like Lepschy sometimes make it out to be. Citing a headline from the Roman newspaper *Il Messagero* (April 9, 1983) about a woman who had just been elected mayor, she noted the ungrammatical jumble: *E' elda Pucci, medico, 51 anni, fanfaniana, la candidata DC a sindaco* (Elda Pucci, physician, 51 years old, affiliated with Fanfani's politics, is the Christian Democratic candidate running for mayor).

The terms for 'physician' (*medico*) and 'mayor' (*sindaco*) are masculine, whereas the term for 'candidate' (*candidata*) and the adjective describing her political affiliations (*fanfaniana*) are feminine. There is resistance to accepting *sindaca* as the feminine form of mayor, so a woman has a choice between adopting the male title or referring to herself as *la donna sindaco* 'woman mayor'.

When evaluating some of these arguments against reform, it is instructive to remember that probably all deliberately proposed innovations are laughed at initially. When, for instance, the title *Frau* was proposed to replace *Madame* in German many years ago, one historian actually rashly predicted that *Frau* would never be accepted, but in fact it has been. Indeed, as a German male colleague confided to me in an amused manner, his young female research assistants were nowadays quite adamant they should be called *Frau*. Of course, traditionally, as young unmarried women, they would have been called *Fräulein*, where the ending *-lein* ('little') is diminutive. There is, however, not surprisingly, no corresponding male term of address, *Herrlein*, for young unmarried men. A German woman who is now a full professor but unmarried told me that her doctoral supervisor was reluctant to address her as *Frau Professor Doktor* (compare the male equivalent *Herr Professor Doktor*) rather than as *Fräulein Professor Doktor*. Women's battle for the right to be addressed as *Frau* continues today. The reason for the replacement of *Madame* with *Frau* many years ago had nothing to do with feminism, but was part of a purification effort to rid German of foreign, especially French, borrowings.

Now some German feminists are suggesting that *frau* should replace the indefinite *man*, which is an androcentric generic when used in contexts such as *man soll das nicht machen* 'one shouldn't do that'. In similar fashion some English-speaking women deliberately use *she* as the generic pronoun to shock their readers. Deborah Cameron, a linguist who adopted this practice, wrote that if there are men who feel uncomfortable about being excluded, they should think of how women feel within minutes of opening most books.

English speakers are sometimes struck by the insistence of German women on being addressed as *Frau* (literally the equivalent of *Mrs.*), while English-speaking women have generally waged a campaign for the insistence of the new title *Ms.*, a designation that does not indicate marital status. To appreciate the different directions reform has taken, we must take a larger view of the semantic and grammatical systems into which existing words fit and how new words relate to them.

In other respects the title *Frau* is not the equivalent of English Mrs. because it is also the word for both *woman* and *wife*. In its meaning of *woman* and *wife*, it forms a pair with *Mann* in its meanings of *man* and *husband*, respectively. As a title, however, it is opposed to *Fräulein*, the equivalent of English Miss, where the ending *-lein* explicitly marks the form as diminutive and makes it grammatically neuter, just as the addition of *-chen* makes *Mädchen* neuter (see chap. 3). The meaning of *Frau* (and likewise *Madame* in French) is being revised from 'married woman' to 'mature woman'.

However, these few examples indicate, as I pointed out in chapter 3, that both the extent and type of reform necessary to rid a language of sexist distinctions will vary depending on the type of language concerned. I also questioned Miller and Swift's (1988) claim that in languages with grammatical gender the impact of gender is much less blatant than in languages like English. English and Norwegian reformers have pushed for gender neutralization (degendering), whereas German and French reformers have campaigned for visibility (engendering or regendering). The Roudy commission I mentioned in chapter 5 proposed two strategies for feminizing job titles, both of which increased the visibility of women. One was the use of the feminine definite article with a masculine or neutral noun, *la professeur*, and the other was to add an *-e* to masculine forms, *la chirugienne*. It rejected, however, the suffix *-esse*.

At the same time, however, some of the resistance to the coining of new female terms appears to come partly from the structure of the language itself. For example, a male cook can be called a *cuisinier* in French, but there is already a feminine-marked form *cuisinière*, which means 'stove'. Here an attempt at reform is blocked by the existence of a word already occupying the semantic slot of 'female cook'. Similarly, in Spanish *verdulero* means a 'male vegetable seller', but the feminine counterpart *verdulera* is already in use to refer to a person of either sex who talks too loudly or behaves impolitely. Another example from Spanish is *abejaro*, meaning 'beekeeper', matched by the feminine form *abejara*, meaning 'beehive'. Here the primary meaning of the feminine form has been depersonalized so that it refers not to a female person performing a particular activity, but to an object related to the activity. As Marina Yaguello (1978) pointed out, however, the blocking of new feminine job titles by the existence of words with different meanings is most evident in nonmanual occupations. In Italian too there are complementary sets of titles with endings in *-ere* for men and *-ea* for women, but these are generally for trades associated with lower status, such as *cameriere/cameriera* 'waiter/waitress'. In any case, language tolerates a great deal of ambiguity and no one is going to confuse a title such as *cuisinière* applied to a female chef with the name of a stove! Once women appropriate the feminine marked forms as titles, the new meanings will become primary.

As far as the replacement of the androcentric generic pronouns is concerned, however, language type seems less important. Both French and Anglo-American feminists have used innovative pronouns (e.g., Michèle Causse, June Arnold, Marge Piercy), as well as traditional pronouns in innovative ways (e.g., Monique Wittig, Ursula Le Guin), as I show in the next chapter. There are nevertheless some influences related to pragmatic conventions on the use of certain pronominal forms. The French third person neuter *on* (which historically is actually derived from the word meaning man) has wider uses in colloquial speech than does its equivalent *one* in English, which sounds quite formal and even archaic in American English. Indeed, French teachers tell their pupils not to use *on* in writing, even though it has virtually replaced the use of the first person plural pronoun *nous* 'we' in speech. Thus, Brawn (1995, p. 177) correctly observed that *one* and *on* are opposites, not equivalents, as far as stylistic level is concerned. I noted in chapter 3 that the political significance of the use of *personne* as a generic, which is feminine in French, is lost when translated into English.

Some instructive cases of successful reform carried out in the context of democratic societies can be found in the modern Scandinavian languages. In both Sweden and Norway as well as in other Nordic countries the position of women is more nearly equal to that of men than in most other parts of the world, thanks to legislation comparable to the proposed but eventually doomed U.S. Equal Rights Amendment. The Icelandic head of state is now a woman and women make up a fourth of cabinet positions. In Norway women make up 40% of the members of parliament and the previous prime minister, who held the office for a considerable number of years, is also female. In Sweden 41% of politicians are women, although figures for female participation in other sectors of society such as management-level positions in business and universities are unfortunately not very high. For example, the number of women holding full professorships in universities is only about 5%.

Both Sweden and Norway recognize a variety of living arrangements that same-sex and different-sex couples may enter into with legally defined benefits and rights with respect to property, children, and so on. The new Norwegian term *samboer* ('together live') refers to a person who lives together with someone in a stable relationship, and *sambo(er)skap*, referring to the relationship itself, may be used of same-sex and different-sex couples.

The use of titles equivalent to *Miss, Mrs.,* or *Mr.* has all but disappeared in both Swedish and Norwegian. However, as far as Norwegian is concerned, Swan (1995) says this is probably due more to democratization than to feminist ideology, which has also all but eliminated the difference between intimate and polite forms of the second person pronoun. Norwegian women seldom take their husbands' names in marriage, as formerly legally required from 1923 to 1961. A 1980 law specified that if married people have different names, the children will automatically receive the mother's name unless the couple informs the authorities otherwise.

The Norwegian feminine suffixes used for nouns referring to women and female occupational titles (e.g., *forfatterinne* 'author', *ekspeditrise* 'saleswoman', *sykepleierske* 'nurse', *kontordame* 'secretary' [literally 'office woman']) have almost become extinct. The new term *sykepleier* without the feminine suffix was introduced for both sexes when men entered the nursing profession. It is official policy to avoid gendered forms. Unlike the case of other European languages I have looked at, however, Norwegian nouns referring to high-status occupations such as that of lawyer, doctor, minister, and so forth are already largely neutral in form.

Nevertheless, like the other Germanic languages, Norwegian does have a high number of androcentric compounds ending in *-mann*, one of the most frequent being the word meaning 'Norwegian person' *nordmann*. The Norwegian Language Council has resisted replacing this word with the neutral *norske*, which would bring Norwegian into conformity with Danish and Swedish, where the words *danske* 'Dane' and *svenske* 'Swede' are used. There is at the moment no other word for a Norwegian of either sex but *nordmann*, a word inherited from Old Norse. Otherwise, as in English, official policy has aimed at replacing forms like *fireman, postman* (Norwegian: *brannmann, postmann*) with neutral forms like *firefighter, postal worker*, and so on. Swan reported that many of these words, with the exception of the word for 'Norwegian', have become obsolete, or have been replaced with neutral terms or compounds containing *-kvinne* 'woman', such as *stortingskvinne* 'woman member of parliament'. Interestingly, there is no sign that the new generic terms are used more often for women, as is the case for some of the English neutral terms I discuss later.

Holmberg (1995) painted a similar picture for Swedish, where feminine job titles as well as feminine suffixes have declined in the usage of the leading newspaper. Neutral terms such as *lärare* 'teacher' and *författare* 'writer' are increasingly replacing the older feminine forms *lärarinna* and *författarinna* used for women. At the same time, however, some titles such as *sjuksköterska* 'nurse who works in a hospital' persist because there is no neutral alternative for them; *skötare* cannot be used because the word already exists and refers to a health professional who has less training than a nurse and does not usually work in hospitals. Thus, the feminine-marked form has in effect become neutral and is used to refer to men. A similar case is that of the word *kassörska* 'cashier', which is feminine, whereas the neutral *kassör* means treasurer. In other cases, however, gender marking persists even where it would be easy to coin a neutral alternative. The term *flygvärdinna* 'flight attendant' is feminine, but instead of replacing it with neutral *flygvärd*, the title *steward* has been borrowed from English and is used for male attendants.

We can now contrast Swedish and Norwegian with two other Scandinavian languages, Icelandic and Faroese, which are somewhat different in structure and spoken in quite different social contexts. Both Icelandic and Faroese have three grammatical genders like German—masculine, feminine, and neuter. In the Faroe Islands the persistence of traditional sex roles has meant that there are few job opportunities for women and therefore fewer chances for women to be financially independent of men. Not surprisingly, most occupational titles are still masculine, as they are also in Icelandic. When a woman does have a masculine job title, grammatical agreement dictates that she is referred to as *hann* 'he' rather than *hon* 'she'. Thus, if a woman were to hold the office of president, she would be referred to with a masculine job title and it would be correct, but odd, to say "The president went to the theatre yesterday and he wore a blue dress."

Both Icelandic and Faroese have compounds ending in *-maður* 'man', that are used for men in addition to their function as androcentric generics. Traditional grammars of Icelandic regard the neuter gender as being unmarked, feminine the most marked, and masculine in between. Grönberg (1995), however, claimed that the masculine is still the unmarked choice. In sentences such as *everyone is welcome* or *nobody is allowed* (to leave the house), the Icelandic words for *everyone* and *nobody* are almost always in the masculine form if the group is mixed, even though the neuter form could be used. Even in job advertisements where the text specifies that the employer is looking for a man or woman, the pronouns used are masculine rather than neuter. The word *maður* also functions the same way as German *mann* in meaning 'one'.

Moreover, there are few feminine words that can be used to refer to men and only a few neuter words referring to people in general, but a large number of masculine words ending in *-maður* (and its plural form *-menn*) are used to refer to women, such as *talsmaður* 'spokesman', and *bankamenn* 'bank employees'. The case of *hjúkrunarkona* 'nurse' is again interesting. The word is marked as a feminine job title through the use of the suffix *-kona* 'woman', as are other terms such as *skúringakona* 'cleaning woman', but the latter had been judged pejorative and replaced by a masculine term translating as 'sanitary technician', and now that men have entered the nursing profession the feminine occupational title has been replaced with a masculine word meaning 'with nursing education.' This shows that what is marked as female is still perceived as abnormal, and this is one reason why some men reject the extension of female job titles. There is also a word meaning 'person' (*manneskja*) that is grammatically feminine and could be used generically. In her study of the largest Icelandic newspaper Grönberg found that masculine nouns, pronouns, and forms ending in *-maður* are in the vast majority of all words denoting human beings.

We can see in this comparison of the Nordic countries that language is not simply a passive reflector of culture, it also creates it. There is a constant interaction between society and language. Otherwise, new terms that are introduced will become incorporated into the existing semantic bias in favor of males. We can see this happening already with some of the supposed sex-neutral terms in English that I examine next. Although a number of studies attest to a decline in sexist usage in public discourse, and there is evidence in computer corpora that the gap between reference to men and women appears to be narrowing (see chap. 4), the success of reform cannot be measured by simply noting the frequency of occurrence of new titles such as *Ms.* or gender-neutral forms such as *chair(person)*.

BUT IS IT MISS OR MRS. REVISITED?

Studies have shown that some of the new neutral terms are used in such a way so as to perpetuate the inequalities expressed by the old sex-marked terms they are supposed to replace. Thus, for example, women are much more likely than men to be referred to as a *chairperson* or *salesperson* or even *Madame Chairperson*, or *Madame Chairman*, which is similar to the French *madame le juge* discussed in chapter 3. Ehrlich and King's (1994) examination of the Canadian newspaper the *Toronto Star* found that the great majority of people referred to over a period of a week were male. In more than 80% of cases, they were called *chairman* or *spokesman*. When women were referred to in the same capacity, they were called *chairpersons* or *chairwomen*, and so forth. Other major newspapers such as the *New York Times* make similar distinctions. In his 1992 State of the Union address, then President George Bush used the term *chairman* to refer to males and *chair* to refer to females. The *Chronicle of Higher Education* also bears out the fact that a woman is a *chairperson* but a man a *chairman*.

The situation appears to be much the same in British English. My examination of the titles *chairman*, *chairperson*, and *chairwoman* in the British National Corpus revealed that *chairman* was still the most frequently used title (1,142 occurrences in a 3 million word sample). The title *chairperson* was used only 130 times, for both men and women, although more often for women. The title *chairwoman* was used only 68 times.

This raises the question of how successful feminist reforms are likely to be. At the moment, sex neutrality is not a recognized category. We can see this reflected in other aspects of society. When we speak of unisex clothing or styles, for instance, what is happening is not really a neutralization of sex-specific styles of dressing, hairstyles, and so on, but an erasing of the distinction in favor of the masculine form. Thus, unisex fashions have fostered greater acceptability for women to wear trousers, and other items of clothing once regarded as for men only. They have not created a social climate of tolerance for men to wear skirts or dresses. Where there is pressure leading to a blurring of sex roles or distinctions, usually women seek to adopt male prerogatives, as is the case with English-speaking women who prefer to be called *chairman*, or the editor of a major news magazine in France who objected to being called *la rédactrice* instead of *le rédacteur* lest people assume she was the editor of a women's magazine.

As Deborah Cameron pointed out (1985, p. 90), "In the mouths of sexists, language can always be sexist." When gender-neutral terms or positive feminine terms are introduced into a society still dominated by men, these words either lose their neutrality or are de- or repoliticized by sexist language practices of the dominant group. The reinterpretation of the feminist term *Ms.* is a good example of how women's meanings can be appropriated and depoliticized within a sexist system. What has happened to *Ms.* is yet another instance of how women's meanings can be subverted in male discourse. Likewise, within what Julia Penelope has called PUD (patriarchal universe of discourse), when a woman says *no* to male sexual advances, she really means *yes*, but is saying *no* to be coy or to play hard to get (see chaps. 8 and 9 for discussion of how a woman's *no* is interpreted as *yes*). McConnell-Ginet (1989) used this particular example to show how linguistic meanings are filtered through the dominant culture's social values and attitudes.

The title *Ms.* has not entirely replaced the marked term *Mrs.*, as was intended. Instead, it has been added as a new term of address alongside the conventional *Mrs.* and *Miss*, or is seen as a replacement for *Miss* and thus is used more often than not in connection with unmarried women. Donna Atkinson's study in Canada indicated that many people used *Mrs.* for married women, *Miss* for women who have never been married, and *Ms.* for divorced women. For some people *Ms.* also carries the connotation that a woman who uses the title is trying to hide the fact that she is single. These examples make clear that the introduction of the new term *Ms.* has not altered the underlying semantic distinction between married and un-married. Only the title used to mark the unmarried distinction has changed. Ehrlich and King (1994) even noted a directive sent out to public infor-mation officers in the state of Pennsylvania which instructed them, "If you use Ms. for a female, please indicate in parentheses after the Ms. whether it's Miss or Mrs." Thus, the title *Ms.* is being used in ways its proposers never intended, to maintain the very distinctions it was supposed to replace. This indicates the high premium that dominant institutions still place on defining women in terms of their relationships with men. Thus, the category of gender gets reconstituted and implemented in a different way with a different set of terms.

In the same way the intended gender-neutral term *chair* or *chairperson* has become in effect a marked term in opposition to *chairman*, which still remains the neutral and unmarked term, an androcentric generic. It is the woman occupying the position referred to by the title who gets singled out by the new term. Like biological reproduction, meaning is sexually repro-duced, and until women figure out a way of reproducing meaning more androgynously, their intended meanings will be reversed (see chap. 11 for discussion of how women's speculative fiction has experimented with re-productive roles). These tendencies are then inherited by the next generation of language users, as is evident in a study Justine Cassell did of 5-, 8-, and 11-year-old French children to see what words they would use for women in formerly male-only professions such as that of doctor, professor, and so on. As I showed in this chapter as well as in chapter 3, language reform has created new feminine titles marked in -*e*, such as *professeure*.

Cassell (1996) independently grouped the children into the categories of high or low gender stereotyping using measures of the kind developed by Sandra Bem (see chap. 2). When told a story about a female doctor, for instance, children who belonged to the high gender stereotyping group reported having heard a story about a nurse. Significantly, it was also these children who were more likely to use the supposedly nonsexist forms such as *docteure*. Cassell claims that this shows how the new forms are still a way of marking deviance from the male norm, even though many women who use them do so with the quite opposite intention of valorizing what is female. As I showed in chapter 6, even whole languages such as Breton and French can have very different symbolic meanings in the context of different value systems.

LANGUAGE REFORM IN PUBLIC AND PRIVATE

When evaluating the success or failure of language reform, we must distinguish between public and private usage. The examples I have cited have shown that reform has affected public usage unevenly and not always in the ways reformers intended. During the 1970s and 1980s many institutions and organizations made serious efforts to eliminate sexist language in their documents. Publications ranging from the Bible to dictionaries and newspapers have begun to reflect the new usage. The U.S. Department of Labor's former Manpower Administration has been renamed the Employment and Training Administration. The Department of Labor revised the titles of almost 3,500 jobs so that they are sex-neutral. Thus, *steward* and *stewardess* are officially "out" and *flight attendant* is in. A *hat-check girl* has become a *hat-check attendant*, a *repairman* a *repairer*, a *maid* a *houseworker*, and so on. The Australian government even has a linguist who acts as an adviser on sexism in its publications. The city of Honolulu adopted a set of guidelines on nonsexist usage prepared by the Committee on the Status of Women.

The *New York Times* stopped using titles like *Mrs.* and *Miss* with the names of women. At first, it resisted the adoption of the new title *Ms.*, but eventually the editor acknowledged that the *New York Times* believed it was now part of the language. The *London Times*, however, still uses androcentric forms such as *spokesman* and the titles *Mrs.* and *Miss*, unless a woman has asked to be referred to as *Ms.* The *Los Angeles Times* has adopted guidelines suggesting alternatives to language that may be offensive to ethnic, racial, and sexual minorities. Such differences in policy are signals of the social and political outlook of editors, who play important roles as gatekeepers in determining which forms they will adopt and thereby help sanction and spread.

In 1978 the *Washington Post* decided to use last names alone on second reference to a person, for example, *Ellen Smith, named to a new position on the Board of Directors of Exxon Corporation, will join the company next week. Smith was one of several contenders for the job.* Previously, the paper would have referred to women with titles. After the change in policy, titled forms of this kind disappeared altogether. Other more subtle aspects of discrimination against women, however, were not the subject of policy change. For example, it is much more common for men to be referred to on first reference with their first and last names together with middle initial. This is much less likely to be the case for women. The addition of the initial, such as Ellen P. Smith, apparently suggests a more important person.

Professional organizations such as the National Council of Teachers of English and the American Psychological Association, along with major publishing houses such as Macmillan, McGraw-Hill, and Holt, Rinehart & Winston, have also adopted guidelines for nonsexist usage. The National Council of Teachers of English deals with sexist language by authorizing the editor to return manuscripts submitted to its journal with a copy of the guidelines and a letter encouraging the author to rewrite the article. If an author refuses to make changes, the article is printed with a note saying that the sexist language appears as the author's express stipulation.

Linguists have generally avoided any involvement in what they call prescriptivism, that is, prescribing norms of language use, insisting instead that linguistics is a descriptive science. Fearing that it would lose credibility as a professional organization if it endorsed prescriptivism, the Linguistics Association of Great Britain, for instance, rejected a proposal to amend its constitution to remove generic masculine pronouns and to rename the office of chairman. The Linguistic Society of America, on the other hand, has embraced reform and issued a set of guidelines as well as established a Committee on the Status of Women in Linguistics.

Such guidelines, however, affect for the most part only written language. In everyday conversation things may be otherwise. For example, although most U.S. airlines have publicly replaced the term *stewardess* with *flight attendant*, as I was writing this book, I spoke with a young woman travel agent in the United States who was still using the older term *stewardess*. British usage, both public and private, lags behind American usage in most respects. For example, in the British National Corpus the female marked form *stewardess* occurred 92 times along with *air hostess* 51 times, whereas the neutral *flight attendant* occurred only 8 times and *cabin crew* 13 times. I have observed many flight attendants on British Airways flights wearing name tags identifying them as *stewardess* or *steward*. Similarly, with respect to French language reform, Fleischman (1994) observes that France lags behind other countries such as Canada and Belgium where French is also spoken. French-speaking Canadians have more readily accepted terms such as *professeure*.

Studies by Rubin, Greene, and Schneider (1994) also measured a decline in sexist language in public discourse of business leaders in the United States between the 1960s and 1980s. Significantly, the biggest decline occurred between the 1960s and 1970s, which predated the widespread introduction of public guidelines for nonsexist usage. Yet men still used three to four times more gender-exclusive language than women. The study also indicated another problem for reformers, namely, that attitudes toward gender equality did not match language usage. Those who had adopted more gender-inclusive language did not necessarily have a more liberal view of gender inequities in language. This means that superficial changes such as a decline in the use of generic *man* and *he* observed in some studies have to be seen in the larger context. If masculine generic terms are simply replaced by sex-specific male terms, then reform is not really successful. Men and women are often still referred to in stereotypical ways. I recall hearing a male colleague very carefully saying "he and she" when making generic references, and on occasions even saying "she" first, but in the same breath referring to the secretarial staff in his departmental office as "girls."

Some experimental evidence supports my suspicion that his reference to "girls" indicates that he has not really changed his mental imagery of women despite having reformed his public use of male androcentric generics. Those who appear more egalitarian in their language are not necessarily so in their thoughts. Groups of undergraduate students at Harvard University who either had or had not reformed their usage in their written work were asked to draw pictures to go with sentences such as *an unhappy person could still have a smile on his/her (or her/their) face.* The findings showed that there were still more male images than female ones, regardless of the pronoun used, and regardless of whether the subject had reformed his/her written usage. However, only women who had reformed their usage produced more female images, and they did so for all three pronouns. Thus, even the men who had ostensibly reformed their usage had done so only superficially and were still androcentric in their thought patterns. In some respects, this shows too that language reforms have had only limited success. Proposed for the most part by women, not surprisingly, it is women for whom they seem to have the greatest effect. Men take more convincing, but then they stand to lose more, and women to gain more from such reform. This example shows again how meaning is socially constructed in line with particular ideologies. This is evident too with respect to other terms such as *rape* and *sexual harassment*, which are understood differently by men and women (see chap. 8).

In another sense, however, the changes are significant if seen from the perspective of earlier experiments in the 1970s in which people were given journal articles to evaluate. Some received articles with the name of a woman author, whereas others received exactly the same articles with men's names. Both men and women judged the same articles as better and more scientific when they thought they had been written by a man than by a woman. Women did not of course need experiments to tell them of this bias. It was partly for this reason that Emily Brontë published *Wuthering Heights* under the male pseudonym of Ellis Bell. All three Brontë sisters wrote under pseudonyms, for as Charlotte Brontë observed, "authoresses are liable to be looked on with prejudice" (Baron, 1986, p. 134). When she wrote to fellow author Robert Southey for advice, he replied that literature could not and ought not to be the business of a woman's life. Indeed, when 17th-century poet Catherine Bernard won the French Academy's highest prize on three occasions, she was ruled out of the competition and prevented from collecting it. Studies have since shown how differently *Wuthering Heights* was interpreted when it became known that a woman was the author. When the critics thought she was a man, Brontë's work was described as bold, strong, masculine stuff. When her identity was revealed, the tone changed and the work became just another female novel, a love story for ladies.

There were similar reactions to the work of Alice Sheldon, who wrote science fiction under the pseudonym of James Tiptree, Jr. (see further in the next chapter). Critic Robert Silverberg (1975) found absurd suggestions that Tiptree was female because there was something "ineluctably masculine" about Tiptree's writing. He was also of the opinion that Jane Austen's novels could not have been written by a man, nor the stories of Ernest Hemingway by a woman.

Men have interpreted experimental results such as these as an indication that women shared the negative image assigned to them by men, and even went so far as to express surprise that "women were prejudiced against women." This is part of the process of being in a subordinate position. It is because the superordinate are more powerful that they impose their own way of thinking (and their language) as the only valid one. The behavior of these women was reminiscent of that of Black children who in experiments conducted in the late 1940s expressed preferences for White over Black dolls, and speakers of nonstandard English who rate standard English speakers as more intelligent, successful, and so forth. Such studies are often used to support the status quo, as, for instance, the producers of children's books, cartoons, and advertisers I discussed in chapters 7 and 9, who say that television reflects society. Later attitudinal studies on accent preference have, however, indicated a reversal of some of these negative attitudes.

Newspapers and television can do more to report the activities of women and to make women more visible. The media do not simply reflect society, they interpret it. Börjeson (1995) reported that a special edition of the second largest newspaper in Sweden devoted one day to news about women written by women. There was no difficulty in finding news items to fill all the usual categories of press coverage, such as international, finance, sports, and so forth. Yet newspapers continue to represent women as marked, as, for instance, this same Swedish newspaper does in its reporting of sports, or other papers do when they have a special women's page. Women's sports are also marked as such, for example, by referring to them as *damfotbol* (women's football), whereas the men's sports are simply sports. Despite the progress women have made in Sweden and Norway, they are still underrepresented in news coverage, and the press still pays more attention to what they wore than what they did. Only nuclear families are referred to as families. An unmarried mother living with her children or a homosexual couple is not called a family.

Many of the language reforms carried out so far do support the more radical approach taken by French feminism, which emphasizes a reordering and revaluing of the differences between men and women. Cosmetic tinkering with the present system will tend to perpetuate the subordinate status of women. There is a certain shock value in making women visible through the positive choice of the female pronoun as the generic (as, for instance, in Cameron, 1990a), and in the femininization of job titles in France. One can always imagine a captain or a doctor to be male, but the masculine interpretation is more difficult when the job title is explicitly marked as feminine as in *la capitaine*. At the same time, however, some women reject the new forms due to the lingering pejorative associations of some of the feminizing suffixes. This reaction is entirely predictable from the results of some of the psycholinguistic studies I discussed in chapter 3, which revealed associations between grammatical gender and attitudes toward men and women.

Yet, as Brawn (1995, p. 251) pointed out, the French reform goes against the current trend in French where gender concord and distinctions in nominal gender are gradually declining. Depending on the context, a slavish observance of the traditional rules for gender concord can indicate that the speaker is a pedantic old-fashioned school teacher, or a postoperative male-to-female transsexual, as well as a radical feminist! Gender markers may thus send conflicting messages; they may support the status quo (as Justine Cassell's, 1993, study showed), oppose it, or subvert it. Similarly, in English, supposedly degendered forms like *chair* can be regendered.

LANGUAGE ENGENDERED/DEGENDERED AND REGENDERED: THE LIMITS OF CHANGE

The examples discussed in this chapter also point to a complex relationship between language, culture, and reality. Sexism is not a property of specific forms. Similarly, societal reform doesn't necessarily go hand in hand with linguistic reform. Although the egalitarian ideology of the former Soviet communist state did create a favorable political climate for the elimination of titles relating to social class distinctions in favor of the address form *comrade*, the symbolic position of women as subordinate to men did not change radically. Even though there are more female than male doctors in the former Soviet Union, the predominance of women physicians has, if anything, devalued the occupational status of doctor. The word for doctor has remained masculine and takes masculine agreement markers even when referring to a woman.

This supports Cameron's (1995, p. 138) claim that it is absolutely untrue that nonsexist language will evolve naturally of its own accord as a reflection of women becoming more visible in an institution or profession. Linguistic change is not an inevitable outcome of a political commitment to equal opportunity. It has to be actively pursued. Male superiority should not be confused with male power. Male superiority is a myth that can be exposed by education and a change in consciousness, but male power has to be challenged in a more radical way in order to effect change.

Although "language" can be planned, discourse cannot be. This suggests that discourse is the real site of political struggle. Revolutionary gains are taken, not given. Because every language serves class interests and reflects the ideology of the dominant group, it is reasonable and necessary to ask whether a liberation not accompanied by a defeat of the linguistic superstructure can be a true liberation of the people who are dominated. Julia Kristeva (1984) and others have argued that a feminist revolution must involve a revolution in discourse. If not, it will amount instead to a liberation of the socially dominant, as is the case with much of the legislation designed to introduce gender equality, such as divorce laws. In other words, all language planning endeavors are limited by the political interests of those in power. This means that those who wish to undertake linguistic reform must be conscious of the larger economic and social policy and the nature of the bureaucratic institutions through which language reform is disseminated.

In Suzette Haden Elgin's (1987) futuristic novel *Native Tongue II: The Judas Rose*, which I deal with in more detail in the next chapter, women linguists disseminate surreptitiously among female networks a new language they have invented. The novel draws its inspiration from the idea that a language reflects the world view of its speakers. If we can change language, then we can change world view. However, it is not that straightforward and the novel ends on a dismal note. In an indirect way, Haden Elgin's book illustrates the difficulty reformers will face in getting their reforms into public usage in a world where media, dictionaries, publishing houses, and so forth are still largely under male control.

Nevertheless, it is instructive in a larger sense (even if somewhat unrealistic) that Haden Elgin's women succeed in reaching so many other women. Some of the most important changes affecting English and other European languages since the 1970s have arisen from changes in society's attitudes toward women prompted by political activism. In many countries, the use of nonsexist language is now legally mandated in certain quarters such as in job advertisements and government publications. At the moment, however, usage is still in flux and where choices exist, they are symbolic of different beliefs and political positions. Compare *Ms. Johnson is the chair(person)* with *Miss Johnson is the chairman.* Although a narrow linguistic analysis would say they mean the same thing and refer to the same person who happens to hold a particular position, choosing one over the other reveals approval or disapproval of, for example, feminism, language reform, political conservatism or liberalism, and so on. There is no way to maintain neutrality now, despite the traditional argument I examined in chapter 4 that *chairman* is generic and therefore gender-neutral. The existence of an alternative forces a reevaluation of the old one. With several alternatives available a woman can sometimes be referred to on the same occasion as *Madame Chairman, chairperson,* and *chairwoman,* as I heard one male conference moderator do all in the space of a few minutes without evidently being aware of it.

It is this impossibility of hiding behind a false illusion of neutrality that annoys people like literary critic C. K. Stead (1989, p. 279):

> My own response to feminist demands for "non-sexist" language was at first to ignore them. I felt that as a writer I had to defend my own sense of style against any and every encroachment. But as time has gone by the complainants have brought about what they said was the case all along. By insisting that the generic "he" is not neuter but masculine, they have made it so; and so for a male writer to go on using it becomes a defiant act which may seem to signal all kinds of irrelevant and untrue things about himself—that he doesn't care about rape, beats his wife, thinks women inferior, and so on. I have therefore struggled (shall I say) manfully to avoid saying "the writer will find that he. . . ." It continues to be difficult; and for reasons which are still not clear to me, but have everything to do with English grammar and nothing to do with gender, I found it impossible and gave up the attempt.

Note that we have now come full circle from the discussion in chapter 3 about the supposed "naturalness" of gender classification in languages like English to the paradoxical position taken by Stead that reform has actually *made* English a language with natural gender. Thus, reformers are in effect only trying to establish what traditional grammarians have always maintained is the case, namely, that there is 100% congruence between gender and sex. If gender assignment had been really natural in the first place, there would have been no need for reform, nor for objections to it.

The changes brought about in the pronoun system in response to feminist activism of the type Stead would prefer to ignore are actually remarkable considering that there have been virtually no major changes in the English pronouns since the Middle English period (1100–1500). Only with the benefit of hindsight, however, will linguists be able to determine what long-term impact linguistic reforms will have, particularly as far as the spoken language is concerned. In the next chapter, however, I turn my attention to what prospects the future holds.

EXERCISES AND DISCUSSION QUESTIONS

1. Examine some newspapers and magazines to see how men and women are referred to. You could also write to the editor to ask what policies the paper has, if any, regarding nonsexist language use. Do not be surprised if you get no response. The editor of *United Airlines* magazine never answered my letter to her about my reaction to some of the examples of sexist usage I discussed in chapters 3 and 9. You may also be able to obtain some copies of back issues of papers and magazines from previous decades for comparison to see how styles of address have changed. Here are some guidelines for choice of publications which might yield interesting contrasts.

   a. "Up market" and "down market" newspapers; for example, in the United Kingdom you might compare usage in *The Financial Times* and *The Daily Mail*, or in the United States, the usage of the *New York Times*, the *Wall Street Journal*, *USA Today*, or the *National Enquirer*, with a less widely circulated newspaper. You could also contrast the norms for usage in publications from different English-speaking countries. What difference does audience make?
   b. Women's magazines such as *Cosmopolitan*, *New Woman*, *Ms.*, *Ladies' Home Journal*, *Family Circle*, *Working Woman*, and so on compared with magazines addressed mainly to men, such as *Popular Mechanics*, *Sports Illustrated*, and *Loaded*.
   c. Other magazines such as *Time*, *Newsweek*, *Forbes*, and *People*.
   d. Official publications and newsletters of universities, colleges, organizations, and so forth.
   e. Romances and other novels.

2. Deborah Cameron (1995, p. 136) documented a complaint that raises interesting questions about our understandings of the word *equality*. When her university published a leaflet on nonsexist usage, it defined sexist language as any item of language that "constitutes a male as a norm view of society by trivializing, insulting or rendering women invisible." Someone suggested changing sex-specific references to sex-inclusive ones, that is, male/female, women/men. The person who wrote the complaint said, "I found the fact that a document, promoting a type of equality, did not in itself treat subjects equally, quite worrying." Many universities in the United States have policies that outlaw racially or sexually stigmatizing remarks. If yours has one, examine what it says.

3. Discuss the policy on manuscript publication being practiced by the National Council of Teachers of English (NCTE). Do you agree with it? In his objection to it one male university dean said the guidelines treated

"the language like an innocent puppy waiting to be neutered for the convenience of his human masters." How would you react to the dean if you were the editor? What changes, if any, would you recommend he make to this statement? The NCTE policy does not authorize the editor to make changes relating to sexist content. Is it possible to separate sexist language from sexist content?

4. Is gender-exclusive language always sexist and is gender-inclusive language the same as nonsexist language? Julia Penelope, among others, has objected to gender inclusive usages such as *spouse beating,* which she claimed is not as accurate as *wife beating* because it obscures the fact that most cases of domestic violence involve men beating women. Is it acceptable to use generic masculine pronouns in connection with groups that are made up exclusively or almost exclusively of men, such as *when a serial killer strikes, his victims are usually not suspicious of his intentions?*

5. Americans have generally regarded freedom of speech as a sacred human right, foundational to the establishment of the United States. Advocates insist that it is essential to a democratic society, even if it offends some people at times. Many feminists, however, have regarded the principle of free speech as a paternalistic weapon used to silence and victimize women. It has been used, for instance, to defend pornography and sexually explicit advertising, as well as to resist feminist language reform. Is freedom of speech part of what Catherine MacKinnon (1987) referred to as the affirmative action plan in favor of men? You may also want to reconsider and discuss the case of virtual rape discussed in chapter 8.

6. Examine these entries from Mary Daly's *Websters' First New Intergalactic Wickedary of the English Language* (1987). Compare them with entries from traditional dictionaries such as the *Oxford English Dictionary, Webster's,* and so on. How likely are Daly's new words and meanings to be adopted? What role do you think dictionaries can and should play in reforming language usage?

Broom: Hag-ridden vehicle propelled by Rage, Transporting Dreadful/Dreadless Women out of the State of Bondage.

Cat/astrophe: an event precipitated by Catty Conspirators that subverts the patriarchal order or system of things.

Chaircrone: any Hag who occupies a chair.

Fall, the: one of patriarchy's Biggest Lies; the biblical story of the "original sin" of Adam and Eve, which projects all guilt upon women, enshrining the myth of feminine evil as revealed by god.

Fembot: female robot: the archetypal role model forced upon women throughout fatherland: the unstated goal/end of socialization into patriarchal womanhood: the totaled woman.

Homesick: 1: sickened by the home. 2: sick of the home; healthily motivated to escape the patriarchal home and family.

Mister-ectomy: guaranteed solution to The Contraceptive Problem; tried and true and therefore taboo birth control method, recommended by Gyn/Ecologists, insisted upon by Spinsters.

Old Maid: a Crone who has steadfastly resisted imprisonment in the Comatose State of matrimony: *survivor*, *Spinster*.

Penis envy: 1: classic reversal and projection propagated by the fraud freud and co.; conceptual cover-up for the male's hidden shame and sense of inadequacy. 2: phallic feeling among fellow members of the cockocratic Men's Association: elementary emotion of males obsessed with measurements of other members' members. 3: motivating emotion behind the missile build-up.

Sisterhood of Man: traditional expression giving a generic weight to the word *sisterhood* while at the same time emasculating the pseudo-generic term *man*. N.B.: This phrase is marked by built-in obsolescence, for, once the expression is understood, the culturally entrenched assumptions it reflects can be discarded. *Man* can no longer pass as a functioning generic and *sisterhood* is freed of the burden of association with this pseudogeneric context.

ANNOTATED BIBLIOGRAPHY AND SUGGESTIONS
FOR FURTHER READING

There are now numerous guides to nonsexist usage in English (see, e.g., Francine Wattman Frank and Paula Treichler, 1989; Ruth King, 1991; Cheris Kramarae and Paula Treichler, 1985; Casey Miller and Kate Swift, 1988, 1991; Rosalie Maggio, 1988) and in other languages (e.g., Marlis Hellinger and Christine Bierbach's 1993 guidelines for German, with a French translation; Alma Sabatini's guidelines for Italian, 1985, 1986; Monique Adriaen and Ruth King on French, 1991). In addition, Marlis Hellinger's (1990) book contains an overview of the efforts of German feminists in language reform and a very useful contrastive analysis of the different problems posed by German, English, and other European languages. Her edited collection (1985) deals with language reform from an international perspective. Deborah Cameron's (1995) book and articles (1990a, 1990b) address theoretical and political issues surrounding reform, as does the work of Cheris Kramarae (1992), Susan Ehrlich and Ruth King (1992, 1993, 1994), Betty Lou Dubois and Isabel Crouch (1987), Nancy Henley (1987), and Sally McConnell-Ginet (1989).

Aileen Pace Nilsen (1987) discusses her experiences with the NCTE policy on nonsexist language and provides an appendix on guidelines for nonsexist usage of language. She also co-edited a 1977 collection of articles about sexism in language, especially textbooks (Nilsen, Bosmajian, Haig, Gershuny, & Stanley, 1977). Fatemeh Khosroshashi's article (1989) reports the results of the study of changing perceptions of usage of generic pronouns at Harvard University. See also Dennis Baron's (1986, pp. 74–76) discussion of Henry James's attack on American women and the article by Luke, McHoul, and Mey (1990) for more general discussion of the limits of language planning.

CHAPTER

11

Writing Feminist Futures

On July 4, 1976, "the Viking probe"—a man-made vessel—will send back pictures to earth to let man see if life is on Mars. For what reason? Man has not mastered his existence here on earth. He cannot live in harmony with his natural environment yet. . . . Man is the only creation that is out of order with the Universal Order of Things. (Kenny Gambles, 1976, sleeve note to Dexter Wansel's album *Life on Mars*)

I believe we must cope courageously and practically, as women have always done, with the here and now, our feet on this ground where we now live. But nothing less than the most radical imagination will carry us beyond this place, beyond the mere struggle for survival, to that lucid recognition of our possibilities which will keep us impatient, and unresigned to mere survival. (Rich, 1980, p. 29)

MALE UTOPIA, FEMALE DYSTOPIA: THE ORIGINS OF FEMINIST FABULATION AND SPECULATIVE FICTION

There is a long tradition of writing about imagined and ideal societies, going back at least to Plato's *Republic* written in the fourth century B.C. Such literature is often called *utopian*, after one such ideal alternative society named Utopia by its author Thomas More (*Utopia, the Best of Republics Sited in the New Island of Utopia*, 1516). Plato's *Republic* was a rare instance among the texts of this genre to grant women equality. His imagined republic was communal and not centered around the nuclear family. Sexual relations were regulated and permitted only at certain times between predetermined partners. Household chores were communal activities, which freed women from domestic burdens. Despite the freedom accorded to women, Plato still believed they were inherently inferior to men. In order to become equal, they would have to participate in male activities, a view still held by many people today.

Yet things were far worse for women in More's Utopia, which from the female point of view was anything but ideal: It was a female dystopia, an anti-Utopia and a difficult place for women. More's utopian vision was strictly patriarchal, with fathers ruling over their wives and children. In her novel *Native Tongue* (1984), Suzette Haden Elgin imagined a futuristic society even more patriarchal than our own contemporary one. Elgin's society, like More's, was a male utopia, but a female dystopia.

In Haden Elgin's writing, as in many other utopian and speculative works, this imaginary society speaks an invented language. Many feminists such as Adrienne Rich have dreamed of a common language, true to women's experience, a "mother" rather than a "father" tongue, as Ursula Le Guin put it (see chap. 10). Imaginary languages in utopian societies tended at first to be conceived of as ideal means of communication designed to serve ideal societies. This reflected the philosophical concern of the 17th and 18th centuries for a perfect and logical universal language that would be a true reflection of thought and reality. In such a language it would be impossible to express a false or illogical idea. Although the language Tetrastichon played but a minor role in More's Utopia, it was supposed to be copious with words, pleasant to the ear, and "for the utterance of a man's mind perfect and sure." Haden Elgin's invented language, as we shall see, is a woman-made language designed by women to express their minds.

The classical utopias were remote in space, but not in time. In other words, they were portrayed as coexisting in the present, but in a different place. More's fictitious island Utopia is in fact a blending of *eutopia* (good place) and *outopia* (no place). Certainly it was no place for women! As I demonstrate, the themes of the utopias women have imagined have for the most part been different from those of men. Women have built their utopias on transformations of gender roles, expectations, and the dream of a common language.

Modern utopias have been portrayed as primarily temporal rather than spatial, as worlds that might exist in the future. Not everyone is of course optimistic about what the future holds in store, nor does everyone agree on what the ideal world would be like. Some authors of novels about futuristic societies, such as Haden Elgin, and George Orwell in his *Ninteen Eighty-Four* (1949), have painted a bleak picture. In Orwell's future, as in Haden Elgin's, a new language plays a key role. Although both novels derive their motitivation from the hypothesis that thought processes are influenced and even determined by language, Orwell's Newspeak goes hand in hand with an oppressive new totalitarian regime, whereas Elgin's Láadan, invented by women for women, provides a means of liberation for women dominated by a patriarchal society. The purpose of Orwell's Newspeak was to make it impossible for the citizens of Ingsoc to think any thoughts diverging from Ingsoc's ideological principles. Ideology precedes language in both cases; the task is to invent and spread a language to encode it.

Similarly, in Jean-Luc Godard's (1965) *Alphaville*, words referring to concepts that have been condemned by the central computer disappear automatically from the dictionaries found in every home. When that happens, people can no longer think of the concepts and things they refer to. In Monique Wittig's novel *Les Guérillères (The Female Warriors, 1969)* women compile a dictionary and revolt against male control of words and their meanings. They say that the vocabulary of every language is to be examined, turned upside down; every word must be screened. As I showed in the previous chapter, this scenario is in line with what many women have seen as one of the tasks of feminism—namely, taking back the language, reclaiming it from male domination, and redefining old words in new ways.

Insofar as some imagined utopias are located in the future, utopian writing can be thought of as overlapping with science fiction or to be more generally part of speculative fiction, a term used by some women writers to include feminist utopias, science fiction, fantasy, and so-called "sword and sorcery." The latter too often incorporates invented languages, as can be seen in J. R. R. Tolkien's *The Lord of the Rings* (1966), where the inhabitants of the imaginary Middle Earth speak languages invented by the author.

As a genre, science fiction draws on past literary traditions, taking something from classical utopian writing as well as from fairy tale, fantasy, myth, and fable. The boundaries among these different genres are far from clear and I do not intend to impose rigid definitions here. No agreed-on name has yet emerged for this new hybrid genre. Donna Haraway uses SF as a useful abbreviation indexing the connections between speculative fiction, science fiction, science fantasy, and speculative feminism. Many critics, however, are unhappy with the label *science fiction, space fiction,* or *feminist science fiction.* Joanna Russ, for instance (whose work I discuss later), prefers to call it simply *what-if literature,* because it attempts to portray things not as they are but as they might be. Marleen Barr (1992), on the other hand, prefers the term *feminist fabulation,* which encompasses science fiction as well as other literary forms. She also fears that calling it *science fiction* will result in its dismissal by those who have negative stereotypes about the genre and do not regard it as "real" literature. Women run the risk of having their work devalued or marginalized by those who might equate the goals of feminism with fantasy. In chapter 6 I showed that fairy tales were essentially a female genre. Despite male appropriation of their authorship in written form by collectors and writers such as Hans Christian Andersen, the Grimm brothers, and Charles Perrault (the first man to write down fairy tales), these stories were generally not regarded as serious literature because they were intended for children and associated with women through domestic images such as that of Mother Goose.

Mainstream critics have similarly dismissed romance novels, a very popular genre aimed specifically at women, who constitute more than half of the book-reading public. Currently one quarter to one third of the approximately 400 paperback titles issued each month in the United States and Britain are romances of one kind or another. It is difficult to know exactly how broad a social spectrum of women they reach because publishers keep most statistics about the demography of their readers secret.

Yet it is evident from Janice Radway's investigation of the reasons why women read romance novels that the genre derives some of its fundamental appeal from the possibilities it provides for escape from a world in which women have responsibilities and duties as caretakers and nurturers without receiving any support from others. Thus, the romance shares this escapist element in common with speculative fiction. In the fictitious world of the romance some of women's needs are met. The essential characteristics of a good romance plot are a happy ending, a romance between a hero and a heroine, which culminates in a perfect union. In many parts of the world where women still do not have the freedom to choose their marriage partners (and even where they do), romantic love is something to fantasize about.

The ideal male in these novels is very masculine but yet nurturing. He falls hopelessly in love with the heroine and needs her. Because he cares so completely for her, she can be passive and allow herself to be taken care of as she was while a child. The women whom Radway interviewed admitted that this was very much a world unlike the real one they inhabited. When reading the romance, women are able to imagine themselves as they often are not in everyday life. By casting themselves as heroines in these love stories, they escape from an unheroic world. Reading the romance supplements the avenues traditionally open to women for emotional gratification by supplying them vicariously with the attention they do not get in everyday life. Some critics have noted that the divorce rate has risen in tandem with the sales of romance novels!

Yet this leisure-time withdrawal leaves women's domestic role in patriarchy virtually intact. These books do not directly address the discontent that gives rise to romance reading in the first place. Thwaite, for instance, examined three Boons and Mills romances and found that women characters more often had things done to them. Males were more often the doers, as is more generally the case in public discourse. Others have pointed out, however, that these fantasies are a kind of empowerment for women because the main female character overpowers the male with uncontrollable passion for her. From the perspective of a theory grounded in women's subjective experiences, reading romances may be one way in which women try to control their anger and aggression toward male power.

As one example of this genre, consider Elisabeth Barr's *The Sea Treasure* (1979), the story of a heroine, Lenora, who is cut off from her family and earlier identity through amnesia. When she is rescued by the hero, Dominic, she has only two distant memories—one of a loving woman, the other of a terrifying man. Because she fears all men as a consequence, she refuses to respond to Dominic, who falls in love with her almost immediately. He embodies an ideal hero's love for his heroine in the image of a mother who stays with her child through a storm to soothe its fears. Lenora is excited by a man who is willing to nurture her in this way.

> He went across to her, and held the shaking body close to his, stroking her hair . . .
> He lay on the coverlet, putting his arm around her and cradling her head against her shoulders. Lenora sighed once, deeply, and her lids fluttered over her eyes. In a little while she slept . . .
> In the fireplace, the dying coals fell with a soft crash, making Lenora start and tremble in her sleep, until he soothed her with the touch of his fingers on her cheek and she slept again. (p. 132)

In the end Lenora accepts his love. Significantly, he also reunites her with her lost mother. The romance transforms traditional masculinity so that it conforms more to female standards. Unrealistically, the male heroes of this genre graft tenderness onto basically unaltered male characters. Thus, traditional roles for men and women are not really challenged as radically as they are in other kinds of feminist fabulation that I examine shortly.

Over the past few decades, writing about future worlds has become increasingly popular with women authors. A kind of mini-boom in feminist utopian and speculative writing is largely contemporaneous with the women's movement. Even in the mid 1970s, however, Suzy McKee Charnas looked for several years to find a publisher willing to publish her book *Motherlines* (1978). The novel had no male characters, and publishers feared that readers would not be interested in a "woman-only" vision of the future. Just as Edwin Ardener and Ivan Illich were told that academic books about women would not sell (see chap. 1), one editor told Charnas (1981), "You know, if this book was all about *men* it would be a terrific story" (p. 103). This reflects some of the findings I discussed in chapters 1, 2, 6, and 7 on male preference for being the subject. Few men are interested in speculative fiction written by women, let alone in the feminist theories that motivate it. Many of the authors are nevertheless committed to making feminist criticism and viewpoints part of mainstream contemporary thought. Critic Jack Zipes (1986a, p. xiii) went so far as to claim that "it is impossible today to be a critic without being a feminist." When this really becomes true, we will have no need to talk of "feminist" critics because the ground rules for criticism will dictate that texts have multiple meanings and that no reading has a claim to privileged status as "objective." Zipes thus appeared to endorse a broad view of feminism that goes beyond a focus on women (see chap. 2).

TO BOLDLY GO WHERE NO WOMAN
HAS GONE BEFORE

As in the case of romance novels, speculative fiction permits a chance for creation of other worlds and escape from one in which women's opportunities and roles are limiting. It offers women the opportunity to explore contentious issues safely. The textual world too has imposed constraints on women because most literary genres have been male dominated, even fairy tales claiming to speak in a woman's voice in the persona of Mother Goose and other female figures. Feminist speculative fiction is more likely to imagine women in charge of a world no longer dominated by men. Fantasy provides one of the few outlets for women to be depicted as heroes, in contrast with the traditional fairy-tale scenario in which females are beautiful princesses, or ugly and wicked stepmothers and witches, whereas men are handsome princes or brave heroes.

Science fiction written by male authors often portrays men overcoming the constraints of nature and conquering the universe as suggested in my opening epigraph to this chapter. This reflects the metaphorization of woman as nature and wilderness, which I discussed in chapter 3. The idea of female space existing outside or apart from a male-dominated society is played out in some feminist speculative fiction, such as Sally Miller Gearhart's *The Wanderground: Stories of the Hill Women* (1978), where women live in a wilderness, and men control the city. The female space is what Elaine Showalter (1985, p. 262) called 'the wild zone' a place where women's values and lifestyle exist outside the dominant male culture. Despite our stereotypical image of utopia as places of warmth, abundance, and so forth, there is also a recurrent setting of frozen landscape found in Margaret Cavendish's early novel (1666) down to the works of more recent authors such as Ursula Le Guin, whose imaginary planet Gethen/Winter has a glacial climate.

Doris Lessing is in some respects typical of women who have made the move from realist to speculative fiction to avail herself of the narrative opportunities possible within the latter genre. In 1979 she began publishing her space fiction with the appearance of *Shikasta*, the first novel of a five-volume series. Although some critics expressed dismay at her "sudden" conversion to science fiction, well over a decade earlier her work contained elements of futuristic speculation, particularly *The Four-Gated City* (1969). Her series asserts an androgynous vision of the future. The inhabitants of Canopus can be either male or female when they visit the corrupt world of Shikasta.

Among the alternative realities women are exploring are matriarchy with or without separatism (i.e., worlds dominated by women, in which men either play a subordinate role or are totally absent from the scene), and androgyny, where masculine and feminine are combined in one person. In these new societies women do not simply gain access to male privileges by acting like men, as Plato would have had it. Both sexes are affected by a new value system. Alternatively, men are excluded from some of these utopias because they are believed to be responsible for violence and in-equality. It is therefore liberating for women to imagine and write about a world without men. Joanna Russ pointed out (1976) that all-male utopias are virtually nonexistent because men do not feel exploited by women. Thus, the themes of male and female utopian writers are strikingly different.

However, the origins of feminist speculative writing go back much farther in time than this recent mini-boom prompted by the modern women's movement. Jane Donawerth and Carol Kolmerten (1994) traced a continu-ous literary tradition of women writing utopian and science fiction from the 17th century to the present. They use the term *literature of estrangement* to refer to texts concerning alienation in a setting displaced in time and/or space. The first woman to write such a utopian novel in English was Margaret Cavendish, author of *The Description of a New World, Called the Blazing-World* (1666). In it she explored a new world located at the north pole, where an Empress has absolute power and undertakes to give women the benefit of education not available to most women outside the Blazing-World.

Around the same time, in France, Marie Catherine d'Aulnoy and Made-leine de Scudéry wrote books in which new idyllic worlds were located on islands, where educated women enjoyed freedom to develop spiritually and intellectually. d'Aulnoy (1690) called her society the Island of Felicity, whose location was unknown to anyone. There women lived in isolation from men until a male intruder discovered them. The absence of men from these early female utopias, as in later ones, is essential in order for women to escape patriarchal authority and values. The women live in harmony and peace on the Island of Felicity, where intimacy rather than hierarchy defines relations among the inhabitants.

d'Aulnoy's plot included elements of romance too. When a Russian prince manages to find Felicity, he falls instantly in love with the ruling

Princess. The two live happily for 300 years until the prince realizes he has been idling with a mistress for so long rather than been engaging in politics and warfare. Once he leaves the island, time catches up with him and he dies. The princess is heartbroken and the story ends unhappily with the moral that there is no perfect felicity as long as men and women have such different values, dreams, and ambitions.

The plot of Sarah Scott's *A Description of Millenium Hall* (1762) shares some similarities. A group of aristocratic women have developed an alternative idealized community that is physically insulated from the rest of society until it is discovered by two male travelers. In Millenium Hall women live in a communal egalitarian society, whose prime interest lies in education and the cultivation of arts.

In the 19th and 20th centuries science and technology provide solutions to societal problems as well as a means of escape from them. Although some recognize Mary Shelley (author of *Frankenstein*, 1818) as the mother of science fiction, prior to 1900 most female characters in the genre were minor. With the exception of Mary Shelley, whose *Frankenstein* was probably the most influential work of science fiction written by a woman, almost all science fiction authors were male and wrote from a male point of view. Not surprisingly, some of the early women writers in the twentieth century used male pseudonyms and wrote from a male point of view too. Today most science fiction is still written by men about male heroes. Many critics have complained of the genre's misogyny. Science fiction, particularly in its so-called "pulp" variety, has, however, long acknowledged the power and male fear of powerful women in the role of aliens such as Amazons or witches with magic abilities. Feminist science fiction seeks to appropriate these images as symbols of female empowerment.

Just because a story has a woman as its main character or is written by a woman does not necessarily make it feminist science fiction. It depends on what we mean by feminism. As I have argued throughout this book, feminism is not a single viewpoint, but allows a wide range of views from androgyny to gynocentrism (see chap. 2). Conversely, if we reject biological essentialism, just because a story is written by a man about male characters, this does not rule out a feminist perspective. At the same time we cannot ignore the fact that a women who dared to write a novel criticizing aspects of the society in which she lived ran far greater risks than a man, not to mention the fact that a woman had fewer opportunities to write (or even speak) to begin with. The very idea of a female voice of authority flouted convention. I noted in the previous chapter critics' reactions to the works of early women novelists such as the Brontë sisters. Authors such as hattie gossett (1981) felt a certain amount of guilt at the self-indulgence of writing, knowing that most of her audience not only could not read but viewed reading as a waste of time. Books such as her own were not going to be sold in ghetto bookshops. Similarly, anthropologist Lila Abu-Lughod (1993) regretted that the Bedouin women whose stories she wrote down were not the audience of her book.

Shortly before his death in 1873, Edward George Earle Bulwer-Lytton (1871) published *The Coming Race or the New Utopia*, and with it began a new era of anti-utopian writing in which imaginary languages became instruments of enslavement or manipulation. The novel was about a superior human civilization living underground for millennia in which women were the more physically powerful and natural rulers. Bulwer-Lytton devoted an entire chapter to the Vril language spoken by the Vril-ya people.

The plot revolved around the attraction between Zee, a woman of the underground world, and the male narrator. Zee combines some of the qualities associated with both male and female. She is physically strong and powerful like a man, yet caring and giving like a woman. Although he rebuffs her advances, Zee saves the narrator by helping him escape back to his world. Bulwer-Lytton thus creates an alternative world to our own, in which male and female have different roles.

The women of Zee's world were early prototypes of the Amazon women, which became popular in later science fiction. Some of these Amazons are, however, negatively portrayed as cruel and hateful to men, as in H. Rider Haggard's novel *She* (1886), where the Queen Ayesha (She who must be obeyed) is evil and wicked. In the works of other male writers, such as Edgar Rice Burroughs (acknowledged by some critics as the "grand-daddy of American science fiction"), scantily dressed and alluring female characters are routinely threatened with sexual assault.

Mary E. Bradley Lane's novel *Mizora: A Prophecy*, which first appeared in serial form in 1880 and 1881, provided an early model of an all female society living in the earth's interior. The men have disappeared as a result of a war between the sexes. The women meanwhile have developed a way of reproduction not dependent on men. In fact, the disappearance of men has resulted in technological advances that make this a superior civilization with no need for security or laws. Violence has disappeared along with the men. In Mizora's classless society everyone is employed and everyone's job is meaningful.

Another early model for a matriarchal society was offered by Mrs. George Corbett's *New Amazonia: A Foretaste of the Future* (1889), set in Ireland in the year 2472. Although men are present, only unmarried women are eligible for ruling positions. Around the same time, Alice Ilgenfritz Jones and Ella Merchant wrote under a pseudonym *Unveiling a Parallel: A Romance* (1893), in which three different worlds coexist, their own Earth society, and two imaginary societies on Mars where women are equal to men. In one of these Martian worlds, however, women have become like men in a negative way. The main character Elodia behaves just like a successful American businessman. In the other, equality has made both sexes kind, loving and generous.

In Charlotte Perkins Gilman's utopian novel *Herland* (1915), men have been extinct for two thousand years and women have established a technologically advanced society. When male explorers accidentally stumble on this all-female world, they assumed that this superior civilization has been built by men. In these early works of utopian and science fiction we can see a variety of themes that have proved useful for contemporary feminist futures.

WOMEN'S SPACE: FROM OUTER SPACE
TO INNER SPACE

One purpose of this new genre of women's fiction, whatever we call it, is to create a positive space for women, a Somewhere that exists in antithesis to a world with Nowhere for women. Although there is a need for reclaiming and rewriting the past, writers of feminist speculative fiction have usually seen more scope for women to take charge of their lives by creating their own futures. Anything can happen in the future, whereas the past requires considerably more reconstruction. As Marge Piercy put it in *Woman on the Edge of Time* (1976), "I want to do something very important. Like fly into the past and make it come out right" (p. 22). Feminist theory and criticism are devoted to revealing how male dominance in the past and present has been constructed on differences seen as natural, inescapable, and therefore morally and scientifically correct. An important tool is the rewriting of the traditional fairy tales and myths of origin within Western and other cultures, such as those I discussed in chapters 2 and 6, that have colonized women and made them Others.

In Jane Yolen's (1977) reworking of the traditional fairy tale of the little mermaid, women return to the sea rather than live in male-governed worlds. In Joanna Russ's (1986) version of the same story the mermaid resists the prince's attempt to transform her into a land princess according to his image of a "real woman." These versions contrast with that of Hans Christian Andersen in which the mermaid's new feet bleed from the pain of having her tail transformed into human legs and feet. The mermaid's sisters exchange their magically beautiful hair in return for a sword from the Sea Witch with which the mermaid must kill the Prince who has enticed her to want human form.

By retelling old stories and narrating new ones, women are breaking the silence. Several fairy tales explicitly deal with silence as punishment. In the tale of the twelve brothers a little girl must keep silent as a condition of her brothers' redemption from the curse that has turned them into birds. The little mermaid has to lose her tongue and suffer great pain in return for human form. Her silence is a precondition for her female form on land. She does not complain when her feet bleed, and she refuses to turn against the prince so that she can become a mermaid again. The moral of the tale is that even having your tongue cut off is not enough to prove your virtue. Self-obliteration is needed: As she throws herself into the ocean she dissolves in air. Dale Spender (1982) and others showed that women have found it difficult to perceive themselves as part of a tradition because women have disappeared from history like the little mermaid who disappears without a trace.

Writing "herstory" or "hystery" is a means of self-definition, a creation of a female subjectivity. I write, therefore I am. If history is properly herstory, hystery is the origin of the womb and the past becomes hysterical. The traditional genre of autobiography, however, has been problematic for some women because it has been shaped by gender ideology that has assumed a male subject. This makes it necessary to create what Stanton (1984) called *autogynography*, or Audre Lorde's (1982) genre of biomythography.

In order to write herstory, women have been engaged in writing feminist critiques of various disciplines, such as anthropology, history, psychology, literature, and linguistics. Feminist perspectives on science have aimed to expose the false universality of the male point of view by taking into account the class, race, culture, and gender of the researcher as important influences on both research methods and findings. Jesse Bernard (1973), for instance, declared sociology a "male science of society" because it equated male subjectivity with scientific objectivity. The establishment of the so-called "hard" sciences has based itself on the ideal of dispassionate objectivity. The linguistic hallmarks of this scientific authority are depersonalized third person discourse (one can see that . . . , the present writer believes), passives (the liquid was poured into a beaker and heated), and so forth. In *De Bello Gallico* Caesar wrote about himself and his conquests in the third person because to have written in the first person would be too personal and more intimate, and therefore unacceptable. To write from the intimate point of view of the first person would be to write less credibly for an audience who vested authority in the objective historian writing in the third person rather than the participant eyewitness. The use of the first person "I" is often said to mean that the text is less objective, but what is objectivity supposed to prevent—intuition, subjectivity? All marks of speaker subjectivity are erased from history, and science written in the third person. It is as if events speak for themselves (see chap. 2, however, for discussion of the illusions behind this assumption). The freeing of the author from participation supposedly allows objective analysis of events and so on to appear from a detached point of view. These are the conventional fictions of objectivity and omniscience that mark Western science, and, for a time, the novel. As I noted in chapter 2, the professional discourse of authority and objectivity is a language of power.

Scholars are supposed to be detached from their work in order to be objective. The problem, as Jane Tompkins (1989, pp. 122–123) put it, is that you're not supposed "to talk about your private life in the course of doing your professional work. You have to pretend that epistemology, or whatever you're writing about, has nothing to do with your life, that it's more important, because it (supposedly) transcends the merely personal." The writer as authority has become divorced from the writer as person in the service of objectivity.

How is the desire for objectivity to be reconciled with the obvious fact that we are all personal participants in our research and have some point of view? Pacific historian J. W. Davidson (1967, p. x) felt he had to explain (apologize?) to his readers that he was a participant in the events he was writing about, and that his participation had been a major personal experience: "If my role as a participant has brought added understanding, it has also created some danger of loss of detachment." Why was Davidson afraid to lose his detachment and to reveal his very obvious personal commitment to the events that led to the independence of Western Samoa?

Tompkins concluded that the reason she feels embarrassed at her own attempts to speak personally is that she's been conditioned to feel that way. Self-knowledge takes on a confessional and anecdotal, even gossipy, tone, which is suspect and certainly not science. Female academics have thus learned to depersonalize their voices in order to be taken seriously (see chap. 7).

In her critique of the language of anthropological discourse, Trinh Minh-Ha (1989) showed how the science devoted to the study of man has constructed both women and natives as Others. Her statement that anthropology is better defined as gossip in which Western men discuss other non-Western men is an ironic dismissal of science's claims to truth and objectivity. By labeling anthropology as gossip, the ultimate of personal and feminine genres (see chap. 6), she underlines the falsehood in its spreading of knowledge about others.

At the moment there are no accepted conventions or solutions to the problem of gendering the academic (or literary) voice in a specifically female way. Lila Abu-Lughod (1993) tried to write ethnography in a different voice by presenting the life experiences of Bedouin women in the form of narratives they themselves had told them. Although feminist anthropology or the anthropology of women is now an important field of research, James Clifford (1986, p. 21) maintained that it has not produced unconventional forms of writing. One reason he suggests is that groups long excluded from positions of institutional power have less freedom to indulge in textual experimentation.

I have often noticed that seniority allows one to speak more personally. To be unconventional, it helps to have tenure! We are all familiar with the keynote speech given by an éminence grise, usually male, in which the speaker recounts "anecdotes," tales of personal experiences and personalities, and so forth (see Geertz, 1995, for a written example of this genre). For a junior scholar to do this would be to risk professional suicide, to be dismissed as having nothing important to say. The embodied knowledge present in personal narratives leads it to be dismissed as anecdotal. I experienced a striking instance of this when a male editor who asked to see a few chapters of this book commented on the "anecdotes" in chapter 8 about women's experience and understanding of sexuality, rape, sexual harassment. The problem Clifford identified as freedom of experientation is actually one of power to define norms. As Dwight Atkinson (1996) showed, the founders of the Royal Society of London, Britain's leading scientific organization, wrote their scientific articles in a more personal style than scientists do today. The personal word of a gentleman sufficed then to convince the audience of his authority on scientific matters.

Postcolonial theory is concerned with the way in which speaking for others in our voice has displaced or appropriated the voices of less powerful others. The representation of others is not easily separable from their manipulation. Is it possible to write about anyone but ourselves without power and dominance entering the picture? Pronouns are indices that position ourselves and others on the contested battleground of discourse. If we do not wish to preempt the right of others to speak for themselves, we must distinguish ourselves from others. But as Donna Haraway (1991, p. 155) asked, who counts as "us" in my own rhetoric? Or as Lorraine Bethel said in her poem "What Chou Mean We, White Girl?" Bethel pointed to the problem I observed in chapter 1 that neither gender nor race nor class can provide the basis for a belief in essential unity.

I am sympathetic to Bakhtin's (1929) view of the self not as a subject or essence in its own right, but as something that can exist only dialogically by virtue of its relation to other selves. Understanding of anything takes place from some point of view. Therefore my point of view is different from yours because I am not you. Because I cannot see the self that I am, I see it in the eyes of others as they must see themselves in my eyes.

If I reject static, essentialism, it follows that I don't believe there is anything irreducibly necessary about "being female" that defines women. That means I cannot by virtue of my female biology speak for all women. So do I say "we," "I," or "they"? I have never much liked the convention of writing "we" when I really mean "I" and have avoided this as much as possible in this book. The first person pronoun and the feminine *she/her* are personal and gender specific, but am I or is anyone else ever just female?

I believe we all search for voices that do not violate the many components of our identity. Haraway (1991, p. 188) wrote that feminist objectivity means simply situated knowledge. Whether I am writing about women, bilingualism, or whatever, I cannot help but leave traces of myself and my personal experiences as a woman, my class, race, nationality, and my debates with myself about the literature that I read. These are the unavoidable conditions, the starting points of my observations.

Feminist critiques have also examined the ways in which the contributions of women have either been ignored or silenced. Ann Oakley (1975a, 1975b) drew attention to housework as a serious activity worthy of study. Within linguistics, Julia Falk (1994) began to document the activities of the women who were founding members of the Linguistic Society of America. Frances Karttunen (1994) examined the lives of a number of non-Western women who were interpreters of their culture to Western explorers in the New World, such as Sacajawea, the Shoshone woman who served as guide and interpreter to the Lewis and Clark expedition, and Doña Marina (known as La Malinche), interpreter for Hernán Cortés in his conquest of Mexico. In so far as Doña Marina's contribution is even acknowledged by historians, she has been generally been charged with the betrayal of indigenous cultures. Karttunen speculated that the explorers may have provided escape for these and other women from the confines of traditional females roles.

Virginia Woolf (1928b, p. 45) pointed out long ago the great gap between women's symbolic position in literature and their representation among the literary establishment when she wrote: "Imaginatively she is of the highest importance; practically she is completely insignificant. She pervades poetry from cover to cover; she is all but absent from history."

Although Woolf modestly pleaded for a room of her own in which to write, feminist science fiction demands even more space, a universe of one's own. Mary Daly's wickedary of words, which I discussed in the previous chapter, contains an entry for *Women's Space*, which she defines as "Space in which women find Rooms, Looms, Brooms of our Own." In women's space there is room to let down your hair and to escape confinement to domestic roles, in contrast to women's portrayal in traditional fairy tales. The shoe, for instance, as an image of women's containment in marriage and domesticity is played out in stories as diverse as the old woman who lived in a shoe with her many children and the glass slipper that fits only Cinderella's foot, as well as in the Chinese tradition of foot binding, and the European custom of giving newlyweds a pair of old shoes.

Given the virtual exclusion of women from careers as pilots and astronauts, the very claiming of outer space itself is symbolic. It is the final male frontier—to boldly go where no man has gone before, as the television epic Star Trek proclaimed. Flying means freedom (as seen in Erica Jong's *Fear of Flying*, 1973), an escape from a male-controlled space, a space threatening to women. Hélène Cixous (1975/1986) also attaches a special significance to flying as a gesture of women's liberation. She points out the double meaning in French *voler*, which means both to fly and to steal.

Women need to fly the coop, to steal away, to fly into the past and seize the future to make it turn out right. In Claudine Hermann's novel (1976) women are *voleuses de langue* (language stealers), taking back the language.

Some praised the highly successful television program *Star Trek*, which first appeared in the mid-1960s, for its pioneering attitude toward women. The ship's communication officer was a woman, as were a number of guest commanders on individual episodes. There were also a number of women in professional roles as geologists, biologists, and so on. Some of these women, however, did not escape stereotypical ideas about female behavior, such as the character of Dr. Janet Lester, who was supposed to have had an unhappy love affair with Captain James Kirk when they were both at the Space Academy. Her ambition to become a space captain had interfered with their romance. She tried to get revenge on Kirk through technology that allowed her to switch minds with him. As the mind of Lester in his body she tried to destroy him because she felt, "It's better to be dead than to live alone in the body of a woman." Kirk explained Lester's motives by saying that she craved power because she didn't "merit" a position as captain. Now she wanted to murder him because "her intense hatred of her own womanhood made [his] life with her impossible." During the course of the episode, however, Lester broke down. She could not handle the pressures of being captain. In the end she appeared as a small child banging her fist and crying because no one would follow her orders. This plot is a familiar one, replayed in films such as *Fatal Attraction*, where the avenging she-devil is defeated in the end.

A central concern of feminine futures is the imagination of a world without gender differentiation and inequality. Naturally, not all writers agree on what consequences would follow from this. For some, gender equality would result in a feminization of society. For others, equality would be based on androgyny. Language has played an important role in these futuristic scenarios. Speaking or narrating in a feminist or gender-neutral language is central to overcoming patriarchy. It becomes a kind of antilanguage, a language of resistance. Margaret Atwood's *The Handmaid's Tale* (1986), for example, speaks in a feminist antilanguage. Her character, Maryann Crescent Moon, a scholar of Caucasian anthropology, gives a lecture at a conference held at the University of Denay located in Nunavit. Nunavit stands for the patriarchal world in which women have "none of it," where "it" means all of the good things and advantages in life. Sheila Finch's novel *Infinity's Web* (1985) also articulated the need for a new nonpatriarchal language, which doesn't limit women's roles, and which creates new names for women's roles. I discuss more examples later.

Although most people think of science fiction as a genre dealing with the exploration of outer space, given the speculative nature of the genre and its future orientation, science fiction is an ideal genre for rewriting of male and female roles and characters. It provides a forum for moral and political allegory. Some authors have used it as a context for exploring inner female space, the outer limits of human potential. The story of a great journey or crusade undertaken in quest of oneself is well established in the Western literary tradition. Usually it has been a male character who embarks on such a journey—Odysseus, for instance, or Prometheus. In chapter 2 I showed how past tales of female seekers of knowledge, like Eve and Pandora, end in disaster. Women's stupidity, wickedness, vanity, and curiosity undermine them, for which their punishment, like that of Lot's wife who could not resist the temptation to look back, has been silence.

The travel into future times and outer space becomes a metaphor for the psychological journey inward, a voyage into what Mary Daly has called "hagocentric space." Women can be and are portrayed as whole beings, free of gender stereotypes and in charge of their own lives. Female utopias set out to challenge the forces that most directly oppress women, such as the low status and pay attached to "women's work." In some cases there is a revaluation of traditional female occupations such as teaching school. Some also assert female power by emphasizing motherhood, the maternal instinct, and female sisterhood.

Twentieth-century feminist science fiction continues to explore gender identity. A number of modern novels involve characters who change their gender. Virginia Woolf's *Orlando* (1928a) is about a man who awakens one morning as a woman. Lois Gould's *A Sea Change* (1976) is the story of Jessie Waterman, who becomes the gunman who raped her during a burglary. Such novels suggest the androgynous potential in all of us. Gender is a social construct rather than biologically fixed.

Joanna Russ's *The Female Man* (1976) underlines the significant impact environment can make. The four main characters are all genetically identical but inhabit parallel universes. Jeannine comes from a 1930s-like America, Joanna from the late 1960s, Jael from a future time when Womanland and Manland are two warring camps, and Janet is a visitor from an all-female universe called Whileaway. Jeannine, Joanna, and Jael live in worlds where humor is used against women. Joanna observes that women's attempts to question or alter their status in society are treated as jokes by men, whereas male violence against women is condoned under the label of good-humored "fun" (see chap. 8). Women's rights are invalidated as jokes. Joanna declares herself to be a "female man" because she has been told so often that words like *man, man-kind,* and *he* refer to all people. Only Janet has experience of a different kind of humor, which does not wound or function to maintain a male hierarchy. In Whileaway a plague wiped out all the men nearly a thousand years before. Until men appear on the planet there is no need to use the word *he*.

Jody Scott's *I, Vampire* (1984) also presents a future scenario in which men and their reproductive role are eliminated. In such societies the word *human* becomes synonymous with *female*. Such worlds are threatening to male dominance in the same way as are worlds where women have psychic powers. Because only women have the power to reproduce, they are essential to the continuation of the male line. Adrienne Rich (1978) explained that the idea of dependence on women for life itself is responsible both for male fear as well as oppression of women.

STRANGE BEDFELLOWS AND THE LANGUAGE OF THE FUTURE

Ursula K. Le Guin's *The Left Hand of Darkness* (1969) takes place on the planet Gethen/Winter, inhabited by humanoids who can involuntarily assume the reproductive functions of either sex. One consequence of not being able to choose whether one will act as a female or male is that rape is no longer possible. Gethen/Winter is a nonviolent society operating under feminist principles of equality. In writing about her work Le Guin describes it as an experiment in eliminating gender in order to see whether real differences exist between men and women. By removing women from their biological role as mothers, Le Guin is able to critique the institution of motherhood, as does Marge Piercy in her novel *Woman on the Edge of Time* (1976). Piercy portrays motherhood and child care as communal activities and not just the responsibility of persons who are biologically female. Each child is assigned three "mothers," to whom it is not related genetically. As I noted in chapter 2, most feminist theorists see the freeing of women from the role of reproduction and child care as necessary for equality.

In our own world technology may have freed women from some of the drudgery and time associated with certain household chores, but not from their domestic role (see chap. 9). Similarly, it has proved easy to invent bottles as substitutes for breast-feeding, and breast pumps to extract the mother's milk, but not to create the social conditions under which men take primary responsibility for child care. Women's economic dependence on men has been supported by governments that provide inadequate maternity leave and child-care arrangements. Because only women become pregnant, failure to take it into account in the workplace automatically disadvantages women and advantages men. The pattern of female employment has followed women's domestic role, where they provide support services to the work done by men. Even the most popular female professions, nursing and teaching, are basically service positions. The most important positions within female-dominated service positions have been generally filled by men. The persons in charge of kitchens and dining room service are likely to be male chefs and headwaiters rather than waitresses.

As long as the debate focuses on the issue of biological difference, we miss the point that women's inequality results from a world so organized that men's needs and rights are implicit, whereas women's are regarded as "special" and in need of explicit justification. This is how difference becomes dominance.

Without using the term "androcentric" to describe such a world, legal scholar Catherine MacKinnon (1987, p. 36) summed it up well when she wrote:

> Virtually every quality that distinguishes men from women is . . . affirmatively compensated in this society. Men's physiology defines most sports, their needs define auto and health insurance coverage, their socially designed biographies define workplace expectations and successful career patterns, their perspectives and concerns define quality in scholarship, their experiences and obsessions define merit, their objectification of life defines art, their military service defines citizenship, their presence defines family, their inability to get along with each other—their wars and rulerships—defines history, their image defines god, and their genitals define sex. For each of these differences from women, what amounts to an affirmative action plan is in effect, otherwise known as the structure and values of American society.

However, this affirmative action plan, as MacKinnon put it, passes for reality, for what is natural. Nevertheless, laws seeking to guarantee women and minorities the rights taken for granted for White males are controversial.

Illich (1982) is pessimistic about feminist dreams of a genderless economy without compulsory sex roles. Economic growth is intrinsically destructive and sexist. Sexism can only be reduced or eliminated at the cost of economic shrinkage (the idea that equality between the sexes must be founded on economic contraction rather than expansion). He is compelled to this conclusion by the fact that legislation has so far not eliminated the sexist exploitation characteristic of industrialized societies. The nation-state is invariably sexist.

If within such a nation-state women's needs are treated as "special," then so are their dilemmas, as is obvious in a "special" issue devoted to retirement by *U.S. News & World Report* (1994), which featured a page devoted to what was termed "A woman's special dilemma." The special dilemma was further described as a "double whammy" in which professional women with four years of college education earned only 63% of the wages earned by men with the same amount of education. The amount a wage earner can put into an employer-sponsored retirement plan and the size of a person's pension and social security benefits all depend on earnings. Half of the elderly women in the United States living alone have incomes of less than $9,500. Divorce rates have gone up, leaving many women and children without support, and there is no guarantee that a woman will get any benefit from her husband's pension.

Some feminists like Andrea Dworkin, who see the traditional family as the source of patriarchal power, want to undermine it, along with other male forms of dominance such as traditional religions based on female subordination and evil, on up to the nation-state. Dworkin (1974, 1981) favors a return to the extended family or tribe as a more egalitarian society, a theme played out in some of the works I mentioned earlier, where women live on their own.

In her book *The Marriages Between Zones Three, Four and Five* (1980), Doris Lessing experimented with a nonseparatist vision in which men and women are not aliens inhabiting different worlds. Lessing initially locates masculine and feminine traits in different zones. Male feminists reside in Zone Three. There women and nonpatriarchal men live together harmoniously, but their relationships are stagnant. They do not wonder what things are like in the other zones. Lessing defines static relationships as unsuccessful ones. Movement between zones is necessary to bring about change and to move beyond separatism. Her message is that gender shouldn't be confined to zones. True to the spirit of French feminism's idea of a feminist text, the series contains no ending. It resists closure.

Lessing touches on some of the dissatisfaction with the concept of androgyny in feminist theory. Critics of the notion have claimed that it reproduces the very gender polarization it endeavors to eliminate. By emphasizing the complementarity of masculine and feminine traits, it assumes these as ideal givens, and thus endorses the naturalness of heterosexuality. As Sandra Bem (1993, p. 124) puts it, androgyny focuses more on the individual's being both masculine and feminine rather than on the cultural creation of the concepts of masculinity and femininity.

Despite her portrayal of a world without fixed sex roles and gender identity, Le Guin has been criticized for her consistent use of the male generic *he* in describing the androgynous inhabitants of Gethen/Winter. For example, in discussing what happens when Gethenians go to the so-called *kemmerhouse*, where mating takes place, she says that the house is open to anyone in *kemmer* so that "he can find a partner."

Le Guin's (1979) initial response was that the novel was not about sex, gender, or feminism and she refused to "mangle English" by inventing a pronoun to replace the traditional *he/she*. She also pointed out that the narrator was a male earthling. However, Le Guin did invent other new terms, for instance, to describe the different kinds of snow and ice found in the planet's glacial climate, so her resistance to innovative pronouns is somewhat curious. In a revised edition of one of her stories set on Gethen and published some years later, Le Guin (1987) changed her mind. Professing that she disliked the "so-called generic pronouns which excluded women from discourse," she changed the pronouns to *they/them* or *she/her*. Nevertheless, Le Guin's novel demonstrates an interesting point. Even though readers expect the unexpected in science fiction, including the invention of androgynous Genthians, our conceptual apparatus is very much guided and circumscribed by the distinctions of our language. Readers felt Le Guin's conventional language was not adequate to match the new world she had narrated. Readers will tend to assume, unless told otherwise, that characters, even androgynous ones, are male. Le Guin's language reinforced that tendency. At the same time, however, she produced a number of clashes similar to ones I discussed in chapter 3. For example, in the first edition of the novel, there are sentences such as *The king was pregnant*, and *It was difficult to imagine him as a young mother*. In the first instance, the anomaly is caused by the semantics of *king*, and in the second by the lack of semantic agreement between *mother* and *him*. Her replacement of the male pronouns with females ones does not solve the Gethenian pronoun problem. In the later edition of her story "Winter's King" set on the planet we have clashes such as *The young king had her back against the wall*, where the semantics of *king* is at odds with the feminine pronoun *her*.

Finally, when a 25th anniversary edition of *The Left Hand of Darkness* appeared in 1995, Le Guin invented a set of pronouns: *e* (for *he/she*), *en* (for *her/him*), *es* (for *his/her/hers*) and *enself* (for *himself/herself*). In an afterword to the book, the author explained how she was led to this solution by the Great Gethenian pronoun problem.

In her transsexual fantasy *In Transit* (1969, p. 69), Brigid Brophy opposed such references to genderless characters when she wrote: "I . . . could hardly . . . commit myself to a main character at whose every appearance in my narrative I would be obliged to write he/she, his/her etc. For which reason I have, dear Sir/Madam, to remain your I" (cited in Brawn, 1995, p. 95). Brophy's protagonist, Pat O'Rooley, has forgotten what sex s/he is and has to try to find out. On hearing evidence that leads him/her to believe s/he is male, Pat enters the men's toilet only to find s/he has no penis. This leads Pat to wonder "Was I perhaps castrato/a?" Here Brophy is parodying some of the feminist reforms to language that try to place the masculine and feminine forms on an equal footing. Yet, as Anna Livia Brawn observed (1995, p. 96), because castration means the removal of the testicles, the *-a* ending would indicate a castrated male rather than a female, so *castrato* and *castrata* in effect refer to the same thing. Pronouns are no use to Pat in trying to figure out sexual identity because *he* can refer generically and gay men and lesbians sometimes refer to themselves by the opposite gender.

However, a number of other authors have tackled in more detail the problem of making language adequate to the task of defining female identity and coping with female experience in future worlds. In her book *The Kin of Ata are Waiting for You* (1971) Dorothy Bryant created a sex-neutral pronoun *kin*. In a world free of sex roles persons are "just Kin, neutral, neuter and unmodified." People nurture each other and work together. In fact, Atans use their language as little as possible. According to the author, it lacks tense distinctions and focuses on the present moment. Yet Bryant does not use the pronoun she invented in the novel itself. She just describes it as part of the language and gives no examples.

Similarly, Piercy's *Woman on the Edge of Time* (1976), a tale of a woman with telepathic access to two possible but conflicting futures, experiments with gender-free language, using, for example, the short form *per* (from *person*) as a generic pronoun (e.g., *per(son) must not do what per(son) cannot do*). In her novel *The Cook and the Carpenter* (1973) June Arnold invented *na*, *nan*, and *naself* as gender neutral pronouns. In David Lindsay's *Voyage to Arcturus* (1920) a man from earth meets people on another planet who are neither man nor woman so he invents a new pronoun *ae* to refer to them. Narratives containing these pronouns are at first jarring, as in this example from Arnold (1973, p. 69): "The boards lay. The carpenter felt that Saturday morning—alone and unrequired by family, job or movement—erotic. Na thought na would write the article after taking a walk with one of the dogs, doing morning things, getting the day in order. Na could structure the article as na went." The author explains in a preface to the novel that she felt it was no longer necessary to distinguish between men and women; therefore she used only one pronoun for both.

Neither Arnold nor Piercy, however, abandons entirely the traditional pronominal paradigm. Each uses the new invented pronouns alongside the old ones. As Brawn (1995) showed, the interplay between the new and old systems is significant in Arnold's novel, which is about a town in Texas into which a group of newcomers arrive whose sexual identities are not revealed. About two thirds of the way into the story the traditional pronouns appear after the newcomers have been taken into custody. A sergeant officer pushes a policewoman to the floor and with "his foot on her back, told the policewoman to take off her shoes, pull down her pants." The switch back to the traditional system indicates a male victory.

Yet the book's publication was a landmark because Arnold founded the publishing company Daughters, Inc., in 1972 as one of the earliest feminist presses in the United States. In doing so, she argued (1976, p. 24) for the exclusion of men from the publishing process, maintaining that her "words will not be sold to his master's voice." This statement conjures up a vivid image of RCA's label stamped on its records showing a dog listening to its master's voice on an old-fashioned gramophone.

Perhaps one of the most linguistically daring attempts to deal with androgyny lies in Anne Garréta's novel *Sphinx* (1986), in which the author attempted to eliminate all grammatical clues to the gender identity of the two main characters, one of whom is the unnamed narrator writing in the first person as *je* (I), a theology student, and the narrator's lover, a dancer, whom she refers to as A***. The title of the novel is itself mysterious and ambiguous. In classical Greek mythology the sphinx is a female monster with the head and breast of a woman, the body of a lion, and the wings of an eagle, but in Egyptian mythology it is a male monster with the head of a man and the body of a lion.

As Brawn (1995) pointed out, Garréta is not the only novelist writing in a language with grammatical gender who has tried to avoid gender marking. Uruguayan novelist Cristina Peri Rossi wrote her book *Solitario de Amor* (1988) in a similar fashion. A parallel exists in English works of fiction dealing with genderless characters, such as Sarah Caudwell's mysteries (e.g., *The Sirens Sang of Murder*, 1989), in which the gender of the narrator, Oxford Professor Hilary Tamar, is never revealed. Garréta's subsequent novels reverted to traditional gender marking, and even within *Sphinx*, it is only the two main characters whose identity is obscure. Minor characters in the novel have conventional sexual identities and Garréta makes use of the usual grammatical system in talking about them.

Garréta wrote her novel in order to show that gender roles were no longer important. Her text was designed as a trap to expose readers' assumptions about gender even when they are not reinforced by conventional grammatical structures such as the sex-differentiated third person pronouns common to both French and English as well as many other languages. As I pointed out in the first chapter, one of the first things we notice or want to know about a person is whether the person is male or female. Readers pick up linguistic clues from the mention of proper names, which are gender specific in French much as they are in English, as I showed in chapter 5, as well as from third person pronouns, *elle* ('she') and *il* ('he'). Naturally, Garréta had to avoid naming the characters or referring to them in the third person, so she chose a first person narrator. This does not, however, entirely avoid the problem of third person reference. In any case, there is much more to gender marking in French, as I showed in chapter 3.

The problems of disguising the gender identity of the narrator and the narrator's lover at first glance appear rather substantial if we remind ourselves of some of the repercussions of grammatical gender in languages like French and Spanish that I examined in chapter 3. The creation of two genderless characters is quite an accomplishment once we realize that gender determines the agreement of a whole range of modifiers and not just the classification of nouns themselves. As Monique Wittig (1986, pp. 64, 72, cited in Brawn, 1995, p. 30) noted, "No other has left its trace within language to such a degree that to eradicate it would not only modify language at the lexical level but would upset the structure itself."

Although there is a decline in the observance of the traditional rules of grammatical concord in everyday spoken French, the written language is more conservative. It is also the case that some of the distinctions of gram-matical gender made in the written language cannot be heard in the spoken language, such as the difference between *mon ami* (masculine) and *mon amie* (feminine) 'my friend'. Some speakers, however, may pronounce the normally silent final -*e* in the feminine form *amie*, or create forms such as *mon ami homme* 'my male friend' to make the gender identity clear. Another site of concord exists between the past participle and the subject, although again, many of the distinctions marked in the written language are not heard in speech due to the silent -*e* marking the feminine, such as *allée* vs. *allé* 'gone'. There is, however, a limited set of forms ending in consonants in the feminine, such as *mettre/mise* 'to put'/'put'. Studies have also shown that agreement is highly variable and generally on the decline in spoken French. Adjectives and part participles that are remote from the nouns they modify tend not to show grammatical agreement. In speech there is no difference in pronunciation between the singular/plural masculine or feminine anyway.

In an unpublished paper "To hell with gender?" Garréta herself described metaphorically the task of avoiding gender reference as running an obstacle course. Nevertheless, she said that once you have identified all the proto-typical situations, it is easy to devise ways around them. Past participles, however, are particularly treacherous. Garréta's success can be measured from the observations of her critics, who did not agree on the sex of the narrator and the narrator's lover. Some said the narrator was male, and others, female, and similarly, some thought the loved one was male, and others, female. There were also critics who thought the narrator and nar-rator's lover were homosexuals or lesbians. Some critics even commented on the prudishness of the text. This suggests that absence of gender marking may indicate not what Garréta intended, but rather that it is so powerful a force, it needs to be muted and unmentioned.

In the absence of linguistic confirmation the critics based their guesses on inferences drawn from the behavior of the characters, none of which actually provides conclusive evidence either. For example, the fact that the narrator has the strength to lift a dead body already weighted down with a heavy piece of masonry and enters a toilet in the company of a male club owner suggests a male identity. Garréta naturally avoided activities or obvious conditions such as pregnancy, which would have been proof of female identity. However, as I pointed out in the last chapter, gender neutrality is not yet a recognized category in society or language. Critics still pressed Garréta to reveal the "true" sex of the narrator and the lover and searched the novel endlessly for clues. Although Garréta can eliminate overt gender marking from the novel, she cannot alter the cultural condi-tions and assumptions against which her text will be read.

Not surprisingly, Garréta's novel is stylistically marked as a result of her attempt to circumvent gender traps. One of her strategies will already be obvious from the expressions that I have had to adopt in writing in English about the novel's characters as the narrator and the narrator's lover. Normally, I would have written *the narrator and her lover* or *the narrator and his lover* because most languages have the convention that once a subject has been introduced into discourse as a noun, it can be referred to on subsequent occasions with a pronoun. Because Garréta had to avoid gender-marked third person pronouns, she used proper names or other words and expressions. Garréta could not write, for example, sentences such as *I told A* * * * *I did not love her/him*. The direct object pronouns *le* and *la* are gender marked, as in *je la voulais* 'I wanted her', but when they appear before verbs beginning with a vowel, they are not because the vowel is omitted, such as in *je l'accusai* 'I accused him/her'.

Nor can the narrator use past participles and adjectives that would reveal his/her identity. The narrator cannot write: *I was happy to meet A* * * * because the adjective *happy* would have to be either *heureux* (masculine) or *heureuse* (feminine). Neither can the narrator use such adjectives in describing A * * *'s states or experiences.

That does not mean, however, that the text avoids descriptive or emotional states. On the contrary, the narrator describes certain features of A * * *'s body and dress in great detail. In this respect, however, Garréta is actually aided by the way in which the conventional French gender-marking system works. Where in English we would have to say *A* * * * *put on his/her new shirt, which matched the color of his/her eyes*, in French the pronouns which modify the nouns *eyes* and *shirt* agree with the gender classification of the noun and not with the sex of the person being referred to. Thus, Garréta (1986, pp. 81–82) could write "A * * * portait un pantalon de cuir . . . qui laissait le modelé musculeux de ses hanches . . . Ses cheveux commençait à repousser . . . Le visage ainsi rendu à sa pure nudité" (A * * * was wearing a pair of leather trousers which showed off the muscular molding of his/her hips . . . His/her hair was beginning to grow again . . . The face thus restored to its naked purity) without using the gender-marked pronouns English requires. The plural pronoun *ses* used with the words meaning 'hips' and 'hair' (which are plural in French) is in any case not marked for gender in French. The modifiers used with the words for 'face' and 'purity' are gender marked but do not reveal the sex of the person referred to because they agree with the gender of the nouns.

Some of Garréta's circumlocutions, such as the constant repetition of A * * *'s name, make the text less cohesive and somewhat disconnected. The fact that A * * * has to be constantly reintroduced into the discourse makes the character seem distant to the reader. A * * * appears as a collection of body parts rather than as a living, active person. All the information about A * * * is filtered through the language of the narrator. Because Garréta had to avoid both subject and direct object pronouns, she also tended to rely more on nouns than verbs. Instead of writing, for instance, *After I kissed him/her*, or *after he/she kissed me*, she substituted *after the kiss*. This makes the novel static. She also avoided the conventional verb forms used for narration and used instead an old-fashioned tense called the simple past, which does not require the gender agreement of the so-called *passé composé* verb forms. The simple past is almost never used in contemporary novels for first or second person narration. Some of Garréta's stylistic choices prompted the critics to say that her style was archaic, whereas others praised her for her elegance.

Brawn (1995, p. 62) concluded that the very concept of selfhood is tenuous without gender. In a language like French where gender spreads beyond the noun, it cannot be eliminated from a text without damaging its cohesiveness. Nevertheless, Brawn (1995, p. 30) also observed that the success of Garréta's experiment does challenge the conventional linguistic analysis of grammatical gender as grammaticalized, or an "obligatory" part of grammar. If Garréta can choose to avoid it, then it must instead be a stylistic option. Moreover, if the gender classification serves primarily syntactic functions, these functions are not essential because they can be dispensed with or can be handled in other ways. This conclusion brings us back full circle to the question of the extent to which grammatical gender is semantically arbitrary, which I raised in chapter 3. If gender marking can be omitted without impairing syntax, then why continue to use it at all?

Monique Wittig (1986, pp. 63–64) also argued for the elimination of gender, which she described as a "primitive ontological concept that enforces in language a division of beings into sexes . . . [it is] a linguistic index of the political opposition between the sexes and of the domination of women." Gender must be destroyed because it grips our minds to such an extent that we cannot think outside it. Unlike Garréta, however, who really did try to eliminate the markings of gender, Wittig attempted to sabotage the system from within by universalizing the already existing pronouns *elles* ('she' plural) and *on* 'one'. In addition, she employed archaic feminine forms and invented new feminine forms where none exist.

In her first novel, *L'Opoponax* (1964), she used the third person singular indefinite *on* 'one' to represent the voice of the narrator, a schoolgirl named Catherine Legrand, through whose eyes Wittig wanted her readers to view the world. Despite being a third person pronoun, *on* carries no mark of gender and can in fact be used to replace all the other pronouns in the system. In *Les Guérillères* (1969) Wittig used the feminine plural *elles* as a universal generic with the meaning 'people in general'. The effect is lost in translation because *they* in English says less than *elles*, whereas the noun phrase *the women* says too much. The absence of men from the first three quarters of the novel establishes the women's perspective as the dominant one.

Michèle Causse carried Wittig's idea further in her novel *Voyages de la grande naine en Androssie* (1993) when she introduced two new third person pronouns, *ille*, which is the feminine counterpart to *il*, and *el* for females who rebel against patriarchal domination but are still trapped in the system. *Elle* is reserved for liberated beings no longer defined by the masculine. Feminist novelist Benoîte Groult, who was head of the French government's commission responsible for feminizing job titles (see chaps. 3, 5, and 10) entitled one of her works *Ainsi soit-elle* ('So be it'/'let it/her be', 1975). As Brawn (1995, p. 174) remarked, the title is well suited for a collection of feminist essays because the meaning suggests that things should remain the way they are, but use of the feminine *elle* subverts the expected masculine generic to suggest that everything should be revolutionized.

In *Lesbian Body* (*Le corps lesbien*, 1973) Wittig rewrote the first person pronoun *I* as *J/e* to symbolize the female *I* cut in two by a language that does not constitute the female self as subject. The *I* symbolized by *je* cannot be *un ecrivain*. For Wittig there is no such thing as feminist writing. The bar through the other first person pronominal forms *m/e, m/a, m/on, m/oi* is a graphic representation of the problematic status of the female subject who has to force herself into an alien language (see chaps. 1 and 2).

As I said earlier in this chapter, there is more to the "pronoun problem" than the literature on language and gender would lead us to suspect, with its focus on questions such as whether male pronouns are generic (see chaps. 2 and 4). A writing style that tries to degender the voice that speaks or writes runs the risk of being taken for masculine by default because the male as unmarked has been assumed to be generic and universal. Moreover, it is not enough to "write women back in" to discussions about "man's" struggle for transcendence (see chaps. 2 and 8). The issue of whether there is or can be a specifically female voice came to light in a controversial way in Australia when in 1996 Aboriginal author Wanda Koolmatrie's (1994) book *My Own Sweet Time* won the prestigious Dobbie award for best first novel by an Australian woman writer. Koolmatrie turned out in fact to be Leon Carren, a 47-year-old White man living in Sydney. If we reject gender essentialism, then any attempt to isolate what is unique to women writers is a misguided exercise. This does not mean that it is impossible to write in what Carol Gilligan (1982) has called a "different voice," only that there is nothing universal in men's or women's experiences, even if some people believe they live in separate worlds, or on different planets!

Brawn pointed out that novels that experiment with gender as a linguistic system can be found primarily in three literary genres: science fiction, detective fiction, and lesbian love stories. Science fiction, as I have argued, is well suited to experimentation and imagination of different worlds. Detective stories deal with puzzles and mysteries, and lesbian love stories challenge the prevailing bipolarized gender system of mainstream society. The need for language change perceived by these and other novelists reflects their belief in the power of language to shape individual and social consciousness. For these women, however, it is not enough simply to steal men's language. A language stolen from others will always remain the other's language, or, as Audre Lorde (1981, p. 99) put it, "The master's tools will never dismantle the master's house."

In Suzette Haden Elgin's novel *Native Tongue* (1984), language change becomes a liberating force for women in the 23rd century. At this time women have become even more subordinated to men than in our own day, thanks to research done by men in 1987 that provided "scientific proof" of the inherent mental inferiority of women. The Equal Rights Amendment had been repealed in 1982 and a new 25th Amendment makes women ineligible to work outside the home without permission of their husbands or male guardians. Under the new law women are minors. They are forced into arranged marriages while still teenagers in order to ensure that there is time for them to bear as many children as possible.

Language learning and linguistics play central roles in the novel because space travel has involved contact with other civilizations in the universe whose inhabitants speak different languages. Children are raised multilingually with a household language such as English, French, Swahili, or other Earth languages, and an alien language that they acquire in order to serve as translators in this new space age. Linguist women seek freedom and privacy through the "Encoding project" within which they invent their own language. Because the men are vigilant for signs of unrest among the women, they have to hide this new tongue. They produce a grossly elaborate language called Langish. Within it is Láadan, a language constructed by women, for women, for the specific purpose of expressing the perceptions of women. Láadan is the means by which they change their reality and liberate themselves from the tyranny of men. A sequel, *Native Tongue II: The Judas Rose* (1987), deals with the women's attempt to spread this language outside the linguist households into the wider world.

Haden Elgin, Láadan's inventor and herself a linguist, worked from the premise that if women had a language adequate to express their own perceptions and experience, it would reflect a different world view from that found in "man-made" languages like English. The name of her invented language comes from *láad* 'to perceive', and *dan* 'language'. She began work on it in 1982, and later in 1988 published a dictionary and grammar as well as a short story in Láadan.

Haden Elgin's work has connections with several different theoretical perspectives on language. One is the idea that language determines or at any rate influences thinking, an idea associated with the work of Edward Sapir (1921) and Benjamin Lee Whorf (1956). Another comes from the anthropological perspective of Edwin and Shirley Ardener, who have written about dominant and muted groups in society (E. Ardener, 1975a, 1975b; S. Ardener, 1975a, 1975b). Each group in society generates its own reality, but in order to articulate its views publically the dominated group is either silenced or forced to translate its reality into the means of communication used by the dominant group. The women linguists in Elgin's novels generate a reality of their own, but have no language to encode it in so they must create their own language. Once they and others start using it, reality changes. A real-life partial analog to Láadan can be found in the secret Liengu (mermaid) language of Bakweri women discussed by Edwin Ardener (1975a).

Láadan attempts to remedy some of the features that feminists see as defects in English. It contains a gender-neutral pronoun *be*, which means 'he', 'she', and 'it'. The word for 'woman' (*with*) also means 'person'. It also has a particle *wa*, which can be added to the end of a sentence to indicate that the speaker believes what she has said to be true because she has seen it with her own eyes. Another particle *wi* means that what is being said is obvious to everyone. The particle *wáa* means that the source of the information reported by the speaker is trustworthy. There are also many words for emotions with separate but related words to indicate 'speaking in anger' (*bíid*), 'in pain' (*bíith*), 'in love' (*bíili*), 'in celebration' (*bíilan*), 'in jest' (*bíida*), 'as a teacher' (*bíidi*), 'in fear' (*bíiya*), and so on. There are also a number of words for different kinds of love, such as *am* 'love for one related by blood', *sham* 'love for a child of her body', *ad* 'love for one respected but not liked', and *ab* 'love for one liked but not respected'. A special sound (indicated in spelling by *lh*) adds a negative meaning to a word (as in the Navajo language, from which Elgin borrowed the idea). Although English has only three degrees of comparison, such as *good, better, best*, Láadan has six. Pronoun forms include four degrees of relation to the speaker: neutral, beloved, honored, despised. These features allow finer discrimination of interpersonal relationships and explicitness of emotions and purpose. Láadan emphasizes internal states and feelings. Commands are very rare except to young children. Láadan is also a tone language (like Chinese, which differentiates words according to the relative pitch with which they are pronounced). It has no consonant clusters, that is, cases where more than one consonant occurs next to another. Therefore in terms of its word structure it is more like Hawaiian and other languages characterized as "feminine" by philologist Otto Jespersen and others (see chaps. 3 and 5).

Other modern novels depicting worlds in which powerful women rule benevolently have also explored the liberating power of creating new words. Andre Norton in her Witch World series (e.g., *Witch World*, 1963) portrays women with magical powers associated with witches, such as the ability to foretell the future, to speak to animals, or to communicate telepathically. In Sally Miller Gearhart's *The Wanderground: Stories of the Hill Women* (1978) the future is gynocentric and separatist. Here a society of women lives in the wilderness without modern technology and no centralized power structure. The City, however, is a totalitarian male-dominated society with poverty, violence, and crime, a place where women have no freedom. Maleness is thus associated with negative qualities and femaleness with positive ones. In their own community outside the City, the Hill women are in closer touch with nature than men. This gives them greater insights and more power, among them telepathic communication and a capacity for psychic healing. Telepathy has a number of names depending on the purpose and quality of communication, such as *shortstretch* versus *longstretch*, *love glow*, and so on. Gearhart also created a number of new words such as *lonth* (a person's untapped reservoir of physical strength, including control of the autonomic nervous system) and *carjery* (lack of harmony).

Some of the future societies imagined by women make reference to myths and religious beliefs, although where these play some role, Christianity with its traditional patriarchal god and hierarchical, largely male priesthood are often replaced with other philosophies. For example, Le Guin imagined two religions on Gethen, one of which had no priests, no hierarchies, no vows or creeds. Gearhart made the earth the source of women's energy and women's ceremonies were all based on a lunar cycle. All women ovulate at the same time in tune with a lunar cycle.

Alice Sheldon (writing under the pseudonym of James Tiptree, Jr.) incorporated a dramatic biological role reversal in her novel *Up the Walls of the World* (1978). Males are equipped with pouches for nurturing children. Fatherhood is the most desirable and revered position, and women dream that one day they will have the right to be fathers and to raise children. Women's position is thus not improved when male patriarchy becomes a male matriarchy. Women still remain powerless. Men believe them to be incapable of rearing children because it is seen as a man's job. Sheldon appears to be saying that even in alternative worlds women's work, whatever it consists of, will be devalued, and men's work will be regarded as having high status. A biological role reversal is not sufficient to bring about equality.

This pessimistic view is also embodied within French feminist theory. Luce Irigaray (1985), for instance, said that if women's aim were simply to reverse the order of things, supposing this were possible, then history would simply repeat itself. Here lies one of the dangers of the "celebration" approach to difference I discussed in chapter 2. If women's liberation takes place within men's language, men's politics, and men's economy, nothing will really change. Irigaray therefore advocated total rejection of the masculine system.

IS THE FUTURE FEMALE?

Not all writers are committed to a particular view of feminism, nor do they share the same vision of a feminist future and the possibilities of nonsexist societies. Just as Láadan proves to be a liberating force for the women in Haden Elgin's novel, so does the writing of speculative feminist fiction have a liberating function for those who engage in it. Although some of the linguistic innovations proposed in these literary experiments have not been adopted, they do raise consciousness about language and gender. Every time readers encounter pronouns such as Wittig's *elles*, Piercy's *per*, or wonder why Garréta has gone to such lengths not to reveal the sex of A***, they will reflect on the reasons the authors had for making these choices. What is important for women, however, is the freedom to imagine all-female utopias and to use them as a means of critiquing gender roles and stereotypes in present and past societies. Speculative fiction provides women both with textual power and textual space. The confining space of the patriarchal mind is expanded by the voyage into outer space. The voyage becomes a corrective to patriarchy's depictions of women.

Nevertheless, Suzette Haden Elgin's *Native Tongue II: The Judas Rose* (1987) ends with a depressing epilogue that again prompts us to reevaluate some of the simplistic claims made about the relationship between language, society, and reality that I discussed in chapters 1 and 10. The Council of the Consortium deliberates the "problem of earth." By this time far in the future contact had been made with many alien civilizations, all of which turned out to be far more technologically advanced than and superior to Earth. The problem with Earth seen from the "alien" perspective was that the Terran males had remained at a primitive stage of evolution, where violence was their primary motivation. Females had evolved beyond this, the Council noted, as was to be expected, given that the female of the human species developed more rapidly toward maturity (and presumably also thanks to the promotion of Láadan). Although the Council had hoped females would be able to lead men with them, males had reacted even more negatively and oppressively. The problem for the rest of the universe was whether to destroy earth entirely to prevent its men from waging war on other planets and wreaking havoc on the universe, to put it under complete quarantine and surveillance, or to interfere with its evolution. All of these options presented ethical problems for the Council because they were out of line with the Council's philosophy of nonviolence. The third alternative had in fact been tried in the year 11,304, but to no avail. Now what?

EXERCISES AND DISCUSSION QUESTIONS

1. Marge Piercy's *Woman on the Edge of Time* (1976) has been described as one of the most reproductively inventive science fiction novels. In her book technological innovations are important in creating an androgynous nonsexist future. Domestic chores are all done by machines, and children are artificially conceived and born in mechanical "brooders." Men

as well as women become "mothers" rather than fathers or parents. Hormone supplements enable men to nurse their children.

> It was part of women's long revolution. When we were breaking all the old hierarchies. Finally there was that one thing we had to give up too, the only power we ever had, in return for no more power for anyone. The original production: the power to give birth. Cause as long as we were biologically enchained, we'd never be equal. And males would never be humanized to be loving and tender. So we all became mothers. Every child has three. To break the nuclear bonding. (p. 105)

Discuss the impact these changes are likely to have on the meanings and uses of terms like *mother, biological mother, birth mother, mothering, fathering*, and so on. Is there a need for new terms in this society? You may need to reread the discussion of these terms in chapter 4.

2. Here is a short lesson in Láadan based on Suzette Haden Elgin's (1988) *A First Dictionary and Grammar of Láadan*. Using the vocabulary list that follows, see if you can translate the English sentences into Láadan, and the Láadan sentences into English. The verb comes first in this language, followed by the subject, then the object, if there is one. There are no words in Láadan for English *a* and *the*.

Translate these sentences from English into Láadan.

    a. The woman is good.

    b. Does the woman speak Láadan?

    c. The woman loves the child (her own child).

    d. Is the food warm?

    e. The food is not warm.

Translate these sentences from Láadan into English:

    f. *Bíi thal háawith.*

    g. *Bíi di ra háawith Láadan.*

    h. *Báa rahal ana.*

    i. *Bíi am háawith mathuleth.*

    j. *Báa bel with anath.*

Vocabulary:

bíi: This word is put at the beginning of a sentence to indicate that what follows is a statement, such as *bíi di le Láadan* 'I speak *Láadan*'.

báa: This word is put at the beginning of a sentence that asks a question, such as *báa di le Láadan* 'do I speak Láadan?'

with 'woman', 'person'.

ra 'no', 'not'

ana 'food'

thal 'to be good'

rahal 'to be bad'

owa 'to be warm'

háawith 'child'

di 'to speak'

am 'love for one related by blood'

sham 'love for a child of her body'

bel 'to take'

mathul 'mother'

le 'I'

-th/eth: An ending put on nouns that function as direct objects, such as *Bíi bel háawith anath* 'The child takes the food'. Here *ana* ('food') is the object of the verb *bel* ('take') and therefore the ending *-th* is added to it. The ending *-eth* is used when the noun it is attached to ends with a consonant. However, some nouns, like *Láadan*, do not need to take the object ending when they are used as objects.

3. Go back to chapter 3 and look at the language invented by King Sevarias. How does it compare to Láadan? Here is a bit more information on the Sevarambian language to help you. The majority of words end in vowels or "easy consonants." This is supposed to make the language the most agreeable sounding in the world. There are "notes" for almost all the tones given to the voice in pronunciation. Some serve to express joy, others grief, anger, doubt, certainty, and almost all the other passions.

4. Feminists such as Adrienne Rich have dreamed of a common language. Discuss the possible interpretations of "common language" and whether this dream is realistic. What does it presuppose about the relationship between language and society and the nature of women's experience?

ANNOTATED BIBLIOGRAPHY AND SUGGESTIONS FOR FURTHER READING

Full details of the novels referred to in this chapter can be found in the references at the end of the book. I have also listed there a number of studies of women's speculative writing and anthologies containing further information. See, for example, the references to the work of Marleen Barr (1981a, 1981b, 1987, 1992), Marleen Barr and Nicholas Smith (1983), Frances Bartkowski (1989), Suzy McKee Charnas (1978, 1981), Jane Donawerth and Carol Kolmerten (1994), Luce Irigaray (1985), Carol Farley Kessler (1984), Margarete Keulen (1991), Robin Roberts (1993), Natalie M. Rosinsky (1984), and Edward Whetmore (1981). The anthropological work of Edwin and Shirley Ardener (E. Ardener, 1975a, 1975b; S. Ardener, 1975a, 1975b) is useful in understanding some of the reasoning behind Suzette Haden Elgin's invention of Láadan. Marina Yaguello's *Lunatic Lovers of Language* (1991) contains a good discussion of imaginary and invented languages. Although Riane Eisler's book, *The Chalice and the Blade*, is a history of cultural evolution rather than a work of speculative fiction, like Suzette Haden Elgin, she sketches the bleak future in store for humanity if we do not manage to transcend the violence and domination typically associated with patriarchal societies.

References[1]

ABU-LUGHOD, L. (1986). *Veiled sentiments: Honor and poetry in a Bedouin society.* Berkeley: University of California Press.

ABU-LUGHOD, L. (1993). *Writing women's worlds: Bedouin stories.* Berkeley: University of California Press.

ADRIAEN, M., & KING, R. (1991). Feminizing French discourse. In R. King (Ed.), *Talking gender: A guide to non-sexist communication* (chap. 6). Toronto: Copp Clark Pittman.

ADVERTISING ADVISORY BOARD. (1976). *Women and advertising: Today's messages—yesterday's images.* Toronto: Author.

ADVERTISING STANDARDS AUTHORITY. (1982). *"Herself appraised," the treatment of women in advertising.* London: Author.

AIKIO, M. (1992). Are women innovators in the shift to second language? A case study of reindeer Sami women and men. In T. Bull & T. Swan (Eds.), Language, sex, and society. *International Journal of the Sociology of Language, 91,* 43–61.

ALCOTT, L. M. (1946). *Little women.* New York: World Publishing. (Original work published 1871)

AMERICAN ASSOCIATION OF UNIVERSITY WOMEN. (1991). *Shortchanging girls, shortchanging America: A call to action. A nationwide poll to assess self-esteem, educational experiences, interest in math and science, and career aspirations of girls and boys ages 9–15.* Washington, DC: Author.

AMERICAN ASSOCIATION OF UNIVERSITY WOMEN. (1993). *Hostile hallways: The AAUW survey of sexual harassment in America's schools.* Washington, DC: Author.

ANDERSEN, E. S. (1992). *Speaking with style: The sociolinguistic skills of children.* London: Routledge.

ARDENER, E. (1975a). Belief and the problem of women. In S. Ardener (Ed.), *Perceiving women* (pp. 1–18). London: Malaby Press.

---

[1]Please note that some references that appear in the reference section are not found in the text. These were deliberately left in the reference section for supplementary reading suggestions.

ARDENER, E. (1975b). The problem revisited. In S. Ardener (Ed.), *Perceiving women* (pp. 19–28). London: Malaby Press.

ARDENER, S. (Ed.). (1975a). *Perceiving women*. London: Malaby Press.

ARDENER, S. (1975b). *Defining females*. New York: John Wiley.

ARIEL, M. (1988). Female and male stereotypes in Israeli literature and media: Evidence from introductory patterns. *Language and Communication, 8*(1), 43–68.

ARNOLD, J. (1973). *The cook and the carpenter: A novel by the carpenter*. Plainfield, VT: Daughters, Inc.

ARNOLD, J. (1976). Feminist presses and feminist politics. *Quest: A Feminist Quarterly, 3,* 18–26.

ATKINSON, D. (1987). Names and titles: Maiden name retention and the use of Ms. *Journal of the Atlantic Provinces Linguistics Association, 9,* 56–83.

ATKINSON, D. (1996). The Philosophical Transactions of the Royal Society of London, 1675–1975: A sociohistorical discourse analysis. *Language in Society, 25,* 333–373.

ATKINSON, J. M. (1984). *Our masters' voices: The language and body language of politics*. London: Routledge.

ATWOOD, M. (1986). *The handmaid's tale*. Boston: Houghton Mifflin.

ATWOOD, M. (1989). *Cat's eye*. London: Bloomsbury Press.

AUSTIN, J. L. (1962). *How to do things with words*. Cambridge, MA: Harvard University Press.

BAKER, C., & FREEBODY, P. (1989). *Children's first schoolbooks*. Oxford: Blackwell.

BAILEY, R. (1991). *Images of English*. Ann Arbor: University of Michigan Press.

BAKHTIN, M. (1973). *Marxism and the philosophy of language* (L. Matejka & I. R. Tituknik, Trans.). New York: Seminar Press. (Original work published 1929)

BARON, D. (1986). *Grammar and gender*. New Haven, CT: Yale University Press.

BARR, E. (1979). *The sea treasure*. New York: Doubleday.

BARR, M. S. (1981a). Charles Bronson, samurai, and other feminine images: A transactive response to *The Left Hand of Darkness*. In M. S. Barr (Ed.), *Future females: A critical anthology* (pp. 138–154). Bowling Green, OH: Bowling Green State University Press.

BARR, M. S. (Ed.). (1981b). *Future females: A critical anthology*. Bowling Green, OH: Bowling Green State University Press.

BARR, M. S. (1987). The *females* do the fathering! Reading, resisting and James Tiptree, Jr. In *Alien to femininity: Speculative fiction and feminist theory* (pp. 19–38). Westport, CT: Greenwood Press.

BARR, M. S. (1992). *Feminist fabulation: Space/postmodern fiction*. Iowa City: University of Iowa Press.

BARR, M. S., & SMITH, N. D. (Eds.). (1983). *Women and utopia: Critical interpretations*. Lanham, MD: University Press of America.

BARTKOWSKI, F. (1989). *Feminist utopias*. Lincoln: University of Nebraska Press.

BARTOS, R. (1982). *The moving target: What every marketer should know about women*. New York: The Free Press.

BEM, S. L. (1993). *The lenses of gender: Transforming the debate on sexual inequality*. New Haven, CT: Yale University Press.

BENEDICT, H. (1992). *Virgin or vamp: How the press covers sex crimes*. New York: Oxford University Press.

BENEKE, T. (1982). *Men on rape: What they have to say about sexual violence*. New York: St. Martin's Press.

BENVENISTE, E. (1971). *Problems in general linguistics II* (E. M. Meek, Trans.). Coral Gables, FL: University of Miami Press.

BERGVALL, V. L. (1996). Constructing and enacting gender through discourse: Negotiating multiple roles as female engineering students. In V. L. Bergvall, J. M. Bing, & A. F. Freed

(Eds.), *Rethinking language and gender research: Theory and practice* (pp. 173–201). Harlow: Longman.

BERNARD, J. (1973). My four revolutions: An autobiographical history of the A.S.A. In J. Huber (Ed.), *Changing women in a changing society* (pp. 11–29). Chicago: University of Chicago Press.

BERNSTEIN, B. (Ed.). (1973). *Class, codes and control: Applied studies towards a sociology of language.* London: Routledge & Kegan Paul.

BERRY, J. W. (1966). Temne and Eskimo perceptual skills. *International Journal of Psychology, 1,* 207–229.

BIOLOGY AND GENDER STUDY GROUP. (1989). The importance of feminist critique for contemporary cell biology. In N. Tuana (Ed.), *Feminism and science* (pp. 172–187). Bloomington: Indiana University Press.

BLOCH, H. R. (1991). *Medieval misogyny and the invention of Western romantic love.* Chicago: University of Chicago Press.

BLUM, S. D. (1997). Naming practices and the power of words in China. *Language in Society, 26,* 357–381.

BLUMENTHAL, M. D. et al. (1972). *Justifying violence: Attitudes of American men.* Ann Arbor: University of Michigan.

BOLINGER, D. (1980). *Language: The loaded weapon.* London: Longman.

BÖRJESON, F. (1995). Ladies' "excuse me." Gender problems in the written press. In P. Holmberg & K. Nordenstam (Eds.), *Language and gender: Case studies from a Swedish seminar* (pp. 63–78). Göteborg: MISS 11 (Meddelanden från Institutionen för Svenska Språket), Göteborg Universitet.

BORNSTEIN, D. (1978). As meek as a maid: A historical perspective on language for women in courtesy books from the Middle Ages. In D. Butturff & E. L. Epstein (Eds.), *Women's language and style* (pp. 132–138). Arkon, OH: Department of English, University of Akron.

BOTTIGHEIMER, R. (1987). *Grimms' bad girls and bold boys: The social and moral vision of the tales.* New Haven, CT: Yale University Press.

BOURDIEU, P. (1977). The economics of linguistic exchanges. *Social Science Information, 16,* 645–668.

BRAWN, A. L. (1995). *Pronoun envy: Literary uses of linguistic gender.* Unpublished doctoral dissertation, University of California at Berkeley.

BROPHY, B. (1969). *In transit.* New York: Putnam.

BROUWER, D., & Van Hout, R. (1992). Gender-related variation in Amsterdam vernacular. In T. Bull & T. Swan (Eds.), Language, sex, and society. *International Journal of the Sociology of Language, 91,* 99–122.

BROWN, P., & LEVINSON, S. (1987). *Politeness: Some universals in language use.* Cambridge: Cambridge University Press.

BROWNMILLER, S. (1975). *Against our will: Men, women, and rape.* New York: Simon & Schuster.

BRYANT, D. (1971). *The kin of Ata are waiting for you.* San Francisco: Moon Books.

BUCHOLTZ, M., LIANG, A. C., SUTTON, L., & HINES, C. (Eds.). (1994). *Cultural performances: Proceedings of the Third Berkeley Women and Language Conference.* Berkeley: Berkeley Women and Language Group.

BULL, T. (1991). Women and men speaking, the roles played by women and men in the process of language shift. *Working Papers on Language, Gender, and Sexism, 1,* 11–24.

BULWER-LYTTON, E. (1871). *The coming race or the new utopia.* London: Routledge.

BURCHFIELD, R. (1989). *Unlocking the English language.* London: Faber & Faber.

BURNS, E. J. (1993). *Bodytalk: When women speak in old French literature.* Philadelphia: University of Pennsylvania Press.

BUSBY, L. (1975). Sex role research on the mass media. *Journal of Communications, 25,* 107–131.

BUTLER, J. (1894). *Memoir of John Gray of Dilston*. Edinburgh.

BUTLER, J. (1990). *Gender trouble: Feminism and the subversion of identity*. London: Routledge.

BUTLER, J. (1993). *Bodies that matter: On the discursive limits of "Sex."* London: Routledge.

BUTLER, S. M., SANERA, M., & WEINROD, W. B. (1984). *Mandate for Leadership II: Continuing the conservative revolution*. Washington, DC: Heritage Foundation.

CAMERON, D. (1985). What has gender got to do with sex? *Language and Communication, 5,* 19–28.

CAMERON, D. (1990a). Making changes: Can we decontaminate sexist language? In *Feminism and linguistic theory* (pp. 72–90). London: Macmillan.

CAMERON, D. (1990b). Why is language a feminist issue? In D. Cameron (Ed.), *The feminist critique of language* (pp. 1–28). London: Routledge.

CAMERON, D. (1992a). "Not gender difference but the difference gender makes"—Explanation in research on sex and language. In T. Bull & T. Swan (Eds.), Language, sex, and society. *International Journal of the Sociology of Language, 91,* 13–26.

CAMERON, D. (1992b). Naming of parts: Gender, culture, and terms for the penis among American college students. *American Speech, 67,* 367–382.

CAMERON, D. (1994). Verbal hygiene for women: Linguistics misapplied? *Applied Linguistics, 15,* 382–398.

CAMERON, D. (1995). *Verbal hygiene*. London: Routledge.

CAMERON, D. (1996). The language-gender interface: Challenging co-optation. In V. L. Bergvall, J. M. Bing, & A. F. Freed (Eds.), *Rethinking language and gender research. Theory and practice* (pp. 31–53). Harlow: Longman.

CAMERON, D., & COATES, J. (1985). Some problems in the sociolinguistic explanation of sex differences. *Language and Communication, 5,* 143–151.

CAMERON, D., & COATES, J. (Eds.). (1988). *Women in their speech communities: New perspectives on language and sex*. London: Longman.

CAMERON, D., & FRAZER, E. (1987). *The lust to kill: A feminist investigation into sexual murder*. Cambridge: Polity Press.

CAPUTI, J. (1991). The metaphors of radiation: Or why a beautiful woman is like a nuclear power plant. *Women's Studies International Forum, 14,* 423–442.

CARGILL, M. (1989, October 29). Corruption of language is no cultural heritage. *Sunday Gleaner,* p. 8A.

CARLSON, M. (1996, March 11). No sleep for the weary. *Time,* p. 16.

CARNEGIE, D. (1957). *How to help your husband get ahead in his social and business life*. New York: Greystone Press.

CASSELL, J. (1996, December 12). Posting to FLING internet discussion list [On-line]. fling@listserv.oit.unc.edu

CASTRO, J. (1992, January 20). Sexual harassment: A guide. *Time,* p. 37.

CAUDWELL, S. (1989). *The sirens sang of murder*. New York: Bantam, Doubleday & Dell.

CAUSSE, M. (1993). *Voyages de la grande naine en Androssie*. Laval: Editions Trois.

CAVENDISH, M. (1966). *The description of a new world, called the blazing world*. A. Maxwell.

CEDERSCHIÖLD, G. (1900). *Om kvinnospråk och andra ämnen* [On women's language and other themes]. Lund: Gleerups.

CHAMBERS, J. (1995). *Sociolinguistic theory*. Oxford: Blackwell.

CHARNAS, S. M. (1978). *Motherlines*. New York: Berkley/Putnam.

CHARNAS, S. M. (1981). A woman appeared. In M. S. Barr (Ed.), *Future female: A critical anthology* (pp. 103–108). Bowling Green, OH: Bowling Green State University Press.

CHAWAF, C. (1987). *L'interieur des heures* [The interior of hours]. Paris: des femmes.

CHESHIRE, J. (1982). *Grammatical variation in an English dialect*. Cambridge: Cambridge University Press.

CHESHIRE, J. (1985). A question of masculine bias. *English Today, 1,* 22–26.

CHODOROW, N. (1978). *The reproduction of mothering: Psychoanalysis and the sociology of gender.* Berkeley: University of California Press.

CIXOUS, H. (1986). *The newly born woman* (B. Wing, Trans.). University of Minnesota Press, Minneapolis, and Manchester University Press. (Original work published 1975)

CLARKE, M. A., LOSOFF, M. D., MCCRACKEN, M. D., & STILL, J. (1981). Gender perception in Arabic and English. *Language Learning, 31,* 159–167.

CLEAVER, E. (1968). *Soul on ice.* New York: Dell-Delta/Ramparts.

CLIFFORD, J. (1986). Introduction: Partial truths. In J. Clifford & G. E. Marcus (Eds.), *Writing culture. The poetics and politics of ethnography* (pp. 1–26). Berkeley: University of California Press.

COATES, J. (1988). *Women, men, and language: A sociolinguistic account of sex differences.* London: Longman.

COATES, J. (1993). *Women, men, and language: A sociolinguistic account of sex differences* (2nd ed.). London: Longman.

COATES, J. (1996). *Women talk: Conversation between women friends.* Oxford: Blackwell.

CODY, M. J., SEITER, J., & MONTAGNE-MILLER, Y. (1995). Men and women in the market place. In P. J. Kalbfleisch & M. J. Cody (Eds.), *Gender, power, and communication in human relationships* (pp. 305–329). Hillsdale, NJ: Lawrence Erlbaum Associates.

CONNELL, R. W. (1989). Cool guys, swots, and wimps: The interplay of masculinity and education. *Oxford Review of Education, 15,* 291–303.

CONNORS, K. (1971). Studies in feminine agentives in selected European languages. *Romance Philology, 24,* 573–598.

CONSTANTINOPLE, A. (1973). Maculinity-femininity: An exception to the famous dictum? *Psychological Bulletin, 80,* 389–407.

COONTZ, S. (1992). *The way we never were. American families and the nostalgia trap.* New York: Basic Books.

COOPER, C. (1995). *Noises in the blood: Orality, gender, and the "vulgar" body of Jamaican culture.* Durham, NC: Duke University Press.

COOPER, R. L. (1984). The avoidance of androcentric generics. *International Journal of the Sociology of Language, 50,* 5–20.

COPENHAGEN AIRPORT SHOPPING CENTER NEWS. (1995, November/December). Santa's greetings from Greenland. p. 10.

CORBETT, G. (1991). *Gender.* Cambridge: Cambridge University Press.

COURTNEY, A. E., & WHIPPLE, T. W. (1983). *Sex stereotyping in advertising.* Lexington, MA: D. C. Heath.

CRENSHAW, K. (1989). Demarginalizing the intersection of race and gendering antidiscrimination law, feminist theory, and antiracist politics. *Chicago Legal Forum, 139.*

CRICHTON, M. (1994). *Disclosure.* New York: Century.

CROSSICK, G. (1991). From gentlemen to the residuum: Languages of social description in Victorian Britain. In P. J. Corfield (Ed.), *Language, history, and class* (pp. 150–178). Oxford: Blackwell.

CRYSTAL, D. (1995). *The Cambridge encyclopedia of the English language.* Cambridge: Cambridge University Press.

CULLUM, J. (1981). *Peer influence on choice of some linguistic variants.* Unpublished master's thesis, University of Birmingham.

CUTLER, A., MCQUEEN, J., & ROBINSON, K. (1990). Elizabeth and John: Sound patterns of men's and women's names. *Journal of Linguistics, 26,* 471–482.

DABNEY, D. (1982, January 18). Wimps? *Toronto Star,* p. A10.

DALE, B., & DALE, J. (1985). *The working woman book.* Kansas City and New York: Andrews, McMeel & Parker.

DALEY, S. (1991, January 9). Girls' self-esteem is lost on way to adolescence, new study finds. *New York Times,* pp. B1, B6.

DALY, M. (1973). *Beyond God the Father: Towards a philosophy of women's liberation.* Boston: Beacon Press.

DALY, M. (1978). *Gyn/ecology. The metaethics of radical feminism.* London: Women's Press.

DALY, M. (1987). *Websters' first new intergalactic wickedary of the English language conjured by Mary Daly in cahoots with Jane Caputi.* Boston: Beacon Press.

DANET, B. (1980). "Baby" or "fetus": Language and the construction of reality in a manslaughter trial. *Semiotica, 32,* 187–219.

DANNEQUIN, C. (1977). *Les enfants baillonnés* [Gagged children]. Paris: CEDIC, Diffusion Nathan.

D'AULNOY, M. C. (1690). *Isle de la Félicité.* No publisher listed.

DAVIDOFF, L. (1973). *The best circles: Society etiquette and the season.* London: Croom Helm.

DAVIDSON, J. W. (1967). *Samoa mo Samoa. The emergence of the independent state of Western Samoa.* Oxford: Oxford University Press.

DAVIES, B. (1982). *Life in the classroom and playground: The accounts of primary school children.* London: Routledge & Kegan Paul.

DAVIES, B. (1989). *Frogs and snails and feminist tales: Preschool children and gender.* London: Allen & Unwin.

DAVIS, A. (1981). *Women, race and class.* New York: Random House.

DEAUX, K., & EMSWILLER, T. (1974). Explanations of successful performance on sex-linked tasks: What is skill for the male is luck for the female. *Journal of Personality and Social Psychology, 29,* 80–85.

DE BEAUVOIR, S. (1968). *The second sex.* New York: Knopf.

DE KLERK, V. (1995). Slang in South African English. In R. Mesthrie (Ed.), *Language and social history: Studies in South African sociolinguistics* (pp. 265–276). Cape Town: David Philip.

DIBBELL, J. (1993, August 3). A rape in cyberspace. *Village Voice,* pp. 33–37.

DIXON, R. M. W. (1972). *The Dyirbal language of North Queensland.* Cambridge: Cambridge University Press.

DONAWERTH, J. A., & KOLMERTEN, C. A. (Eds.). (1994). *Utopian and science fiction by women. Worlds of difference.* Syracuse, NY: Syracuse University Press.

DOUGLAS, M. (1966). *Purity and danger.* New York: Praeger.

DOUGLAS, S. J. (1994). *Where the girls are: Growing up female with the mass media.* New York: Time Books.

DUBOIS, B. L., & CROUCH, I. (1975). The question of tag questions in women's speech: They don't really use more of them, do they? *Language in Society, 4,* 289–294.

DUBOIS, B. L., & CROUCH, I. (1987). Linguistic disruption: He/she, s/he, he or she, he-she. In J. Penfield (Ed.), *Women and language in transition* (pp. 28–35). Albany, NY: State University of New York Press.

DULLAK, S. (1983). *Je serai elle.* Paris: presses de la cité.

DURANTI, A. (1994). *From grammar to politics. Linguistic anthropology in a Samoan village.* Berkeley: University of California Press.

DWORKIN, A. (1974). *Woman hating.* New York: E.P. Dutton.

DWORKIN, A. (1981). *Pornography: Men possessing women.* London: Women's Press.

DYNAMIC, ACTIVE, MASCULINE VECTOR OF NEW LIFE. (1987, March 25). *New York Times,* p. 20.

EASLEY, B. (1983). *Fathering the unthinkable: Masculinity, scientists, and the nuclear arms race.* Concord, MA: Pluto Press.

ECKERT, P. (1988). *Jocks and burnouts: Social categories and identity in high school.* New York: Teachers College Press.

ECKERT, P. (1989). The whole woman: Sex and gender differences in variation. *Language Variation and Change, 1,* 245–267.

ECKERT, P. (1993). Cooperative competition in adolescent "girl talk." In D. Tannen (Ed.), *Gender in conversational interaction* (pp. 32–61). New York: Oxford University Press.

ECKERT, P., & MCCONNELL-GINET, S. (1992). Think practically and look locally: Language and gender as community-based practice. *Annual Review of Anthropology, 21,* 461–490.

EDELSKY, C. (1977). Acquisition of an aspect of communicative competence: Learning what it means to talk like a lady. In S. Ervin-Tripp & C. Mitchell-Kernan (Eds.), *Child discourse* (pp. 225–243). New York: Academic Press.

EDELSKY, C. (1981). Who's got the floor? *Language in Society, 10*(3), 383–421.

EDWARDS, J. (1979). Social class differences and the identification of sex in children's speech. *Journal of Child Language, 6,* 121–127.

EHRENREICH, B., & ENGLISH, D. (1978). *For her own good: One hundred and fifty years of the experts' advice to women.* New York: Anchor.

EHRLICH, S., & KING, R. (1992). Gender-based language reform and the social construction of meaning. *Discourse and Society, 3,* 151–166.

EHRLICH, S., & KING, R. (1993). Feminist meanings and sexist speech communities. In K. Hall, M. Bucholtz, & B. Moonwoman (Eds.), *Locating power: Proceedings of the Third Berkeley Conference on Women and Language.* Berkeley: University of California.

EHRLICH, S., & KING, R. (1994). Feminist meanings and the (de)politicization of the lexicon. *Language in Society, 23,* 59–76.

EHRLICH, S., & KING, R. (1996). Consensual sex or sexual harassment: Negotiating meaning. In V. L. Bergvall, J. M. Bing, & A. F. Freed (Eds.), *Rethinking language and gender research. Theory and practice* (pp. 153–172). Harlow: Longman.

EISLER, R. (1987). *The chalice and the blade.* New York: HarperCollins.

ELLIS, S. S. (1839). *The women of England, their social duties, and domestic habits* (3rd ed.). London.

EPSTEIN, J. F. (1990). Either/or–neither/both: Sexual ambiguity and the ideology of gender. *Genders, 7,* 99–142.

ERVIN, S. (1962). The connotations of gender. *Word, 18,* 249–261.

EVANS, H. (1985). A feminine issue in contemporary French usage. *Modern Languages, 4,* 231–236.

FALK, J. (1994). The women Foundation Members of the Linguistic Society of America. *Language, 70,* 455–490.

FALUDI, S. (1991). *Backlash: The undeclared war against American women.* New York: Crown.

FASOLD, R., YAMADA, H., ROBINSON, D., & BARISH, S. (1990). The language planning effect of newspaper editorial policy: Gender differences in the *Washington Post. Language in Society, 19,* 521–539.

FAUSTO-STERLING, A. (1985). *Myths of gender: Biological theories about women and men.* New York: Basic Books.

FAY, E. A. (1994). *Eminent rhetoric: Language, gender, and cultural tropes.* Westport, CT: Bergin & Garvey.

FELDMAN, R. S. (1993). *Understanding psychology.* New York: McGraw-Hill.

FERGUSON, C. (1972). Diglossia. In P. Gigliolo (Ed.), *Language and social context* (pp. 232–252). Harmondsworth, England: Penguin. (Original work published 1959)

FINCH, S. (1985). *Infinity's web.* New York: Bantam.

FINLAYSON, R. (1995). Women's language of respect: Isihlonipho sabafazi. In R. Mesthrie (Ed.), *Language and social history. Studies in South African sociolinguistics* (pp. 140–153). Cape Town: David Philip.

FISHMAN, P. M. (1978). Interaction: The work women do. *Social problems, 25,* 397–406. Also in B. Thorne, C. Kramarae, & N. Henley (Eds.). (1983). *Language, gender, and society* (pp. 89–102). Rowley, MA: Newbury House.

FITZPATRICK, M. A., & MULAC, A. (1995). Relating to spouse and stranger: Gender-preferential language use. In P. J. Kalbfleisch & M. J. Cody (Eds.), *Gender, power, and communication in human relationships* (pp. 213–231). Hillsdale, NJ: Lawrence Erlbaum Associates.

FLEISCHMAN, S. (1994). Eliminating gender bias in French: A case of language ideologies in conflict. In M. L. Bucholtz, A. C. Liang, L. Sutton, & C. Hines (Eds.), *Cultural performance: Proceedings of the Third Berkeley Women and Language Conference* (pp. 187–196). Berkeley: Berkeley Women and Language Group.

FLEXNER, S. B., & WENTWORTH, H. (1975). *Dictionary of American slang.* New York: Crowell.

FODOR, I. (1959). The origin of grammatical gender. *Lingua, 8,* 1–41, 186–214.

FOUCAULT, M. (1972). *The archaelogy of knowledge and the discourse on language.* New York: Pantheon.

FOURNIER, H. S., & RUSSELL, D. W. (1992). A study of sex-role stereotyping in the *Oxford English Dictionary* 2E. *Computers and the Humanities, 26,* 13–20.

FOWLER, H. W. (1927). *A dictionary of modern English usage.* Oxford: Clarendon Press.

FRANK, F., & ANSHEN, F. (1983). *Language and the sexes.* Albany: State University of New York Press.

FRANK, F., & TREICHLER, P. (1989). *Language, gender and professional writing.* New York: Modern Language Association.

FREED, A. F. (1993). We understand perfectly: A critique of Tannen's view of cross-sex communication. In K. Hall, M. Bucholtz, & B. Moonwoman (Eds.), *Locating power: Proceedings of the Third Berkeley Conference on Women and Language* (pp. 144–152). Berkeley: University of California.

FREED, A. F. (1996). Language and gender research in an experimental setting. In V. L. Bergvall, J. M. Bing, & A. F. Freed (Eds.), *Rethinking language and gender research: Theory and practice* (pp. 54–76). Harlow: Longman.

FREUD, S., & BREUER, J. (1955). *Studies on hysteria.* (J. Strachey with A. Freud, Trans.). New York: Basic Books.

FRIEDAN, B. (1963). *The feminine mystique.* New York: Norton.

FRIEDAN, B. (1981). *The second stage.* New York: Summit Books.

FUNK, C. E. (1938). *The new comprehensive standard dictionary of the English language.* New York: Funk & Wagnalls.

GABRIEL, S. L. (1990). Gender, reading, and writing: Assignments, expectations, and responses. In S. L. Gabriel & I. Smithson (Eds.), *Gender in the classroom: Power and pedagogy* (pp. 127–139). Urbana: University of Illinois Press.

GAL, S. (1991). Between speech and silence: The problematics of research on language and gender. In *Gender at the crossroads of knowledge: Feminist anthropology in the postmodern era* (pp. 175–203). Berkeley: University of California Press.

GALLAGHER, M. (1981). *Unequal opportunities: The case of women in the media.* Paris: UNESCO.

GANDER, P. (1989). *Father Gander's nursery rhymes for the nineteen nineties: The alternative Mother Goose.* New York: Oleander Press.

GARRÉTA, A. (1986). *Sphinx.* Paris: Grasset.

GEARHART, S. M. (1978). *The Wanderground: Stories of the hill women.* Watertown, MA: Persephone Press.

GEERTZ, C. (1995). *After the fact: Two countries. Four decades. One anthropologist.* Cambridge, MA: Harvard University Press.

GEIS, M. L. (1982). *The language of television advertising.* New York: Academic Press.

GILBERT, S. M., & GUBAR, S. (1979). *The mad woman in the attic: The woman writer and the nineteenth-century imagination.* New Haven, CT: Yale University Press.

GILLIGAN, C. (1982). *In a different voice: Psychological theory and women's development.* Cambridge, MA: Harvard University Press.

GILMAN, C. P. (1914). *The man-made world, or our androcentric culture.* New York: Charlton Company.

GILMAN, C. P. (1915). *Herland.* New York: Pantheon Books.

GINZBURG, R. (1989). Uncovering gynocentric science. In N. Tuana (Ed.), *Feminism and science* (pp. 69–84). Bloomington: Indiana University Press.

GLEASON, J. B., & GREIF, E. B. (1983). Men's speech to young children. In B. Thorne, C. Kramarae, & N. Henley (Eds.), *Language, gender, and society* (pp. 140–150). Rowley, MA: Newbury House.

GLEASON, J. B. (1987). Sex differences in parent-child interaction. In S. U. Philips, S. Steele, & C. Tanz (Eds.), *Language, gender, and sex in comparative perspective* (pp. 189–199). Cambridge: Cambridge University Press.

GODARD, J.-L. (1965). *Alphaville* [film]. Paris.

GOFFMAN, E. (1976). *Gender advertisements.* New York: Harper & Row.

GOLDIN, C. (1990). *Understanding the gender gap: An economic history of American women.* New York: Oxford University Press.

GOODCHILDS, J. D. (1991). *Psychological perspectives on human diversity in America.* Washington, DC: American Psychological Association.

GOODWIN, M. H. (1980). Directive-response speech sequences in girls' and boys' task activities. In S. McConnell-Ginet, R. Borkar, & N. Furman (Eds.), *Woman and language in literature and society.* New York: Praeger.

GOODWIN, M. H. (1988). Cooperation and competition across girls' play activities. In A. D. Todd & S. Fisher (Eds.), *Gender and discourse: The power of talk* (pp. 55–94). Norwood, NJ: Ablex.

GOODWIN, M. H. (1990). *He said–she said. Talk as social organization among Black children.* Bloomington: Indiana University Press.

GOODWIN, M. H. (in press). !Ay Chirriona!: Co-construction in Latina girls' hop scotch. In S. Hoyle & C. T. Adger (Eds.), *Language practices of older children.* New York: Oxford University Press.

GORDON, E. (1994). Sex, speech, and stereotypes: Why women's speech is closer to the standard than men's. In M. Bucholtz, A. C. Liang, L. Sutton, & C. Hines (Eds.), *Cultural performance: Proceedings of the Third Berkeley Women and Language Conference* (pp. 242–250). Berkeley: Berkeley Women and Language Group.

GOSSETT, H. (1981). Who told you anybody wants to hear from you? You ain't nothing but a Black woman! In C. Morraga & G. Anzaldua (Eds.), *This bridge called my back: Writings by radical women of color.* Watertown, MA: Persephone Press.

GOULD, L. (1976). *A sea change.* New York: Avon Books.

GOULD, S. J. (1981). *The mismeasure of man.* New York: Norton.

GRADDOL, D., & SWANN, J. (1989). *Gender voices.* Oxford: Basil Blackwell.

GRAY, J. (1992). *Men are from Mars, women are from Venus: A practical guide for improving communication and getting what you want in your relationships.* New York: HarperCollins.

GREER, G. (1971). *The female eunuch.* London: Paladin.

GREER, G. (1986). Lady love your cunt. In *The madwoman's underclothes: Essays and occasional writings 1968–1985* (pp. 74–77). London: Pan Books.

GREGERSEN, E. A. (1979). Sexual linguistics. In J. Orasanu, M. K. Slater, & L. L. Adler (Eds.), *Language, sex, and gender: Does "la difference" make a difference?* (pp. 3–22). New York: New York Academy of Sciences.

GRÖNBERG, A. G. (1995). Konan er líka maður. An analysis of generic masculine in modern Icelandic. In P. Holmberg & K. Nordenstam (Eds.), *Language and gender. Case studies from a Swedish seminar* (pp. 79–88). Göteborg: MISS 11, Göteborg Universitet.

GROULT, B. (1975). *Ainsi soit-elle*. Paris: Grasset.

GUARDIAN. (1986, April 1). Why perfume ads stink. pp. 16–17.

GUIORA, A. Z., BEIT-HALLAHMI, B., FRIED, R., & YODER, C. (1982). Language environment and gender identity attainment. *Language Learning, 32*, 289–304.

GUIRAUD, P. (1978). *Le langage de la sexualité*. Tome 1. *Dictionnaire Erotique*. Tome 2. *Semiologie de la sexualité*. Paris: Payot.

GUPTA, A. F., & YIN, A. L. S. (1990). Gender representation in English langage textbooks used in Singapore primary schools. *Language and Education, 4*, 29–50.

HAGGARD, H. R. (1860). *She*. London: Longman, Green & Co.

HAIMAN, J. (1979). Hua: Papuan language of New Guinea. In T. Shopen (Ed.), *Languages and their speakers* (pp. 35–91). Cambridge, MA: Winthrop.

HALL, E. T. (1983). *The dance of life: The other dimension of time*. New York: Anchor/Doubleday.

HALL, K., & O'DONOVAN, V. (1996). Shifting gender positions among Hindi-speaking hijras. In V. L. Bergvall, J. M. Bing, & A. F. Freed (Eds.), *Rethinking language and gender research: Theory and practice* (pp. 228–266). Harlow: Longman.

HAMILTON, E. (1940). *Mythology*. New York: Little, Brown.

HAMILTON, M. C., HUNTER, B., & STUART-SMITH, S. (1994). Jury instructions worded in the masculine generic. In C. Roman, S. Juhasz, & C. Miller (Eds.), *The women and language debate: A sourcebook* (pp. 340–347). New Brunswick, NJ: Rutgers University Press.

HARAWAY, D. J. (1991). *Simians, cyborgs, and women: The reinvention of nature*. New York: Routledge.

HARRAGAN, B. L. (1977). *Games mother never taught you: Corporate gamesmanship for women*. New York: Warner.

HARVEY, P. (1994). The presence and absence of speech in the communication of gender. In P. Burton, K. K. Dyson, & S. Ardener (Eds.), *Bilingual women: Anthropological approaches to second language use* (pp. 44–64). Oxford: Berg.

HAUGEN, E. (1966). *Language conflict and language planning, the case of modern Norwegian*. Cambridge, MA: Harvard University Press.

HAYDEN ELGIN, S. (1984). *Native tongue*. New York: DAW.

HAYDEN ELGIN, S. (1987). *Native tongue II: The Judas rose*. New York: DAW.

HAYDEN ELGIN, S. (1988). *A first dictionary and grammar of Láadan* (2nd ed.). Madison, WI: Society for the Furtherance and Study of Fantasy and Science Fiction.

HAYDEN ELGIN, S. (1993). *Genderspeak: Men, women, and the gentle art of verbal self defense*. New York: John Wiley & Sons.

HEILBRUN, C. (1973). *Toward a recognition of androgyny*. New York: Norton.

HELLINGER, M. (1980). For men must work and women must weep: Sexism in English language textbooks used in German schools. In C. Kramarae (Ed.), *The voices and words of women and men* (pp. 267–275). Oxford: Pergamon Press.

HELLINGER, M. (1990). *Kontrastive Feministische Linguistik: Mechanismen sprachlicher Diskriminierung im Englischen und Deutschen* [Contrastive feminist linguistics: Mechanisms of linguistic discrimination in English and German]. München: Max Hueber Verlag.

HELLINGER, M., & BIERBACH, C. (1993). *Eine Sprache für beide Geschlechter: Richtlinien für einen nicht-sexistischen Sprachgebrauch* [A language for both sexes: Guidelines for non-sexist language use]. Bonn: Deutsche Unesco-Kommission. Also in French translation (1989), *Pour un langage non sexiste* [Guidelines on non-sexist language]. Paris: Unesco.

HEMINGWAY, E. (1968). Up in Michigan. In *The first forty-nine stories*. London: Jonathan Cape.

HENLEY, N. (1977). *Body politics: Power, sex, and non-verbal communication*. New York: Prentice-Hall.

HENLEY, N. (1987). This new species that seeks a new language: On sexism in language and language change. In J. Penfield (Ed.), *Women and language in transition* (pp. 3–27). Albany, NY: State University of New York Press.

HENLEY, N. (1995a). Ethnicity and gender issues in language. In H. Landrine (Ed.), *Handbook of cultural diversity in feminist psychology*. Washington, DC: American Psychological Association.

HENLEY, N. (1995b). Body politics revisited: What do we know today? In P. J. Kalbfleisch & M. J. Cody (Eds.), *Gender, power, and communication in human relationships* (pp. 27–61). Hillsdale, NJ: Lawrence Erlbaum Associates.

HERBERT, R. K. (1990a). Hlonipha and the ambiguous woman. *Anthropos, 85*, 455–473.

HERBERT, R. K. (1990b). Sex-based differences in compliment behavior. *Language and Society, 19*(2), 201–224.

HERDT, G. (1993). Sexual repression, social control, and gender hierarchy in Sambia culture. In B. Miller (Ed.), *Sex and gender hierarchies* (pp. 193–211). Cambridge: Cambridge University Press.

HERMANN, C. (1976). *Les voleuses de langue* [The tongue snatchers]. Paris: Payot.

HERRING, S. C. (1995). Gender and democracy in computer-mediated communication. In I. Broch, T. Bull, & T. Swan (Eds.), *Proceedings of the Second Nordic Conference on Language and Gender* (pp. 1–20). Tromsø, Norway: Tromsø University Working Papers on Language and Linguistics, No. 23.

HERRING, S. C. (1996a). Freedom of speech or freedom of harassment? *The College* (magazine of the University of Texas at Arlington College of Liberal Arts), *1*, 7–8.

HERRING, S. C. (1996b, December 11). Posting to FLING internet discussion list [On-line]. fling@listserv.oit.unc.edu

HEY, V. (1996). *The company she keeps. An ethnography of girls' friendships*. Buckingham: Open University Press.

HILL, A. O. (1986). *Mother tongue, father time: A decade of linguistic revolt*. Bloomington: Indiana University Press.

HINES, C. (1994). Let me call you "sweetheart": The *woman as dessert* metaphor. In M. L. Bucholtz, A. C. Liang, L. Sutton, & C. Hines (Eds.), *Cultural performance: Proceedings of the Third Berkeley Women and Language Conference* (pp. 295–303). Berkeley: Berkeley Women and Language Group.

HINES, C. (1995, July). *Foxy chicks and Playboy bunnies: A case study in metaphorical lexicalization*. Paper given at the Fourth International Cognitive Linguistics Association, University of New Mexico, Albuquerque, NM.

HIRAGA, M. (1991). Metaphors Japanese women live by. *Working Papers on Language, Gender, and Sexism, 1*, 38–57.

HINTON, L. (1994). *Flutes of fire: Essays on California Indian languages*. Berkeley, CA: Heydey Books.

HITE, S. (1987). *Women and love: A cultural revolution in progress*. New York: Knopf.

HOCHSCHILD, A. (1983). *The managed heart: Commercialization of human feeling*. Berkeley: University of California Press.

HOCHSCHILD, A. (WITH A. MACHUNG). (1989). *The second shift: Working parents and the revolution at home*. New York: Viking.

HOLMBERG, P. (1995). On female job titles in modern Swedish. In P. Holmberg & K. Nordenstam (Eds.), *Language and gender: Case studies from a Swedish seminar* (pp. 63–78). Göteborg: MISS 11, Göteborg Universitet.

HOLMES, J. (1986). Functions of *you know* in women's and men's speech. *Language in Society, 15*, 1–22.

HOLMES, J. (1994). *Women, men and politeness*. London: Longman.

HOLMES, J. (1995). Glottal stops in New Zealand English: An analysis of variants of word final /t/. *Linguistics, 33*, 433–463.

HON. H. H. (1866). *Poor letter H. Its use and abuse* (40th ed.). London: John F. Shaw.

hooks, b. (1981). *Ain't I a woman: Black women and feminism.* Boston: South End Press.

hooks, b. (1984). *Feminist theory: From margin to center.* Boston: South End Press.

hooks, b. (1989). *Talking back: Talking feminist, talking Black.* Boston: South End Press.

hooks, b. (1993). *Sisters of the yam: Black women and self-recovery.* Boston: South End Press.

hooks, b. (1995). *Killing rage: Ending racism.* New York: Henry Holt.

HORVATH, B. (1985). *Variation in Australian English: The sociolects of Sydney.* Cambridge: Cambridge University Press.

HOUDEBINE, A.-M. (1987). Le français au feminin. *Le Linguistique, 23,* 13–34.

HUGHES, L. A. (1993). "You have to do it with style": Girls' games and girls' gaming. In S. T. Hollis, L. Pershing, & M. J. Young (Eds.), *Feminist theory and the study of folklore* (pp. 130–148). Urbana: University of Illinois Press.

HULME, K. (1984). *The bone people.* Auckland: Hodder & Staughton.

HUME, E., & MCELHINNY, B. (1993). *Language and gender syllabi collection.* Washington, DC: Linguistic Society of America.

HUNTER, D. (n.d.) Teaching the social skills to modern-day Eliza Doolittles! [local free newspaper]

HUXLEY, A. (1921). *Crome yellow.* London: Chatto & Windus.

ILLICH, I. (1982). *Gender.* New York: Pantheon Books.

IRIGARAY, L. (1985). *The sex which is not one.* (C. Porter, Trans.). Ithaca, NY: Cornell University Press.

IRVINE, J. T. (1990). Registering affect: Heteroglossia in the linguistic expression of emotion. In C. Lutz & L. Abu-Lughod (Eds.), *Language and the politics of emotion* (pp. 126–161). Cambridge: Cambridge University Press.

IRVINE, J. T. (1995). The family romance of colonial linguistics: Gender and family in nineteenth century representations of African languages. *Pragmatics, 5,* 139–155.

JACOBS, S.-E., & CROMWELL, J. (1992). Visions and revisions of reality: Reflections on sex, sexuality, gender and gender variance. *Journal of Homosexuality, 23,* 43–71.

JAMES, D. (1996). Women, men and prestige speech forms: A critical review. In V. L. Bergvall, J. M. Bing, & A. F. Freed (Eds.), *Rethinking language and gender research. Theory and practice* (pp. 98–126). Harlow: Longman.

JAMES, D., & CLARKE, S. (1993). Women, men and interruptions: A critical review. In D. Tannen (Ed.), *Gender in conversational interaction* (pp. 231–280). New York: Oxford University Press.

JAMES, D., & DRAKICH, J. (1993). Understanding gender differences in amount of talk: A critical review of research. In D. Tannen (Ed.), *Gender in conversational interaction* (pp. 281–312). New York: Oxford University Press.

JAMES, H. (1906–1907). The speech of American women. *Harper's Bazaar, 40,* 979–982, 1103–1106; *41,* 17–21, 113–117.

JESPERSEN, O. (1922). The woman. In *Language, its nature, development, and origin* (pp. 237–254). London: Allen & Unwin/New York: Holt. Reprinted in D. Cameron (Ed.), 1990, *The feminist critique of language* (pp. 201–220). London: Routledge.

JESPERSEN, O. (1949). *A modern English grammar on historical principles, Part VII, Syntax.* Copenhagen: Ejnar Munksgaard.

JOHNSON, S., & MEINHOF, U. H. (Eds.). (1996). *Language and masculinity.* Oxford: Blackwell.

JOHNSTONE, B. (1993). Community and contest: Midwestern men and women creating their worlds in conversational storytelling. In D. Tannen (Ed.), *Gender in conversational interaction* (pp. 62–80). New York: Oxford University Press.

JOHNSTONE, J. (1973). *Lesbian nation: The feminist solution.* New York: Simon & Schuster.

JONES, A. I., & MERCHANT, E. (1991). *Unveiling a parallel: A romance.* Syracuse, NY: Syracuse University Press. (Original work written 1893)

JONES, D. (1917). *An English pronouncing dictionary.* London: Dent.

JONG, E. (1973). *Fear of flying; A novel.* New York: Holt, Rinehart & Winston.

JOYCE, J. (1917). *A portrait of the artist as a young man.* The Egoist.

JUDD, J. (1989, July 9). Church of our fathers is asked to watch its language. *Sunday Observer,* p. 3.

JUNKER, M.-O. (1992). Metaphors we live by: The terminology of linguistic theory. *Natural Language and Linguistic Theory, 10,* 141–145.

JURAFSKY, D. (1996). Universal tendencies in the semantics of the diminutive. *Language, 72,* 533–579.

KALBFLEISCH, P. J., & KEYTON, J. (1995). Power and equality in mentoring relationships. In P. J. Kalbfleisch & M. J. Cody (Eds.), *Gender, power, and communication in human relationships* (pp. 189–212). Hillsdale, NJ: Lawrence Erlbaum Associates.

KALCIK, S. (1975). . . . Like Ann's gynecologist or the time I was almost raped. In C. R. Farrer (Ed.), *Women and folklore* (pp. 3–11). Austin: University of Texas Press.

KANFER, S. (1972, October 23). Sisspeak: A Msguided attempt to change herstory. *Time,* p. 79.

KANTROWITZ, B. (1996, November 4). Gay families come out. *Newsweek,* pp. 50–56.

KARTTUNEN, F. (1994). *Between worlds. Interpretors, guides and survivors.* New Brunswick, NJ: Rutgers University Press.

KAYSER, A. (1936). *Nauru grammar* (K. Rensch, Ed.). Yarralumla: Embassy of the Federal Republic of Germany in Australia. (Original work published 1936)

KEENAN, E. (1974). Norm makers, norm breakers: Use of speech by men and women in a Malagasy community. In J. Sherzer & R. Bauman (Eds.), *Explorations in the ethnography of speaking* (pp. 125–143). Cambridge: Cambridge University Press.

KELLAWAY, L. (1994, October 10). Bumping into office etiquette. *Financial Times.*

KESSLER, C. F. (Ed.). (1984). *Daring to dream: Utopian stories by United States women, 1836–1919.* Boston: Pandora.

KESSLER, S. J., & MCKENNA, W. (1978). *Gender: An ethnomethodological approach.* Chicago: University of Chicago Press.

KEULEN, M. (1991). *Radical imagination: Feminist conceptions of the future in Ursula Le Guin, Marge Piercy and Sally Miller Gearhart.* Frankfurt: Peter Lang.

KEY, M. R. (1975). *Male/female language.* Metuchen, NJ: Scarecrow Press.

KHOSROSHASHI, F. (1989). Penguins don't care, but women do: A social identity analysis of a Whorfian problem. *Language in Society, 18,* 505–526.

KILBOURNE, J. (1987). *Still killing us softly: Advertising's image of women* [videotape]. Cambridge, MA: Cambridge Documentary Films.

KING, B. (1984). *Women of the future: The female main character in science fiction.* Metuchen, NJ: Scarecrow Press.

KING, J., & STOTT, M. (1977). *Is this your life? Images of women in the media.* London: Virago.

KING, R. (Ed.). (1991). *Talking gender: A guide to non-sexist communication.* Toronto: Copp Clark Pittman.

KIPERS, P. S. (1987). Gender and topic. *Language in Society, 16,* 543–557.

KJELLMER, G. (1986). "The lesser man": Observations on the role of women in modern English writings. In J. Aarts & W. Meijs (Eds.), *Corpus linguistics II: New studies in the analysis and exploitation of computer corpora* (pp. 163–176). Amsterdam: Rodopi.

KLEINFELD, J. S. (1995). The boys on the bus: Bad language or sexual harassment? In J. S. Kleinfeld & S. Yerian (Eds.), *Gender tales: Tensions in the schools* (pp. 149–155). New York: St. Martin's Press.

KLEINFELD, J. S., & YERIAN, S. (Eds.). (1995). *Gender tales: Tensions in the schools.* New York: St. Martin's Press.

KNOTTS, L. (1991, May 28). Job-hunting advice for women: Talk like a man. *Baltimore Evening Sun.*

KONISHI, T. (1994). The connotations of gender: A semantic differential study of German and Spanish. *Word, 45,* 317–328.

KOOLMATRIE, W. (1994). *My own sweet time.* Broome, WA: Magabala Books.

KRAMARAE, C. (Ed.). (1980). *The voices and words of women and men.* Oxford: Pergamon Press.

KRAMARAE, C. (1981). *Women and men speaking: Frameworks for analysis.* Rowley, MA: Newbury House.

KRAMARAE, C. (1992). Punctuating the dictionary. In T. Bull & T. Swan (Eds.), Language, sex, and society. *International Journal of the Sociology of Language, 91,* 135–154.

KRAMARAE, C., & TREICHLER, P. (Eds.). (1985). *A feminist dictionary.* Boston: Pandora Press.

KRAMER, C. (1975). Stereotypes of women's speech: The word from cartoons. *Journal of Popular Culture, 8*(3), 624–638.

KRISTEVA, J. (1984). *Revolution in poetic language* (M. Walker, Trans.). New York: Columbia University Press.

LABOV, W. (1966). *The social stratification of English in New York City.* Washington, DC: Center for Applied Linguistics.

LABOV, W. (1972a). *Sociolinguistic patterns.* Philadelphia: University of Pennsylvania Press.

LABOV, W. (1972b). Rules for ritual insults. In *Language in the inner city* (pp. 297–353). Philadelphia: University of Pennsylvania Press.

LABOV, W. (1990). The intersection of sex and social class in the course of linguistic change. *Language Variation and Change, 2,* 205–254.

LAFRANCE, M., & HAHN, E. (1994). The disappearing agent: Gender stereotypes, interpersonal verbs and implicit causality. In C. Roman, S. Juhasz, & C. Miller (Eds.), *The women and language debate: A sourcebook* (pp. 348–362). New Brunswick, NJ: Rutgers University Press.

LAKOFF, G. (1987). *Women, fire and dangerous things: What categories reveal about the mind.* Chicago: University of Chicago Press.

LAKOFF, G. (1996). *Moral politics: What conservatives know that liberals don't.* Chicago: University of Chicago Press.

LAKOFF, R. (1975). *Language and woman's place.* New York: Harper & Row. (Out of print)

LAKOFF, R. (1990). *Talking power: The politics of language.* New York: Basic Books.

LAKOFF, R. (1992). The rhetoric of reproduction. *Conscience, XIII,* 2–12.

LAKOFF, R., & COYNE, J. (1993). *Father knows best. The use and abuse of power in Freud's use of Dora.* New York: Teachers College Press.

LAKOFF, R., & SCHERR, R. L. (1984). *Face value: The politics of beauty.* London: Routledge & Kegan Paul.

LANE, M. E. B. (1975). *Mizora: A prophecy.* Boston: Gregg Press. (Original work written 1889)

LARCHE, D. W. (1986). *Father Gander nursery rhymes: Traditional nursery rhymes updated for the 1980s.* Watford, England: Exley Publications.

LARSON, K. (1982). Role playing and the real thing: Socialization and standard speech in Norway. *Journal of Anthropological Research, 38,* 401–410.

LAWSON, D. (1994, November 3). *The salon.* Broadcast discussion on political correctness chaired by Sarah Dunant, BBC Radio 4.

LEAP, W. L. (1996). *Word's out: Gay men's English.* Minneapolis: University of Minnesota Press.

LEECH, G. (1974). *Semantics.* Harmondsworth, England: Penguin.

LEES, S. (1983). How boys slag off girls. *New Society, 13,* 51–53.

LEES, S. (1986). *Losing out: Sexuality and adolescent girls.* London: Hutchinson.

LE GUIN, U. K. (1969). *The left hand of darkness.* New York: Ace Books.

LE GUIN, U. K. (1979). Is gender necessary? In *The languages of the night: Essays on fantasy and science fiction* (pp. 161–171). New York: Putnam.

LE GUIN, U. K. (1986). The mother tongue. *Bryn Mawr College Alumnae Bulletin.*

LE GUIN, U. K. (1987). Is gender necessary? Redux. In *Dancing at the edge of the world: Thoughts of words, women and places* (pp. 7–16). New York: Grove Press.

LE GUIN, U. K. (1995). Afterword. *The left hand of darkness.* New York: Ace.

LEHTONEN, J., & SAJAVAARA, K. (1985). The silent Finn. In D. Tannen & M. Saville-Troike (Eds.), *Perspectives on silence* (pp. 193 201). Norword, NJ: Ablex.

LEPSCHY, G. (1987). Sexism and the Italian language. *The Italianist,* 158–169.

LEPSIUS, K. L. (1863). *Standard alphabet for reducing unwritten languages and foreign graphic systems to a uniform orthography in European letters* (2nd ed.). London: Williams & Norgate.

LESSING, D. (1969). *The four-gated city.* New York: Bantam Books.

LESSING, D. (1979). *Shikasta.* New York: Vintage Books.

LESSING, D. (1980). *The marriages between zones three, four and five.* New York: Random House.

LESTER, P. M. (Ed.). (1996). *Images that injure: Pictorial stereotypes in the media.* Westport, CT: Praeger.

LEVENSON, H. et al. (1975). Are women still prejudiced against women? *Journal of Psychology, 89,* 67–71.

LEVER, J. R. (1978). Sex differences in the complexity of children's play and games. *American Sociological Review, 43,* 471–483.

LEVERE, J. (1974, June 8). Portrayal of women in ads defended by top ad women. *Editor and Publisher,* p. 11.

LEVIN, I. (1972). *Stepford wives: A novel.* New York: Random House.

LEVINE, B. (1996, November 4). Milk is macho. How to allay men's fear of milk. *Newsweek,* special advertising section.

LEVINSON, R. M. (1975). From Olive Oyl to Sweet Poly Purebread: Sex role stereotypes and televised cartoons. *Journal of Popular Culture, IX,* 561–572.

LILLIAN, D. (1996, December 14). Posting to Fling internet discussion list [On-line]. fling@listserv.oit.unc.edu

LINDSAY, D. (1920). *Voyage to Arcturus.* London: V. Gollancz.

LIVIA, A., & HALL, K. (Eds.). (1996). *Queerly phrased: Language, gender and sexuality.* New York: Oxford University Press.

LORDE, A. (1981). The master's tools will never dismantle the master's house. In C. Morraga and G. Anzaldua (Eds.), *This bridge called my back: Writings by radical women of color.* Watertown, MA: Persephone Press.

LORDE, A. (1982). *Zami: A new spelling of my name.* Trumansburg, NY: Crossing Press.

LOVELOCK, J. E. (1985). Gaia, the powerful goddess. In N. Myers (Ed.), *The Gaia atlas of planet management* (pp. 105–122). London: Pan Books.

LUKE, A., MCHOUL, A. W., & MEY, J. L. (1990). On the limits of language planning: Class, state and power. In R. Baldauf, Jr., & L. Allan (Eds.), *Language planning and education in Australasia and the South Pacific* (pp. 25–46). Clevedon, Avon: Multilingual Matters.

LUTZ, C. (1990). Engendered emotion: Gender, power, and the rhetoric of emotional control in American discourse. In C. Lutz & L. Abu-Lughod (Eds.), *Language and the politics of emotion* (pp. 69–91). Cambridge: Cambridge University Press.

LYONS, J. (1968). *Introduction to theoretical linguistics.* Cambridge: Cambridge University Press.

LYONS, J. (1977). *Semantics.* Cambridge: Cambridge University Press.

MACAULAY, R. K. S. (1978). The myth of female superiority in language. *Journal of Child Language, 5,* 353–363.

MACCOBY, E. E., & JACKLIN, C. N. (1974). *The psychology of sex differences.* Stanford, CA: Stanford University Press.

MACDONALD, R. H. (1994). *The language of empire: Myths and metaphors of popular imperialism, 1880–1918.* Manchester: Manchester University Press.

MACKAY, D. G. (1980). On the goals, principles and procedures for prescriptive grammar. *Language in Society, 9,* 349–367.

MACKAY, D. G., & KONISHI, T. (1980). Personification and the pronoun problem. In C. Kramarae (Ed.), *The voices and words of women and men.* Oxford: Pergamon Press.

MACKINNON, C. A. (1987). "Difference and dominance: On sex discrimination. In C. A. MacKinnon (Ed.), *Feminism unmodified: Discourses on life and law* (pp. 32–45). Cambridge, MA: Harvard University Press.

MACKINNON, C. A. (1989). *Toward a feminist theory of the state.* Cambridge, MA: Harvard University Press.

MAGGIO, R. (1988). *The nonsexist word finder: A dictionary of gender-free usage.* Boston: Beacon Press.

MALTZ, D. N., & BORKER, R. A. (1982). A cultural approach to male-female miscommunication. In J. J. Gumperz (Ed.), *Language and social identity* (pp. 195–217). Cambridge: Cambridge University Press.

MARTEL, B. (1981). *Né homme, comment je suis devenue femme.* Montréal: Québecor.

MASTERS, W. H., & JOHNSON, V. E. (1966). *Human sexual response.* Boston: Little, Brown.

MATHIOT, M., & ROBERT, M. (1979). Sex roles as revealed through referential gender in American English. In M. Mathiot (Ed.), *Ethnolinguistics: Boas, Sapir and Whorf revisited* (pp. 1–47). The Hague: Mouton.

MATISOFF, J. A. (1991). The mother of all morphemes: Augmentatives and diminutives in areal and universal perspective. In M. Ratliff & E. Schiller (Eds.), *Papers from the First Annual Meeting of the Southeast Asian Linguistics Society* (pp. 293–349). Tempe, AZ.

MATOESIAN, G. (1993). *Reproducing rape: Domination through talk in the courtroom.* Chicago: University of Chicago Press.

MATTHEWS, G. (1987). *"Just a housewife": The rise and fall of domesticity in America.* New York: Oxford University Press.

MAURER, D. (1981). *Language of the underworld* (A. W. Futrell & Charles B. Wordell, Eds. & Collectors). Lexington: University Press of Kentucky.

MCCOMBIE, M. (1996, Spring). Material gal, Barbie: The anatomy of a cash cow. *Bryn Mawr Alumnae Bulletin,* pp. 15–19.

MCCONNELL-GINET, S. (1983). Review article. *Language, 59,* 373–391.

MCCONNELL-GINET, S. (1989). The sexual (re)production of meaning. In F. Frank & P. Treichler (Eds.), *Language, gender and professional writing* (pp. 35–50). New York: Modern Language Association.

MCCONNELL-GINET, S., BORKAR, R., & FURMAN, N. (Eds.). (1980). *Women and language in literature and society.* New York: Praeger.

MCDONALD, M. (1994). Women and linguistic innovation in Brittany. In P. Burton, K. Dyson, & S. Ardener (Eds.), *Bilingual women: Anthropological approaches to second language use* (pp. 85–110). Oxford: Berg.

MEAD, M. (1935). *Sex and temperament in three primitive societies.* New York: William Morrow.

MEAD, M. (1949). *Male and female.* New York: William Morrow.

MEDRICH, E. A., ROIZEN, J., RUBIN, V., & BUCKLEY, S. (1982). *The serious business of growing up: A study of children's lives outside school.* Berkeley: University of California Press.

MICHEL, A. (1986). *Down with stereotypes! Eliminating sexism from children's literature and school textbooks.* Paris: UNESCO.

MILL, J. S. (1869). *The subjection of women.* (no publisher).

MILLER, B. (Ed.). (1993). *Sex and gender hierarchies.* Cambridge: Cambridge University Press.

MILLER, C., & SWIFT, K. (1988). *The handbook of nonsexist writing* (2nd ed.). New York: Harper & Row. (Original work published 1980)

MILLER, C., & SWIFT, K. (1991). *Words and women: New language in new times.* New York: HarperCollins.

MILLS, J. (1989). *WomanWords: A dictionary of words about women.* New York: Free Press.

MILROY, J., MILROY, L., & HARTLEY, S. (1994). Local and supralocal change in British English: The case of glottalization. *English World-Wide, 15,* 1–34.

MILROY, L. (1980). *Language and social network.* Oxford: Blackwell.

MILROY, L. (1992). New perspectives in the analysis of sex differentiation in language. In K. Bolton & H. Kwok (Eds.), *Sociolinguistics today: International perspectives* (pp. 163–179). London: Routledge.

MINH-HA, T. T. (1989). *Woman, native, other: Writing postcoloniality and feminism.* Bloomington: Indiana University Press.

MOI, T. (1985). *Sexual/textual politics: Feminist literary theory.* London: Methuen.

MONTAGUE, A. (1968). *The natural superiority of women.* London: Macmillan.

MOORE, H. (1989). *Feminism and anthropology.* Minneapolis: University of Minnesota Press.

MORGAN, M. (1993). No woman no cry: The linguistic representation of African American women. In K. Hall, M. Bucholtz, & B. Moonwoman (Eds.), *Locating power: Proceedings of the Third Berkeley Conference on Women and Language.* Berkeley: University of California.

MORGAN, R. (1982). *The anatomy of freedom.* Oxford: Martin Robertson.

MORRIS, J. (1974). *Conundrum.* New York: Signet.

MOYNIHAN, D. P. (1986). *Family and nation.* New York: Harcourt, Brace, Jovanovich.

MUGGLESTONE, L. (1995). *"Talking proper": The rise of accent as a social symbol.* Oxford: Oxford University Press.

MUNRO, A. (1983). *The moons of Jupiter.* Harmondsworth, England: Penguin.

MURRAY, J. A. H. (1900). *The evolution of English lexicography.* Oxford: The Romanes Lecture.

MURRAY, S. O. (1985). Toward a model of members' methods for recognizing interruptions. *Language in Society, 13,* 31–41.

MURRAY, S. O., & COVELLI, L. (1988). Women and men speaking at the same time. *Journal of Pragmatics, 12,* 103–111.

MYERS, N. (1990). Gaia: The lady becomes ever more acceptable. *Geography Review, 3,* 3–5.

NATIONAL ADVERTISING REVIEW BOARD. (1975). *Advertising and women: A report on advertising portraying or directed to women.* New York: Author.

NEWMAN, J. (1982). *Girls are people too! A bibliography of nontraditional female roles in children's books.* Metuchen, NJ: Scarecrow Press.

NEWMAN, M. (1996). What can pronouns tell us? A case study of English epicenes. *Studies in Language.*

NEWSWEEK. (1984, May 28). What is "le mot juste" in an age of feminism? p. 23.

NEWSWEEK. (1983, October 24). Scrubbing the scriptures. p. 49.

NEWSWEEK. (1994, May 16). Men, women and computers.

NEWSWEEK. (1996a, September 23). Children of hate: Born under a bad sign. pp. 49–51.

NEWSWEEK. (1996b, November 4). Crossing over. p. 66

NICHOLS, P. (1983). Linguistic options and choices for Black women in the rural South. In B. Thorne, C. Kramarae, & N. Henley (Eds.), *Language, gender and society* (pp.). Rowley, MA: Newbury House.

NILSEN, A. P. (1987). Guidelines against sexist language: A case history. In J. Penfield (Ed.), *Women and language in transition* (pp. 37–64). Albany, NY: State University of New York Press.

NILSEN, A. P., BOSMAJIAN, H. H., GERSHUNY, L., & STANLEY, J. (1977). *Sexism and language.* Urbana, IL: National Council of Teachers of English.

NORDENSTAM, K. (1992). Male and female conversational style. In T. Bull & T. Swan (Eds.), Language, sex, and society. *International Journal of the Sociology of Language, 94,* 73–98.

NORDENSTAM, K. (1994). Women and gossip. *Working Papers on Language, Gender and Sexism, 4,* 69–77.

NORDENSTAM, K. (1996). *Skvaller i kvinnliga och manliga gruppsamtal* [Gossip in female and male group conversation]. Göteborg: MISS 12, Göteborg Universitet.

NORTON, A. (1963). *Witch world.* New York: Ace Books.

OAKLEY, A. (1972). *Sex, gender and society.* New York: Harper & Row.

OAKLEY, A. (1975a). *Women's work: The housewife, past and present.* New York: Pantheon.

OAKLEY, A. (1975b). *The sociology of housework.* New York: Pantheon.

OAKLEY, A. (1982). *Subject women.* London: Fontana.

O'BARR, W., & ATKINS, B. (1980). Women's language or powerless language? In S. McConnell-Ginet, R. Borker, & N. Furman (Eds.), *Women and language in literature and society* (pp. 93–109). New York: Praeger.

OCHS, E. (1992). Indexing gender. In A. Duranti & C. Goodwin (Eds.), *Rethinking context* (pp. 335–358). Cambridge: Cambridge University Press.

OFFEN, K. (1988). Defining feminism: A comparative historical approach. *Signs: Journal of Women in Culture and Society, 14,* 119–157.

OPIE, I., & OPIE, P. (1959). *The lore and language of schoolchildren.* Oxford: Oxford University Press.

ORBACH, S. (1978). *Fat is a feminist issue: The anti-diet guide to permanent weight loss.* New York and London: Paddington Press.

ORENSTEIN, P. (1994). *Schoolgirls: Young women, self-esteem, and the confidence gap.* New York: Doubleday.

ORTNER, S. B. (1974). Is female to male as nature is to culture? In M. Z. Rosaldo & L. Lamphere (Eds.), *Woman, culture, and society* (pp. 67–87). Stanford, CA: Stanford University Press.

ORTNER, S. B., & WHITEHEAD, H. (Eds.). (1981). *Sexual meanings: The cultural construction of sexuality.* Cambridge: Cambridge University Press.

ORWELL, G. (1949). *Nineteen eighty-four: A novel.* London: Secker & Warburg.

OSTLING, R. N. (1992, October 26). A somewhat less fatherly God. *Time,* p. 72.

OXFORD UNIVERSITY PRESS. (1995). *New Testament and Psalms.* Oxford, England: Author.

PATTERSON, P. (1996). Rambos and Himbos: Stereotypical images of men in advertising. In P. M. Lester (Ed.), *Images that injure: Pictorial stereotypes in the media* (pp. 93–96). Westport, CT: Praeger.

PAUWELS, A. (Ed.). (1987). *Language, gender and society in Australia and New Zealand.* Melbourne: River Seine Publications.

PENELOPE, J. (1990). *Speaking freely: Unlearning the lies of the father's tongues.* New York: Pergamon Press.

PENFIELD, J. (Ed.). (1987). *Women and language in transition.* Albany, NY: State University of New York Press.

PEOPLE WEEKLY. (1993, April 12). The body counters. pp. 34–37.

PERI ROSSI, C. (1988). *Solitario de amor.* Grijalbo.

PERSSON, G. (1990). *Meanings, models and metaphors: A study in lexical semantics in English.* Stockholm: Almqvist & Wiksell International.

PETERSON, K. (1994, December 16–19). Full "Disclosure": Film on harassment puts woman in wolf's clothing. *USA Today,* pp. 1–2.

PHILIPS, S. U., STEELE, S., & TANZ, C. (Eds.). (1987). *Language, gender, and sex in comparative perspective*. Cambridge: Cambridge University Press.

PHILIPSEN, G. (1975). Speaking like a man in Teamsterville: Culture patterns in role enactment in an urban neighborhood. *Quarterly Journal of Speech, 61,* 13–22.

PHILLIPS, K. C. (1984). *Language in Victorian England*. Oxford: Blackwell.

PIERCY, M. (1976). *Woman on the edge of time*. New York: Fawcett Crest.

PINTER, J. D. (1995, August). Boeing beauty. *Hemispheres,* p. 17.

POLANYI, L., and STRASSMANN, D. (1996). Story telling and gatekeepers in economics. In V. L. Bergvall, J. M. Bing, & A. F. Freed (Eds.), *Rethinking language and gender research: Theory and practice* (pp. 126–152). Harlow: Longman.

POYNTON, C. (1989). *Language and gender: Making the difference*. Oxford: Oxford University Press.

PUSCH, L. F. (1984). *Das Deutsche als Männersprache* [German as men's language]. Frankfurt: Suhrkamp.

QUIRK, R., GREENBAUM, S., LEECH, G., & SVARTVIK, J. (1985). *A comprehensive grammar of the English language*. London: Longman.

RADFORD, J., & RUSSELL, D. E. (1992). *Femicide: The politics of woman killing*. Milton Keynes: Open University Press.

RADWAY, J. (1991). *Reading the romance: Women, patriarchy and popular literature*. Chapel Hill: University of North Carolina Press.

RAFFERTY, F. (1994, May 1). Trading faces. *Sunday Times*.

RAIDT, E. H. (1995). Women in the history of Afrikaans. In R. Mesthrie (Ed.), *Language and social history: Studies in South African sociolinguistics* (pp. 129–139). Cape Town: David Philip.

RAMSAY, E., & STEFANOU-HAAG, E. (1991). On lies and silence: Cross-cultural perspectives on the construction of women's oppression through linguistic omission. *Working Papers on Language, Gender and Sexism, 1,* 31–42.

REINHOLTZ, R. K., MUEHLENHARD, C. L., PHELPS, J. L., & SATTERFIELD, A. T. (1995). Sexual discourse and sexual intercourse: How the way we communicate affects the way we think about sexual coercion. In P. J. Kalbfleisch & M. J. Cody (Eds.), *Gender, power, and communication in human relationships* (pp. 141–162). Hillsdale, NJ: Lawrence Erlbaum Associates.

RICH, A. (1978). *The dream of a common language*. New York: W. W. Norton.

RICH, A. (1980). *On lies, secrets, and silence: Selected prose 1966–1978*. London: Virago.

RICHERT, S. (1990). *Boys and girls apart: Children's play in Canada and Poland*. Ottawa: Carleton University Press.

RISCH, B. (1987). Women's derogatory terms for men: That's right, "dirty" words. *Language in Society, 16,* 353–358.

ROBERTS, R. (1993). *A new species: Gender and science in science fiction*. Chicago: University of Chicago Press.

RODGERS, E. M., HIRATA, T. M., CHANDRAN, A. S., & ROBINSON, J. D. (1995). Television promotion of gender equality in societies. In P. J. Kalbfleisch & M. J. Cody (Eds.), *Gender, power, and communication in human relationships* (pp. 277–304). Hillsdale, NJ: Lawrence Erlbaum Associates.

ROMAINE, S. (1982). *Socio-historical linguistics: Its status and methodology*. Cambridge: Cambridge University Press.

ROMAINE, S. (1984). *The language of children and adolescents: The acquisition of communicative competence*. Oxford: Blackwell.

ROMAINE, S. (1996). Clothes make the man, but language makes the woman: Socio-historical reflections on women and standard speech. In L. Elmevik, B. Melander, & M. Thelander (Eds.), *Samspel and variation* (pp. 393–403). Uppsala: University of Uppsala, Institutionen för Nordiska Språk.

ROMAINE, S. (1997a). Grammar, gender and the space in between. In H. Kotthoff & R. Wodak (Eds.), *Communicating gender in context* (pp. 51–76). Amsterdam: John Benjamins.

ROMAINE, S. (1997b). War and peace in the global greenhouse: Metaphors we die by. *Metaphor & Symbolic Activity, 11*, 175–194.

ROMAINE, S. (1998). Why ladies are supposed to talk properly: The glamour of grammar. In N. Warner, J. Ahlers, L. Bilmes, M. Oliver, S. Wertheim, & M. Chen (Eds.), *Gender and belief systems* (pp. 633–645). Berkeley, CA: Berkeley Women and Language Group.

ROMAINE, S. (forthcoming). Women, land and language: Shifting metaphors and shifting languages. To appear in *Proceedings of the Fifth Berkeley Women and Language Conference*. University of California, Berkeley: Berkeley Women and Language Group.

ROMAN, C., JUHASZ, S., & MILLER, C. (Eds.). (1994). *The women and language debate: A sourcebook*. New Brunswick, NJ: Rutgers University Press.

ROSALDO, M. Z., & LAMPHERE, L. (Eds.). (1974). *Woman, culture, and society*. Stanford, CA: Stanford University Press.

ROSSER, P. (1989). *The SAT gender gap: Identifying the causes*. Washington, DC: Center for Women Policy Studies.

ROSINSKY, N. M. (1984). *Feminist futures: Contemporary women's speculative fiction*. Ann Arbor, MI: UMI Research Press.

ROYKO, M. (1979, January 17). Ain't love grand? *The Oregonian*, p. D5.

RUBIN, D. L., GREENE, K., and SCHNEIDER, D. (1994). Adopting gender-inclusive language reforms: Diachronic and synchronic variation. *Journal of Language and Social Psychology, 13*, 91–114.

RUSS, J. (1976). *The female man*. New York: Bantam.

RUSS, J. (1986). Russalka, or the Seacoast of Bohemia. In J. Zipes (Ed.), *Don't bet on the prince: Contemporary fairy tales in North America and England* (pp. 88–94). New York: Methuen.

RYSMAN, A. (1977). How the "gossip" became a woman. *Journal of Communication, 27*, 176–180.

SABATINI, A. (1985). Occupational titles in Italian: Changing the sexist usage. In M. Hellinger (Ed.), *Sprachwandel und feministische Sprachpolitik: Internationale Perspektiven*. Opladen: Westdeutscher Verlag.

SABATINI, A. (1986). *Raccomandazioni per un uso non sessista della lingua italiana* [Recommendations for nonsexist usage in the Italian language]. Commissione Nazionale per la Realizzazione della Parità tra Uomo e Donna. Rome: Presidenza del Consiglio dei Ministri.

SAFIRE, W. (1992, July 5). On language: Disagreeing to agree. *The New York Times Magazine*, p. 6.

SAID, E. W. (1993). *Culture and imperialism*. New York: Alfred A. Knopf.

SANDAY, P. R. (1981). *Female power and male dominance: On the origins of sexual inequality*. Cambridge: Cambridge University Press.

SANDAY, P. R. (1990). *Fraternity gang rape: Sex, brotherhood, and privilege on campus*. New York: New York University Press.

SANDAY, P. R., & GOODENOUGH, R. G. (Eds.). (1990). *Beyond the second sex: New directions in the anthropology of gender*. Philadelphia: University of Pennsylvania Press.

SAPIR, E. (1921). *Language, an introduction to the study of speech*. New York: Harcourt, Brace & Co.

SCHEIDLER, J. (1985). *Closed: 99 ways to stop abortion*. San Francisco: St. Ignatius Press.

SCHIEFFELIN, B. (1987). Do different words mean different worlds? In S. Philips, S. Steele, & C. Tanz (Eds.), *Language, gender, and sex in comparative perspective* (pp. 249–262). Cambridge: Cambridge University Press.

SCHNEIDER, J. W., & HACKER, S. L. (1973). Sex role imagery and use of the generic "man" in introductory texts: A case in the sociology of sociology. *American Sociologist, 8*, 12–18.

SCHWARTZ, D. (1996). Women as mothers. In P. M. Lester (Ed.), *Images that injure: Pictorial stereotypes in the media* (pp. 75–80). Westport, CT: Praeger.

SCHWARTZ, P., PATTERSON, D., & STEEN, S. (1995). The dynamics of power: Money and sex in intimate relationships. In P. J. Kalbfleisch & M. J. Cody (Eds.), *Gender, power, and communication in human relationships* (pp. 253–274). Hillsdale, NJ: Lawrence Erlbaum Associates.

SCOTT, J. (1984). *I, vampire*. New York: Ace.

SCOTT, S. (1995). *A description of Millenium Hall*. Broadview Press. (Original work written 1762)

SEGAL, L. (1988). *Is the future female? Troubled thoughts on contemporary feminism*. New York: Peter Bedrick Books.

SELLERS, S. (1991). *Language and sexual difference: Feminist writing in France*. New York: St. Martin's Press.

SHAYWITZ, B. A., SHAYWITZ, S. E., & GORE, J. C. (1995). Sex differences in the functional organization of the brain for language. *Nature, 373*, 607–609.

SHELDON, A. (1993). Pickle fights: Gendered talk in preschool disputes. In D. Tannen (Ed.), *Gender in conversational interaction* (pp. 83–109). New York: Oxford University Press.

SHELLEY, M. W. (1990). *Frankenstein*. New York: Dover. (Original work written 1818)

SHIBAMOTO, J. S. (1985). *Japanese women's language*. New York: Academic Press.

SHOWALTER, E. (1985). Feminist criticism in the wilderness. In E. Showalter (Ed.), *The new feminist criticism: Essays on women, literature, and theory* (pp. 243–270). New York: Pantheon.

SHUMAN, A. (1986). *Storytelling rights: The uses of oral and written texts by urban adolescents*. Cambridge: Cambridge University Press.

SILVERBERG, R. (1975). Who is Tiptree, What is he? In J. Tiptree, Jr., *Warm worlds and otherwise*. New York: Ballantine Books.

SIMON, J. (1980). *Paradigms lost. Reflections on literacy and its decline*. New York: Clarkson N. Potter.

SISTREN (WITH H. F. SMITH). (Ed.). (1986). *Lionheart gal: Life stories of Jamaican women*. London: Women's Press.

SMITH, P. (1985). *Language, the sexes and society*. New York: Basil Blackwell.

SOLSKEN, J. W. (1993). *Literacy, gender, and work in families and in school*. Norwood, NJ: Ablex.

SPENDER, D. (1980a). *Man made language*. London: Routledge & Kegan Paul.

SPENDER, D. (1980b). Talking in class. In D. Spender & E. Sarah (Eds.), *Learning to lose: Sexism and education*. London: Women's Press.

SPENDER, D. (1982). *Invisible women: The schooling scandal*. London: Writers and Readers Publishing Cooperative.

SPIRO, M. E. (1993). Gender hierarchy in Burma: Cultural, social, and psychological dimensions. In B. Miller (Ed.), *Sex and gender hierarchies* (pp. 316–333). Cambridge: Cambridge University Press.

STANGER, C. A. (1987). The sexual politics of the one-to-one tutorial approach and collaborative learning. In C. Caywood & G. Overing (Eds.), *Teaching writing: Pedagogy, gender, and equity*. Albany: State University of New York Press.

STANLEY, J. P. (1977). Paradigmatic woman: The prostitute. In D. L. Shores & C. P. Hines (Eds.), *Papers in language variation*. Tuscaloosa: University of Alabama Press.

STANLEY, J. P. (1977). Passive motivation. *Foundations of Language, 13*, 25–39.

STANLEY, J. P., & ROBBINS, S. W. (1976). Truncated passives: Some of our agents are missing. *Linguistic Theory and the Real World, 1*, 33–37.

STANLEY, J. P., & ROBBINS, S. (1978). Sex-marked predicates in English. *Papers in Linguistics, 11*, 487–516.

STANNARD, U. (1977). *Mrs. man*. San Francisco: Germainbooks.

STANTON, D. (1984). Autogynography: Is the subject different? In D. Stanton (Ed.)., *The female autograph: Theory and practice of autobiography from the tenth to the twentieth century*. Chicago: University of Chicago Press.

STATE OF NEW JERSEY. (1984). *Women in the courts*. The First Year Report of the New Jersey Supreme Court Task Force on Women in the Courts. Trenton: Author.

STEAD, C. K. (1989). *Answering to the language: Essays on modern writers*. Auckland, New Zealand: Auckland University Press.

STEINEM, G. (1990, September). Sex, lies and advertising. *Ms.*, p. 24.

STENSTRÖM, A.-B. (1991). Expletives in the London-Lund corpus. In K. Aijmer & B. Altenberg (Eds.), *English corpus linguistics: Studies in honour of Jan Svartvik* (pp. 239–254). London: Longman.

STEVENSON, R. L. (1988). *The lantern bearers and other essays* (J. Treglown, Ed.). New York: Farrar, Straus & Giroux.

STEWART, D. (1987). Forms for women in Italian. *The Italianist*, 170–192.

STRASSER, S. (1982). *Never done: A history of American housework*. New York: Pantheon.

STRATHERN, M. (1988). *The gender of the gift: Problems with women and problems with society in Melanesia*. Berkeley: University of California Press.

SVARTENGREN, T. H. (1927). The feminine gender in Anglo-American. *American Speech, 3*, 83–113.

SWAN, T. (1992). Women's language in Sweden: Review of Kerstin Thelander, 1986. *Politikerspråk in könsperspektiv* [Political language in gender perspective]. Stockholm: Liber Forlag. In T. Bull & T. Swan (Eds.), Language, sex, and society. *International Journal of the Sociology of Language, 94*, 173–184.

SWAN, T. (1995). Gender and language change: The case of Norwegian. In I. Broch, T. Bull, & T. Swan (Eds.), *Proceedings of the Second Nordic Conference on Language and Gender* (pp. 298–315). Tromsø, Norway: Tromsø University Working Papers on Language and Linguistics No. 23.

SWANN, J. (1992). *Girls, boys, and language*. Oxford: Blackwell.

SWEET, H. (1890). *A primer of spoken English*. Oxford: Clarendon Press.

TALBOT, M. (1995). Randy fish boss branded a stinker: Coherence and the construction of masculinities in a British tabloid. In I. Broch, T. Bull, & T. Swan (Eds.), *Proceedings of the Second Nordic Conference on Language and Gender* (pp. 259–270). Tromsø, Norway: Tromsø University Working Papers on Language and Linguistics No. 23.

TANAKA, J. (1996, October 28). No boys allowed. *Newsweek*, pp. 82–84.

TANAKA, K. (1994). Images of women. In K. Tanaka (Ed.), *Advertising language: A pragmatic approach to advertisements in Britain and Japan* (pp. 107–131). London: Routledge.

TANNEN, D. (1990a). Who's interrupting? Issues of dominance and control. In *You just don't understand: Women and men in conversation* (pp. 188–215). New York: William Morrow.

TANNEN, D. (1990b). Gender differences in conversational coherence: Physical alignment and topical cohesion. In B. Dorval (Ed.), *Conversational organization and its development* (pp. 167–206). Norwood, NJ: Ablex.

TANNEN, D. (1992). Reply to Senta Troemel-Ploetz. *Discourse and Society, 3*, 249–254.

TANNEN, D. (1993a). Where'd all the fun go? *The Washington Post Book World, XXIII*(47), 1, 10–11.

TANNEN, D. (1993b). The relativity of linguistic strategies: Rethinking power and solidarity in gender and dominance. In D. Tannen (Ed.), *Gender in conversational language* (pp. 165–188). New York: Oxford University Press.

TANNEN, D. (Ed.). (1993c). *Gender in conversational interaction*. New York: Oxford University Press.

TANNEN, D. (1994a). Interpreting interruption in conversation. In D. Tannen (Ed.), *Gender and discourse* (pp. 53–83). New York: Oxford University Press.

TANNEN, D. (Ed.). (1994a). *Gender and discourse*. New York: Oxford University Press.

TANNEN, D. (1994b). *Talking from 9 to 5: How women's and men's conversational styles affect who gets heard, who gets credit, and what gets done at work.* New York: William Morrow.

TANNEN, D. (1994c, May 16). Hi-tech gender gap. *Newsweek*, pp. 52–53.

TANNEN, D., & SAVILLE-TROIKE, M. (Eds.). (1985). *Perspectives on silence.* Norwood, NJ: Ablex.

TAYLOR, J. (1991, January 21). Are you politically correct? *New York*, pp. 32–40.

THELANDER, K. (1986). *Politikerspråk in könsperspektiv* [Political language in gender perspective]. Stockholm: Liber Forlag.

THORNE, B. (1994). *Gender play: Girls and boys in school.* New Brunswick, NJ: Rutgers University Press.

THORNE, B., & HENLEY, N. (Eds.). (1974). *Language and sex: Difference and dominance.* Rowley, MA: Newbury House.

THORNE, B., KRAMARAE, C., & HENLEY, N. (Eds.). (1983). *Language, gender and society.* Rowley, MA: Newbury House.

THOVERON, G. (1987). *How women are represented in television programmes. Part one: Images of women in news, advertising and series and serials.* Luxembourg: Office for Official Publications of the European Community.

THWAITE, A. (1983). *Sexism in Three Mills and Boon romances.* Unpublished thesis, Department of Linguistics, University of Sydney.

TIME. (1959, May 23). Free press and fair trial.

TIME. (1992a, January 20). Why are men and women different: It isn't just upbringing. New studies show they are born that way.

TIME. (1992b, March 9). Fighting the backlash against feminism: Susan Faludi and Gloria Steinem sound the call to arms.

TIMES HIGHER EDUCATION SUPPLEMENT. (1994, February 18). Gender studies: Men bite back. p. 12.

TIPTREE, J., JR. (1978). *Up the walls of the world.* New York: Berkley.

TODOROV, T. (1984). *The conquest of America: The question of the other* (R. Howard, Trans.). New York: Harper & Row.

TOGEBY, O. (1992). Is there a separate women's language? In T. Bull & T. Swann (Eds.), Language, sex, and society. *International Journal of the Society of Language, 94,* 63–73.

TOLKIEN, J. R. R. (1966). *The lord of the rings.* London: Grafton.

TOMPKINS, J. (1989). Me and my shadow. In L. Kauffman (Ed.), *Gender and theory: Dialogues on feminist criticism* (pp. 121–139). Oxford: Blackwell.

TREVELYAN, G. O. (1878). *The life and letters of Lord Macaulay by his nephew George Otto Trevelyan* (Vols. 1 & 2). London: Longman, Green & Co.

TROEMEL-PLÖETZ, S. (1991). Selling the apolitical: Review of *You just don't understand* by D. Tannen. *Discourse & Society, 2,* 489–502. (Reprinted in *Language and gender: A reader*, pp. 446–459, by J. Contes, Ed., 1998, Oxford: Blackwell)

TRUDGILL, P. (1972). Sex, covert prestige and linguistic change in the urban British English of Norwich. *Language in Society, 1,* 179–195.

TRUDGILL, P. (1974). *Sociolinguistics.* Harmondsworth, England: Penguin.

TRUDGILL, P. (1983). *On dialect.* Oxford: Blackwell.

TUANA, N. (1989). *Feminism and science.* Bloomington: Indiana University Press.

TUANA, N. (1993). *Less noble sex: Scientific, religious, and philosophical conceptions of women's nature.* Bloomington: Indiana University Press.

TUKIA, P., & TUKIA, M. (1988). Structure linguistique et identification sexuelle chez les enfants de 16 à 42 mois, analyse psychométrique et linguistique pour tester l'hypothèse Sapir-Whorf. *Contrastes: La différence sexuelle dans le langage* (pp. 19–28). Acts du colloque ADEC-Université Paris III.

TWAIN, M. (1935). The awful German language. *A tramp abroad.* New York: Harper & Brothers.

UCHIDA, A. (1992). When "difference" is "dominance": A critique of the "anti-power-based" cultural approach to sex differences. *Language in Society, 21*(4), 547–568.

U.S. NEWS & WORLD REPORT. (1994, June 13). A woman's special dilemma. p. 93.

U.S. NEWS & WORLD REPORT. (1995, September 11). Playing women for suckers. p. 60.

U.S. NEWS & WORLD REPORT. (1995, September 25). Street talk, simplicity and PC.

U.S. SURGEON GENERAL. (1991, May 1). *Washington Spectator,* p. 3.

VALENTINE, J. (1995). Naming the other: Calling, becalling and the inflation of euphemisms. *Language in Society.*

VERBRUGGE, L. M., & MADENS, J. H. (1985, March). Women's roles and health. *American Demographics,* p. 36.

VESTERGAARD, T., & SCHRODER, K. (1985). *The language of advertising.* Oxford: Blackwell.

VOYAGER. (1995, May/June). Tribes that travel: Supermodels (Magazine of British Midland Airlines). p. 50.

WAKSLER, R. (1995). She's a mensch and he's a bitch: Neutralizing gender in the 1990s. *English Today, 42,* 3–6.

WALL STREET JOURNAL. (1978, August 28–September 22). Women at work: Let's get rid of "The Girl."

WALL STREET JOURNAL. (1994, July 5). Space cadet at 3,000 ft.: Woman pilot chronicles alleged harassment. p. 1.

WALSH, B. (1993). Women at Oxford, now and then. *Oxford Magazine, 98,* 7–14.

WALSH-CHILDERS, K. (1996). Women as sex partners. In P. M. Lester (Ed.), *Images that injure. Pictorial stereotypes in the media* (pp. 81–85). Westport, CT: Praeger.

WARD, R. L. (1979). *Curing on Pohnpei: A medical ethnography.* Doctoral dissertation, Tulane University, New Orleans, LA.

WARNER, M. (1985). *Monuments and maidens: The allegory of the female form.* New York: Atheneum.

WARNER, M. (1994). *From the beast to the blonde: On fairy tales and their tellers.* New York: Farrar, Straus & Giroux.

WARREN, C. (1987). *Madwives: Schizophrenic women in the 1950s.* New Brunswick, NJ: Rutgers University Press.

WARSHAW., R. (1988). *I never called it rape: The Ms. report on recognizing, fighting, and surviving date and acquaintance rape.* New York: Harper & Row.

WEBB, S. L. (1992). *Step forward: Sexual harassment in the workplace.* New York: Master-Media.

WEEDON, C. (1987). *Feminist practice and poststructuralist theory.* Oxford: Blackwell.

WEEKEND AUSTRALIAN. (1988). When it's everyone for himself/herself. p. 21.

WEIGEL, S. (1990). *Topographien der Geschlechter: Kulturgeschichtliche Studien zur Literatur* [Topographies of the sexes: Cultural-historical studies in literature]. Reinbeck bei Hamburg: Rowohlt Taschenbuchverlag.

WEIKEL, B., & YERIAN, S. (1995). Tough Anna. In J. S. Kleinfeld & S. Yerian (Eds.), *Gender tales. Tensions in the schools* (pp. 77–81). New York: St. Martin's Press.

WENDT, A. (1978). *Leaves of the banyan tree.* Auckland, New Zealand: Longman Paul.

WEST, C. (1985). When the doctor is a "lady": Power, status and gender in physician–patient encounters. In *Proceedings of the First Berkeley Women and Language Conference* (pp. 62–83). Berkeley: Women and Language Group.

WEST, C., & ZIMMERMAN, D. (1983). Small insult: A study of interruptions in cross-sex conversations between unacquainted persons. In B. Thorne, C. Kramarae, & N. Henley (Eds.), *Language, gender and society* (pp. 102–117). Rowley, MA: Newbury House.

WEST, C., & ZIMMERMAN, D. H. (1987). Doing gender. *Gender and Society, 1,* 125–151.

WHALEN, M. R. (1995). Working toward play: Complexity in children's fantasy activities. *Language in Society, 24,* 315–348.

WHETMORE, E. (1981). A female captain's enterprise: The implications of *Star Trek's* "turnabout murder." In M. S. Barr (Ed.), *Future females: A critical anthology* (pp. 157–161). Bowling Green, OH: Bowling Green State University Press.

WHITING, B. B., & EDWARDS, C. P. (1988). *Children of different worlds.* Cambridge, MA: Harvard University Press.

WHORF, B. L. (1956). *Language, thought and reality: Selected writings of Benjamin Lee Whorf* (J. B. Carroll, Ed.). Cambridge, MA: MIT Press.

WIERZBICKA, A. (1986). Does language reflect culture? *Language in Society, 15,* 349–374.

WILLIAMS, W. (1988). *The spirit and the flesh: Sexual diversity in American Indian culture.* Boston: Beacon Press.

WILLINSKY, J. (1994). *Empire of words: The reign of the OED.* Princeton, NJ: Princeton University Press.

WILLIS, P. (1977). *Learning to labor: How working class kids get working class jobs.* New York: Columbia University Press.

WILMS, D., & COOPER, I. (Eds.). (1987). *A guide to non-sexist children's books, Vol. II: 1976–1985.* Chicago: Academy Chicago Publishers.

WILSON, T. (1909). *The art of rhetoric.* London: Clarendon Press. (Original work written 1553)

WISSELINCK, E. (1986). *Hexen.* München: Frauenoffensive.

WITTGENSTEIN, L. (1958). *Philosophical investigations* (G. E. M. Anscombe, Trans.). New York: Macmillan.

WITTIG, M. (1964). *L'Opoponax.* Paris: Minuit. Also *The Opoponax* (H. Weaver, Trans.). London: Peter Owen.

WITTIG, M. (1969). *Les guérillères.* Paris: Minuit. Also *The female warriors* (D. le Vay, Trans.). New York: Viking Press.

WITTIG, M. (1973). *Le corps lesbien.* Paris: Minuit. Also *The lesbian body* (D. le Vay, Trans.). Boston: Beacon Press.

WITTIG, M. (1992). The mark of gender. In *The straight mind and other essays.* Boston: Beacon.

WOLF, N. (1990). *The beauty myth: How images of beauty are used against women.* London: Vintage.

WOLFRAM, W. (1974). *A sociolinguistic description of Detroit Negro speech.* Washington, DC: Center for Applied Linguistics.

WOLFSON, N., & MANES, J. (1980). Don't dear me! In S. McConnell, R. Borkar, & N. Furman (Eds.), *Woman and language in literature and society* (pp. 79–82). New York: Praeger.

WOLLSTONECRAFT, M. (Ed.). (1978). *A vindication of the rights of women.* Harmondsworth, England: Penguin. (Original work published 1792)

WOOD, J. (1984). Groping towards sexism: Boys' sex talk. In A. McRobie & M. Nava (Eds.), *Gender and generation.* London: Macmillan.

WOOLF, V. (1928a). *Orlando: A biography.* London: Hogarth Press.

WOOLF, V. (1928b). *A room of one's own.* London: Hogarth Press.

WULFF, H. (1988). *Twelve girls: Growing up, ethnicity, and excitement in a South London micro-culture.* Stockholm: University of Stockholm.

WYLD, H. C. (1934). *The best English: A claim for the superiority of Received Standard English.* Society for Pure English, tract 39. Oxford: Clarendon Press.

YAGUELLO, M. (1978). *Les mots et les femmes* [Words and women]. Paris: Payot.

YAGUELLO, M. (1989). L'élargissement du Capitaine Prieur. *Contrastes: La différence sexuelle dans la langue,* 73–78.

YAGUELLO, M. (1991). *Lunatic lovers of language: Imaginary languages and their inventors* (C. Slater, Trans.). London: Athlone Press.

YOKOYAMA, O. T. (1986). Lexical frequency and its implications: The case of contemporary edited Russian. *Slavic and East European Journal, 30*, 147–166.

YOLEN, J. (1977). *The hundredth dove and other tales.* New York: Crowell.

ZHANG, H. (1992). Spare a woman a beating for three days, they will stand on the roof and tear the house apart. In K. Hall, M. Bucholtz, & B. Moonwoman (Eds.), *Locating power: Proceedings of the Third Berkeley Conference on Women and Language* (pp. 601–609). Berkeley: University of California.

ZIMMERMAN, D., & WEST, C. (1974). Sex roles, interruptions and silences in conversations. In B. Thorne & N. Henley (Eds.), *Language and sex: Difference and dominance* (pp. 105–129). Rowley, MA: Newbury House.

ZIPES, J. (Ed.). (1986a). *Don't bet on the prince: Contemporary fairy tales in North America and England.* New York: Methuen.

ZIPES, J. (1986b). A second gaze at Little Red Riding Hood's trials and tribulations. In J. Zipes (Ed.), *Don't bet on the prince: Contemporary fairy tales in North America and England* (pp. 227–260). New York: Methuen.

ZITA, J. N. (1989). The premenstrual syndrome: "Dis-easing" the female cycle. In N. Tuana (Ed.), *Feminism and science* (pp. 188–210). Bloomington: Indiana University Press.

ZUBIN, D. A., & KÖPCKE, K.-M. (1981). Gender: A less than arbitrary grammatical category. In R. A. Hendrick, C. A. Masek, & C. F. Miller (Eds.), *Papers from the Seventeenth Regional Meeting of the Chicago Linguistic Society* (pp. 439–449). Chicago: Chicago Linguistics Society.

Author Index

Subject Index